Social Behavior in Context

Adrian Furnham
University of London

Allyn and Bacon, Inc.

Boston   London   Sydney   Toronto

For MICHAEL ARGYLE

Library of Congress Cataloging in Publication Data
Main entry under title:
Social behavior in context.

    Bibliography: p.
    Includes index.
    1. Social psychology—Addresses, essays, lectures.
  2. Social interaction—Addresses, essays, lectures.
  3. Personality and situation—Addresses, essays, lectures.
I. Furnham, Adrian.
HM251.S67114 1986   302   84-18413
ISBN 0-205-08378-1

Production Coordinator: Helyn Pultz
Editorial Production Services: Wordsworth Associates

Printed in the United States of America.

10 9 8 7 6 5 4 3 2 1 90 89 88 87 86 85

Contents

    Rom Harre

        Theory   155
        Method   160
        References   166

III. Applications: Clinical, Community, Environmental, and Linguistic Psychology   167

7. Social Fit and Misfit: An Interactional
    Account of Social Difficulty   *169*
    Peter Trower

        Introduction   169
        Surveys of social difficulty   170
        Speculations on a model of social difficulty   177
        Conclusion   191
        References   191

8. Cooperation Dilemmas   *195*
    Richard Price

        Introduction   195
        Alternative formulations   196
        Some problems with contemporary research
            on settings and situations   199
        Cooperation dilemmas in the
            community context   201
        Coping strategies   202
        Social problem solving and
            cooperation dilemmas   205
        References   206

9. Putting Situations in Their Place   *208*
    David Canter

        A role for the physical context   208
        The concept of place   214
        Place roles and rules   218
        Places in the home   222
        The structure of building interpretations   226

Preface

For the social psychology of this century reveals a major lesson: often it is not so much the kind of person that a person is, as the kind of situation in which he finds himself that determines how he will act. (Milgram 1974)

The 1970s and 1980s have been quite an interesting period for social psychology and personality theory. Although this period has seen much questioning and doubt about the viability of theories and the appropriateness of methodology, a new spirit of optimism and change now prevails. *Social Behavior in Context* reflects two topics characterizing research in this period.

The first topic stresses social cognition and moves away from examining actual social behavior to studying the mental representations of external features. The second topic concerns the relationship between personality and social behavior and such related issues as the consistency of behavior over situations and the stability of behavior over time. Much of this concern involves a social learning theory critique of trait theory. The realization that powerful determinants of social behavior are not objective external stimuli but how individuals perceive situations and attribute them with meaning means these two strands of research have come together.

Many authors and researchers in different fields have pointed to an emerging paradigm in social psychology and related disciplines. This paradigm concerns the analysis of the structure and function of behavioral processes and action within naturally occurring social episodes, situations, and settings. That is, it has been argued that all behavioral processes in the real world are embedded in episodes unfolding within specific social situations and defined settings. These processes influence and are influenced by the definition, meaning, and structure of the situation in which they are embedded. There is therefore a widespread movement to recontextualize the study of social behavior. Thus, *Social Behavior in Context*— the title of this volume.

This paradigm shift has occurred for many empirical, philosophical, and applied reasons. Empirically, results from laboratory experiments or observations in vacuo do not generalize to the real-life situation. Also, predictions about social behavior in a range of social situations made from exclusively intrapersonal (trait, type) variables are poor and situational determinants of behavior are important. Philosophically, important criticisms of psychology and social psychology's methodology and fundamental theoretical positions attacked the predominant model of people as passive reactors to social stimulus rather than as active creators of the social world. Action is meaningful, and the meanings attributed to behavior sequences can vary between observers and actors from different groups with different perspectives or needs. This behavior occurs in real time and has a definite sequential and structural pattern. These criticisms have major consequences for the methods appropriate to studying social behavior. Finally, applied researchers have become disappointed by academic researchers' inability and unwillingness to consider applied research problems in which the variables are messier and more complex than in the laboratory.

One beneficial consequence of this paradigm shift, partly in response to what is fashionably called the "crisis in contemporary psychology," is that various disciplines and research areas are considering closely related problems. Generally, this problem is how various forms of social behavior are influenced by the context in which they occur. There are also moves toward a theoretical framework for studying behavior in contexts that cross disciplinary lines.

An open and constructive dialogue must exist between social scientists from different areas. Each, of course, considers different social processes at different levels of analysis, has a different set of methodological and practical problems, is aware of a different literature and research tradition, and yet is concerned with the same overriding issues. Many of the chapters in *Social Behavior in Context* have a historical note indicating various past errors and biases that may be overcome in the future. *Social Behavior in Context* provides the diversity of approaches to the same central theme and offers a more integrated theoretical framework with clearly defined emerging themes to serve as a template for further research.

I am, of course, greatly indebted to many people who have helped me in the course of this work. First and foremost, I owe a great deal to my doctoral supervisors, Michael Argyle and Jos Jaspars, for their advice, insight, criticism, and other benefits of their experience as researchers in social psychology. I was also greatly intellectually stimulated by discussions with other people, including Stephen Bochner, Michael Brenner, Peter Collett, Sharon Foster, Hilde Himmelwent, Jerry Ginsburg, Rom Harré, Jim McCloskey, and Larry Pervin. Other more distant academics provided useful feedback, and I am happy to acknowledge Robert M. Arkin, University of Missouri; Robert A. Baron, Lafayette, Indiana; Joseph Forgas, University of Sydney; and Norman Endler, York University, Canada.

A number of personal friends at Oxford, especially David Pendleton, Miles Hewstone, Monika Henderson, and Jean Graham, shared with me both ideas and anxieties concerning the nature of *Social Behavior in Context*. I received financial support from the Rotary International, the Social Science Research Council, Wolfson College Oxford, and the Tregastris Bequest. Finally, I would like to acknowledge Ann McKendry and Mellissa Li, whose expert and efficient typing helped my delay-of-gratification problems.

A.F.

Introduction

The past decade has been an exciting one for social psychology. A number of substantive issues have occupied academics and continue to be debated and researched. These issues include much soul searching by academic social psychologists, as well as by philosophers of science, who have challenged the epistemological and empirical status of social psychological research and theory. Something of a cognitive revolution in social psychology has also occurred, with the focus of research moving from social behavior to information-processing and the attribution and explanation of social behavior. A third, hotly debated and much researched issue, the topic of *Social Behavior in Context*, concerns the internal (personality) and external (situational) determinants of social behavior. At the interface of personality (correlational) and social (experimental) psychology, this issue touches on some of the most fundamental questions in the discipline as a whole, such as the temporal and situational consistency of behavior and the measurement of individual differences.

It would be naïve to presume that the protagonists and researchers in these various 'new' areas were ignorant of each other's work. Indeed, the opposite is true, for there has been much cross-fertilization of ideas among attribution theorists, personality researchers, historians and philosophers of psychology and others to the benefit of the discipline as a whole. It would also be incorrect to believe that these substantive issues are new. The scientific status of psychology and the everyday understanding of social behavior can be traced to the beginnings of psychology as an academic discipline. These issues and others are like deep, subterranean rivers of knowledge surfacing at various points, sometimes in small springs and at other times as great pools. The water is the same. Each new eruption seems to be a cause for celebration and investigation, until more detailed investigation reveals it to be not a new river but an eruption of the older stream.

A consequence of the faddishness of some social psychological issues is usually much rhetoric and proselytizing. However, after a time, reviewers and even protagonists of one approach or theory appraise the state of the art, the applications of the new research, and glance optimistically into the future. Progress in the discipline can be most accurately assessed in these more reflective periods.

The person-situation debate, or interactional psychology, continues to stimulate research and discussion. Yet, after more than twenty years of innovative research and lively discussion, many scholars have felt it

1

time for a reappraisal of the evidence for personality differences, situational determinants, and interaction effects. Furthermore, the usefulness and relevance of the new concepts, theories, and methodologies need to be assessed. One feature of this book is a state-of-the-art appraisal of interactional psychology and related issues. Chapters by Endler, Furnham, and Jaspars discuss the nature of progress to date.

The energy provoked by important debates can be an important source of creativity and activity. Many researchers have had to reappraise their work, justify their previously accepted axioms, and defend their approach. Some have marshaled better support for their position; others have developed new themes. Still others searched the past for important but ignored ideas, salient to the topic, and some turned away different disciplines in the hope of new inspiration. Chapters by Eysenck, Pervin, Stebbins, and Harré represent these different responses. A second feature of this volume is the juxtapositioning of personality theorists and psychological social psychologists with philosophers of science and sociologists to examine different perspectives on the same problem.

Because of the importance of the internal-external issue to all areas of psychology, researchers in other fields have been interested in the ideas arising from research in this area. Many have used these ideas in their work, often highlighting the context of social behavior and its importance in eliciting, shaping and controlling of that behavior. Thus it is not only personality and social psychology that has been concerned with the context of social behavior but also community, clinical, environment and linguistic psychology, to name but a few. A third feature of this volume is a section on the applications of interactional psychology to applied areas of research. Chapters by Price, Canter, Trower, and Giles and Hewstone represent some important applications of interactional psychology.

Finally, this volume attempts to be geographically and epistemologically eclectic. European psychologists complain that American psychologists do not read their work, and vice versa. Although they often share similar interests, certain differences are apparent between the two in how they conceptualize and experiment on psychological issues. Four contributors to this volume are North American (two from Canada and two from the United States); the other eight are European.

OVERVIEW

Social Behavior in Context is divided into four sections. The two chapters in the first section review the current status of interactional psychology. The first chapter, by Endler, is a theoretical review, looking both into the past and into the future. The second chapter, by Furnham, is primarily a methodological review.

It is fitting that Norman Endler's chapter is first in this volume as his work (with colleagues) in the 1960s provoked empirical work on the person-situation interaction issue. He has continued this research since the early 1960s and has also attempted to appraise the progress in an area he named—interactional psychology. After an introduction to the historical, political, and philosophic aspects of the debate, Endler examines some of the more important theoretical issues in interactional psychology and the nature of the evidence used to support various ideas. The latter half of the chapter discusses how personality and social psychologists can consider the context of social behavior and the role of situations in personality.

Endler is concerned with the direction interactional psychology should take, arguing that we should develop strategies and methods focusing on the structure of mechanistic interactions and the processes in dynamic interactions. He also points to the need for more work on the description, classification, and systematic analysis of social situations. Endler recognizes the need for a balanced approach: the study of individual differences and personality is as important as more recent research into situational determinants of behavior; laboratory studies are essential but should be complemented by real-life studies; traditional research strategies, though useful, should be enhanced by new methodologies. The lessons of the past, if acknowledged, can be beneficial for the future.

The second chapter, by Adrian Furnham, is concerned specifically with the evidence for interactional psychology, reviewing and criticizing the S (situation) – R (response) studies that provoked interest in interactional psychology. Furnham criticizes previous reviews, explores the prototypical format of these studies, then looks at the two-, three-, and four-way analysis of tabulated variance studies. The studies were criticized because they confounded actors and observers; because of how the response modes were chosen; because of the comparability of hypothetical, imagined situations; and for the large variance in the variance component. Various reanalyses are also performed on the existing data to show that the conclusions drawn from the original studies were not always justified. The range of the dependent variances in these studies and the journals in which they are published attest to the interest in interactional psychology.

Part II of *Social Behavior in Context* contrasts psychological and sociological approaches to examining the context of social behavior. Despite their differences of emphasis of concepts and of background literature, recurrent themes include the goal-oriented nature of social behavior, the difference between shared and nonshared perceptions of the social world, and the need for explanatory models as well as descriptive studies.

Lawrence Pervin, author of many books on personality theory, argues in chapter 3 for an interactional approach to studying social behavior. A study is then reported with the hypothesis that people will respond to situations similarly to the extent they perceive them as similar in their reinforcement contingencies. Evidence is found for the hypothesis though Pervin notes that behavior is regulated by normative and personal standards to varying degrees. Pervin then offers propositions for a goal theory, arguing that our behavior in and choice of social situations can only be understood in terms of their place in a goal-directed system. These goals, like attitudes, have cognitive, affective, and behavioral properties and vary over time and in complexity, content, and salience. These goals are acquired or learned on the basis of the association of effects and can be activated by external or internal stimuli. Pervin's theory of goals, like Kelly's construct theory, thus attempts to understand social behavior within the goals system of individuals.

In chapter 4, Hans Eysenck is also concerned with individuals and their personality. Though acknowledging the importance of situational and contextual determinants of social behavior, he is primarily concerned with individual differences in reaction to identical situations. He attempts to explain as well as describe individual differences. To defend his theory, he marshals impressive evidence from cross-cultural comparisons and genetic determinants of behavior. Here and elsewhere, Eysenck rebuffs the situationist critique of personality theories; he believes they are misplaced or use poor data to support their position. He then sets out his theory of the biological foundations of personality and social behavior, impressive because of the diverse studies he has conducted to illustrate the theory. More than any other psychologist, Eysenck has bridged the two disciplines of scientific psychology—experimental and correlational—and believes both are necessary to establish a scientific psychology. He thinks the recent emphasis on the context of behavior, the situational determinants, rather than on individual differences, is misplaced. Despite his defense of some personality theories, he is an interactionist.

In chapter 5, Robert Stebbins considers the context of behavior from a different perspective, offering a critical and historical review of the sociological literature on the definition of the situation. He contrasts the symbolic interactionist, ethnomethodological, and social psychological approaches to the concept. The stress on goal and action orientation of the symbolic interactionists is similar to Pervin's ideas, though they rely on different bodies of knowledge for support. In his section on social psychological approaches, Stebbins concentrates on the Oxford school, particularly on the work of Harré and Argyle. Chapter 5 illustrates from a historical sociological perspective some major different emphases on such microsociological approaches as the culturally shared nature of situational definitions currently discussed by social psychologists.

In Chapter 6, Rom Harré, a philosopher of science, offers an ethogenic analysis of everyday situations episodes. Strongly influenced by symbolic interactionists and ethnomethodologists, Harré argues that we need to make explicit the analytical models through which we investigate the context of social behavior. Like Eysenck, Harré notes the analysis of action and the explanation of action are logically independent activities. His methodology aims to uncover peoples' understanding and beliefs; he is particularly interested in shared, as opposed to individual, beliefs, outlining four kinds of episodes distinguished by location (public/private) and display (individual/collective). Harré then explains the ethnogenic method for analyzing social episodes. His contribution is innovative, challenging, and critical of traditional methodology in social psychology.

In Part III of *Social Behavior in Context*, Peter Trower is concerned specifically with applying the person-situation debate to clinical psychology. As others have done, Trower, in chapter 7, approaches the issue in terms of a positive fit between person and situation. To explain the problems of a negative fit, he reviews studies of social difficulty in everyday situations. He then identifies problem persons (socially unskilled individuals experiencing difficulty in everyday situations) and problem situations (everyday situations that are difficult for different groups). He isolates such various dimensions of problematic situations as scripted vs. unscripted, and explicit vs. implicit rule structure that attempt to define the properties of situations making them difficult for people. Trower also tries to specify such dimensions of problem persons as restricted vs. elaborated skill repertoires, appropriate vs. inappropriate, and self vs. other schemes that help explain what sort of people have interactional problems. Trower returns to his original theme in trying to explain the interactional fit or misfit between person and situation in terms of the key characteristics both of the individual and the situation he or she inhabits.

In chapter 8, Richard Price uses situational theory to understand social problems. He uses the commons dilemma as a useful heuristic to illustrate the short-term individual interests and advantage on the one hand and long-term collective interest on the other. He then specifies some problems with contemporary research in person-situation interaction and explores the potential usefulness of the cooperation dilemma paradigm to explain these problems. Price believes this paradigm explains some situational aspects of many social problems that otherwise would seem unrelated, illustrating this point by different examples. The cooperation dilemma paradigm is used to understand and solve social problems. Just as Argyle stressed the importance of applying situational analysis to every social problem, so Price used research in community psychology to understand the nature of social problems.

Chapter 9, by environmental psychologist David Canter, begins with a warning based on the history of environmental psychology. Social psychologists, he argues, are bringing back from environmental psychologists many concepts and methodologies they brought from social and experimental psychologists a generation earlier, but without recognizing the research or thinking in environmental psychology. Canter develops the concept of place, which provides a useful basis on which to build the bridges between social and environmental psychology. The concept of place has three sets of properties that make them distinctive: activities or behaviors associated with time, the evaluation or conception of them, and their physical properties. Specific attention is paid to place rules—their stability and reliability; places in the home illustrate the points. Canter draws on such other areas of psychology as social skills training to illustrate his point. He offers interesting suggestions for future research on such things as place cognition and place prototypes. Most impressive is his attempt to build bridges across various ravines in psychology rather than to erect fences.

Chapter 10, by Howard Giles and Miles Hewstone, is concerned with speech and language as an independent variable in defining and redefining the nature of the situation for the individuals involved. They review previous approaches to speech and social situations as well as social psychological literature on intergroup relations and social situations. Central to the chapter is the authors' theoretical model with two components: speech as a dependent variable and speech as an independent variable of social situations. They illustrate how social situations determine speech patterns and vice versa and also develop a series of testable propositions, examined in some detail. They want to extend the previous research on objective taxonomies of situations for understanding speech variations to produce a cognitive model focusing on the mediating role of speakers' own cognitive representations of the situation as an important set of forces determining speech variation. The importance of this chapter is therefore twofold: it relates the work on psycho- and sociolinguistics to the person-situation debate and also offers a clear, dynamic conception of the interrelationship between behavior—in this case, speech and social situations.

Chapter 11, the final chapter in *Social Behavior in Context*, is not an epilogue or overview but a look ahead with regard to the lessons of the past. Jos Jaspars begins by looking at relationships between social psychology and other social sciences. Central to his thesis is that social psychologists have never developed a theory to explain our universal findings in order to apply them to particular individuals or special cultural or structural situations. The historical development of social psychology has seen a continual narrowing of the social issues to be studied and a miniaturizing of the social environment so it could be studied scientifically. Much current research and debate in social psychology can be understood in terms of the past. Much criticism concerns the relevance of social psychology, which is seen not to possess any universality because research has been done so often in highly unrepresentative and unrealistic situations.

Jaspars, however, believes many of these criticisms misplaced and much of the pessimism unnecessary. What we need, he argues, is a psychological taxonomy of social situations allowing us to explain how social, cultural, and situational factors affect social psychological laws. The second half of the last chapter is devoted to some taxonomic proposals and research strategies and methods. Through illustrations of various types of data and reanalysis, Jaspars suggests that it is possible to predict situational transformations of general social psychological laws, so providing universality.

I

Interactional Psychology

1. Origins of Interactional Psychology[1]

NORMAN S. ENDLER[2]
York University

INTRODUCTION

The field of personality has shown much promise during the last decade, but not as much fulfillment. Nevertheless, conceptual, theoretical, methodological and empirical advances occurred in the 1970s. As Endler and Magnusson (1976c) noted, the four major personality models, which have had the greatest influence in guiding theory and research, have been the trait model, the psychodynamic model, situationism, and interactionism.

The model making the greatest strides during the 1970s was interactionism, both in theorizing and research. An examination of personality texts and psychological journals of the 1970s indicates the importance of and interest in interactionism, as do various international conferences and symposia on interactionism, consistency, and the situational context in personality (see Endler 1982).

Ekehammar (1974) and Endler (1982, 1983) discussed and reviewed the historical antecedents of modern interactionism. This chapter summarizes some highlights of these reviews.

Interactionism as a theoretical concept can be traced to the times of Aristotle (see Shute 1973), Descartes, and other philosophers.

In the modern era, Kantor (1924, 1926) was most likely the first person to present a psychological interpretation of interactionism. "No biological fact may be considered as anything but the mutual interaction of the organism and the environment" (Kantor 1926, 369). The unit of analysis, according to Kantor, was "the individual as he interacts with all the various types of situations which constitute his behavior circumstances" (1924, 92). He believed that "a personality conception must be predominantly functional and must place great emphasis upon the stimuli conditions and the interaction of the person with them" (Kantor, 1924, 91). Although he emphasized the physical environment, Kantor (1924, 1926, 1969) was one of the first writers to distinguish between the physical and psychological environments. Field theorists, such as Lewin (1936), and the theories of most interactionists empha-

11

size the psychological environment. However, Kantor's behavioristic field theory focused on the reciprocal interaction between the environment and the person.

Koffka (1935) and Lewin (1935, 1936) also emphasized the distinction between the physical environment and the psychological environment. For Lewin, the various elements within the person-situation relationship were mutually interdependent and characterized by a reciprocal interaction between the environment and the person. Murray (1938) also focused on the interaction of personal and situational factors within the context of his need-press theory of personality. "Since at every moment, an organism is within an environment which largely determines its behavior, and since the environment changes— sometimes with radical abruptness—the conduct of an individual cannot be formulated without a characterization of each confronting situation physical and social" (Murray 1938, 39). Murray distinguished between *Alpha* press (physical environment) and *Beta* press (psychological environment) and also used the parallel constructs of needs and presses for persons and environments, respectively.

Angyal (1941) proposed that the person and the situation interpenetrate one another so pervasively that it is not feasible to unravel them without destroying their unity or wholeness. He suggested that the person-by-environment system was an inseparable holistic entity, the *biosphere.* Tolman (1935/1951), on the other hand, believed that the various components were independent. He focused on the physical environment, whereas Lewin, Koffka, and Angyal emphasized the psychological environment. However, Tolman conceptualized behavior as related to the organism's stimulus setup, heredity, training, and the physiological state.

Murphy (1947) proposed the *biosocial* theory of personality, basically an interactional theory. Personality is a function of two factors, one within the biological organism, and the other within the social environment. Rotter (1954), within the context of his social learning theory of personality, suggested that the basic unit of analysis for examining personality should be the interaction of the individual and his or her meaningful environment—the psychological environment. Jessor (1956, 1958) also focused on the psychological environment, which he attempted to relate to phenomenological theories of personality. In most instances, the psychological environment means the individual's perception of the situation.

Basic, fundamental empirical research on interactionism began in the 1950s and 1960s, even though the prime theoretical formulations about person-by-situation interactions initially had appeared in the 1920s, 1930s, 1940s, and 1950s. Much of the empirical research was conducted independently of the theoretical bases of the person-by-situation interaction issue. The early empirical studies on interactionism by Raush, Dittmann, and Taylor (1959a, 1959b), and Endler and Hunt (1966) offer no evidence for any apparent relationship with the theorizing of Kantor, Koffka, Lewin, or Murray.

Renewed interest in the theoretical apsects of interactionism did not develop until the mid- and late-1960s and the 1970s (e.g., Endler 1976; Endler and Hunt 1969; Endler and Magnusson 1976b, 1976c; Hunt 1965; Magnusson and Endler 1977; Raush 1965). Concomitantly, there have also been comprehensive reviews of the empirical literature on interactionism, with special emphasis on the consistency versus specificity issue (e.g., Argyle and Little 1972; Bowers 1973; Ekehammar 1974; Endler and Magnusson 1976b, 1976c; Magnusson 1976; Magnusson and Endler 1977; Mischel 1973; Pervin 1968).

EXTRASCIENTIFIC FACTORS INFLUENCING PERSONALITY THEORY AND RESEARCH

Most early research and theorizing on personality, which was based on work related to individual differences (psychometrics), underestimated the role of situation factors and overestimated the role of person factors. Specifically, social and experimental psychology emphasized situational factors, while theorizing and research in personality emphasized person factors. Ichheiser (1943) pointed out that this state of affairs has its roots in general in sociopolitical factors; specifically, in the social system and ideology of nineteenth century liberalism. This nineteenth century philosophy proclaimed that "our fate in social space depended exclusively, or at least predominantly, on our individual qualities—that we, as individuals, and not the prevailing social conditions shape our lives" (Ichheiser 1943, 152). During the last half century, such sociopolitical and sociopsychological factors as the depression, unemployment, World War II, the Cold War, Viet Nam, the Third World forces, inflation, and the revolution of rising expectations have altered the research and theoretical emphasis from a focus on personal factors toward explaining behavior in terms of social conditions.

Research and theory in personality is not value-free and is influenced by personal, political, and social forces (Endler 1981a, 1981b). Pervin (1978a, 280) noted that all "Scientific pursuits have a historical context and a political context." Furthermore, even research methodology and research tactics are affected by personal and social forces (Endler 1981a, 1981b). By being aware of these extrascientific considerations, it is possible to minimize their contaminating effects.

Both theory and research in the field of personality have been guided, directed, and influenced primarily by the trait model. The trait model has emphasized traits (inner factors) as the major and basic determinants of behavior. Thus, there has been more emphasis on investigating traits than on examining situations. Research on situations has focused on the role of situations as experimental stimuli. One force shifting research toward investigating the role of situations in personality research has been the interaction model of personality (Endler and Magnusson 1976c). Nevertheless, this model does not neglect the role of person factors in its research and theorizing.

According to Endler (1977, 1981a, 1981b, 1982), Magnusson (1976, 1980), and Endler and Magnusson (1976c), the two basic tasks or problems for an interactional psychology of personality are (1) the examination of how persons and situations interact in determining behavior; and (2) the description, classification, and systematic analyses of situations, including stimuli, and environments. The character and nature of person-by-situation interactions and the role of situations have been discussed in detail by Endler and Magnusson (1976c), Magnusson and Endler (1977), Endler (1981a, 1981b, 1982), and Magnusson (1976, 1980). This chapter summarizes some major points but focuses particularly on the psychological examination of situations in terms of the role of situational factors for interactional psychology. Basically, we discuss the description, classification, and systematic analyses of stimuli, situations, and environments. We examine both the within situation factors and the between situation factors in personality theory and research (Endler 1982; Magnusson 1980; Magnusson and Endler 1977).

THE PERSON-BY-SITUATION INTERACTION DEBATE

Endler and Magnusson (1976c) pointed out the four basic models in personality theory and research: (1) the trait model; (2) the psychodynamic model; (3) the situationism model; and (4) the interaction model. After a brief summary of each model, this chapter focuses on the interaction model of personality.

The Trait Model

The trait model postulates that behavior is primarily determined by stable, latent dispositions; that is, by factors internal to the person. For example, Cattell (1957) and Guilford (1959) believe that traits serve as a predispositional basis for response-response consistencies of behavior in many situations.

Basically, the trait model recognizes the impact of situations because its adherents do not believe that persons behave the same way in various situations. The model nevertheless assumes that the rank order of persons for a specific personality variable (such as anxiety) is the same across different situations.

Allport (1937) proposed that traits were general and enduring predispositions to respond and that they were not linked to specific stimuli or responses. Trait theorists disagree as to the specific structures, numbers, and types of traits. However, they agree that traits are the basic units of personality and are dispositions accounting for cross-situational consistency. Situations interact with traits in determining behavior.

The Psychodynamic Model

The psychodynamic models, primarily psychoanalysis, focus on the internal determinants of behavior and thus are similar to the trait models. They also differ from the trait models in many important ways. The psychodynamic models propose a basic personality core that serves as a predispositional basis for behavior in different situations. For example, psychoanalysis focuses on the personality structure (id, ego, and superego), dynamics, and development (Freud 1959).

The dynamics of personality emphasize the continuous interaction of and conflict among the id, ego, and superego. One consequence of this conflict is anxiety. The individual develops defense mechanisms, which are motives defending the self-concept against this potentially debilitating anxiety. Freud believed that, developmentally, experiences serve primarily to modify the expression of instinctual impulses. The neo-Freudians (e.g., Erikson 1963; Fromm 1955; Horney 1945; Sullivan 1953), on the other hand, de-emphasized the psychosexual stages and the role of instincts and emphasized social factors, the ego, and psychosocial stages of development.

The trait model assumes a one-to-one positive monotonic relationship between reactions and underlying intervening variables or hypothetical constructs; psychodynamic models propose that a one-to-one relationship may not necessarily exist between overt behavior and hypothetical constructs. In some instances, for example, because of defense mechanisms, consistency at the mediating level (e.g., the hypothetical construct of anxiety) may not always result in consistency at the response level (e.g., anxious behavior).

The Model of Situationism

Dewey and Humber (1951) and Dollard and Miller (1950), proponents of classical social learning theory, provided prototypic examples of situationism. The situationism model emphasizes external factors, primarily stimulus situations, as the basic determinants of behavior. The different social learning theories provide a heterogeneous viewpoint (Endler and Edwards 1978). For example, Dollard and Miller (1950), the classical behavior theorists, emphasize situations and the importance of learning, but they also study such organismic variables as drives, motives, and conflict.

The modern behavior theorists (Bandura 1971, 1977; Mischel 1973; and Rotter 1975) are interested in the person's behavior rather than in attributes, traits, and motives. They focus on situations, but they include person factors in their theories (e.g., see Bandura 1977 on self-efficacy; Mischel 1973 on cognitive factors; and Rotter 1975 on expectancy).

The Interaction Model

The interaction model of personality (see Bowers 1973; Endler 1977; Endler and Magnusson 1976c, Magnusson 1980; and Magnusson and Endler 1977) emphasizes the role of situation-by-person interactions in personality. This model postulates a continuous interaction between the individual and the situations encountered. Individuals select the situations or behavioral contexts in which they act and subsequently influence the routine and character of these situations. This behavior implies an ongoing process whereby situations influence people, who, in turn, affect these situations.

Interactionism emphasizes how persons and situations interact in promoting or restricting behavior, rather than whether persons or situations are a major source of behavioral variance. The person-versus situations or internal-versus-external determinants of behavior is largely a false issue.

According to Endler and Magnusson (1976c), modern interactionism has four major postulates: (1) behavior is primarily a function of the continuous, ongoing, and multidimensional process of person-by-situation interactions; (2) the individual is an intentional and active agent in this process; (3) cognitive, emotional, and motivational factors play essential roles as person factors in this process; and (4) the psychological meaning or the person's perception of the situation is an essential determining factor in the behavioral process.

RESEARCH AND THEORETICAL ISSUES
FOR INTERACTIONAL PSYCHOLOGY

Controversial issues in interactionism have fueled the significant research in this field of personality. These issues include (1) situation specificity versus cross-situational consistency, (2) persons versus situations, (3) reaction variables versus mediation variables, and (4) the fundamental distinction between psychological models and their measurement models.

Measurement Models, Psychological Process Models,
and Personality Theories

Psychologists often fail to distinguish between personality theories that are models of psychological process and the measurement models assessing these theories (Endler 1977, 1981a; Magnusson 1976; Magnusson and Endler 1977). They also often do not distinguish between the reactions or responses they are studying and the methods they use to collect data (Magnusson and Endler 1977). For example, measures of overt behavior can be obtained by ratings, self-reports, or objective measures.

One basic assumption of the trait measurement model is that a true (error free) trait score exists for each individual. This assumption means that individual positions on a trait dimension are stable across situations. This assumption implies that the behavior (test score) indicating this trait is also stable across a variety of situations. The trait measurement model therefore assumes that the rank order of persons for behavior indicating a trait dimension is also stable across various situations.

However, very little empirical evidence supports trans-situational consistency (Endler 1973, 1981a, 1981b; Mischel 1968, 1969). Critics of trait theories, basing their position on empirical results, have pointed their arguments against the trait measurement model. On the other hand, adherents of traits have emphasized the trait personality (psychological process) theory.

Trait and psychodynamic models emphasize person (internal) factors as the major determinants of behavior, but they differ in their measurement models. In the trait measurement model, a positive and linear monotonic relationship exists between overt responses and underlying mediating variables. The psychodynamic model instead suggests that an increase in a mediating variable, such as aggressiveness, may, at a certain level of intensity, lead to a decrease in overt aggressive responses because of defensiveness. That is, the psychodynamic model suggests a curvilinear relationship between mediating variables and reaction variables.

Reaction Variables and Mediating Variables

Magnusson and Endler (1977) emphasized the need to distinguish between reaction (response) variables and mediating variables, in terms of both personality theory and research. Consistency at the mediating variable level is not always reflected in consistency at the reaction variable level.

Reaction variables. Magnusson and Endler (1977) posit at least four types of reactions (or responses): physiological reactions, covert reactions (feelings, emotions, etc.), overt behavior, and artificial behavior (role playing, test behavior, etc.). Physiological reactions can be assessed by ratings, self-report measures, and objective measures. Covert reactions can be assessed by self-report measures. Overt behavior can be assessed by ratings, self-report measures, and objective measures. Artificial behavior can be assessed by ratings, standardized test methods, and objective measures.

Mediating variables. Hypothetical constructs or mediating variables are inferred from behavioral observations and from phenomenological self-reports. Traits and motives, which are mediating variables, help us understand, explain, and predict the processes through which both stored information and concurrent stimuli are selected. Magnusson and Endler (1977) suggest three types of mediating variables: structural, content, and motivational.

Structural variables. They refer to such concepts as abilities, cognitive complexity, competence, and intelligence. Within the normal range of situational effects, structural variables are not easily modified by situational factors. However, evidence suggests that under extreme situations, such as threatening conditions, structural variables are modified. Mischel (1968, 1969) and Rushton and Endler (1977) have found evidence for the consistency of structural variables. Since intelligence is a structural variable, it is not surprising that intelligence in one situation (e.g., school) is highly predictive of intelligence in another situation (e.g., work).

Content variables. These variables include stored information or situationally determined information. An example is the content of anger-arousing situations. In a specific situation, the content that the mediating system processes is determined both by the stored information activated by sensory stimulation and by the specific stimulus cues selected by (or imposed on) the individual. Situational factors influence the content of the mediating process, which can lead to inconsistency of behavior across situations.

Motivational variables. They refer to motives, needs, drives, attitudes and values. These variables influence the arousal, maintenance, and direction of behavior. They affect how an individual selects and treats information and are concerned with why a person reacts or responds as he or she does. Varying contexts affect different motivational variables, which are altered by situational factors. The mediating system processes (and selects) content and motivational factors in a regulated and consistent style. However, the expression of these motivational and content variables differs in a variety of situations.

The Relative Effects of Situations and Persons

Are persons (internal determinants) or situations (external determinants) the major source of response variability? Endler (1973) suggested that this issue is really a pseudo-issue since the crucial question is how persons and situations interact in influencing behavior.

On one hand, social psychologists, social learning theoriests, and sociologists (e.g., Cooley 1902; Cottrell 1942a, 1942b; Dewey and Humber 1951; Mead 1934; Mischel 1968, Rotter 1954; Skinner 1953) have held that situations and the perception or meaning of situations are the prime determinants of behavior. On the other hand, person-ologists, personality trait theorists (e.g., Allport 1966; Cattell 1946; Guilford 1959; and McClelland 1951), and clinicians (e.g., Freud 1959; Rapaport, Gill, and Schafer 1945) have held that traits and their dynamic sources within persons are the prime determinants of behavior.

However, as indicated, the trait theorists now recognize the role of external situational factors in personality; and the situational theorists recognize the role of internal person factors in personality. This issue is now primarily one of historical interest, because most personality theorists recognize the roles of both person and situation factors in personality. Obviously, both persons and situations are essential factors. Nevertheless, the person-versus-situation issue has relevance for the most controversial issue in personality theory and research—the issue of trans-situational consistency versus situational specificity.

Situational Consistency (Stability) and Inconsistency (Specificity)

The issue of consistency versus specificity has probably been the most controversial and productive issue of personality research and theory. As indicated, no necessary one-to-one relationship exists between consistency at the reaction variable level and consistency at the mediating variable level. Magnusson and Endler (1977) and Endler (1977, 1981a) describe three different meanings of consistency at the reaction variable level: absolute consistency, relative consistency, and coherence.

Absolute consistency. This type of consistency postulates that an individual manifests a specified behavior (e.g., dependency) to the same extent in various situations. The obverse of this would be variability. Absolute consistency can be investigated for one individual at a time (Magnusson and Endler 1977). No empirical evidence supports this type of consistency.

Relative consistency. This type of consistency postulates that the rank order of persons for a specified behavior (e.g., anxiousness) is stable across various situations. This type of consistency is typically investigated by studying groups of individuals across situations. Most empirical studies on the consistency-versus-specificity issue have investigated relative consistency. "In order for the relative consistency hypothesis about stable rank orders to be valid, the correlations between measures for different situations should approach 1.0, except for errors of measurement" (Magnusson and Endler 1977, 7).

Coherence. This type of consistency postulates that behavior is inherent and predictable, without necessarily being stable in either absolute or relative terms. Coherence refers to sequences or patterns of behavior "that may vary across situations of various kinds but in which the behavior is coherent and lawful all the same" (Magnusson and Endler, 1977, 7). Coherence refers to the notion that "the *rank order* of a person's behavior in various situations with respect to a number of variables is stable and predictable, but his (or her) rank order may differ from another person's rank order of the situations" (Endler 1977, 348). For example, person *A* may manifest different levels of anxiety in different situations, but his or her rank order of anxiety responses in various situations is stable and consistent. Person *B* may rank order anxiety responses differently than person *A*, but person *B*'s rank order is stable and consistent. Coherence implies that behavior is regulated and lawful rather than random.

Consistency of behavior can be described in terms of temporal (longitudinal) factors or of spatial (cross situational) factors. That is, persons can be consistent across situations over different time periods (months or years) or across different situations occurring over a relatively short time. It is probably more meaningful to differentiate consistency on the basis of reactions to similar versus dissimilar situations since temporal and spatial factors are obviously not independent.

Typically, cross-sectional studies have been concerned with consistency across dissimilar situations (usually over a very short time span). Longitudinal studies have been concerned with consistency of individuals across similar situations, ontogenetically over time. Investigations conducting longitudinal research have studied the correlation for a specific personality variable (e.g., anxiety) over two different time periods (e.g., childhood and adolescence) and have generally ignored specific situational variables.

Block (1977), for example, has analyzed comprehensive personality case histories and test results on several hundred Oakland and Berkeley, California, residents. The original data were first gathered (by others) in the 1930s, when the persons were in junior high school. The Berkeley Institute of Human Development tracked these students when they were in their late teens, in their mid-thirties, and again when they were in their mid-forties (in the 1960s). The data include transcripts of interviews with the persons, their parents, teachers, and spouses, as well as attitude checklists. Different sets of materials were collected at each of the four time periods. Block (1977) clearly demonstrated the existence of longitudinal stability and consistency for a number of variables, including cheerfulness, social poise, self-defeating attitude, and mood swings.

Cross-sectional studies have investigated the correlation for a specific personality variable (e.g., friendliness) in two different situations (e.g., at home and on the tennis courts), usually occurring over a short time span. The evidence for cross-situational consistency with respect to social and personality variables is not very strong. The average correlations for cross-situational consistency for personality and social variables has been about 0.30 (e.g., see Endler, 1973, 1975a, 1975b; Mischel 1968, 1969).

Consistency of structural, content, and motivational variables is an index of consistency or coherence of mediating processes. Structural variables would be consistent and coherent in the style or manner in which they initially select and subsequently process both content and motivational variables. Nevertheless, the expression of the content and motivational variables frequently varies due to different situations.

Social learning processes and other behavioral processes are important for the consistent or coherent style of processing both content and motivational factors. Consistency of mediating processes does not mean that the behavioral expression (or response) of these underlying processes is consistent. As indicated, situational factors usually modify the expression of content and motivation variables and under extreme circumstances can modify the expression of structural variables. For example, persons suffering from test anxiety can have their level of academic performance lowered on an important examination they perceive as threatening. It is important to relate reaction variables to mediating variables.

EMPIRICAL INVESTIGATIONS OF
THE CONSISTENCY VS. SPECIFICITY ISSUE

Three strategies have been used to study the consistency versus specificity issue: (1) multidimensional variance components techniques; (2) correlations; and (3) personality-by-treatment experimental designs. For comprehensive empirical reviews of this issue, see Argyle and Little (1972), Bowers (1973), Endler (1973, 1977), Endler and Magnusson (1976c), Magnusson (1976), and Magnusson and Endler (1977).

Multidimensional Variance Components Studies

This strategy analyzes variance of the data and determines the amount of variance due to such different sources as persons, situations, and person-by-situation interactions. This approach has empirically demonstrated interactions, but it does not explain them.

Raush, Dittmann, and Taylor (1959a, 1959b) and Endler and Hunt (1966, 1969) were among the first to conduct personality studies using this strategy. Raush et al., using ratings of observed behavior in six different situations for delinquent boys, demonstrated that the person-by-situation interaction accounted for more response variance than either situations or persons per se.

Endler and Hunt (1966, 1969), using the S-R Inventory of Anxiousness (Endler, Hunt, and Rosenstein 1962) as their data base, analyzed subjects' responses nested in various situations for twenty-two males and twenty-one females. Persons accounted for 4.44 percent of the variance for males and 4.56 percent of the variance for females; situations accounted for 3.95 percent for males and 7.78 percent for females; and person-by-situation interactions accounted for about 10 percent of the variance.

In Bowers's (1973) summary of eleven studies using the variance components strategy, the person-by-situation interactions accounted for more behavioral variance than either persons or situations for fourteen out of eighteen comparisons.

Endler and Magnusson (1976c) suggested that although the variance components technique indicates no absolute consistency, it has certain limitations with respect to relative consistency. They noted that it is possible for the stability of rank orders to be of a high magnitude even in cases in which the variance due to persons is small (see also Endler 1977; Epstein 1977). In those cases of low interaction variance, the demonstration that both person and situation variance is also low may not have any direct implications for situationism or for trait psychology. However, strong person-by-situation interactions are indirect evidence for the lack of stable rank orders (i.e., the lack of consistency). These results provide direct evidence for interactionism. The variance components technique demonstrates the existence of strong interactions. However, other approaches are needed to explain and predict the nature of interactions (e.g., personality-by-treatment experimental designs).

Correlations

Correlational research strategy directly tests the assumption of cross-situational consistency or stability. Hartshorne and May (1928) originally investigated cross-situational consistency in their classic study of honesty in school children across different siuations. Their results did not support the consistency assumption of trait theory; they found correlations of honesty in different situations to average about 0.30. Almost fifty years later, Rushton (1976), in his review of social altruism studies with children, found the average correlations of altruism across various situations was also about 0.30. In Newcomb's (1931) study of introversion-extroversion behavior reactions over thirty situations with a sample of delinquent boys, the average correlation of introversion-extroversion across these situations was ± 0.30.

Cross-situational stability in ratings of cooperative ability, self-confidence, and leadership, and objective measures of talking time were investigated by Magnusson and his colleagues (Magnusson, Gerzén, and Numan 1968; Magnusson and Heffler 1969; and Magnusson, Heffler, and Nyman 1968). Systematically varying the situation variables of group composition and tasks, they found that when the situations were similar, the correlations were about 0.70; when the situations were dissimilar, the correlations were zero.

As indicated, Block (1977) demonstrated the existence of consistency in his longitudinal studies. Similarly, Olweus (1979) found consistency with respect to aggressiveness in boys in a longitudinal study. It may be that in longitudinal studies, various situations are not that dissimilar. Since to a certain extent people select the situations in which they interact, they may select situations similar to those that have been rewarding. Magnusson and his colleagues, in their cross-sectional studies, showed evidence for consistency in similar situations but no evidence for relative consistency in dissimilar situations.

Factor analytic techniques have also been used to examine the trait hypothesis about trans-situational consistency. Trait theorists would predict that most of the total variance could be explained by one major factor. Burton (1963) reanalyzed the Hartshorne and May (1928) honesty data. Similarly, Nelson, Grinder, and Mutterer (1969) factor analyzed their own honesty data. Honesty was only moderately consistent across varying tasks. Endler, Hunt, and Rosenstein (1962), Endler and Okada (1975), and Endler and Magnusson (1976a) factor analyzed anxiousness in varying situations and could not demonstrate trans-situational consistency. Anxiousness was multidimensional. Endler and Hunt (1968) obtained analogous results for hostility data.

Personality-by-Treatment Experimental Designs

The third stategy relevant to the consistency vs. specificity issue is the personality-by-experimental treatment design. The correlational and variance components strategies point out that interactions exist and are important but do not provide insights as to why (Sarason, Smith, and Diener 1975) or how situations and persons interact in eliciting behavior (Endler 1973). If investigations are guided by theory, then experimental studies incorporating both situational and personality variables in their designs help predict the nature of interactions. For example, Fiedler (1971, 1977) found that leadership style (a person variable) interacts with situational variables in affecting group effectiveness. Berkowitz (1977) and Moyer (1973) found an interaction of person and situation variables.

Person-by-situation interaction studies have examined the consequences of congruence and incongruence between the locus of control (Rotter 1966, 1975) in the situation and the individual's generalized locus of control (internal or external) expectancy. When the situational locus of control is operationally defined as a chance versus skill task description or perception, situation-by-person interactions influence reward value (e.g., Lefcourt, Lewis, and Silverman 1968), information seeking (e.g., Davis and Phares 1967), and performance (e.g., Houston 1972). Baron and Ganz (1972) and Baron, Cowan, Ganz, and MacDonald (1974) demonstrated that locus of control (I-E) interacted with type of reinforcement (intrinsic versus extrinsic) to influence performance. Sherman (1973) demonstrated that I-E interacted with various attitude change procedures (e.g., writing a counter-attitudinal essay versus reading or persuasive communication) to affect the degree of attitudinal change. For more details on the locus of control studies, see Endler and Edwards (1978).

Endler (1966) and Endler and Hoy (1967) studied the effects of reinforcement, a situational factor on conforming behavior. Both reinforcement and sex (a person factor) affected conformity, but the person (sex)-by-situation (reinforcement) interactions were not significant. Witkin and Goodenough (1976), reviewing the literature on field dependence, a person variable, and conforming behavior, found that the relationship between field dependence and conforming behavior was influenced by situational factors.

Using a person-by-experimental treatment design, a number of studies tested Endler's (1975b, 1980) interaction model of anxiety. Endler and Okada (1974) found an interaction between physical danger trait anxiety (a person variable) and a physically threatening situation in affecting state anxiety for female college students. Endler and Magnusson (1977); Endler, King, Kuczynski, and Edwards (1980); and Phillips and Endler (1980) evaluated the interaction model of anxiety in a real-life examination situation. They found an interaction between trait anxiety (A-trait) and a congruent interpersonal or social evaluation examination stress in influencing state anxiety (A-state). Endler, Edwards, and McGuire (1979) found a trend toward an interaction between social evaluation A-trait and the congruent situational stress of a live stage performance for actors in eliciting changes in A-state. Diveky and Endler (1977), examining middle-management male bankers in both stressful on-the-job situations and nonstressful off-the-job situations, found a significant interaction between social evaluation A-trait and congruent social evaluation situational job stress in influencing A-state arousal. Flood and Endler (1980) found an interaction between a stressful track meet (social evaluation) situation and the social evaluation dimension of A-trait in affecting A-state. King and Endler (1980) demonstrated significant interactions between a medical intervention procedure (dilation and curettage or laparoscopy) and the ambiguous, physical danger and social evaluation facets of A-trait with respect to A-state. Kendall (1978) compared the Spielberger (1972) state-trait anxiety model with the Endler (1975b, 1980) interaction model of anxiety. The results of the Kendall experiments supported the interaction model of anxiety. Interactions occurred only in instances when the facets of A-trait were congruent with the situational stressors.

MECHANISTIC AND DYNAMIC INTERACTION

These studies on personality-by-treatment experimental designs focused on mechanistic interaction and did not examine the processes occurring in dynamic interaction. In general, the interaction concept has been defined and used in various ways. For example, Olweus (1977) described four different meanings of the term *interaction:* (1) in a very general sense to indicate how persons and situations combine or connect (unidirectional interaction); (2) on the basis of the interdependency reciprocal action; (3) on the basis of reciprocal action; and (4) in terms of its use in the analysis of variance. The first and fourth meanings refer to undirectional interaction. The fourth meaning is basically in a methodological subset of the first meaning.

Olweus (1977) described three kinds of interaction: unidirectional (mechanistic), reciprocal (dynamic), and a third type in which one cannot realistically separate persons from situations. Due to the present lack of methodological sophistication, it is not feasible empirically to investigate this last type of interaction. Therefore, we have two meaningful conceptions of interaction: mechanistic (unidirectional) and dynamic (reciprocal action).

Mechanistic Interaction

The mechanistic model of interaction focuses on interactions of such main factors as persons, situations, and modes of response within the context of a data matrix. It uses analysis of variance techniques in its measurement model. This model clearly distinguishes between independent and dependent variables and assumes a linear and additive relationship between person and situation factors (independent variables) in determining behavior.

Within the mechanistic model, interaction describes the interdependency of determinants of behavior. It does not focus on the interaction between independent and dependent variables. "Interaction is not between cause and effect, but between causes" (Overton and Reese 1973, 78). Mechanistic interaction is not concerned with the process of interaction. It is concerned with the structure of interaction.

As indicated, person (P)-by-situation (S) interactions, person (P)-by-modes-of-response (M-R) interactions, situation (S)-by-modes-of-response (M-R) interactions, situation (S)-by-modes-of-response (M-R) interactions, and P-by-S-by M-R interactions have all been examined by variance components techniques and by person-by-experimental treatment analysis of variance techniques. Most emphasis has been on P-by-S interactions, and the variance components technique has demonstrated but not explained interactions. The person-by-treatment experimental designs enable us to explain interactions. However, both the person-by-treatment designs and the variance components approach represent a mechanistic model. They are necessary strategies but are not sufficient for examining the dynamic interaction process occurring within the interaction model of personality.

Dynamic Interaction

The dynamic or organismic model of interaction is concerned with the reciprocal interaction between situational (environmental) events and behavior, with reciprocal causation and the relationship between independent and dependent variables. "*Reciprocal causation* means that not only do events affect the behavior of organisms but the organism is also an active agent in influencing environmental events" (Endler and Magnusson 1976c, 969). Multidimensional dynamic interaction refers "to the mutual interdependence of person-situations and behavior so that persons-situations influence behavior and vice versa" (Endler 1975a, 18). Dynamic interaction is process oriented. This model attempts to integrate situations, mediating variables, and person-reaction variables.

The usual distinction between independent and dependent variables in personality research may not be very fruitful, according to Raush (1977). Perhaps we should use the person-by-situation interaction as a basic unit of analysis. Most empirical research on interaction has been concerned with mechanistic interaction because we have not fully developed the strategies, techniques, and measurement models needed by investigating dynamic interaction.

According to Endler (1982), the two prime tasks for an interactional psychology of personality are (1) the examination of how persons and situations interact in determining behavior and (2) the description, classification, and systematic analyses of stimuli, situations, and environments. Let us now examine the role of stimuli, situations, and environments.

THE ROLE OF SITUATIONS IN PERSONALITY

A basic problem with the analyses of situations is the failure to define and explicitly differentiate among the concepts *stimuli, situations,* and *environments* (Pervin 1978b). According to Frederiksen (1972, 115), "We need a systematic way of conceptualizing the domain of situations and situation variables before we can make rapid progress in studying the roles of situations in determining behavior."

It is possible to make a rough distinction among environments, situations, and stimuli (see Endler 1981b). Basically, the environment is the persistent and general context within which behavior is manifested. The situation is the transient or momentary context or background. Stimuli can be defined as the elements within a situation. Endler (1981b) suggested that this definition is analogous to the trait-state distinction. The environment is the enduring background (trait), and the situation (state) is the momentary or transient background. A stimulus is a component or element within the situation. As will be discussed, it is possible to compare elements within a situation and determine how this influences behavior. It is also possible to perform a comparison between situations and assess the effects of situations as wholes on behavior.

Although in theory it is possible to distinguish among environments, situations, and stimuli, in practice, the borderline between any two is frequently fuzzy. Stimuli often spill over into situations, and situations into environments. One individual's environment may be another individual's situation; one person's situation may be another person's stimulus. The individual perception of the situation (or environment, or stimulus), as will be discussed, seems to be an essential determinant of behavior. A specific situation (or environment, or stimulus) can and does have a different effect on different people.

The concepts *environment, situation,* and *stimulus* have been used interchangeably, frequently without being adequately defined. Pervin (1978b, 79) noted that "The major distinction appears to have to do with the scale of analysis—ranging from the concern with molecular variables in the case of stimulus to molar variables and behaviors in the case of the environment." In practice, however, as Pervin pointed out, this is not always the case.

Perception psychologists (and many experimental psychologists) have focused on the stimulus. Personality psychologists, who have emphasized person-by-situation interactions, have focused on the situation. Ecologists and environmental psychologists have focused on the environment. An important issue about situations is whether one can define the situation (or stimulus, or environment) independently of the perceiver. Since the significance or meaning of a situation is an essential determinant of behavior, it is necessary to examine the perception of situations when investigating the person-by-situation interaction issue. How do individuals construe the situations they select or have imposed on them and with which they interact?

Sells (1963a, 1963b) defined situations on the basis of objectively measured external characteristics. Rotter (1955) and Barker (1965) also defined situations in terms of objective characteristics. Frederiksen (1972), on the other hand, defined situations in terms of the reactions of behaviors associated with the situations. Endler and Magnusson (1976c), Endler (1981a, 1981b), and Magnusson (1978) defined the situation in terms of the individual's perception of the situation. According to Pervin (1978b, 77), "The situation-perception approach leads to definitions of situations in terms of their perceived properties or dimensions, as opposed to their objectively defined properties or their behavior-eliciting properties."

Individuals react to situations as well as affecting the situations in which they interact. Bowers (1973, 32), noted that "Situations are as much a function of the person as the person's behavior is a function of the situation." A dynamic, continuous, and constant interchange occurs beween situations and individuals, and it is necessary to assess the ongoing process. Endler (1983) suggested that one way to classify situations is on the basis of those we decide to encounter versus those imposed on us.

If we are born or decide to live in a rural area instead of a city, we are more likely to experience and encounter large distances between homes, unpolluted air, and farm animals and are less likely to have experiences and interactions with tall buildings, subways, and areas of high population density. Endler (1981b, 1982, 1983) noted that an individual who plans to attend college will probably not become a farmhand, an assembly-line operator, or be involved in (manual) labor occupations. Furthermore, a college-educated person will probably not socialize with individuals in these occupations.

These types of career choices affect not only the work that individuals do but also the kinds of homes they purchase, how they spend leisure time, the books they read, and recreational activities. We are all basically creatures of habit. Except for unusual events, such as marriages, divorces, death of a relative, and vacations, we usually are involved in the same kinds of situations from day to day and from weekend to weekend.

Much of the consistency in behavior probably occurs because we are involved in similar situations, both at work and at play, from day to day. We affect our environment, but our environment also affects us. Longitudinal studies have demonstrated consistency, which probably occurs because the situations experienced are usually similar. Cross-sectional studies have not typically demonstrated consistency of behavior, perhaps because the situations are often dissimilar. Throughout life, we frequently select situations that are rewarding and satisfactory. If we like to play tennis, we will select situations involving tennis. We look for situations that reward us and avoid those that are unpleasant. Such activity may restrict and limit the situations we encounter, but it facilitates consistency of behavior.

STRATEGIES AND METHODS FOR ASSESSING SITUATIONS

What strategies and methods are most appropriate for assessing situations, stimuli, and environments? Moos (1973) described six methods for characterizing environments: (1) ecological dimensions (e.g., architectural-physical variables, meteorological-geographical variables); (2) behavior settings, including both ecological and behavioral parameters; (3) parameters of organizational structure; (4) personal and behavioral characteristics of the environmental inhabitants; (5) psychosocial, climate, and organizational variables; and (6) variables relevant to functional analyses of environments or reinforcement. These six methods are not independent of one another. Feshbach (1978) discusses two levels of the environment of personality: (1) the situational level; and (2) the sociocultural level. He describes a third level, related to the theories, perspectives, and viewpoints that influence and determine a scientist's research program.

According to Ekehammar (1974, 1041–1042), the five major methods for studying the problems of situational classification and description are "(a) a priori defined variables of *physical* and *social* character; (b) *need* concepts; (c) some *single reaction* elicited by the situations; (d) individuals' *reaction patterns* elicited by the situations; and (e) individuals' *perceptions* (cognitions) of situations."

A number of researchers (e.g., Ekehammar 1974; Endler and Magnusson 1976b, 1976c; Magnusson 1978; and Pervin 1978) proposed a basic distinction between the objective (physical, external) factors and the subjective (psychological, internal) factors of situations and environments. As indicated, Kantor, Koffka, Lewin, and Murray made similar distinctions in the 1920s and 1930s.

Is it possible to define fully the situation (or stimulus or environment) independent of the perceiver? This is an important issue for interactional psychology since the significance or meaning of the situation is an important variable affecting behavior. It is therefore necessary to examine the perception of situations.

Actual behavior occurs in a situation or that part of the ecology (the physical and social environment) a person perceives and reacts to immediately (Murray 1938) or the momentary situation (Lewin 1936). The perception of the environment (the subjective world) can be described and discussed at different levels of generality (Endler and

Magnusson 1976b; Magnusson 1978). Similarly, the objective external world, independent of the person's perceptions of the environment, can be discussed at different levels of generality, including micro- and macroenvironments, and also physical and social factors.

The physical macroenvironment is exemplified by parks, lakes, and cities. The physical microenvironment is exemplified by single stimulus variables. Examples of the social macroenvironment are norms, cultural values, and roles common to the whole society. Examples of the social microenvironment are norms, values, habits, and attitudes common to the specific groups and individuals whom the person encounters directly, specifically at home, work, or school. The social microenvironment is part of the person's idiosyncratic milieu and is based primarily on his or her unique life experiences interacting with experiences common to the culture. The social environment is obviously more ambiguous and fluid than the physical environment.

Differential Psychology and Situations

Differential psychology usually refers to the study of individual differences. As an analogue, Magnusson (1978, 1980) proposed a differential psychology of situations to complement the differential psychology of persons. A differential psychology of situations can be discussed on the basis of a number of different dimensions, namely, impact, complexity, objectiveness, relevance, and/or subjectiveness. It is desirable, however, to obtain an adequate and representative sampling of situations.

Since personologists have attempted to develop taxonomies of traits, one can question whether it is desirable to develop taxonomies of situations. One danger of classifying both traits and situations is that different psychologists may emphasize different attributes and thus develop different taxonomies. This problem can be partially avoided by developing taxonomies on the basis of theory rather than in an arbitrary fashion. This would not necessarily ensure a homogeneity of taxonomies because different psychologists would probably propose different theories of situations (or traits). Endler (1983) proposed that a classification system should be based primarily on the situations individuals encounter and on their perceptions of these situations.

A possible strategy for assessing situations is to have individuals keep logs or diaries of their daily activities and of the situations they encounter. One could determine how individuals perceive their daily life experiences, which situations they consider pleasurable, and which ones they consider stressful. The personal projects of individuals can also be assessed. All people have projects and goals in life (e.g., preparing for a career, finding a spouse, having children, buying a home, buying a car, going on a vacation). These projects can vary over a number of parameters, including size, intensity, relevance, and scope. Situations should be examined on the basis of their meaning and on the basis of how they affect people's lives.

Pervin (1977) sampled situations ecologically in terms of people's natural habitats. Examining people's free responses of their perceptions and their affective and behavioral responses to their daily routines, he classified the variables on the basis of a factor analysis. Pervin concluded that the person-by-situation interaction was the most relevant unit of analysis. Magnusson (1978, 8) indicated that the actual situation is central for "understanding the development process and actual behavior."

Situation Perception and Situation Reaction Empirical Studies

Much research on situations has used the situation perception and situation reaction research strategies (see Ekehammar 1974). Endler and Magnusson (1976b, 15) noted that "The psychological significance of the environment can be investigated by studying the individual's *perception* of the situation (the meaning he assigns to a situation) and *reaction* to a situation (a specific situation or the general environment)."

Magnusson (1971, 851) pointed out that "individuals differ not mainly with regard to certain stable characteristics of behavior but particularly regarding their specific characteristic ways of adjusting to the varying characteristics of different situations." Magnusson and Ekehammar (1973), using an empirical psychophysical method for studying the perception of situations (developed by Magnusson 1971), investigated situations common to university students. They found two bipolar dimensions (positive versus negative, and active versus passive) and one unipolar dimension (social). In a subsequent study (Ekehammar and Magnusson, 1973) with stressful situations, they obtained basically the same results. The meaning or perception of the situation was an important determinant of behavior.

A number of investigators have conducted situation-reaction studies. According to Frederiksen (1972) and Rotter (1954), situations can be classified on the basis of the similarity of behavior evoked in persons; the goal is to develop taxonomies of situations. Most situation-reaction studies used data from questionnaires or inventories originally developed for research purposes (e.g., S-R Inventory of Anxiousness—Endler, Hunt, and Rosenstein 1962; Interactional Reactions Questionnaire—Ekehammar, Magnusson, and Ricklander 1974; Magnusson and Ekehammar 1975a; Stressful Situations Questionnaire—Hodges and Felling 1970). Endler et al. (1962), factor analyzing the situations of the S-R Inventory of Anxiousness, found three situational factors: interpersonal threat, inanimate physical danger, and ambiguous. Endler and Magnusson (1976a) obtained similar results for a factor analysis of the S-R Inventory of General Trait Anxiousness (Endler and Okada 1957).

Magnusson and Ekehammar (1975b, 1978) and Ekehammar, Shalling, and Magnusson (1975) studied the relationship between situation perception and situation reaction for the same individuals. The relationship between perceptions and reactions has implications for interactional psychology because reactions to situations are to a great extent influenced by the perception of the situations.

Magnusson and Ekehammar (1975b) and Ekehammar, Schalling, and Magnusson (1975) collected situation-perception and situation-reaction data on the same group subjects. The congruence between categories of situation and categories of reactions for three of the four a priori groups of situations was about .90; for the fourth group, it was about .70. Magnusson and Ekehammar (1978), analyzing individual data rather than group data, obtained essentially the same results.

Studies on the psychological aspects of situations indicate that it is important to distinguish between the perception of and the reaction to situations. Although two persons may perceive a situation as threatening, one may react by withdrawing and the other by attacking the situation. Furthermore, at different periods the same person may react differently to the same specific situation. At time A, an individual may withdraw from a threatening situation, whereas at time B, the same person may attack a similar threatening situation. Contextual, motivational, and experiential factors also affect the relationship between the perception of and the reaction to situations. New situations are perceived differently than familiar ones.

Between and Within Situations

One can compare elements (stimuli) within a situation and evaluate how they affect behavior, and/or one can make a comparison between situations and determine the effects of situations as wholes on behavior. Most empirical research on situationism and interactionism has investigated the situation as a whole and performed a comparison between situations. However, it is possible to examine the situational cues or elements within a situation. The elements within a situation interact with one another and change in the process (Magnusson and Endler 1977).

During a debate, for example, Bill's reaction to Jim, as opponent, is affected by Jim's reaction to Bill; and both of their reactions to their interaction (the situation) are probably affected by the audience and the nonverbal cues they receive from the audience. Ideally, we should examine this continuous and ongoing process (Endler 1978; Magnusson 1976), but we usually assess a cross-sectional portion of it at one particular time. "One can construe a situation as a dynamic process in which a person selects certain elements or events (primarily other persons) and is in turn affected by these other elements" (Endler 1977, 356). Elements of situations in interactional psychology refer to both person-by-situation interactions and person-by-person interactions.

UNITS OF SITUATIONAL ANALYSIS

How do we decide on the most appropriate units of analysis for environments and situations? Psychologists have usually been scrupulous about obtaining representative samples of persons in their research. However, they have taken little care to obtain representative and unbiased samplings of situations and environments. About thirty years ago, Brunswik (1952, 1956) emphasized the need to obtain representative samplings of situations. Now, in the 1980s, his suggestions have gone largely unheeded. There are definitional and conceptual problems in addition to the problem of sampling. What should be the basic unit of analysis? Do situations vary in their relative impact? Can individuals respond independently of situations? When does a situation begin and when does it end? How long does a situation last? (See Endler 1983.)

What are the most appropriate size and kind of units in personality research? In the investigation of persons, traits have been the most prominent units of analysis, but some research has studied motives and defenses. There have not been many systematic investigations of the most appropriate units for classifying stimuli, situations, and environments. Nevertheless, there has been a dramatic increase in studying the roles of situations and environments in personality research. A number of psychologists have proposed that the person-by-situation interaction unit is the best one for personality research (e.g., Endler 1981b; Murray 1938; Pervin 1977; Raush 1977). Murray (1938) suggested that need-press (person-situation) units or themes are most appropriate for personality research. Now, more than forty years later, no one has yet conducted systematic studies of the person-by-situation interaction unit.

Using the person as the basic unit of analysis, there have been systematic longitudinal and/or intensive investigations of persons (e.g, Block 1977, 1981; Levinson 1978; White 1966, 1976). No one has yet conducted programmatic longitudinal investigations of the situations people encounter, nor longitudinal studies of person-by-situation interactions.

Since the 1970s, social psychologists (including ecologists) and personologists have conducted some studies emphasizing person-by-situation interactions. Environmental psychologists have studied how individuals perceive situations and environments. Stokols (1972) defined crowding as a perceptual or phenomenological variable rather than as a physical density variable. Density refers to physical space limitations, but crowding refers to the person's perception of the restricting aspects of these space limitations. Crowding is basically concerned with the interaction among social, environmental, and personal variables. A number of studies on anxiety, locus of control, and conformity have been done within the context of person-by-treatment (situation) experimental design. (See earlier in this chapter for a summary; see also Endler and Edwards 1978 for more details.)

Person-by-situation interactions also include person-by-person interactions as a subset. Other individuals with whom we interact serve as our situational context or stimuli to which we react. Patterson and Moore (1978) define interactionism in terms of person-by-person interactions because other people provide important cues for our behavior and are an important ingredient of our situational encounters. In interaction with others, our behavior is largely influenced by our anticipation of how others will react to our behavior. The reactions of others serve as stimuli for our own behavior. Interaction is a continuous and ongoing process.

The interaction process is characterized by a dynamic change of ongoing events. However, for research purposes, we abstract relevant situation and person variables and arbitrarily assess a shorter slice of this continuous process. Individuals actively seek out and select the other persons and situations with which they interact. They also have situations imposed on them, and situations have a profound effect on people (Endler 1982, 1983). Individuals, however, are not passive victims of situations and environments; they are active and intentional stimulus-seeking organisms.

Although it is important to continue conducting laboratory studies, it is essential to conduct real-life studies. Although real-life studies are costly, complex, difficult, and lack the precision of laboratory studies, they have a higher degree of relevance for what really happens in the complex interaction process. Laboratory and real-life studies complement one another; both are necessary.

ORIGINS AND FUTURE OF INTERACTIONAL PSYCHOLOGY

This chapter has reveiwed the historical theoretical and historical and current empirical facets of interactionism. What direction should interactional psychology take in terms of theory and research?

Progress has been made in isolating some theoretically important and relevant variables of interactional psychology. However, we are just beginning to explain and understand the effective functional relationship between antecedent conditions (independent variables) and the behavior they control or influence (dependent variables). (See Endler and Edwards 1978; Endler 1981a.) Along with making progress on these two goals of science, we should attempt to examine behavioral processes to explain and predict behavior (see Endler 1981a). We should simultaneously investigate both mechanistic and dynamic interactions.

The variance components studies of mechanistic interaction are descriptive rather than predictive. The results do not explain interactions. Nevertheless, the person-by-treatment (situation) experimental studies enable us to predict the nature and direction of mechanistic interpretations, especially if the studies are formulated within the context of a theory. For example, the studies summarized in this chapter of the differential hypotheses of the multidimensional interaction model of anxiety (Endler 1980) enable us to make specific predictions about the nature of interactions. However, the results of these studies are incomplete because they focus on two specific periods of time and do not tell anything about the continuous dynamic interaction process. We need to develop methods and strategies for investigating dynamic processes.

Interaction Strategies and Methods

Initially, the best strategy for investigating interactions is to focus on the structure of interactions (i.e., mechanistic interactions). This focus enables us to understand the effective and predictive (independent) variables and the behavioral reactions (dependent variables) they affect. The anxiety studies summarized in this chapter provide a valiant start in this direction. However, these studies need to be supplemented by studies of interaction processes and dynamic interactions.

The concepts of consistency (stability) and change are complex and have relevance not only for the field of personality but also in the investigation of developmental processes. Endler (1983) noted that although organisms change in the course of development, this change occurs within a context of continuity and stability (or consistency). Rules or regularities guide change; there is a lawfulness or orderliness or coherence to behavior. If there were not, then human behavior and interaction would be chaotic.

Perhaps we should focus on rules and strategies of interaction rather than on content. The understanding and meaning of a tennis game, for example, is largely determined by the game's rules and strategies rather than by the specific content of a single game. Rather than making specific predictions about the specific contents of social interaction, Argyle (1977) proposed that we examine and analyze the generative rules of social interaction. Mischel (1973) recommended that we study the encoding and decoding strategies people use. Similarly, we should infer the rules and strategies that people use in interactions with others and with situations.

The Relationship among Theory, Content, and Method

During the 1970s and and early 1980s, various methods were developed and used for investigating the dynamic interaction process and for studying individuals intensively. Peterson (1977) studied person-by-person interactions in married couples. Raush (1977) used Markov chains for studying interactions, and Argyle (1977) studied rules and strategies for social interaction in order to infer generative rules of interaction. Mischel (1973) discussed encoding and decoding strategies, and Epstein (1979, 1980) studied aggregates of behavior during thirty-day periods. Pervin (1977) developed techniques for having individuals generate their own situations, and Block (1977, 1981) conducted intensive longitudinal studies.

Content (subject matter), methodology (technology), and theory are inextricably intertwined and enhance one another's development (Endler 1981a, 1983). At present, we are limited by a lack of fully developed and appropriate methodologies for studying interactions, but promising starts have been made. Recent developments in causal modeling, including cross-lagged correlations and path analysis (see Asher 1976) and the use of Markov changes in personality research can enhance our investigations of interaction processes and the development of interactional theories of personality. Person-by-situation interactions may be more appropriate units of analysis in preference to persons or situations per se. We should also examine chains of events continuously rather than a few discrete events. It is important to assess the dynamic interplay between people and situations and to determine both how situations affect people and how people affect situations.

Methods of Investigating Situations

As indicated, the two major tasks for an interactional psychology of personality are an assessment of interactions and the description, classification, and systematic analyses of situations.

For situations, it is essential to distinguish between the perceptions of situations and the reactions to situations and to differentiate the objective from the subjective aspects of situations. It is also necessary to distinguish between the situation as a whole and the specific elements within a situation. Much research on situations has focused on their macro aspects and has emphasized differences between situations rather than specific elements within a specific situation.

Future research on situations should ensure a representative and random sampling of situations to avoid biased conclusions. The multidirectional and multicausal elements within a siuation and the chain of events or process of interaction also need to be studied. Chains of events include other people as well as situations because other individuals serve as situational cues for us and influence and are influenced by our behavior. Chains of person-by-situation units need to be studied to understand the interaction process.

SUMMARY AND CONCLUSIONS

Personality research and theory showed a lot of promise during the 1970s but not much fulfillment. However, conceptual, theoretical, empirical, and methodological advances have occurred. Theory and research have been guided by four major models: trait psychology, psychodynamics, situationism, and interactionism. Although trait psychology has had the major influence, the model making the greatest strides in terms of theory and research during the 1970s and early 1980s has been interactionism.

The discussion of historical antecedents of modern interactionism pointed out that the empirical research of the 1950s and 1960s developed almost independently of the theoretical foundations of the 1920s, 1930s, 1940s, and 1950s. The research in the 1970s and early 1980s has been related to earlier theoretical formulations.

Extrascientific factors influencing personality theory and research were discussed; science is not value-free but is influenced by personal, political, and social factors. Most early work in personality related to studies of individual differences and underestimated the role of situation factors while overestimating the role of person factors. During the last half century, social and political factors shifted the emphasis toward situational factors, but today most personologists recognize the role of both situational and personal factors and their interactions.

The two basic tasks for an interactional psychology of personality are (1) the examination of how persons and situations interact in determining behavior; and (2) the description, classification, and systematic analysis of situations, including stimuli, and environments. The person-by-situation interaction debate was discussed in the context of comparing the trait, psychodynamic, situationism, and interaction models of personality.

Controversial issues of interactionism have largely fueled the significant recent research in personality. These issues include situational specificity versus cross-situational consistency, persons versus situations, reaction variables versus mediation variables, and the basic distinction between psychological process models and their measurement models. Distinctions were made among absolute consistency, relative consistency, and coherence.

A survey of the empirical literature regarding the consistency versus specificity issue indicated that three major research strategies have been used: multidimensional variance components techniques, correlations, and personality-by-treatment experimental designs. The results indicate that even though evidence exists for longitudinal consistency for the consistency of the mediating structural variable (but not for the mediating content and motivational variables), little evidence exists for cross-situational consistency of personality and social variables. Person-by-situation interactions seem to be important predictors of behavior.

The distinction was made between mechanistic (structural) and dynamic (process) interaction; most empirical studies investigated mechanistic interaction. Future studies should focus on dynamic interaction.

The role of situations in personality was evaluated; there is often a failure to distinguish among stimuli, situations, and environments. People are influenced by situations and to a great extent select and influence the situations with which they interact. Strategies and methods for assessing situations were described and results of situation perception versus situation reaction were discussed. A distinction was also made comparing between situation studies and within situation studies. The problem of the basic unit of analysis was evaluated; a need exists for a differential psychology of situations.

The present and future status of interactional psychology were evaluated; although progress had been made in isolating effective and predictive variables and in examining the functional relationships between antecedent conditions and the behavior they control, little progress had been made in examining behavioral processes. Strategies for studying interactions were presented; recent promising developments have occurred in using causal modeling techniques and Markov chains for studying interactions. Rushton, Jackson, and Paunonen (1981) in a reply to Kenrick and Stringfield (1980), who opt for an idiographic approach, noted that the nomothetic approach to personality may be predictive of consistency of behavior when aggregates of responses are used. This may be related to our emphasis on the need to study processes. However, intensive studies of individuals and ideographic approaches can complement the nomothetic approach.

The discussion of relationships among theory, method, and content noted that perhaps we should concentrate on rules and strategies of interaction rather than on content. It is necessary to develop new strategies and new methodologies for studying dynamic interaction processes and for investigating situations. Until we develop new research strategies and new methodologies, and until we develop new ways of conceptualizing the important problems and issues of personality research, progress in an interactional psychology of personality will be limited.

ENDNOTES

1. The author thanks Jean M. Edwards for her comments and assistance in compiling the references.

2. This chapter was completed while the author had a Research Fellowship from the Faculty of Arts, York University, Toronto, Ontario, Canada.

REFERENCES

Allport, G. W. *Personality: A psychological interpretation.* New York: Holt, Rinehart and Winston, 1937.

Allport, G. W. Traits revisited. *American Psychologist,* 1966, *21,* 1-10.

Angyal, A. *Foundations for a science of personality.* Cambridge: Harvard University Press, 1941.

Argyle, M. Predictive and generative rules models of P × S interaction. In D. Magnusson & N. S. Endler (Eds.), *Personality at the crossroads: Current issues in interactional psychology.* Hillsdale, N.J.: Lawrence Erlbaum Associates, 1977.

Argyle, M., & Little, B. R. Do personality traits apply to social behaviour? *Journal for the Theory of Social Behaviour,* 1972, *2,* 1-35.

Asher, H. B. *Causal modeling.* Sage University Paper Series on Quantitative Applications in the Social Sciences series No. 07-003. Beverly Hills, Calif., and London: Sage Publications, 1976.

Bandura, A. (Ed.). *Psychological modeling: Conflicting theories.* New York: Aldine-Atherton, 1971.

Bandura, A. Self-efficacy: Toward a unifying theory of behavioral change. *Psychological Review,* 1977, *84,* 191-215.

Barker, R. G. Explorations in ecological psychology. *American Psychologist,* 1965, *20,* 1-14.

Baron, R. M., Cowan, G., Ganz, R. L., & McDonald, M. Interaction of locus of control and type of performance feedback. Considerations of external validity. *Journal of Personality and Social Psychology,* 1974, *30,* 285-292.

Baron, R. M., & Ganz, R. L. Effects of locus of control and type of feedback on the task performance of lower-class black children. *Journal of Personality and Social Psychology,* 1972, *21,* 124-130.

Berkowitz, L. Situational and personal conditions governing reaction to aggressive cues. In D. Magnusson & N. S. Endler (Eds.), *Personality at the crossroads: Current issues in interactional psychology.* Hillsdale, N.J.: Lawrence Erlbaum Associates, 1977.

Block, J. Advancing the psychology of personality: Paradigmatic shift or improving the quality of research. In D. Magnusson & N. S. Endler (Eds.), *Personality at the crossroads: Current issues in interactional psychology.* Hillsdale, N.J.: Lawrence Erlbaum Associates, 1977.

Block, J. Some enduring and consequential structure of personality. In A. I. Rabin, J. Aronoff, A. M. Barclay, & R. A. Zucker (Eds.), *Further explorations in personality.* New York: John Wiley and Sons, 1981.

Bowers, K. S. Situationism in psychology: An analysis and a critique. *Psychological Review,* 1973, *80,* 307–336.

Brunswik, E. *The conceptual framework of psychology.* Chicago: University of Chicago Press, 1952.

Brunswik, E. *Perception and the representative design of psychological experiments.* Berkeley: University of California Press, 1956.

Burton, R. V. Generality of honesty reconsidered. *Psychological Review,* 1963, *70,* 481–499.

Cattell, R. B. *The description and measurement of personality.* New York: World Book, 1946.

Cattell, R. B. *Personality and motivation structure and measurement.* Yonkers-on-Hudson, N.Y.: World Book, 1957.

Cooley, C. H. *Human nature and the social order.* New York: Scribner's, 1902.

Cottrell, L. S., Jr. The adjustment of the individual to his age and sex roles. *American Sociological Review,* 1942, *7,* 618–625. (a)

Cottrell, L. S., Jr. The analysis of situational fields. *American Sociological Review,* 1942, *7,* 370–382. (b)

Davis, W. L., & Phares, E. J. Internal-external control as a determinant of information seeking in a social influence situation. *Journal of Personality,* 1967, *35,* 547–561.

Dewey, R., & Humber, W. J. *The development of human behavior.* New York: Macmillan, 1951.

Diveky, S., & Endler, N. S. *The interaction model of anxiety: State and trait anxiety for banking executives in normal working environments.* Unpublished manuscript, York University, Toronto, 1977.

Dollard, J., & Miller, N. E. *Personality and psychotherapy: An analysis in terms of learning, thinking and culture.* New York: McGraw-Hill, 1950.

Ekehammar, B. Interactionism in personality from a historical perspective. *Psychological Bulletin,* 1974, *81,* 1026–1048.

Ekehammar, B., & Magnusson, D. A method to study stressful situations. *Journal of Personality and Social Psychology,* 1973, *27,* 176–179.

Ekehammar, B., Magnusson, D., & Ricklander, L. An interactionist approach to the study of anxiety: An analysis of an S-R inventory applied to an adolescent sample. *Scandinavian Journal of Psychology*, 1974, *15*, 4–14.

Ekehammar, B., Schalling, D., & Magnusson, D. Dimensions of stressful situations: A comparison between a response analytical and a stimulus analytical approach. *Multivariate Behavioral Research*, 1975, *10*, 155–164.

Endler, N. S. Conformity as a function of different reinforcement schedules. *Journal of Personality and Social Psychology*, 1966, *4*, 175–180. (a)

Endler, N. S. The Effect of Person by Situation Interactions on Anxiety. Research Grant Proposal to the Canada Council, August 1973.

Endler, N. S. The case for person-situation interactions. *Canadian Psychological Review*, 1975, *16*, 12–21. (a)

Endler, N. S. A person-situation interaction model of anxiety. In C. D. Spielberger & I. G. Sarason (Eds.), *Stress and anxiety* (Vol. 1). Washington, D.C.: Hemisphere Publishing Corporation (Wiley), 1975. (b)

Endler, N. S. Grand illusions: Traits or interactions? *Canadian Psychological Review*, 1976, *17*, 174–181.

Endler, N. S. The role of person by situation interactions in personality theory. In I. C. Uzgiris & F. Weizmann (Eds.), *The structuring of experience*. New York: Plenum Press, 1977.

Endler, N. S. The interaction model of anxiety: Some possible implications. In D. M. Landers & R. W. Christina (Eds.), *Psychology of motor behavior and sport—1977.* Champaign, Ill.: Human Kinetics, 1978.

Endler, N. S. Person-situation interaction and anxiety. In I. L. Kutash & L. B. Schlesinger (Eds.), *Handbook on stress and anxiety: Contemporary knowledge, theory and treatment*. San Francisco, Calif.: Jossey-Bass, 1980.

Endler, N. S. Persons, situations and their interactions. In A. I. Rabin (Ed.), *Further explorations in personality*. New York: Wiley,1981.(a)

Endler, N. S. Situational apsects of interactional psychology. In D. Magnusson (Ed.), *Toward a psychology of situations: An interactional perspective*. Hillsdale, N.J.: Lawrence Erlbaum Associates, 1981. (b)

Endler, N. S. Interactionism comes of age. In M. P. Zanna, E. T. Higgins, & C. P. Herman (Eds.), *Consistency in social behavior: The Ontario Symposium* (Vol. 2). Hillsdale, N.J.: Lawrence Erlbaum Associates, 1982.

Endler, N. S. Interactionism. In N. S. Endler and J. McV. Hunt (Eds.), *Personality and the behavior disorders* (2nd ed.). New York: John Wiley and Sons, 1983.

Endler, N. S., & Edwards, J. Person by treatment interactions in personality research. In L. A. Pervin & M. Lewis (Eds.), *Interaction between internal and external determinants of behavior.* New York: Plenum Press, 1978.

Endler, N. S., Edwards, J., & McGuire, A. *The interaction model of anxiety: An empirical test in a theatrical performance situation.* Unpublished manuscript, York University, Toronto, 1979.

Endler, N. S., & Hoy, E. Conformity as related to reinforcement and social pressure. *Journal of Personality and Social Psychology,* 1967, *7,* 197–202.

Endler, N. S., & Hunt, J. McV. Sources of behavioral variance as measured by the S-R Inventory of Anxiousness. *Psychological Bulletin,* 1966, *65,* 336–346.

Endler, N. S., & Hunt, J. McV. S-R inventories of hostility and comparisons of the proportions of variance from persons, responses and situations for hostility and anxiousness. *Journal of Personality and Social Psychology,* 1968, *9,* 309–315.

Endler, N. S., & Hunt, J. McV. Generalizability of contributions from sources of variance in the S-R Inventory of Anxiousness. *Journal of Personality,* 1969, *37,* 1–24.

Endler, N. S., Hunt, J. McV., & Rosenstein, A. J. An S-R Inventory of Anxiousness. *Psychological Monographs,* 1962, *76,* No. 17 (Whole No. 536), 1–33.

Endler, N. S., King, P. R., Kuczynski, M., & Edwards, J. Examination induced anxiety: An empirical test of the interaction model. *Department of Psychology Reports,* York University, 1980, No. 97.

Endler, N. S., & Magnusson, D. Multidimensional aspects of state and trait anxiety: A cross-cultural study of Canadian and Swedish college students. In C. D. Spielberger & R. Diaz Guerrero (Eds.), *Cross-cultural anxiety.* Washington, D.C.: Hemisphere Publishing Corporation (Wiley), 1976. (a)

Endler, N. S., & Magnusson, D. Personality and person by situation interactions. In N. S. Endler & D. Magnusson (Eds.), *Interactional psychology and personality.* Washington, D.C.: Hemisphere Publishing Corporation (Wiley), 1976. (b)

Endler, N. S., & Magnusson, D. Toward an interactional psychology of personality. *Psychological Bulletin,* 1976, *83,* 956–974. (c)

Endler, N. S., & Magnusson, D. The interaction model for anxiety: An empirical test in an examination situation. *Canadian Journal of Behavioural Science,* 1977, *0,* 101–107.

Endler, N. S., & Okada, M. An S-R Inventory of General Trait Anxiousness. *Department of Psychology Reports*, York University, Toronto, 1974, No. 1.

Endler, N. S., & Okada, M. A multidimensional measure of trait anxiety: The S-R Inventory of General Trait Anxiousness. *Journal of Consulting and Clinical Psychology*, 1975, *43*, 319–329.

Epstein, S. Traits are alive and well. In D. Magnusson & N. S. Endler (Eds.), *Personality at the crossroads: Current issues in interactional psychology*. Hillsdale, N.J.: Lawrence Erlbaum Associates, 1977.

Epstein, S. The stability of behavior: I. On predicting most of the people much of the time. *Journal of Personality and Social Psychology*, 1979, *37*, 1097–1126.

Epstein, S. The stability of behavior: II. Implications for psychological research. *American Psychologist*, 1980, *35*, 790–806.

Erikson, E. *Childhood and society* (2nd ed.). New York: Norton, 1963.

Fleshbach, S. The environment of personality. *American Psychologist*, 1978, *33*, 447–455.

Fiedler, F. E. Validation and extension of the contingency model of leadership effectiveness: A review of empirical findings. *Psychological Bulletin*, 1971, *76*, 128–148.

Fiedler, F. E. What triggers the person situation interaction in leadership? In D. Magnusson & N. S. Endler (Eds.), *Personality at the crossroads: Current issues in interactional psychology*. Hillsdale, N.J.: Lawrence Erlbaum Associates, 1977.

Flood, M., & Endler, N. S. The interaction model of anxiety: An empirical test in an athletic competition situation. *Journal of Research in Personality*, 1980, *14*, 329–339.

Frederiksen, N. Toward a taxonomy of situations. *American Psychologist*, 1972, *27*, 114–123.

Freud, S. *Collected papers.* Vols. I–V. New York: Basic Books, 1959.

Fromm, E. *The sane society.* New York: Rinehart, 1955.

Guilford, J. P. *Personality.* New York: McGraw-Hill, 1959.

Hartshorne, H., & May, M. A. *Studies in the nature of character:* 1. *Studies in deceit.* New York: Macmillan, 1928.

Hodges, W. F., & Felling, J. P. Types of stressful situations and their relation to trait anxiety and sex. *Journal of Consulting and Clinical Psychology*, 1970, *34*, 333–337.

Horney, K. *Our inner conflicts.* New York: W. W. Norton, 1945.

Houston, B. K. Control over stress, locus of control, and response to stress. *Journal of Personality and Social Psychology*, 1972, *21*, 249–255.

Hunt, J. McV. Traditional personality theory in the light of recent evidence. *American Scientist*, 1965, *53*, 80–96.

Ichheiser, G. Misinterpretations of personality in everyday life and the psychologist's frame of reference. *Character and Personality*, 1943, *12*, 145-160.

Jessor, R. Phenomenological personality theories and the data language of psychology. *Psychological Review*, 1956, *63*, 173-180.

Jessor, R. The problem of reductionism in psychology. *Psychological Review*, 1958, *65*, 170-178.

Kantor, J. R. *Principles of psychology* (Vol. 1). Bloomington, Ill.: Principia Press, 1924.

Kantor, J. R. *Principles of psychology* (Vol. 2). Bloomington, Ill.: Principia Press, 1926.

Kantor, J. R. *The scientific evolution of psychology* (Vol. 2). Chicago: Principia Press, 1969.

Kendall, P. C. Anxiety: States, traits—situations? *Journal of Consulting and Clinical Psychology*, 1978, *46*, 280-287.

Kenrick, D. T., & Stringfield, D. O. Personality traits and the eye of the beholder: Crossing some traditional philosophical boundaries in the search for consistency in all of the people. *Psychological Review*, 1980, *87*, 88-104.

King, P. R., & Endler, N. S. Medical intervention and the interaction model of anxiety. *Department of Psychology Reports*, York University, 1980, No. 98.

Koffka, K. *Principles of Gestalt psychology*. New York: Harcourt, 1935.

Lefcourt, H. M., Lewis, L., & Silverman, I. W. Internal vs. external control of reinforcement and attention in a decision making task. *Journal of Personality*, 1968, *36*, 663-682.

Levinson, D. J. *The seasons of a man's life*. New York: Alfred A. Knopf, 1978.

Lewin, K. *A dynamic theory of personality. Selected papers*. New York: McGraw-Hill, 1935.

Lewin, K. *Principles of topological psychology*. New York: McGraw-Hill, 1936.

Magnusson, D. An analysis of situational dimensions. *Perceptual and Motor Skills*, 1971, *32*, 851-967.

Magnusson, D. The person and the situation in an interactional model of behavior. *Scandinavian Journal of Psychology*, 1976, *17*, 253-271.

Magnusson, D. On the psychological situation. *Reports from the Department of Psychology*, University of Stockholm, 1978, No. 544.

Magnusson, D. Personality in an interactional paradigm of research. *Zeitschrift fur Differentialle und Diagnostiche Psychologie*, 1980, *1*, 17-34.

Magnusson, D., & Ekehammar, B. An analysis of situational dimensions: A replication. *Multivariate Behavioral Research*, 1973, *8*, 331-339.

Magnusson, D., & Ekehammar, B. Anxiety profiles based on both situational and response factors. *Multivariate Behavioral Research*, 1975, *10*, 27-43. (a)

Magnusson, D., & Ekehammar, B. Perceptions of and reactions to stressful situations. *Journal of Personality and Social Psychology*, 1975, *31*, 1147-1154. (b)

Magnusson, D., & Ekehammar, B. Similar situations—similar behaviors? *Journal of Research in Personality*, 1978, *12*, 41-48.

Magnusson, D., & Endler, N. S. Interactional psychology: Present status and future prospects. In D. Magnusson & N. Endler (Eds.), *Personality at the crossroads: Current issues in interactional psychology*. Hillsdale, N.J.: Lawrence Erlbaum Associates, 1977.

Magnusson, D., Gerzén, M., & Nyman, B. The generality of behavioral data: I. Generalization from observations on one occasion. *Multivariate Behavioral Research*, 1968, *3*, 295-320.

Magnusson, D., & Heffler, B. The generality of behavioral data: III. Generalization potential as a function of the number of observation instances. *Multivariate Behavioral Research*, 1969, *4*, 29-42.

Magnusson, D., Heffler, B., & Nyman, B. The generality of behavioral data: II. Replication of an experiment on generalization from observation on one occasion. *Multivariate Behavioral Research*, 1968, *3*, 415-422.

McClelland, D. C. *Personality*. New York: Wm. Sloane Assoc. (now Holt, Rinehart & Winston), 1951.

Mead, G. H. *Mind, self and society*. Chicago: University of Chicago Press, 1934.

Mischel, W. *Personality and assessment*. New York: Wiley, 1968.

Mischel, W. Continuity and change in personality. *American Psychologist*, 1969, *24*, 1012-1018.

Mischel, W. Toward a cognitive social learning reconceptualization of personality. *Psychological Review*, 1973, *80*, 252-283.

Moos, R. H. Conceptualizations of human environments. *American Psychologist*, 1973, *28*, 652-665.

Moyer, K. E. The physiology of violence. *Psychology Today*, 1973, *7*, 35-38.

Murphy, G. *Personality: A biosocial approach to origins and structure*. New York: Harper, 1947.

Murray, H. A. *Explorations in personality*. New York: Oxford University Press, 1938.

Nelson, E. A., Grinder, R. E., & Mutterer, M. L. Sources of variance in behavioural measures of honesty in temptation situations: Methodological analyses. *Developmental Psychology*, 1969, *1*, 265-279.

Newcomb, T. M. An experiment designed to test the validity of a rating technique. *Journal of Educational Psychology*, 1931, *22*, 279-289.

Olweus, D. A critical analysis of the modern interactionist position. In D. Magnusson & N. S. Endler (Eds.), *Personality at the crossroads: Current issues in interactional psychology*. Hillsdale, N.J.: Lawrence Erlbaum Associates, 1977.

Olweus, D. Stability of aggressive reaction patterns in males: A review. *Psychological Bulletin*, 1979, *86*, 852-875.

Overton, W. F., & Reese, H. W. Models of development: Methodological implications. In J. R. Nesselroads & H. W. Reese (Eds.), *Life span developmental psychology: Methodological issues*. New York: Academic Press, 1973, 65-86.

Patterson, G. R., & Moore, D. R. Interactive patterns as units. In S. J. Suomi, M. E. Lamb, & G. R. Stevenson (Eds.), *The study of social interaction: Methodological issues*. Madison: University of Wisconsin Press, 1978.

Pervin, L. A. Performance and satisfaction as a function of individual-environment fit. *Psychological Bulletin*, 1968, *69*, 56-68.

Pervin, L. A. The representative design of person-situation research. In D. Magnusson & N. S. Endler (Eds.), *Personality at the crossroads: Current issues in interactional psychology*. Hillsdale, N.J.: Lawrence Erlbaum Associates, 1977.

Pervin, L. A. *Current controversies and issues in personality*. New York: Wiley, 1978. (a)

Pervin, L. A. Definitions, measurements, and classifications of stimuli, situations, and environments. *Human Ecology*, 1978, *6*, 71-105. (b)

Peterson, D. R. A functional approach to the study of person-person interactions. In D. Magnusson & N. S. Endler (Eds.), *Personality at the crossroads: Current issues in interactional psychology*. Hillsdale, N.J.: Lawrence Erlbaum Associates, 1977.

Phillips, J. B., & Endler, N. S. Academic examinations and anxiety: The interaction model empirically tested. *Department of Psychology Reports*, York University, 1980, No. 99.

Rapaport, D., Gill, M., & Schafer, R. *Diagnostic psychological testing*. Chicago: Year Book, 1945 (2 volumes).

Raush, H. L. Interaction sequences. *Journal of Personality and Social Psychology*, 1965, *2*, 487-499.

Raush, H. L. Paradox, levels and junctures in person-situation systems. In D. Magnusson & N. S. Endler (Eds.), *Personality at the cross-*

roads: Current issues in interactional psychology. Hillsdale, N.J.: Lawrence Erlbaum Associates, 1977.

Raush, H. L. Dittmann, A. T., & Taylor, T. J. The interpersonal behavior of children in residential treatment. *Journal of Abnormal and Social Psychology,* 1959, *58,* 9-26. (a)

Raush, H. L., Dittmann, A. T., & Taylor, T. J. Person, setting and change in social interaction. *Human Relations,* 1959, *12,* 361-378. (b)

Rotter, J. B. *Social learning and clinical psychology.* Englewood Cliffs, N.J.: Prentice-Hall, 1954.

Rotter, J. B. The role of the psychological situation in determining the direction of human behavior. In M. R. Jones (Ed.), *Nebraska Symposium on Motivation.* University of Nebraska Press, Lincoln, 1955, 245-268.

Rotter, J. B. Generalized expectancies for internal versus external control of reinforcement. *Psychological Monographs,* 1966, *80* (1, Whole No. 609).

Rotter, J. B. Some problems and misconceptions related to the construct of internal versus external control of reinforcement. *Journal of Consulting and Clinical Psychology,* 1975, *43,* 56-67.

Rushton, J. P. Socialization and the altruistic behavior of children. *Psychological Bulletin,* 1976, *83,* 898-913.

Rushton, J. P., & Endler, N. S. Person by situation interactions in academic achievement. *Journal of Personality,* 1977, *45,* 297-309.

Rushton, J. P., Jackson, D. N., & Paunonen, S. V. Personality: Nomothetic or idiographic? A response to Kenrick and Stringfield. *Psychological Review,* 1981, *88,* 582-589.

Sarason, I. G., Smith, R. E., & Diener, E. Personality research: Components of variance attributable to the person and the situation. *Journal of Personality and Social Psychology,* 1975, *32,* 199-294.

Sells, S. B. Dimensions of stimulus situations which account for behavior variances. In S. B. Sells (Ed.), *Stimulus determinants of behavior.* New York: Ronald Press, 1963. (a)

Sells, S. B. An interactionist looks at the environment. *American Psychologist,* 1963, *18,* 696-702. (b)

Sherman, S. J. Internal-external locus of control and its relationship to attitude change under different influence techniques. *Journal of Personality and Social Psychology,* 1973, *26,* 23-29.

Shute, C. Aristotle's interactionism and its transformations by some 20th century writers. *Psychological Record,* 1973, *23,* 283-293.

Skinner, B. F. *Science and human behavior.* New York: Macmillan, 1953.

Spielberger, C. D. Anxiety as an emotional state. In C. D. Spielberger (Ed.), *Anxiety: Current trends in theory and research* (Vol. 1). New York: Academic Press, 1972.

Stokols, D. On the distinction between density and crowding: Some implications for future research. *Psychological Review*, 1972, *79*, 275–277.

Sullivan, H. S. *The interpersonal theory of psychiatry.* New York: Norton, 1953.

Tolman, E. C. Psychology versus immediate experience. In E. C. Tolman, *Collected papers in psychology.* Berkeley: University of California Press, 1951. (Reprinted from *Philosophy of Science*, 1935, *2*, 356–380.)

White, R. W. *Lives in progress* (2nd ed.). New York: Holt, Rinehart and Winston, 1966.

White, R. W. *The enterprise of living: A view of personal growth* (2nd ed.). New York: Holt, Rinehart and Winston, 1976.

Witkin, H. A., & Goodenough, D. R. Field dependence and interpersonal behavior. *Research Bulletin of the Educational Testing Service*, Princeton, N.J.: 1976.

2. Interactionism in Psychology: A Critical Analysis of the S-R Inventories

ADRIAN FURNHAM
University of London

INTRODUCTION

Like philosophy, psychology has many central questions that are fashionable to discuss and debate. One of the oldest is the extent to which stable internal (personality) or external (situational) factors determine social behavior. This debate and research area have received much attention during the last fifteen years in personality and social psychology (Argyle, Furnham, and Graham 1981; Furnham and Argyle 1981). It is now more than twenty years since Endler, Hunt, and Rosenstein (1962) published their seminal study that was a watershed in the area.

The rise in interest in the person-situation debate has been due in part to the proliferation of a particular type of experimental design. Though not the first (those of Raush, Dittmann, and Taylor 1959; and Raush, Farbman, and Llewellyn 1959 preceded it), the study generating most research in this area was Endler, Hunt, and Rosenstein's (1962) thirty-one-page monograph, "An S-R Inventory of Anxiousness." S stood for situation and R for response. Since then, nearly thirty studies have used the same format and method of analysis. These studies used the analysis of variance model in a novel way—instead of simply testing for a significant F, they partitioned the sources of variance into various components so that one can determine the percentages of variance due to persons (individual differences), situations (interpersonal episodes) or responses (behavioral reactions), and the interaction effects.

By this method it was hoped to prove statistically to what extent social behavior was determined by personality variables or situational characteristics. However, these studies proved neither; instead, they led directly to the rise of interactional psychology (Magnusson and Endler 1977).

49

Much of the attack on trait theory and situationalism has been based on the results of these studies (Endler and Magnusson 1976). Furthermore, they are regularly quoted as evidence for an interactionist conception of personality. The seriousness, therefore, of the attack on trait theory and the evidence supporting interactionism must therefore largely be judged on the appropriateness and soundness of S-R studies that continue to be done.

This chapter reviews most of the S-R studies. They have been published in widely diverse journals, ranging from the *International Journal of Sport Psychology* to the *Journal of Marketing Research*, and were located by computer searches, a review of *Psychological Abstracts* and other journals that abstract current literature. Despite these attempts to be comprehensive, some published studies using the S-R format might not be included here. Nevertheless, this review remains fairly comprehensive, reflecting the state of the art.

The S-R studies will be compared and evaluated since they differ in many respects. A critique will then put the results of these studies into proper perspective.

PREVIOUS REVIEWS OF S-R STUDIES

Even though they appear to be a cornerstone in the person-situation debate, there have been few comparative reviews of S-R studies. The reviews of Bowers (1973) and Sarason, Smith, and Diener (1975) are notable exceptions.

Although Bowers's (1973) review was more theoretical than methodological, he did attempt to review the empirical evidence for person-situation interaction. He stated that he found only eleven articles published since 1959, though curiously he did not tabulate the Endler, Hunt, and Rosenstein (1962) study, the first of its type. Bowers suggested that these studies can be divided into three types:

1. Self-reports of ratings in hypothetical situations by subjects whose past experience with similar situations is the basis for their ratings.
2. Self-observation of reactions in real stimulus situations by subjects who fill out questionnaires soon after participating in various situations.
3. Observation of actual behavior in specific situations.

Bowers concluded that "irrespective of whether the dependent variable consists of behavior or self-ratings, both the trait and situationist hypotheses seem seriously compromised" (321). Averaging over all the studies, he found 12.71 percent of the variance accounted for by the person, 10.17 percent by the situation, and 20.77 percent by the interaction of person and situation. Eleven out of the nineteen comparisons showed the percentage of variance due to situations is less than variance due to person. The interaction of person and situation accounts for a higher percentage of variance than either main effect in fourteen of eighteen possible comparisons; and in eight of the eighteen, the interaction term accounts for more variance than the sum of the main effects. However, this includes error variance in some of the studies.

Bowers pointed out two major implications of this part of his review. The first relates to the sampling of subjects. Bowers noted that the careful selection of subjects and situations can easily be used to find support for either a trait or situationist position, though he did not believe this had happened in S-R studies. However, he did believe these experiments had not paid sufficient attention to individual differences or subject variables, which he believed were of relatively minor interest to current investigators in personality research. A second implication is that behaviors differ in their vulnerability to situational influences. Consequently, it cannot simply be assumed that success in changing one kind of behavior will mean similar success in changing another kind of behavior. "Nevertheless, one could almost wish for a metric that would indicate just how much expenditure of effort and resources is necessary to change a given problematic behavior. The size of this index could then be employed as a rough measure of the degree to which the behavior in question was originally attributable to characteristics of the person instead of to evoking and maintaining conditions" (323).

Bowers's review did not revolve around the S-R studies. They served only to illustrate his points. Many studies are missing; others are not comparable because they use different analytic techniques; in some, an arbitrary selection of results has been made. Nevertheless, his review was a useful first attempt to compare the findings from many S-R studies at the height of their popularity.

Bowers (1973) had been selective in his review, choosing to assess only the S-R studies he could find; Sarason, Smith, and Diener (1975) went to the opposite extreme. They surveyed the top four American personality journals from 1950 to 1972 to find the components of variance attributable to the person and the situation. However, they did not restrict their work to S-R studies, preferring to survey all the literature. They found an increase in the percentage of studies that permitted the determinants of interaction effects between individual difference and experimental variables (5 percent in 1950; 14 percent in 1960; 25 percent in 1970). Of the 147 studies involving only situational independent variables, 95.2 percent showed significant effects (at the 0.5 level or beyond); of the 59 studies involving only personality independent variables, 83.0 percent showed significant effects; and of the 12 studying only demographic independent variables, 83.3 percent showed significant results. In studies incorporating both situational and personality variables within factorial designs, the magnitude of the statistically significant effects were tabulated: 65.5 percent for situational effects, 31 percent for individual difference effects, and 59.9 percent for interaction effects. Thus, situational variables yielded significant results twice as frequently as did individual difference variables and were nearly four times as likely to be the most potent variable in the analysis. The authors also noted the high frequency with which significant interactions were obtained between situational and individual difference variables as well as the relatively high percentage of cases in which the interaction was the most potent effect.

They also reanalyzed 102 studies to determine the omega square, which can be used to estimate the amount of response variance that can be accounted for by each main and interaction effect in an analysis of variance. On the average, individual difference variables accounted for only a small proportion of the variance, either alone (± 11 percent) or in interaction with the other variables (± 8 percent). Much the same result occurred for the situation variables, either alone (± 13 percent) or in interaction with the other variables (± 8 percent). Further interactions involving situational and individual difference variables account for less variance than does either main effect.

In most studies, the independent variables account for little of the variance. It therefore appears either that they are studying relatively subtle psychological phenomena or that the measurement techniques are poor. The authors favored the first interpretation. They also appear to be aware of some limitations of a review such as theirs, notably the extreme heterogeneity of the variables, subjects, and research designs compared.

Despite these two reviews, no attempt has been made to evaluate critically and compare all the S-R studies that have been the focus of the person-situation debate. Before this is done, it is worthwhile to investigate more clearly the first S-R inventory.

THE PROTOTYPICAL FORMAT:
THE S-R INVENTORY OF ANXIOUSNESS

Because it proved to be a prototype for all subsequent studies of this type, the first study (Endler, Hunt, and Rosenstein 1962) is worth a detailed analysis.

What provoked the study was the lack of agreement among raters of any given trait or characteristic exhibited by a person or group of persons. They maintained that any rater bases his or her judgments not only on personal predilections concerning the response criteria of the trait in question, but also on the sample of situations afforded by his or her observational vantage point. Also, this vantage point often involves the rater as an important part of the situation in which the rated subjects are seen, and therefore the personality of the rater becomes important. Yet curiously, in their analyses Endler and colleagues confound actors and observers in this and later studies, not mentioning that systematic attributional errors might occur (Furnham, Jaspars, and Fincham 1983).

They maintained that the purpose of the study was to answer six questions:

1. What are the relative contributions of persons, situations, and modes of response to the variance in reported intensity?
2. How reliable are the total score, the situation, and the mode of response scales?
3. How well do total scores from the S-R inventory correlate with scores from other instruments?
4. Are the interpersonal correlations homogeneous among the scores from seven other scales?
5. Do situation scales comprise a single factor or several?
6. Do the response mode scales comprise a single factor or several?

The first question attracted most attention by later readers. From the analysis of variance results, they found that the variance contributed by the response mode contributed about twice the amount of variance as this particular sampling of situations, and that these situations contribute nearly four times the amount of variance as the person variable. Persons-situations interaction contributed almost no variance (a hundredth of the response mode factor). To some extent, Endler et al. recognised why these results occurred: the modes of response were varied (compare 'Enjoy the challenge' and 'Experience nausea'), the situations were all anxiety-provoking, and the subjects homogeneous. Yet they conclude, "The predominance of situational variance over S variance clearly supports the contention of social psychologists that knowing the situation is more important for predicting behavior, than knowing personal idiosyncracies" (29).

The answers to the other questions regarding validity, reliability, and factor structure provide some evidence for the usefulness of the S-R inventory. The alpha reliability of the scales was acceptably high, and the inventory correlated significantly highly with the scores of other inventories. Factor analyses of the situations and response modes revealed three readily interpretable factors for each. What is noticeable about this paper are the haphazard, atheoretical way situations and modes of response were selected and the large amount of descriptive statistical work devoted to investigating the patterns or types of these two factors. It would have been more sensible to spend more time on the theoretical and conceptual work needed beforehand and less on the subsequent analyses. However, this is easy to say with the benefit of hindsight.

The conclusions to this paper were not nearly as wide-ranging or provocative as in later Endler papers (Endler and Hunt 1968; Endler and Hunt 1969; Endler and Magnusson 1976), which were based on the same methodology and findings. In fact, person-situation interaction was not mentioned in the discussion section, which is not surprising given the percent of variance accounted for by this interaction. Most of the subsequent S-R papers were based on this design and method of analysis and hence share its problems. Some, but not all, of these problems appear to have been recognized in the paper. The most important criticism the authors recognize was in the sampling methods—selecting the situations and modes of response. Factor analysis of the situation and response scales after constructing the inventory is an unsatisfactory way to construct tests. In fact, the authors contradict themselves in the paper, at first suggesting the sampling was nonrandom (indeed the opposite) and then using an all-random ANOVA model. Endler (1966) later recognized the inconsistency.

Other problems such as the meaning of the mode of response factor were not mentioned. However, Endler et al. (1962) did recognize a serious problem in this study—one that provoked it in the first place. They wrote: "Obviously, the validity of such an inventory depends, as is true of all inventories, upon the conditions of the respondents and upon the degree to which they can report what they have done, what they do or what they would do in the situations described" (4). This statement is misleading because in these self-report studies the observer and the actor are now confounded.

Overall, this early study did not contain the self-assurance of later studies like it, though it was perhaps more thorough in its analysis. It is to be regretted that later researchers did not read this study in detail; they seemed to have glossed over many of its problems, some of which were highlighted by the authors themselves, and ignored its original aim.

Yet this study did open up a new research tradition and can be considered innovative. Notwithstanding its faults, its conclusions are still accepted today.

THE S-R STUDIES

To help evaluate the existing empirical literature, the S-R studies have been tabulated in Tables 2-1, 2-2, and 2-3. The results in the tables cannot be directly compared without consulting the text because many points specific to each study cannot be easily summarized. This fact means that comparisons such as those of Bowers (1973) are misleading.

The studies are grouped according to the number of factors that have been varied. Table 2-1 presents the P × S × R, the most popular studies; Table 2-2 presents the P x S studies; and Table 2-3 summarizes more complex studies, including factors P x S x R x O (other). Within each table, the studies are classified according to the dependent variables studied. Information also is supplied on the sample, the method of analysis, and whether the situations were hypothetical (that is, were assessed by self-report) or actual (assessed by observation). Most studies used a variance component analysis and expressed the amount of variance explained in W^2 ratios for all components. Most criticisms and analyses will be directed to studies in Table 2-1.

The most striking observation of the variance components is that the P x S interaction effect is not very outstanding. In fact, for the twenty studies in Table 2-1, the mean variance accounted for by the P x S interaction effect is 10.8 percent, whereas it was 10.74 percent for the P variable. Yet the entire debate has revolved around the person-situation interaction effect. The fact that the residual variance accounts for more than one-third of the variance is also striking, but this no doubt occurs because the three-way interaction is often mixed with error variance. Thirdly, the range of dependent variables studied according to this format is surprising—from movie attendance to conformity—yet there appears to be no theoretical model for determining which dependent variables are most suitably studied by this method.

The Person x Situational Studies (Two-Way ANOVAs)

The simplest designs appear in Table 2-2, the person x situation studies. Note that in comparing them to the more common person x situation x response mode studies, three-quarters of the studies in Table 2-2 were observational studies (Moos 1969, 1970; Raush et al. 1959; Nelson et al. 1969) even though the observers are not treated as a separate factor in the design. In Moos's studies of psychiatric patients, the subjects are nested under observers (each patient was observed by only one observer); thus, some variance due to the person main effect or person x situation interaction may be due to the differences between observers. Although the reliability of the observers' work is satisfactory, the main effects of the observers should not be confounded with the person variance.

In all these studies, except that by Nelson et al. (1969), more than one response was observed, which would have permitted a P x S x R analysis; yet this was not done. The use of single responses in these analyses implies that there must be a great deal of within-situation or error variance, which is evident from the observation studies by Moos, the only person to calculate within variance. That is, single observations are unreliable. This conclusion accounts for the fact that the response mode as a main effect and in interactions accounts for so much of the variance.

TABLE 2-1

Three-Way Analysis of Variance: Proportions of Variance in S-R Inventories

Psychological Process	Study	Hypothetical/ Actual Situations	ANOVA Model	Subjects	Sample	Sources of Variance as Percent						
						P	S	R	P×S	P×R	S×R	Residual
Academic Achievement	Rushton & Endler, 1977	Hypothetical	Random effects	School Children (N= 241)	10-12 yr. olds	49.1	3.8	0.3	19.2	1.9	0.8	24.6
					15-17 yr. olds	52.8	0.9	0.0	23.5	1.9	0.0	20.7
					Mean	50.8	2.3	0.1	21.3	1.9	0.4	22.6
	Endler & Hunt, 1966	Hypothetical	Random effects	Students (N= 189)	Illinois	10.4	7.2	19.5	9.8	17.0	6.4	29.3
					Penn St.,	5.7	5.2	24.4	9.9	11.1	6.5	36.8
					York	6.8	6.0	23.5	10.0	11.1	6.8	35.5
					Mean	7.6	6.1	20.2	9.9	13.0	6.5	33.8
	Endler & Hunt, 1968	Hypothetical	Random effects	School Children Students, Adults (N = 2,873)	Male	4.4	3.9	24.7	9.1	10.3	7.5	37.0
					Female	4.5	7.7	26.6	9.3	11.0	6.9	34.3
					Mean	4.4	5.8	25.6	9.2	10.6	7.2	35.6
Anxiety	Ekehammar, Magnusson & Ricklander, 1974	Hypothetical	Random effects	School Children (N= 116)	Male	5.5	5.7	16.5	12.0	12.5	5.0	42.4
					Female	9.1	5.7	20.9	8.2	13.7	6.1	36.1
					Mean	7.3	5.7	18.7	10.1	13.1	5.5	39.2
	Fisher, Horsfall, & Morris, 1977	Hypothetical	Mixed effects	Athletes (N= 147)	Males	9.0	10.0	6.0	10.0	8.0	15.0	42.0
	Furnham, 1980	Hypothetical	Random effects	School Children Students, Adults (N= 143)	Adults	20.3	2.3	8.9	10.4	10.4	3.5	42.0
					Students	17.0	2.4	11.2	14.0	8.2	7.9	39.1
					Therapists	12.5	5.9	20.5	9.0	7.0	10.9	34.6
					School Children	13.1	4.1	11.4	11.2	11.1	6.0	42.7
					Mean	15.6	3.8	12.2	11.9	10.2	6.3	40.6
	Mellstrom, Zuckerman & Cicala, 1978	Both	Mixed effects	Students (N= 114)	Hypothetical	32.2	0.0	4.6	14.0	16.8	2.5	26.8
					Actual	29.0	0.6	5.7	21.5	11.7	0.7	30.8
					Mean	30.6	0.3	5.1	17.5	14.5	1.6	28.8

		Effects									
Cinema Attendance	Belk 1974 b	Hypothetical	Students (N = 100)		0.9	0.5	15.6	7.0	1.9	33.7	39.4
	Furnham, 1980	Hypothetical	Students, housewives (N = 180)	Students Q1	1.4	5.0	19.3	1.0	11.6	10.2	51.1
				Q2	1.2	1.2	15.5	1.5	14.2	15.8	50.2
				Housewives Q1	5.7	1.4	17.4	0.6	12.6	13.3	49.3
				Q2	0.0	1.3	18.2	1.7	11.7	16.1	50.6
Conformity				Mean	3.9	2.2	17.6	1.2	12.5	13.8	50.4
	Dworkin & Kihlstrom, 1978	Hypothetical	Students (N = 182)	Harvard Male	11.2	8.1	7.2	21.0	9.0	4.0	39.6
				" Female	8.8	7.3	7.4	23.8	8.7	4.7	39.3
				Wellesley Mixed	8.6	4.8	7.2	25.9	8.0	2.8	42.6
				Mean	9.5	6.7	7.3	23.5	8.5	3.8	40.5
Drinking	Sandell, 1968	Hypothetical	Students (N = 31)	Male	0.5	2.7	14.6	2.7	11.8	39.8	37.8
Eating	Belk 1974 a	Hypothetical	Adults (N = 100)		4.6	5.2	15.0	2.9	9.7	26.2	36.4
	Belk 1974 b	Hypothetical	Students (N = 100)		6.7	0.4	6.7	6.1	22.4	18.7	39.0
	Belk 1975	Hypothetical	Housewives (N = 98)		8.1	2.2	13.4	2.2	20.1	15.3	38.7
Group Participation	Moos, 1968	Actual	Patients (N = 12)	Anxiety	17.7	0.0	0.0	18.1	1.4	0.3	62.0
				Vigor	0.5	0.0	1.1	47.5	0.0	1.5	49.4
				Pleasantness	16.3	0.5	0.0	16.1	5.9	5.2	56.0
				Worth	5.8	1.0	0.0	38.2	0.9	0.9	53.2
				Therapeutic Benefits	13.6	0.5	1.2	51.2	1.1	0.0	32.4
				Participation	0.0	0.0	4.5	20.1	28.3	1.2	45.1
				Affiliation	7.3	0.0	0.0	17.4	0.0	0.0	67.9
				Leadership	6.6	0.0	0.0	34.4	0.0	0.0	59.2
				Mean	8.4	0.2	0.8	30.3	5.6	1.1	53.1

TABLE 2-1 (cont.)

Psychological Process	Study	Hypothetical/ Actual Situations	ANOVA Model	Subjects	Sample	Sources of Variance as Percent						
						P	S	R	P×S	P×R	S×R	Residual
Hostility	Endler & Hunt, 1968	Hypothetical	Random effects	Students (N = 262)	Male	19.0	4.6	13.9	10.4	12.6	3.0	32.1
					Female	14.8	7.0	15.3	11.4	16.2	3.9	29.2
					Mean	16.9	5.8	14.6	10.9	14.4	3.4	30.6
Institutional Living	Moos, 1968	Hypothetical	Random effects	Patients and staff (N = 40)	Patients Factor 1	39.5	0.9	0.2	18.6	1.7	0.9	37.8
					Staff Factor 1	7.1	8.7	0.0	18.6	0.0	12.0	53.3
					Mean	23.3	4.8	0.1	18.6	0.8	6.4	45.0
Leisure Activity	Bishop & Witt, 1970	Hypothetical	Random effects	Students (N = 140)	Male	5.2	1.9	8.5	4.6	22.7	10.0	47.8
					Female	3.6	2.0	9.6	3.8	19.6	16.7	43.5
					Mean	4.4	1.9	9.1	4.2	21.1	13.3	45.6
Self-Disclosure	McCloskey, 1978	Hypothetical	Random effects	Students (N = 107)	1	7.7	22.9	17.2	13.1	13.7	2.7	22.4
					Quest 2	15.0	11.9	25.7	10.0	17.6	1.9	17.7
					3	9.3	16.8	26.6	10.0	10.2	3.4	23.4
					Mean	10.6	17.2	23.1	11.0	13.8	2.6	21.1
Social Appropriateness	Price & Bouffard, 1974	Hypothetical	Random effects	Students (N = 52)		6.1	16.8	17.9	5.8	7.6	14.7	31.0

Source: Reprinted with permission from *Personality and Individual Differences*, Vol. 4, No. 6, by A. Furnham and J. Jaspars, "The Evidence for Interactionism in Psychology: A Critical Analysis of the Situation-Response Inventories," Copyright 1983, Pergamon Press Ltd.

TABLE 2-2
Two-Way Analysis of Variance: Proportions of Variance in Studies

Psychological Process	Study	Hypothetical/ Actual Situations	Analysis	Subjects	Scales	Sources of Variance as Percent			
						P	S	P×S	Within
Affectional/ Status Behavior	Raush, Dittmann & Taylor, 1959	Actual	Multivariate Attribute Analysis	Disturbed children (N = 6)	Affectional				
					To Peers: Early phase	8.4	7.2	8.7	
					Later phase	11.7	15.4	17.9	
					To Adults: Early phase	8.5	9.5	11.4	
					Later phase	12.2	11.9	14.9	
					Status				
					To Peers: Early phase	8.0	5.5	10.0	
					Later phase	7.1	8.5	9.9	
					To Adults: Early phase	7.1	8.7	20.0	
					Later phase	6.4	6.2	8.1	
					Mean	8.6	9.1	11.3	
Dyactic Interaction	Argyle & Little, 1972	Hypothetical	ANOVA	Students (N = 23)	Mean	16.1	43.6	40.2	
Nonverbal Behavior	Moos, 1969	Actual	ANOVA	Patients (N = 16)	Hand & arm movement	16.8	11.9	31.9	39.4
					Foot & leg	27.4	10.0	26.7	35.9
					Scratch, pick, rub	30.7	13.1	24.5	31.9
					General movement	17.3	1.4	47.1	34.1
					Nod yes	4.2	42.9	33.5	25.6
					Smile	35.3	3.6	35.4	25.6
					Talk	10.5	68.3	13.9	7.4
					Smoke	41.9	7.1	20.7	30.2
					Mean	20.3	19.7	29.2	27.9

TABLE 2-2 (cont.)

Psychological Process	Study	Hypothetical/Actual Situations	Analysis	Subjects	Scales	Sources of Variance as Percent			
						P	S	P×S	Within
Nonverbal Behavior	Moos, 1970	Actual	ANOVA	Patients (N = 12)	Smile	20.2	2.1	35.5	42.2
					Talk	2.8	5.5	37.3	54.4
					Nod yes	8.2	7.0	52.1	32.0
					General movement	4.4	2.5	13.9	79.2
					Hand & arm movement	3.6	0.0	28.7	67.7
					Foot & leg movement	13.0	0.0	37.0	50.0
					Scratch, pick, rub	17.7	4.5	20.7	57.5
					Mean	9.9	3.0	32.1	54.7
Honesty	Nelson, Grinder, & Mutterer, 1969	Actual	ANOVA	School children— 47 boys 59 girls	Interval Scores				
					Random effects	18.1	14.3		67.5
					Mixed effects	26.4	12.9		60.7
					Dichotomous Scores				
					Random effects	14.7	15.5		69.8
					Mixed effects	23.6	13.4		62.5
					Mean	20.7	14.1		65.5
Anxiety	Van Heck & Van der Leeuw, 1975	Hypothetical	ANOVA	School children (N = 98)	*SELF*				
					Heart beats faster	40.73	11.67	8.48	39.11
					Begin to perspire	39.26	9.59	14.20	36.96
					Become immobilized	28.24	11.58	17.99	42.19
					Mean of all 8 scales	34.1	7.98	14.1	43.51
					OTHER				
					Heart beats faster	42.74	9.71	6.86	40.68
					Begin to perspire	41.54	6.09	5.21	47.10
					Become immobilized	29.58	11.63	12.34	46.45
					Mean of all 8 scales	37.1	7.0	8.00	47.4

Source: Reprinted with permission from *Personality and Individual Differences*, Vol. 4, No. 6, by A. Furnham and J. Jaspars, "The Evidence for Interactionism in Psychology: A Critical Analysis of the Situation-Response Inventories," Copyright 1983, Pergamon Press Ltd.

TABLE 2-3
Four-Way Analysis of Variance: Proportions of Variance in Studies

Psychological Process	Study	Hypothetical/Actual Situations	Analysis	Subjects	Sample	Person	Situation	T.P.	Sex	P×Sit	P×T.P.	Sex×T.P.	Sex×Sit	T.P.×Sit	Sex×T.P.×Sit	P×T.P.×Sit
Cross-Cultural Interaction	Argyle, Shimoda, & Little, 1978	Hypothetical	ANOVA	School Children (N = 100)	English	7.4	28.2	35.0	12.3	1.2	3.6	3.1	2.9	1.9	1.2	0.8
					Japanese	6.7	37.2	21.3	12.2	1.6	2.9	4.9	3.3	5.7	1.0	0.9
					Mean	7.0	32.7	28.1	12.1	1.4	3.2	4.0	3.1	3.8	1.1	0.8

Psychological Process	Study	Hypothetical/Actual Situations	Analysis	Subjects	Sample	Person Type	Person
Rule Breaking	Edinger & Auerbach, 1978	Hypothetical and Actual	ANOVA	Prisoners (N = 84)	Self-Report	2.4	58.7
					Observation	0.1	4.8
					Mean	12.3	31.7

Situation	Response	Sanction	P×S	P×R	P×Sa	S×R	S×Sa	R×Sa	P×S×R	P×S×Sa	P×R×Sa	S×R×R	P×S×R×Sa	Residual
0.2	2.5	1.7	0.0	0.6	0.7	0.5	0.0	0.2	0.0	0.0	0.0	0.0	0.0	02.1
	2.7	0.0	0.0	0.0	0.8	0.0	1.0	0.0	0.0	0.0	0.0	0.0	0.0	90.4
0.1	2.6	0.8	0.0	0.3	0.7	0.2	0.5	0.1	0.0	0.0	0.0	0.0	0.0	61.2

Source: Reprinted with permission from *Personality and Individual Differences*, Vol. 4, No. 6, by A. Furnham and J. Jaspars, "The Evidence for Interactionism in Psychology: A Critical Analysis of the Situation-Response Inventories," Copyright 1983, Pergamon Press Ltd.

61

Also note that few other studies attempted to consider the error factor separately from the interaction effect. One exception is the study by van Heck and van der Leeuw (1975), which calculated also within-situation variance. In this study, however, observer and observed are completely confounded.

Also consider the nature of the responses studied in these experiments. Only studies by Nelson et al. (1969) and van Heck and van der Leeuw (1975) attempt to measure the same latent disposition (hostility and anxiety, respectively); in all other studies, the responses are a curious mixture of a variety of behaviors. Many behaviors appear to reflect temporary emotional states (general movement, smiling, affectionate behavior) or any behavior primarily a function of the (social) situation in which it occurs (talking, mutual gaze, nodding yes). These latter responses have never exclusively been considered as manifestations of latent invariant dispositions in traditional personality theory or measurement and thus do not appear to be strictly relevant.

Finally, note that in all the P × S studies, with the exception of Nelson, subjects were not exposed to the same situations. Subjects in Moos's observational study were exposed to similar situations, not the same circumstances. Individual therapy sessions may vary considerably from one person to the next, and free-time activities are likely to be entirely different for different patients. The P × S interactions might therefore reflect that the patients were exposed to different situations. The same is true for the study by Raush et al., since the children were observed one at a time.

Another similar complication arises in the study by Argyle and Little (1972), where subjects are asked to report about situations in which they interacted with persons who were role-related in terms of some category. Since we can assume that there was little similarity between the interpersonal situations for different subjects, this study relies on the social psychological similarity of the situations for the subjects. Since this is also a self-report study, it becomes difficult to know how to interpret the interaction between person and situation. Different subjects may be talking about different interpersonal situations that they select, perceive, and report about in unique ways. As Cooper (1981) pointed out: "Fantasizing about imaginary introspection under hypothetical circumstances is not, however, a method renowned for its prediction of actual behavior and although one may perhaps evaluate the state and trait components of imagined anxiety by such means, the generalization to the specific characteristic ways of adapting the various characteristics of different situations may be premature" (135).

The best controlled study in this respect is Nelson's experiment, in which children are exposed to the same experimentally created situations and response variance and covariance is analyzed before the analysis of variance is presented. This study contains a strong main effect of the task or situation factor and a barely significant person effect; but because there were more subjects than tasks, the variance component for persons is roughly equal to, or larger than, the variance component for situations. In other studies reported here, the ratio of persons to situations is more in favor of the situations. Because of these differences, it is important to report the variances of the variance components, yet this is rarely done (one exception is Furnham, Jaspars, and Fincham 1983). Nelson was aware of this problem, however.

The Person × Situation × Response Studies (Three-Way ANOVAs)

Most problems noted in the two-way ANOVA studies (confusion of actors and observers; variety within the response mode; comparability of situations; and the large variance of the variance components) are also found in the more numerous three-way ANOVA studies.

The most important point about the studies in Table 2-1 is that the majority are self-report studies. Attribution theorists have pointed out some differences in the perceptions of actors and observers. This distinction is consistently confounded in interactional studies because of the use of self-report methods. Therefore, in the S-R inventories, subjects report as observers on how they would probably behave as an actor in various situations. Since subjects in S-R inventories are not asked actually to attribute their own behavior to stimuli inherent in the situations, one would predict from attribution theory that they would rate their own behavior as less consistent over situations than the behavior of others. This result has been demonstrated by van Heck and van der Leeuw (1975) who found the percentage of variance accounted for by persons was greater for judgments of others than for self-judgments, whereas the percentage of variance accounted for by person × situation interaction was smaller for judgments of others than for self-judgments.

S-R experiments that have not confounded actor and observer (i.e., observational studies) have a different pattern of results from those that confounded these factors (i.e., self-report studies). To see if this held over all the studies, an analysis was done of all three-way inventories to determine the nature of the studies where variance percentages were at extremes.

Table 2-4 clearly illustrates this point. Studies that experimented with actual situations (i.e., that used O or T data) showed highest P variance and lowest R and S × R variance; studies that experimented with hypothetical situations showed highest S variance, R variance, and lowest P × S variance. Remember, however, that these studies are not experimenting with the same behaviors. With one or two exceptions, the pattern of studies in Table 2-4 is clear. (Note that the Mariotto [1978] study is not in Table 2-1.)

TABLE 2-4

Extremes of Variance Proportions Accounted for by Each Source in the Three-Way S-R Inventories

The mean percentage score for each source of variance in each of the three-way studies was calculated. The three studies that had the highest percentage and the lowest percentage in each of the sources of variance were calculated. (A) signifies studies that experimented with ACTUAL situations. (H) signifies studies that experimented with HYPOTHETICAL situations.

Sources of Variance	Highest		Extremes	Lowest	
PERSON	1. Rushton & Endler 1977	(A)	(A)	1. Sandell 1968	(H)
	2. Mellstrom et al. 1978	(A)	(A)	2. Belk 1974	(H)
	3. Mariotto 1978	(A)	(A)	3. Endler & Hunt 1966	(H)
SITUATION	1. McClosky 1978	(H)	(A)	1. Moos 1970	(A)
	2. Moos 1968	(H)	(H)	2. Belk 1974	(H)
	3. Fisher et al. 1978	(H)	(H)	3. Belk 1975	(H)
RESPONSE	1. Endler & Hunt 1968	(H)	(H)	1. Rushton & Endler 1977	(A)
	2. McCloskey 1978	(H)	(H)	2. Mariotto 1978	(A)
	3. Endler & Hunt 1968	(H)	(H)	3. Moos 1970	(A)
PERSON × SITUATION	1. Moos 1970	(A)	(A)	1. Furnham 1980	(H)
	2. Moos 1968	(H)	(H)	2. Belk 1975	(H)
	3. Rushton & Endler 1977	(A)	(A)	3. Price & Bouffard 1974	(H)
PERSON × RESPONSE	1. Belk 1975	(H)	(H)	1. Rushton & Endler 1977	(A)
	2. Mariotto 1978	(A)	(A)	2. Moos 1968	(H)
	3. Belk 1974	(H)	(H)	3. Moos 1970	(A)
SITUATION × RESPONSE	1. Sandell 1968	(H)	(H)	1. Mariotto 1968	(A)
	2. Belk 1975	(H)	(H)	2. Rushton & Endler 1977	(A)
	3. Fisher et al. 1978	(H)	(H)	3. Moos 1970	(A)

Source: Reprinted with permission from *Personality and Individual Differences*, Vol. 4, No. 6, by A. Furnham and J. Jaspars, "The Evidence for Interactionism in Psychology: A Critical Analysis of the Situation-Response Inventories," Copyright 1983, Pergamon Press Ltd.

64

The existence of attribution errors resulting from the confounding of actor and observer in nearly all S-R inventories means these results must be treated with caution. However, although this bias tends to accentuate situational variance, it appears to reduce the amount of variance accounted for by person × situation interaction. According to attribution theory, though, person × situation variance would be accentuated by self-report, which does not appear to be borne out by Table 2–4.

Observation studies seem to provide more valid data on the nature of person × situation interaction (Argyle 1976). Certainly, studies done tend to find large P variance and P × S variance and relatively small S variance (Mellstrom et al. 1978; Moos 1968). But these studies have faults, which could also bias the results. As in the Moos study, subjects were observed by only one observer in equivalent situations. No attempt was made to establish observer reliability. Mellstrom et al., on the other hand, asked observers to rate the same subjects in the same situations but tended to restrict their ratings to global observations (neuroticism, social anxiety) on a restricted sample of situations.

Secondly, as in the two-way studies, many experimenters mixed the response factors in the three-way studies. Consider, for instance, Dworkin and Kihlstrom's (1978) response scale 6, 'Take the lead in figuring out what to do' vs. scale 11, 'Others ask me to decide what should be done,' which hardly constitutes a response. Price and Bouffard's (1974) response scales also vary widely from 'Jump' to 'Kiss' and do not appear to be chosen according to any logical theory. Predictably, Endler and Hunt (1968) have extremely varied responses (e.g., 'perspire,' 'swear,' and 'grimace'). Other studies, such as Bishop and Witt (1970), however, have a unidimensional response scale comprising only leisure activities. It is therefore not surprising that the response mode accounts for so much of the variance, particularly in the studies of Endler and Hunt (1968, 1969) and Price and Bouffard (1974).

Because the subjects are required to indicate on a questionnaire their likelihood of response to various social situations, we assume they are responding to functionally equivalent situations. However, these situations are often chosen a priori and with little or no preliminary work to determine their appropriateness or the subject experience of these situations. Thus, much variance can occur because of the differences in the imagined stimuli. Unless subjects are chosen from a closely homogeneous group, or the situations fully described or shown on video equipment, this problem will continue to occur. In all studies in this chapter, this point must be remembered. Yet many of the studies used homogeneous groups (i.e., students), which, in turn, leads to problems of generalization to other groups. Furthermore, attempts to ensure homogeneity might lead to an unrepresentative reduction in the person variance.

Perhaps the most unusual aspect of the three-way analysis is that these studies have usually been concerned within an interactionist framework in order to determine primarily the amount of variance accounted for by person, situation, and the interaction of person and situation. The response factor, the response × situation, and the response × person interactions have usually been ignored (Fisher et al. 1977). As will be shown later, it has been suggested that it is inappropriate to include any response in the S-R inventories since people respond through, not to, a response mode (Cartwright 1975).

Furthermore, as Argyle (1976) pointed out, the third source of variance (response mode) and its interaction with the other modes accounts for a lot of the variance and accordingly suppresses percentages of variance from the other sources, though it is not clear which. Olweus (1977) reanalyzed the original Endler, Hunt, and Rosenstein (1962) data that showed the amount of variance for person rose from 5.8 percent in the three-way to 26.5 percent in the two-way, while that for situation rose from 5.3 percent to 22.9 percent, and that for the interaction of person and situation rose from 10.0 percent to 50.7 percent.

Because so much of the debate has depended on the percentages of variance accounted for by these three factors, it was decided to recalculate the three-way ANOVAs into two-way ANOVAs.

Table 2-5 shows the percentages of variance accounted for by the P, S, and P × S factors as analyzed originally by three-way and then by two-way ANOVAs. This was done by converting the sum of squares of each effect in order to remove the adjustment for the third factor. By eliminations, this process is reduced simply to multiplying the mean square for each effect by the number of levels of the deleted factor. The adjusted means are then used in the random effects two-way model and the components calculated by the standard formuli.

Before discussing these results, however, note these three limitations: (1) not all S-R studies could be recalculated, as some had not provided sufficient information (about N, response modes of, etc.) to allow for recalculation; (2) the person × situation interaction includes both error variance and the two-way effect, which cannot be separated; (3) Table 2-1 (from which Table 2-5 was derived) consists of studies with different assumptions about the nature of the effects model (random vs. fixed) that cannot be answered with the original data, which were not available. However, a nonadditivity, random effects model was assumed for calculating the proportions.

Despite these problems, Table 2-5 shows some interesting findings. In seventeen of the twenty-four studies, the person variance accounts for more than the situation variance; and in fourteen studies, the person × situation effects account for most of the variance. For all three effects, the standard deviation is high, suggesting large differences in person × situation interaction across different dependent variables.

TABLE 2-5
Reanalysis of the Three-Way ANOVAs as Two-Way ANOVAs

Process	Study	Source of Variance	Original Three Way	Reanalyzed Two Way
	Endler and Hunt (1966)	Person	5.7	26.5
		Situation	5.2	22.9
	Penn State sample	Person × Situation	9.9	50.7
	Ekehammar et al. (1974)	Person	5.5	23.5
		Situation	5.7	22.3
	Males	Person × Situation	12.0	54.2
	Females	Person	9.1	38.0
		Situation	5.7	23.0
		Person × Situation	8.2	39.0
Anxiety	Fisher et al. (1978)	Person	9.0	25.0
		Situation	10.0	25.0
		Person × Situation	10.0	50.0
	Mellstrom et al. (1978)	Person	29.5	43.0
		Situation	8.6	0.0
	Hypothetical Situation	Person × Situation	21.8	57.0
	Actual Instances	Person	29.0	7.0
		Situation	0.6	2.0
		Person × Situation	21.5	91.0
	Furnham (1979)	Person	15.0	44.0
		Situation	2.8	9.0
	Total Population	Person × Situation	11.9	47.0
Academic	Rushton & Endler (1977)	Person	52.6	61.0
Achievement		Situation	0.9	5.0
	(15–17 yrs.)	Person × Situation	21.3	34.0

67

TABLE 2-5 (cont.)

Process	Study	Source of Variance	Original Three Way	Reanalyzed Two Way
Cinema Going	Belk (1974)	Person	0.9	1.0
		Situation	0.5	8.0
		Person × Situation	1.9	81.0
Conformity	Furnham (1979)	Person	1.4	44.0
		Situation	5.0	13.0
	Questionnaire 1	Person × Situation	1.0	43.0
Drinking	Sandell (1968)	Person	0.5	12.0
		Situation	2.7	48.0
		Person × Situation	2.7	40.0
Dominance	Dworkin & Kihlstrom (1978)	Person	11.2	27.0
		Situation	8.1	17.0
	Harvard sample	Person × Situation	21.0	54.0
Eating	Belk (1974) Meat Products	Person	4.6	27.0
		Situation	5.2	33.0
		Person × Situation	2.9	40.0
	Belk (1975) Fast Foods	Person	8.1	48.0
		Situation	2.2	15.0
		Person × Situation	2.2	37.0
Group Participation	Moos (1970	Person	8.4	27.0
		Situation	0.2	0.0
		Person × Situation	30.3	73.0
	Endler & Hunt (1968)	Person	19.6	51.0
Hostility	York (Males)	Situation	4.9	13.0
		Person × Situation	11.5	36.0
	York (Females)	Person	14.0	10.0
		Situation	8.5	6.0
		Person × Situation	12.9	84.0

Category	Study	Component		
	Moos (1968) Staff Factor 1	Person	7.1	14.0
		Situation	8.7	23.0
		Person × Situation	18.6	64.0
Institutional Living	Patients Factor 1	Person	39.5	55.0
		Situation	0.9	43.0
		Person × Situation	18.6	2.0
	Mariotto (1978)	Person	41.9	58.7
		Situation	0.4	40.7
		Person × Situation	28.9	0.6
	Bishop & Witt (1970)	Person	6.4	38.0
		Situation	3.3	19.0
		Person × Situation	5.4	43.0
Leisure	Kentucky Male	Person	1.9	44.0
		Situation	3.3	20.0
		Person × Situation	4.5	36.0
	Kentucky Female	Person	7.7	15.0
		Situation	22.9	52.0
		Person × Situation	13.1	33.0
Self-Disclosure	McCloskey (1978) Sample 1	Person	6.1	19.0
		Situation	16.8	56.0
		Person × Situation	5.8	25.0

			Mean	SD	Mean	SD
Social Appropriateness	Price & Bouffard (1974)	Person	13.94	14.12	31.61	17.19
		Situation	5.33	5.44	21.49	16.38
		Person × Situation	12.28	8.74	46.90	20.07

69

Source: Reprinted with permission from *Personality and Individual Differences*, Vol. 4, No. 6, by A. Furnham and J. Jaspars, "The Evidence for Interactionism in Psychology: A Critical Analysis of the Situation-Response Inventories," Copyright 1983, Pergamon Press Ltd.

However, differences seem readily interpretable. Compare Rushton and Endler's (1977) study in which the person factor accounted for 61 percent of the variance and Belk's (1974) paper in which the person factor accounted for 1 percent of the variance. Rushton and Endler (1977) were measuring academic performance at different academic tasks (situations); Belk (1974), measuring movie attendance, found a large person x situation effect. That is, the large person variance in Rushton and Endler's (1977) study may be due to a strong general intelligence factor, whereas the large person x situation variance in Belk's (1974 a) experiment shows that people have particular tastes in movies. But although there is evidence of considerable difference in the relative percentage of variance accounted for by the two main and one interaction effect across different variables, there is also evidence of some consistency in findings within an area. Thus, the findings from the seven anxiety studies are similar, with the exception of the Mellstrom et al. (1978) studies, which are not representative, as mentioned.

Overall, then, the reanalyzed three-way studies provide strong support for the interactionist position. Remember also that the interaction variance in the reanalyzed ANOVAs contains both the interaction and error terms, and that in most studies subjects are allowed to define their own situations (i.e., they are self-report studies). This statement must be qualified since it seems to rely on the dependent variable studied and the method used. The person-situation debate has traditionally been concerned with personality or individual difference variables such as anxiety, hostility, conformity, and self-disclosure. However, more than half of these studies appear to measure aspects of behavior (eating, drinking, movie attendance) that are beyond the bounds of the debate. These social behaviors may also be a function of person-situation interaction, but findings in these experiments cannot be used as support for evidence against trait, situations, or interactionist conceptions of social behavior.

Person X Situation X Response X Other Variable Studies (Four-Way ANOVAs)

Two four-way ANOVA studies have been very different in their hypotheses and methodology.

Argyle et al. (1978) asked Japanese and English school children to rate five role-related target people as they behaved in four situations. A four-way ANOVA was computed, but it was not discussed or considered important. A two-way ANOVA (person x situation) was computed on each rating scale for the two populations, presumably collapsed over target people. The main hypothesis, that there 'would be relatively more P variance for English subjects, and relatively more S variance for Japanese subjects,' was supported. The problems highlighted in two- and three-way ANOVAs are equally apparent in this study: confounding actors and observers; having a multidimensional response mode (compare, for instance, rating scale—'concerned with appearance' vs. 'tense'); having similar but not necessarily the same stimulus situations vaguely described and therefore encouraging error variance; and an inappropriate analysis. This study is also complicated by cultural differences.

Edinger and Auerbach (1978), on the other hand, developed a person × situation × response mode × reinforcer sanction model to account for infractions of rules by prisoners. The nature of the population, situations, and modes of response limit the generalizability of the results. Furthermore the study involved only two situations and four highly varied response modes. More importantly, the responses referred not to how the subjects responded in these situations but to how others responded to them. The ANOVA showed a large person effect. Previous studies (Endler and Hunt 1968, 1969) treated all individual differences (state, trait, error) as person variance. This study, however, specifically measured individual differences (MMPI) as person variance and the unmeasured trait, state (etc.) differences among subjects as error variance. Surprisingly, the person × situation interaction accounted for none of the variance, and yet an interactionist conception was one of the study's conclusions.

These two studies are too different to draw many conclusions about four-way ANOVAs. These studies appear to contain many problems found in the two- and three-way studies, with the added difficulty that four-way interactions are difficult to interpret.

PROBLEMS WITH THE S-R INVENTORIES

Despite their popularity, the S-R inventories have been criticized. Many theoretical criticisms mentioned in chapter 1 and in the review of the variance study have been directed specifically at claims based on the results of S-R studies. More importantly, four criticisms have been directed to methodological issues surrounding the S-R inventories.

The Representativeness of the Situations, Subjects, and Responses Sampled

Bowers (1973), Argyle (1976), Olweus (1977), and others have pointed out that the proportions of variance derived from S-R inventories and around which much debate has centered are heavily dependent on the representativeness of the situations, responses, and subjects sampled. That is, it is easy to determine the pattern of the variance components by carefully selecting the P, S, and R variables to suit one's own end. If a homogeneous sample of mental patients are asked to indicate their responses to a variety of mundane, everyday situations, the P variance is likely to be low; but if a heterogeneous sample of normal adults are asked to indicate their responses to a variety of potentially anxiety-provoking social situations where the threat might be both social or physical, the situation (and perhaps the response) variance is likely to be high.

Mischel (1973) argued that studies therefore could be designed to demonstrate almost any outcome desired by the experimenter to support a theoretical viewpoint. Furthermore, subject populations appear to have been selected more according to their availability than their respresentativeness (with some notable exceptions, such as Endler and Hunt 1968). As a result, the implicit or explicit theories of the experimenters, as regards P × S interaction, may have been confirmed by a nonrandom, unrepresentative sampling of subjects and questionnaire items. Even when attempts are made to sample appropriately, it is difficult to obtain a comparable range of person and situation factors.

Systematic Biases in Different Kinds of Data

Much work in attribution theory has shown that systematic differences exist in the perception of actors and observers. That is, individuals act like trait theorists in describing other people and like social behaviorists in describing themselves. This effect was demonstrated by van Heck and van der Leeuw (1975), who asked subjects to fill out the S-R Inventory for Anxiety twice: once for themselves and once for a friend. They found the percentages of variance accounted for by person (indicating cross-situational consistency) were greater for judgments of others than for self-judgments. However, the percentages of variance accounted for by situations (indicating cross-situational variability) and the interaction of person and situation were smaller for judgments of others than for self-judgments.

Most interactional experiments, however, have confounded the actor and observer by using the self-report methods. That is, in interactional experiments, the subjects are both actor and observer—they report as an observer on how they would probably behave as an actor in various situations. Studies that have not confounded the actor and the observer, such as those by Moos (1969, 1970), show a different pattern of variance. Despite the variability in the results across scales, it appears that observational studies produce a higher percentage of person and person × situation variance, whereas self-report studies produce a higher percentage of situation variance.

Therefore, before any conclusions can be drawn from S-R studies about the nature of person-situation interaction, the biases in the data must be considered. Most S-R studies have used self-report data which, it has been suggested, would lead to higher situational variance. Schmitt and Saari (1978) found that neither situational factors nor situation-behavior interactions explained much variance in leadership behavior, but that differences between raters and behaviors accounted for most of the explained variance, possibly because different raters (peers, subordinates, superiors) rated subjects on different dimensions.

The Inclusion of the Response Mode as a Separate Factor

Cartwright (1975) was puzzled that although S-R inventories show the person only accounts for about 5 percent to 10 percent of the variance, other anxiety scales (not having specific situational components) show 95 percent reliability scores, which can be considered an index of person variance. Cartwright concluded that the incorrect inclusion of the mode of response factor in the three-way ANOVA accounted for this, for two reasons.

First, subjects do not respond to but through a mode of response. It thus is questionable whether variance due to such a component should enter the total aginst which the proportion of variance due to individual differences is evaluated. Thus, possibly due to the inclusion of this factor (which in many cases accounts for much of the variance), the variance accounted for by the person factor is greatly reduced. Second, Cartwright maintained that the mode of response factor in the S-R inventories is actually two factors. "The mode of response factor therefore appears to be a condensation of the two factors, namely type of emotion and modes of response, with modes nested under types of emotion" (p. 410).

To illustrate his point, Cartwright showed that even though subjects rank-order the situations (from the S-R inventory) in identical ways, they varied considerably in rank-ordering the modes of response. Further, a two-way ANOVA showed that situations accounted for 15.19 percent of the variance, whereas people accounted for nearly three times as much (44.09 percent). That is, most of the response mode variance went into the person variance. According to Cartwright, this fact solved the puzzle: "the inventory allows large quantities of variance from unjustified sources to enter into the total variance against which the individual difference component is evaluated. By summing across modes of response the proportion of variance due to individual differences becomes relatively larger since variation due to the modes factor is eliminated from the total. By summing across situations (as in computing a total score on the inventory) variation due to situation is also eliminated from the total" (414).

If excluding the response mode as a separate factor produced such drastic changes in results, as in Cartwright's sample, this would lend strong support to the trait position. However, Cartwright neglected to explain why S-R inventories thus analyzed show person variance accounting for about 45 percent of the variance, whereas earlier inventories account for 95 percent (as calculated by reliability scores) of the person variance. That is, despite the high increase in P variance found by a two-way ANOVA, there is still considerable evidence of situational factors in anxiety (see Table 2–5). Furthermore, Golding and Knudson (1975) actually demonstrated that traditional anxiety inventories psychometrically outperform the S-R inventory.

The Correct Analysis of the S-R Inventories

There have been many criticisms of how the early S-R inventories were analyzed. Endler (1966) himself pointed out that the early analysis of his 1962 data was incorrect in that he had used a random, rather than a mixed, analysis of variance model. Because it is difficult to define and sample a universe of persons, situations, and modes of response, the mixed effects model appears more appropriate than the random effects model for estimating variance components from mean squares. However, as Endler himself showed, the actual difference in the estimated variance components from the two models is small, ranging from .05 percent to 2.5 percent. Nevertheless, it is important to use the correct model.

Golding (1975), on the other hand, said that the ratios used to calculate variance rather than the ANOVA model should be questioned. He argued that coefficients of generalizability and not omega-square ratios should be used. Generalizability coefficients for person index the percentage of observed score variation due to individual differences, whereas omega-square ratios index the percentage of total variation accounted for by the variance due to individual differences.

> While individuals differ in absolute *amount* of dominance-submission demonstrated in various situations, they maintain perfectly their rank ordering. Hence, there is perfect consistency in the sense that the ordering of, and distance between, universe scores is perfectly predictable from a sample observation, and the generalizability co-efficient should be unity. This property of the data is not reflected in the omega-squared ratios. In order to index consistency across situations in the rank order sense, differences among situations in their tendency to elicit different magnitudes of behavior in question (situation main effects) are irrelevant. Thus, while omega-square ratios do *technically* index the percentage total variation, they do not index the theoretically desired property of consistency. (p. 280)

Other authors have recognized the importance of this point and used generalizability coefficients in their calculations (Furnham, Jaspars, and Fincham 1983). Yet it should be pointed out that when Golding reanalyzed the Endler et al. (1962) data, much the same results appeared, although this conclusion may be due to these particular data.

More importantly, perhaps, Golding appears to doubt the usefulness of ANOVA designs. He believes they are not suited to showing the important patterns in the data.

> Numerous multivariate clustering techniques that would be well suited to the task of uncovering meaningful patterns exist. With the exception of Argyle and Little's (1972) attempt at clustering and Tucker's (1964) preliminary application of three mode factor analysis to some Endler-Hunt data, investigations of the theoretically important questions of person x situation interactions have rather uniformly ignored systematic interpretations of these interactions. In applying multivariate clustering techniques to the problem of person x situation x mode of response interactions the goal would be the search for person subclusters that are relatively homogeneous with respect to either the pattern of response in a particular situation, or the pattern of responses across situations.... the existence of interactive terms cannot be uncritically accepted as supportive of the interactionist viewpoint unless they are shown to be non-artifactual, replicable and meaningfully patterned. (287)

Olweus (1971), however, noted that although Golding's general conclusions appear to be correct, the use of generalizability coefficients does not solve the person-situation debate or provide an adequate test of the theoretical positions involved. Yet, he also stresses the need for multivariate classification that would discover regularities in the person-by-situation interaction patterns; for instance, by sorting the individuals into relatively homogeneous subgroups.

Various techniques have been mentioned. Lantermann (1978) suggested a polynomial conjoint measurement model; Golding and Knudson (1975), a multivariable-multimethod convergence approach; and Kuhl (1978), a stochastic test model.

There has also been some debate as to the replicability of some established S-R findings. Lazzerini et al. (1979) replicated Magnusson and Ekehammar's (1975) study to find evidence of a general anxiety trait independent of situational influences, which accounted for five times as much variance as situational factors. Cooper (1981), on the other hand, reanalyzed both Magnusson and Ekehammar's (1975) and Lazzerini et al.'s (1979) data and found the presence of two replicable situational factors in addition to the general factor of anxiety. Cooper (1981) suggested that the use and interpretation of factor analysis by both authors were inappropriate; he also criticized the S-R inventories for being psychometrically inadequate.

CONCLUSIONS FROM THE S-R STUDIES

It has been pointed out that many common statements regarding the relative size of the variance components to be expected on the basis of a trait and a situationist position are incorrect because they are based on misconceptions of the positions in question. This chapter has suggested that misconceptions also exist about the appropriateness of the analysis of variance techniques as used to analyze S-R inventories. It is impossible to institute adequate tests of the three (trait, situationist, interactionist) positions by an ANOVA, as several different outcomes are compatible with some or all of the positions. We therefore could argue that the variance component technique has brought more confusion than clarity and that many conclusions drawn in this literature about interactionism canot be accepted.

Nevertheless, the S-R inventories have stimulated considerable research and interest in this field. Dissatisfaction with the S-R format has led to the development of other techniques (Bem and Funder 1978) and to a close examination of the issues in person-situation interaction. As a result, many important issues in personality theory and social psychology have been highlighted.

REFERENCES

Argyle, M. Personality and social behaviour. In R. Harré (Ed.), *Personality*. Oxford: Blackwell, 1976.

Argyle, M., Furnham, A., & Graham, J. *Social situations*. Cambridge: Cambridge University Press, 1981.

Argyle, M., & Little, B. Do personality traits apply to social behaviour? *Journal for the Theory of Social Behaviour*, 1972, *2*, 1-35.

Argyle, M., Shimoda, K., & Little, B. Variance due to personal and situations in England and Japan. *British Journal of Social and Clinical Psychology*, 1978, *17*, 335-337.

Belk, R. An exploratory assessment of situational effects in buyer behaviour. *Journal of Marketing Behaviour*, 1974, *11*, 156-163. (a)

Belk, R. Application and analysis of the behavior differential inventory for assessing situational effects in consumer behavior. In J. Ward and P. Wright (Eds.), *Advances in consumer research*. Champagne-Urbana, Ill.: ACR, 1974. (b)

Belk, R. Situational variables and consumer behavior. *Journal of Consumer Behavior*, 1975, *2*, 157-164.

Bem, D., & Funder, D. Predicting some of the people some of the time: The search for cross-situational consistencies in behavior. *Psychological Review*, 1978, *85*, 485-501.

Bishop, D. & Witt, P. Sources of behavioural variance during leisure time. *Journal of Personality and Social Psychology*, 1970, *16*, 352-360.

Bowers, K. Situationism in psychology: An analysis and a critique. *Psychological Review*, 1973, *80*, 307-334.

Cartwright, D. Trait and other sources of variance in the S-R Inventory of Anxiousness. *Journal of Personality and Social Psychology*, 1975, *32*, 408–414.

Cooper, C. The utility of a general anxiety trait: Some methodological considerations. *British Journal of Social Psychology*, 1981, *20*, 135–139.

Dworkin, R., & Kihlstrom, J. An S-R inventory of dominance for research on the nature of person-situation interaction. *Journal of Personality*, 1978, *46*, 43–56.

Edinger, J., & Auerbach, S. Development and validation of a multidimensional multivariate model for accounting for infractions in a correction setting. *Journal of Personality and Social Psychology*, 1978, *36*, 1472–1499.

Ekehammar, B., Magnusson, D., & Ricklander, L. An interactionist approach to the study of anxiety: An analysis of an S-R inventory applied to an adolescent sample. *Scandinavian Journal of Psychology*, 1974, *15*, 4–14.

Endler, N. Estimating variance components from mean squares for random and mixed effects analysis of variance models. *Perceptual and Motor Skills*, 1966, *22*, 559–570.

Endler, N., & Hunt, J. S-R inventories of hostility and comparisons of the proportions of variance from persons, responses, and situations for hostility and anxiousness. *Journal of Personality and Social Psychology*, 1968, *9*, 309–315.

Endler, N. & Hunt, J. Generalizability of contributions from source of variance in the S-R Inventory of Anxiousness. *Journal of Personality*, 1969, *37*, 1–24.

Endler, N., Hunt, J., & Rosenstein, A. An S-R Inventory of Anxiousness. *Psychological Monographs*, 1962, *536*, 1–31.

Endler, N., & Magnusson, D. Toward an interactional psychology of personality. *Psychological Bulletin*, 1976, *83*, 956–974.

Fisher, A., Horsfall, J., & Morris, H. Sport personality assessment: A methodological re-examination. *International Journal of Sport Psychology*, 1977, *8*, 92–102.

Furnham, A. An S-R inventory for conformity research. Unpublished paper, 1980.

Furnham, A. A social S-R inventory of anxiousness. In M. Argyle, A. Furnham, and J. Graham (Eds.), *Social situations*. Cambridge: Cambridge University Press, 1981.

Furnham, A., & Argyle, M. (Eds.). *The psychology of social situations*. New York: Pergamon, 1981.

Furnham, A., Jaspars, J., & Fincham, F. Professional and naive psychology: Two approaches to the explanation of social behaviour. In J.

Jaspars, F. Fincham, & M. Hewstone (Eds.), *Attribution theory and research*, Vol. 1. London: Academic Press, 1983.

Golding, S. Flies in the ointment: Methodological problems in the analysis of the percentages of variance due to persons and situations. *Psychological Bulletin*, 1975, *82*, 278–288.

Golding, S., & Knudson, B. Multivariable-multimethod convergence in the domain of interpersonal behaviour. *Multivariate Behavioural Research*, 1975, *10*, 425–443.

Kuhl, J. Situations-, reaktions-, under personbezongene konsistenz des leislungsmotivs bei der messungmittels des heckhausen-TAT. *Archiv fur Psychologie*, 1978, *130*, 35–52.

Lantermann, E. Polnomusch-verbundene messung van personer, situationen und reakhonen auf der grundlage van S-R fragebogen. *Archiv fur Psychologie*, 1978, *130*, 342–351.

Lazzerini, A., Cox, T., & Mackay, C. Perceptions of and reactions to stressful situations: The utility of a general anxiety trait. *British Journal of Social and Clinical Psychology*, 1979, *18*, 363–369.

Magnusson, D., & Ekehammar, B. Anxiety profiles based on both situational and response factors. *Multivariate Behavioral Research*, 1975, *10*, 27–43.

Magnusson, D., & Endler, N. (Eds.). *Personality at the crossroads*. Hillsdale, N.J.: Lawrence Erlbaum Associates, 1977.

Mariotto, M. Interaction and the person and situation effects for chronic mental patients: A two-year follow-up. *Journal of Abnormal Psychology*, 1978, *87*, 676–679.

McCloskey, J. An interactional approach to self-disclosure. Paper presented at the BPS Social Psychology sections, Wales, 1978.

Mellstrom, M., Zuckerman, M., & Cicala, G. General vs specific traits in the assessment of anxiety. *Journal of Consulting and Clinical Psychology*, 1978, *46*, 423–431.

Mischel, W. *Personality and assessment*. New York: Wiley, 1968.

Mischel, W. Toward a cognitive social learning reconceptualization of personality. *Psychological Review*, 1973, *80*, 335–344.

Moos, R. Situational analysis of a therapeutic community milieu. *Abnormal Psychology*, 1968, *73*, 49–61.

Moos, R. Sources of variance in responses to questionnaires and in behavior. *Journal of Abnormal Psychology*, 1969, *74*, 405–412.

Moos, R. Differential effects of psychiatric ward settings on patient changes. *Journal of Mental and Nervous Diseases*, 1970, *151*, 316–321.

Nelson, E., Grinder, R., & Mutterer, M. Sources of variance in behavioral measures of honesty in temptation situations: Methodological analyses. *Developmental Psychology*, 1969, *1*, 265–279.

Olweus, S. "Modern" interactionism in personality psychology and the analysis of variance components approach. In D. Magnusson and N. Endler (Eds.), *Personality at the crossroads.* Hillsdale, N.J.: Lawrence Erlbaum Associates, 1977.

Price, R., & Bouffard, D. Behavioral appropriateness and situational constraints as dimensions of social behavior. *Journal of Personality and Social Psychology*, 1974, *30*, 579–586.

Raush, H., Dittmann, A., & Taylor, T. Person, setting and change in social interaction. *Human Relations*, 1959, *12*, 361–378.

Raush, H., Farbman, I., & Llewellyn, L. The interpersonal behavior of children in residential treatment. *Journal of Abnormal and Social Psychology*, 1959, *58*, 9–26.

Rushton, J., & Endler, N. Person by situation interactions in academic achievement. *Journal of Personality*, 1977, *45*, 297–309.

Sandell, R. Effects of attitudinal and situational factors on reported choice behavior. *Journal of Marketing Research*, 1968, *5*, 391–397.

Sarason, I., Smith, R., & Diener, E. Personality research: Components of variance attributable to the person and the situation. *Journal of Personality and Social Psychology*, 1975, *32*, 199–204.

Schmitt, N., & Saari, B. Behavior situation and rater variance in descriptions of leader behaviors. *Multivariate Behavioral Research*, 1978, *13*, 483–496.

Van Heck, G., & Van Der Leeuw, E. Situatie en dispositie als variateikomponenten in zelfbeourdeling en beoorderling van die ander. *Gedrag, tydschrift voor Psychologie*, 1975, *4*, 202–214.

Vleeming, R. Some sources of behavioural variance as measured by an S-R inventory of Machiavellianism. *Psychological Reports*, 1981, *48*, 359–368.

II

Psychological (Individual) and Sociological (Collectivistic) Approaches

3. Personal and Social Determinants of Behavior in Situations

LAWRENCE A. PERVIN
Rutgers University

INTRODUCTION

The history of psychology is filled with controversy focusing on extreme positions taken by competing points of view. The nature-nurture controversy illustrates this tendency; the recent person-situation controversy is another example. A common theme running through many controversies is the internal-external controversy (Pervin 1978a; Pervin and Lewis 1978).

This issue has been formulated in various ways. Allport (1955) found this issue, above all others, to divide psychologists: whether behavior is governed from within or from without. He attributed these differences to commitment of either a European, Leibnitzian tradition (i.e., an emphasis on internal causes, as in Freud and the gestalt psychologists) or an Anglo-American, Lockean tradition (i.e., an emphasis on external causes, as in Skinner and the association psychologists). Murray (1938) drew a similar distinction between centralists (viewing people as active and influenced by internal energies) and peripheralists (viewing people as mainly responsive to external stimuli). More recently, Harré and Secord (1973) drew attention to this tendency toward a dichotomy between an emphasis on environment contingencies as opposed to a view of the organism as self-directed and self-maintaining—the mechanistic model vs. the anthropomorphic, humanistic model.

In most specific areas of controversy, attention has gradually shifted from an emphasis on which is the cause of behavior to how much of each determines behavior, and ultimately to how internal and external factors interact to determine behavior. This sensible interactionist position provides the basis for investigating many questions, such as: How does the person retain some structural consistency and integrity while varying his or her behavior to meet the demands of the situation? How do people retain their individuality while conforming to the demands of society?

THE PERSON, SOCIETY, AND THE
RELATION BETWEEN THE TWO

An issue with some parallels to the internal-external question is the extent to which behavior is regulated by societal norms and rules, or by environmental constraints, as opposed to behavior's being regulated by person needs and wishes. Concepts such as the former emphasize what is common to the behavior of group members—homogeneity; concepts such as the latter emphasize what is specific to each individual—heterogeneity. Obviously, both are in most aspects of behavior (e.g., most people walk when the light is green, but they walk at different speeds and with different styles). The tendency, however, has been to focus either on what is common to people or on what is idiosyncratic. The perspective appears to be partly responsible for professional divisions such as those between sociologists and psychologists, or between social psychologists and clinical psychologists.

As indicated, sociologists in particular tend to emphasize concepts associated with similarities in behavior across individuals. The emphasis is on ways in which institutional goals can be met and on how reliable expectancies can exist concerning behavior. Such concepts as norms, roles, and rules are used to capture these regulatory aspects of social behavior. Goffman (1963) similarly focuses on the rules people learn and generally share in common in their daily social behavior.

Among psychologists, Barker (1968) has clearly articulated the view that environments and situations shape behavior along particular lines. According to Barker, the physical and social environments select and shape the people who inhabit them. These environments have structural and dynamic properties to which people must adapt. The same environmental unit provides different inputs to different persons, and the differing motives and cognitions of the inhabitants result in differing perceptions; nonetheless, the environment generates and maintains characteristic behavior patterns despite the great variety of internal conditions. Environments are viewed as homeostatic systems that maintain their characteristic patterns within preset limits by means of control mechanisms, just as a road has corrective mechanisms for driving too slow or too fast regardless of the individual's internal world.

For Barker, the concept of behavior setting expresses the intimate relation between environment and extra-individual patterns of behavior. These behavior patterns are independent of the participation of particular persons since they are characteristic of people en masse in that setting rather than of individuals. Individuals may change; the behavior pattern remains the same. The setting retains structural integrity despite change. Individuals may show considerable diversity in aspects of their behavior; Barker, however, emphasizes the similarities in behavior as they are related to the structural features of the environment.

In terms of the issue under consideration, note that Barker recognized that much of an individual's behavior in a setting does not conform to the behavior en masse. He described (1965) Maud's drugstore behavior as harmonious with and appropriate to the drugstore setting but also noted that much of her behavior did not conform to common social inputs: "Maud's relation to her environment was quite different in the large than in the small. If we look upon this as a test of Maud's drugstore behavior, we see that Maud failed most of the items, but she passed the test" (Barker 1965, 8).

Basing their efforts on Barker's work, Wicker (1972) and Price (1974) investigated how a congruence between behavior and environment is achieved. They emphasized processes orienting behavior toward goals, the specification of behavior to be acted, and the use of devices to counter deviation. The concept of situational constraint (Price 1974; Price and Bouffard 1974) expresses the extent to which the situation calls for or demands certain behaviors and not others. Barker's emphasis is mainly on how the physical environment regulates behavior; the emphasis here is on how social aspects (i.e., expectations, rules, norms) combine to regulate behavior. Similarly, Argyle (1977, 1980) attempts to understand the "deep structure" of situations through an analysis of the rules that "specify what should and should not happen, including who may be present, what should be worn, and appropriate sequences of behavior" (1977, 364).

These approaches all emphasize the organization and patterning of common forms of social behavior. An interdependence between person and environment is recognized, but emphasis is placed on forces in the environment that act on the person. The focus is on how the setting acts on people as opposed to how the people act on the setting or on the reciprocal relationship between the two. The environment selects and shapes behavior! The world of internal perceptions, cognitions, and feelings is recognized, but attention is drawn exclusively to attributes of overt behavior.

In contrast with such sociological, ecological, and social psychological analyses are the analyses by personality and clinical psychologists. The differences are remarkable, not only in terms of such concepts as traits and needs, but also in terms of the types of behaviors and situations emphasized. Rather than looking at behavior on the turnpike, attention is drawn to responses to the Rorschach. Even within the latter, particular interest is in the unusual rather than the popular response. The clinician is interested in the uncommon in the unstructured situation rather than in the common in the structured situation.

Analyzing ecobehavioral entities and situational constraints involves disregarding individual differences to highlight environmental and normative regulations; analyzing traits and character structure involves disregarding normative behavior and variations in behavior across situations to highlight individual regularities. In the one, emphasis is on the games people play with one another and with the rules followed to lead to social goals; in the other, emphasis is on the games people play with themselves and the rules they follow to attain personal goals. The one emphasizes the deep structure of settings and social interaction; the other emphasizes the deep structure of people and the relationships among parts within the person.

As noted, an exclusive focus on one or another domain of inquiry not only leads to a distorted sense of behavior but also dismisses the opportunity for investigating individual-environment, personal-social relationships. To a certain extent, Jung drew attention to this issue when he considered the relationship between the individual's persona or mask developed in response to society's demands and the private self that develops in response to internal demands. Part of the human dilemma is to be able to integrate a public personality with a private personality, to conform to the demands of social convention without becoming alienated from personal experience and genuine feeling.

In a broader analysis of the issue, and as part of an attempt to develop a general theory of action, Parsons and Shils (1951) suggested that the relationship between personality and social role is a critical question facing the social sciences. Using a systems perspective, they drew attention to the issue of articulation between the personality and the social system, between personal needs or goals and societal role expectations or norms. Roles keep the person's behavior within narrow limits and provide for shared expectations, but they have a significance and an effect on motivation different for different personalities. Commenting further, "an important feature of a large proportion of social roles is that the actions which make them up are not minutely prescribed and that a certain range of variability is regarded as legitimate. . . . This range of freedom makes it possible for actors with different personalities to fulfill within considerable limits the expectations associated with roughly the same roles without undue strain" (24).

They emphasize two aspects of behavior in their focus on the person. The first, motivational orientation, refers to the influence of need-dispositions on behavior. The second, value orientation, refers to the influence of norms or social standards on behavior. The effort of both society and the person must be to provide for some integration between the two. In demanding conformity to role expectations, the society must provide for need satisfaction. In satisfying needs of pursuing personal goals, the individual must function within the context of social norms. In other words, an intimate relationship between the social and the personal may be associated with varying degrees of strain or malintegration.

Whether one prefers terms such as *role expectations* and *need dispositions*, as suggested by Parsons and Shils, or other terms, the point is that attention can be drawn to the articulation of personality and social systems. Although for certain purposes it may be useful to consider behavioral regularities associated with norms and roles, and for other purposes it may be useful to consider individual regularities associated with traits or needs, for many purposes it may be useful to focus on the relation between the two. In a broader context, this focus means recognizing that behavior is always a function of the person and the situation, the personal and the social, or the internal and the external.

PERSONAL AND SOCIAL DETERMINANTS— SOME RELEVANT ANALYSES

The data here are an extension of data gathered by Champagne. They relate to the issues raised and suggest directions for future research. The study on which the data build involves testing the social learning hypothesis that a person will respond to situations similarly to the extent that they are perceived as similar in their reinforcement contingencies.

To test this hypothesis, each of six subjects completed the following tasks:

1. Listing twenty situations representative of their current life; each situation was defined in terms of who is there, where it occurs, when it occurs, and what is going on.
2. Rating the probability of their expressing each of fourteen behaviors in each of the twenty situations.
3. Rating the probability of receiving each of nine reinforcers for each of the fourteen behaviors in each situation.
4. Rating the value of each of the nine reinforcers in each situation. All probability and value ratings were made on a four-point scale: very likely, somewhat likely, somewhat unlikely, very unlikely for probability ratings; and very important, somewhat important, somewhat unimportant, and very unimportant for value ratings.
5. Paired comparison rating of the similarity of pairs of situations.
6. Paired comparison rating of the similarity of their behavior in pairs of situations.
7. Completing semantic differential ratings for each situation, the scales involving characteristics of the situation (e.g., formal-informal), feelings in the situation (e.g., happy-sad), and behavior in the situation (e.g., hostile-friendly).

Four distinguishing characteristics and preliminary findings are worth noting. First, the study involved considerable data with a few subjects, with at least some data being unique to the subject (e.g., listing twenty personal situations). My emphasis had been on an idiographic approach to research (Pervin 1977). Through such an approach, I can present tasks of greater interest and meaning to subjects than would otherwise be the case, while still testing principles in a systematic way. Obviously, an idiographic approach is not suitable for all questions, and one must be able to suggest generalizations across subjects, but I have found it a useful procedure for many questions concerning individual-environment interaction.

Second, the data involved perceptions of situations, feelings, and behaviors, all seen as important though somewhat independent aspects of responses to situations. Of course, data concerning actual behavior would also be desirable; such data are difficult to obtain given the representative nature of the situations.

Third, the reinforcers listed included both external sources of reinforcement (e.g., receive praise or receive criticism) and internal sources of reinforcement (e.g., self-praise or self-criticism), the importance of which relates to the personal-social issue emphasized and to which we shall return later. Finally, the analyses in many cases involved patterns of scores rather than individual scores or sums of scores, providing a more realistic picture of how people perceive and respond to situations.

The preliminary analyses of these data, involving multidimensional scaling analyses, suggest that people respond similarly to situations perceived to be similar in their reinforcement contingencies. In another approach to data analysis, I reported evidence suggesting that the probability of a behavior is a function of the probability of positive reinforcers multiplied by their values minus the probability of unpleasant, undesirable reinforcers multiplied by their values, as suggested by social learning theory. However, the exceptions to this overall pattern appear to be due to the potential for an effective response to override the anticipated response consequences. Thus, for example, a subject is not likely to smile when with a sick grandfather, even though such a response would be followed by positive consequences, because the subject is overcome with grief and sadness (Pervin 1980). Reinforcers, external and internal, are important but not all-determinant.

In the study of the relationship between behavioral probabilities and anticipated consequences, four situations were chosen at random if they met the criterion of being associated with behaviors of varying probability for each situation. These same four situations were used in the research reported here, involving the extent to which other individuals could anticipate the subjects' responses to each of the four situations used in the earlier analysis (i.e., meeting with friends in the dormitory; riding in the car with a date; at the deathbed of a grandfather; on the phone with mother).

Eight subjects, four female and four male, were asked to predict the responses of the average female college student to each situation on each of three tasks: (1) probability of each behavior in each situation; (2) probability of each reinforcer for each behavior in each situation; (3) value of each reinforcer in each situation. The assumption here was that if behavior is normatively regulated, then the eight subjects should agree concerning the probabilities of the behaviors in each situation as well as the probabilities and values of the reinforcers. Such agreement should also match what the subject reports. An absence of agreement among the raters would suggest that norms, rules, or shared expectations do not exist, and a lack of predictive accuracy would suggest either that norms do not exist or that the person reports the likelihood of unusual or deviant behavior. In addition, since both internal and external reinforcers are included, the data offer the opportunity for comparing agreement and accuracy of these two categories of reinforcement.

In terms of data analysis, criteria for agreement and accuracy needed to be determined. For agreement, the percent of agreement among the four raters was defined in terms of the number of pairs of raters that agreed in their rating of the specific probability of a behavior, reinforcer, or value of a reinforcer and the number of pairs of raters that agreed in the next closest probability cell on the same side of the likely-unlikely or important-unimportant continuum. With eight raters, there were 28 possible pairs of agreement. Thus, for example, if two people rated a behavior as very likely and four as somewhat likely, the percent agreement would be 25 percent (6 of 28 pairs = 21 percent plus 2 pairs of a possible 28 = 4 percent), regardless of whether the two remaining raters agreed that the behavior (or reinforcer) was somewhat unlikely or very unlikely. For accuracy of prediction, the criterion used was the percentage of the eight raters that accurately predicted the subject's actual response. Again, if behaviors in these situations are normatively defined, one should get high agreement and high accuracy whereas low scores would suggest that there is not normative agreement or, in the case of accuracy, that the subject responded in a deviant fashion.

The first question is about the amount of agreement concerning the probability of each of the fourteen behaviors in each of the four situations. The relevant data appear in Table 3-1 and these conclusions are suggested:

1. Some difference in agreement among the situations exists across the fourteen behaviors, but not a great deal. Across the four situations, there is 43 percent agreement; the situation "On the phone with mother" shows the least agreement concerning the probability of the various behaviors.

2. Within each situation, there is considerable agreement concerning the probabilities of some behaviors and disagreement concerning the probabilities of other behaviors. For example,

TABLE 3-1
Mean Percent Agreement and Mean Percent Accuracy
in Estimates of the Probabilities of
Behaviors in Each of Four Situations

	Situation			
	1	2	3	4
Mean Percent Agreement	47	46	47	33
Mean Percent Accuracy	46	46	49	25

1 = Visiting friends in the dormitory
2 = Riding in car with a date
3 = At the deathbed of grandfather
4 = On the phone with mother

everyone agrees that it is very likely that the person will smile a
lot while "visiting friends in the dormitory," but there is little
agreement about whether the person will act involved or be
submissive in that same situation.

3. In a certain sense, each situation can be defined by a few behaviors that people agree are very likely or very unlikely. For
example, in the situation "visiting friends in the dormitory"
there is good agreement that the person is very likely to be
friendly and smile a lot and that the person is unlikely to be
hostile, detached, or formal. Thus, over the sample of fourteen
behaviors, there may be agreement concerning the likelihood of
a few behaviors, the unlikelihood of a few other behaviors, and
disagreement concerning the majority of the behaviors. Thus, it
may be that high, though not absolute, agreement concerning a
few defining characteristics is all that is necessary for people to
define or classify most situations. While this conclusion may be
surprising, in that intuitively we might sense there is greater
agreement, such efforts toward simplifying and categorizing
would accord with other evidence of the functioning of prototypes for objects and people (Cantor and Mischel 1979). Also
note that we are speaking of agreement concerning the likelihood of various behaviors and not of accuracy, a point we will
return to. As Cantor and Mischel (1979) point out, categories
or prototypes require some match to reality but an absolute
match is not required for them to exist and be used.

4. Considering the behaviors across the four situations, we can see
that some variation in agreement exists about the overall probability of various behaviors (see Table 3-2). Thus, for example,

people are generally in greater agreement concerning the likelihood of the person's being active in these four situations than they are concerning the likelihood of the person's being submissive, passive, or expressing disagreement. Whether, in general, people are more in agreement concerning the likelihood of "desirable" behaviors than "undesirable" behaviors is an interesting question. In any case, probably more striking than the average agreement across the four situations is the variation in agreement for each behavior according to the particular situation. Whereas people are sure the person will be friendly and smile a lot while "visiting friends in the dorm," they are not nearly so sure about these behaviors when the person is "talking on the phone with mother." To return to the previous point, each situation may have some of its own defining behavioral characteristics, but the particular behaviors that are

TABLE 3–2
Mean Percent Agreement and Mean Percent Accuracy
in the Probability Estimates of Behaviors
across Four Situations

Behavior	Mean Percent Agreement	Mean Percent Accuracy
Act friendly	53	35
Act involved	48	50
Submissive	26	44
Aloof, detached	38	50
Active	76	47
Formal, rigid	35	38
Dominant	38	41
Hostile, unfriendly	53	60
Passive	31	22
Informal, open	32	50
Talk a lot	49	41
Express disagreement	31	10
Smile a lot	59	32
Express opinions	38	29

salient in their prescription or proscription vary from situation to situation. It is likely that some behaviors are generally more key for defining and classifying situations than are other behaviors, but every behavior may be a key defining characteristic for at least some situations.

The second question concerns the accuracy of the raters' predictions of the behavioral probability responses; that is, to what extent were they accurate in predicting the subject's response concerning the probability of each behavior? The relevant data in Tables 3-1 and 3-2 suggest these conclusions:

1. Across the fourteen behaviors, three situations are similar in average amount of accuracy, and the fourth, "on the phone with mother," shows considerably less accuracy (Table 3-1). This result may be partially due to the lesser amount of agreement concerning the likelihood of various behaviors in this situation or to the more unusual responses of the subject herself.

2. As with agreement, in each situation, some responses are predicted quite accurately and others are not (Table 3-2). These results bear some relationship to the agreement figures, but the relationship is not absolute. Thus, for example, though all eight raters agreed that it was very likely that the subject would smile a lot "while visiting with friends in the dormitory," the subject rated this behavior as only somewhat likely. In the same situation, seven of the eight raters thought it very or somewhat unlikely that the person would be passive, while the subject rated herself as somewhat likely to behave in this way; and whereas six of the eight raters thought it likely that she would express disagreement in this situation, the subject reported it somewhat unlikely that she would do so. In the second situation, "riding in the car with my date," the raters are in fair disagreement concerning the likelihood of her expressing disagreement and none of them accurately predicted her response of very likely doing so.

3. Looking at the fourteen behaviors, we again find individual variations in ease of predictability of response, but perhaps more impressive is the extent to which almost every behavior shows a high degree of predictability in one situation and a low degree of predictability in another.

To summarize these data concerning accuracy of prediction of response, we can say that situations and behaviors vary in their overall degree of predictability. This conclusion should not be surprising. Further, however, some relationship may exist between rater agreement about the likelihood of a response and accuracy of prediction, but this relationship is not absolute. In relatively few cases are behaviors so prescribed or proscribed that prediction is perfect; people often do the unexpected or behave differently from how they or others feel they should behave (Deutscher 1973). Norms can exist even though they are frequently ignored.

Turning to behavioral consequences, we can ask whether raters agree about the probable consequences for the various behaviors in the situations; that is, to what extent do people agree about the probability of various behaviors being reinforced in various situations, and to what extent do they agree about the values of these reinforcers? As noted, social learning expectancy × value theories emphasize that the probability of a behavior is a function of the expected consequences of that behavior and the value of these consequences. Furthermore, as also noted, a particularly significant aspect of current social learning theory (Bandura 1977) and some forms of current attitude theory (Bentler and Speckart 1979; Fishbein and Ajzen 1975) emphasize internal as well as perceived external sources of reinforcement.

In social learning theory, self-control or self-regulation is exercised through maintaining internal standards used as the basis for self-reinforcement in the form of self-praise or self-criticism. Such internal, self-control mechanisms are distinguished from regulation by external sources of reinforcement, such as praise and criticism from others. Similarly, the Fishbein-Ajzen theory of attitude-behavior relations suggests that behavior intention (i.e., the subjective probability of a behavior), which is seen as a close prediction of actual behavior, is a function of the expectancy × value total for internal and perceived external consequences of a behavior. The concept of subjective norm is used for the latter source of reinforcement.

Here, we can consider the agreement about the probable consequences for the various behaviors in the four situations and the agreement about the expected value of these reinforcers for the subject. If our own behavior is largely, though not totally, determined by such an expectancy × value relationship, then perhaps our expectancies of the behaviors of others are also a function of how we think they will perceive the probable consequence of each behavior and the value of those consequences. We can proceed, then, by calculating the agreement among the eight raters for the probability and value of each reinforcer (N = 9), for each behavior (N = 14), in each situation (N = 4), and then consider the overall agreement for situations and reinforcers. The relevant data in Tables 3–3 and 3–4 suggest these conclusions:

1. Do the situations differ in the extent to which raters agree, overall, in their rating of the expected consequences for the various behaviors? The data suggest greater overall agreement

TABLE 3-3
Mean Percent Agreement and Mean Percent Accuracy
in the Prediction of Probable Consequences
of Behaviors in Four Situations and of the
Value of these Consequences

	Situation			
	1	2	3	4
Mean Percent Agreement				
Probable Consequences	40	43	29	33
Value Reinforcers	33	43	38	25
Mean Percent Accuracy				
Probable Consequences	45	49	34	35
Value Reinforcers	52	61	38	38

1 = Visiting friends in the dormitory
2 = Riding in car with a date
3 = At the deathbed of grandfather
4 = On the phone with mother

about the probable consequences for the behaviors in situations 1 and 2 (Table 3-3). In terms of agreement concerning the value of the nine reinforcers in each situation, generally there is greater agreement for the first three situations than for the fourth situation. Of course, there is variation in agreement concerning the probability and value of the various reinforcers in each situation, though in general one can see that agreement consequences for behavior in a situation such as "riding in car with date" is greater than that for behavior in a situation such as "talking on the phone with mother." Not surprisingly, this result parallels that found in the study of agreement concerning the probability of the behaviors in these situations. Each situation has behaviors more or less clearly associated with specific consequences, with situations varying in the overall extent to which people can agree on these consequences.

A note can be made about agreement on internal as opposed to external reinforcers. Overall differences in agreement were not found for the probability of internal and external consequences for the various behaviors, but a striking difference was found in agreement about the value of external reinforcers (56 percent for receive love, affection and 34 percent for receive disapproval) as opposed to agreement concerning the value of internal reinforcers (31 percent for self-approval and 15 percent for self-disapproval). This difference was found in each of the four situations. In other words, in predicting how people will estimate the consequences of their behavior, it may be more difficult to estimate their internal standards than to estimate their perception of external standards. Of course, here, too, there will be variation. Predicting internal standards would be easier to the extent that we know a person well, when we know their attitudes in Fishbein and Ajzen's terms. Predicting external standards would be difficult when interacting with someone from a different culture, when we are unclear about the subjective norm in Fishbein and Ajzen's terms.

2. Turning to agreement and accuracy concerning the consequences associated with the specific behaviors (across the four situations and nine reinforcers), we again see considerable variability (Table 3-4). At the extremes, a fair amount of agreement exists among the raters and between them and the subject about the probable consequences of being hostile or unfriendly; but much lesser agreement exists among the raters as to the probable consequences of being dominant and much less agreement between the rates and the subject about the consequences of behaving in an aloof, detached manner. Again, these means mask the considerable variability that exists for the various behaviors and expected consequences in the different situations. Consensus might exist about the consequences of a behavior in one situation, but not about the consequences of a behavior in another situation, or agreement concerning the probability of some reinforcers for behavior in a situation but disagreement concerning the probability of other reinforcers for that behavior in the same situation. As noted, agreement and accuracy can be greater or lesser for internal as opposed to external reinforcers in each situation.

What, then, are we to conclude from these data? We have considered only eight raters each predicting the response of one subject to fourteen behaviors and nine reinforcers in each of four situations. Other raters, behaviors, situations, and reinforcers could be considered, but the general nature of the conclusions would not differ. The three conclusions here make intuitive, empirical and theoretical sense.

First, behavior is regulated by normative and personal standards to varying degrees. Such variation exists in situations, behaviors, and people. Each situation has behaviors more or less clearly associated with specific consequences, with situations varying in the overall extent to which people can agree on these consequences. Each behavior is more

TABLE 3-4

Mean Percent Agreement and Mean Percent
Accuracy for Probability of Reinforcement
Ratings across Nine Reinforcers and
Four Situations

Behavior	Mean Percent Agreement	Mean Percent Accuracy
Act friendly	43	50
Act involved	34	41
Submissive	31	34
Aloof, detached	44	28
Active	33	44
Formal, rigid	35	34
Dominant	30	35
Hostile, unfriendly	54	51
Passive	37	42
Informal, open	37	45
Talk a lot	31	42
Express disagreement	36	40
Smile a lot	35	44
Express opinions	35	36

or less clearly associated with specific consequences in specific situations, with behaviors varying in the overall extent to which people can agree on their consequences. Finally, though not indicated in the data, we know that people vary in the extent to which different behaviors can be predicted in different kinds of situations (Bem and Allen 1974). In other words, situations, behaviors, and people can be more or less predictable.

Second, it has been suggested that only a few behaviors in a situation need to be perceived as having high consensus in probability or improbability for there to be a sense that behavior in that situation is normatively regulated or for there to be a sense of typical or appropriate behavior for the situation. Such prototypes, like person and physical object prototypes, leave considerable room for elements (behaviors) outside the domain of the prototype and even for elements (behaviors) that in specific cases violate the prototype. Norms continue to exist despite our recognition that we do not always do what we are supposed to do or what we say we will do. If we were to subject our predictions of behavior in social situations to the same tests that we do our predictions based on psychological tests, we would probably find them to be of questionable reliability and validity—yet sufficiently useful to get on with the business of life.

Third, it has been suggested that a useful distinction can be made between the person's expectations and valuing of consequences emanating from internal standards as opposed to those perceived as coming from the surrounding environment. Internal and perceived external standards may be more or less important in different situations and in different people. For example, Carver (1979) suggested a cybernetic model in which behavior can be matched to internal and external standards. Snyder (1979) found that some people monitor their behavior closely according to the demands of the situation whereas other people rely to a greater extent on internal cues. As noted, internal and external standards can be predicted to varying degrees depending on our knowledge of the individual and the culture of which he or she is a part. Finally, the concepts of internal and external standards can be useful in analyzing conflict within the individual or between the individual and society.

Though these data and the associated anayses only begin to answer the question of the relation between internal standards and the perception of external standards, or the relation between internal standards and actual external norms, they suggest the kinds of data and analyses that can be considered. An overall theoretical context within which such issues can be viewed follows.

SITUATIONAL BEHAVIOR WITHIN THE CONTEXT OF A THEORY OF GOALS

Understanding behavior in situations and the importance of internal and external standards for reinforcement can occur within the context of a theory of goals. This section sketches some propositions toward a theory of goals, drawing heavily on cybernetics and general systems theory (see Pervin 1978 a), affect theory, and social learning theory and is similar to recent formulations in psychoanalytic theory (Holt 1976; Rosenblatt and Thickstun 1977). The propositions currently being considered follow:

1. *Behavior in situations and the choice of situations to be in are primarily directed toward obtaining goals.* This proposition sets forth the purposive, intentional, goal-directed quality of human life. Cybernetics theory, with its emphasis on goals, feedback loops, and self-control

mechanisms, has provided the basis for a purposive, nonteleological view of human behavior. If you were to log your behavior throughout the day, considering the situations you are in and your behavior in them, you would be impressed with this goal-directed quality.

Most situations are chosen at least in part because they serve as part of a plan in acquiring or achieving a goal. In this sense, often they cannot be understood in and of themselves but, instead, can only be understood in terms of their place in a goal-directed system. Similarly, behaviors and situations are rarely activated or caused by specific stimuli, in particular environmental stimuli. Rather, they occur within the context of goal selection. If no one is home, the dog sleeps all day, unless disturbed by the mail carrier or a passing car. A person home alone works according to the goals set forth that can realistically be accomplished in the time available.

2. *Goals have cognitive, affective, and behavioral properties.* The cognitive component of a goal involves mental representations (images) of goals and constructions of paths (plans) toward these goals. These representations and constructions can be more or less developed and more or less available to awareness. The goal's affective component involves the association of the goal and relevant plan with affect. The goal and movement toward and away from it are associated with affect.

The goal's behavioral component involves the behaviors necessary for goal acquisition. The cognitive and affective components can be strong or weak, in absolute and relative terms. A goal with strong cognitive and weak affective components has the quality of a belief. A goal with strong affective and weak cognitive components has the quality of an urge, wish, or desire. A goal without a defined plan has the quality of a fantasy.

3. *Goals vary in content, time span, complexity, and importance.* Since almost anything can be associated with affect and thereby take on goal qualities, it is impossible to develop an absolute list of goals or a functional classification that will hold across all individuals. This emphasis on the varied content or focus of goals despite their similarity of basis in affect is similar to Freud's emphasis on the object of instincts and wishes being variable relative to their source and aim. Goals can be long-range or short-range, the former involving greater cognitive importance.

4. *Personality can be considered in terms of the individual's goal system, including its stable and fluid (dynamic) qualities and its qualities of integration and conflict.* Goals function in relation to one another in terms of a system. Any person's goal system may contain many or few goals, many or few levels in the goal hierarchy, and simple or complex relationships among goals. The overall goal system has stable

properties, but relationships among goals can vary depending on changes inside the person (e.g., mood) and environmental circumstances (e.g., barriers or incentives in the situation). Goals function in terms of a hierarchical system, but the system need not be fixed and certainly there is no absolute ordering of goal priority across individuals. Survival goals may be critical for most individuals, but for some people, these goals become secondary to those of patriotism and altruism, for example. The various goals within the person's goal system can be integrated or in conflict with one another.

5. *Goals are acquired or learned on the basis of the association of affects with specific people, objects, events, symbols, or processes.* In terms of the importance of affect in goals, goals are acquired or learned primarily on the basis of classical conditioning and vicarious learning. In the course of development, the goal system becomes increasingly complex (differentiation and integration), includes a greater time span (e.g., delay of gratification), and is associated with greater affective complexity due to important cognitive developments. Cognitive developments are not critical to the basic affects, but they do provide for differentiation of particular affects (e.g., the development of affects such as guilt and jealousy require certain cognitive developments not required for affects, such as anxiety and excitement). A particularly important aspect of goal development is developing internal standards for self-control and self-regulation (e.g., self-praise and self-criticism), considered in psychoanalytic theory under the terms *ego ideal* and *super-ego.* Individuals differ in the importance of internal standards (i.e., internal goals) and external standards (i.e., goals dependent on responses from others).

6. *Goal-directed functioning can be considered in terms of the variables influencing their activation, selection, maintenance, and termination.* Goals can be activated by external or internal stimuli. The former are more important for lower-order species and children; the latter are generally more important for higher-order species and adults.

Where movement toward achieving more than one goal is possible, the person may choose one goal over another, find some compromise, or develop a plan leading to the achievement of more than one goal. In general, the choice among goals is based on an optimizing or instrumentality principle (i.e., the importance of each goal and the potential for achieving it) involving cognitive, affective, and behavioral elements. Selection often is a complex process since situations generally provide for the achievement of many goals (i.e., multidetermination) and for conflict among goals. Since many goals involve considerable time, delay, frustration, and the person's ability to put them aside and retrieve them, mechanisms for retaining a goal in memory (image) and for keeping the person goal-directed are important. Concepts such as intermittent reinforcement may be important here; it is more likely, however, that developing subgoals and internal mechanisms for self-control are more important in accounting for the perseverence often associated with goal-directed behavior. Activity toward a goal is terminated when the goal is achieved, when it is blocked, or when attention is directed toward another, more important, or more possible goal.

7. *Psychopathy and interpersonal conflict can be understood in terms of conflicts among goals and/or among plans.* Individual psychopathology consists of conflicted or nonintegrated system functioning. For the individual, conflict can exist between goals (e.g., between wishes or between wishes and fears in psychoanalytic terms) or between paths toward a goal. A dyadic or family system can be considered to be integrated to the extent that goals and plans are shared or different but compatible with one another. If this is not the case, then conflict and strain exist within the system. Members of a group share the same values and norms to the extent that they share common goals and plans; that is, certain objects, symbols, and patterns of behavior have similar affective significance for the group members. This is what culture is about. Deviance and individual-society conflict exist when the person pursues goals in conflict with societal goals or pursues shared goals in ways that conflict with society's prescribed plans. In terms of the individual's relation to society, conflict can exist within the individual between internal standards and perceived external standards or between individual and societal goal systems.

These propositions are suggested as providing the basis for a formulation of personality and behavior that considers the purposive nature of human functioning and focuses on cognition, affect, and behavior without making one the ruler of the others. People, in terms of their goal systems, are seen as both stable and fluid, as preserving their structural integrity while influencing and adapting to life's varied events. The propositions emphasize the system aspects of individual, interpersonal, and societal functioning. The particular issues considered here offer the basis for investigating goal-complementarity and goal-conflict within the person, goal-complementarity and goal-conflict between actors in a situation, as illustrated in the work of Argyle, Furnham, and Graham (1981) and for investigating goal-complementarity and goal-conflict between the person and society.

> The constraints imposed on us by the expectations we learn to develop of the natural world, of each other, and of ourselves correspond to three common verbs. They help to define for us what we can and cannot do, must and must not do, and should and should not do. Conflicts may occur within each of these categories and between any of them....

To resolve or contain such conflicts is the main activity of individual and collective human life, and the ability to do so is its main enlargement, perhaps the only dimension along which anything worth calling progress is open to humankind. So it is especially important that the psychosocial sciences should not state the problem in trivial or misleading terms. (Vickers 1973, 248)

REFERENCES

Allport, G. W. *Becoming: Basic considerations for a psychology of personality.* New Haven: Yale, 1955.

Argyle, M. Predictive and generative rules models of P × S. In D. Magnusson & N. S. Endler (Eds.), *Personality at the crossroads.* Hillsdale, N.J.: Lawrence Erlbaum Associates, 1977.

Argyle, M. The experimental study of the basic features of situations. In D. Magnusson (Ed.), *Toward a psychology of situations.* Hillsdale, N.J.: Lawrence Erlbaum Associates, 1980.

Argyle, M., Furnham, A., & Graham, J. *Social situations.* Cambridge: Cambridge University Press, 1981.

Bandura, A. *Social learning theory.* Englewood Cliffs, N.J.: Prentice-Hall, 1977.

Barker, R. G. Explorations in ecological psychology. *American Psychologist,* 1965, *20,* 1–14.

Barker, R. G. *Ecological psychology.* Stanford, Calif.: Stanford University Press, 1968.

Bem, D. J., & Allen, A. On predicting some of the people some of the time: The search for cross-situational consistencies in behavior. *Psychological Review,* 1974, *81,* 506–520.

Bentler, P. M., & Speckart, G. Models of attitude-behavior relations. *Psychological Review,* 1979, *86,* 452–464.

Cantor, N., & Mischel, W. Prototypes in person perception. In L. Berkowitz (Ed.), *Advances in experimental social psychology.* New York: Academic, 1979.

Carver, C. S. A cybernetic model of self-attention processes. *Journal of Personality and Social Pscyhology,* 1979, *8,* 1251–1281.

Deutscher, I. *What we say/What we do.* Glenview, Ill.: Scott-Foresman & Co., 1973.

Fishbein, M., & Ajzen, I. *Belief, attitude, intention and behavior.* Reading, Mass.: Addison-Wesley, 1975.

Goffman, E. *Behavior in public places.* Glencoe, Ill.: Free Press, 1963.

Harré, R., & Secord, P. F. *The explanation of social behavior.* Totowa, N.J.: Littlefield, Adams & Co., 1973.

Holt, R. R. Drive or wish? A reconsideration of the psychoanalytic theory of motivation. *Psychological Issues*, 1976, *9*, 158–197.

Murray, H. A. *Explorations in personality.* New York: Oxford University Press, 1938.

Parsons, T., & Shils, E. A. (Eds.). *Toward a general theory of action.* Cambridge, Mass.: Harvard University Press, 1951.

Pervin, L. A. *Current controversies and issues in personality.* New York: Wiley, 1978. (a)

Pervin, L. A. Theoretical approaches to the analysis of individual-environment interaction. In L. A. Pervin & M. Lewis (Eds.), *Perspectives in interactional psychology.* New York: Wiley, 1978. (b)

Pervin, L. A. The relation of situations to behavior. In D. Magnusson (Ed.), *Toward a psychology of situations.* Hillsdale, N.J.: Lawrence Erlbaum Associates, 1980.

Pervin, L. A., & Lewis, M. (Eds.). *Perspectives in interactional psychology.* New York: Wiley, 1978.

Price, R. H. The taxonomic classification of behavior and situations and the problem of behavior-environment congruence. *Human Relations*, 1974, *27*, 567–585.

Price, R. H., & Bouffard, D. L. Behavioral appropriateness and situational constraints as dimensions of social behavior. *Journal of Personality and Social Psychology*, 1974, *30*, 579–586.

Rosenblatt, A. D., & Thickstun, J. T. Modern psychoanalytic concepts in a general psychology. *Psychological Issues*, 1977, *11*, Monograph 42/43.

Snyder, M. Self-monitoring processes. In L. Berkowitz (Ed.), *Advances in experimental social psychology.* New York: Academic, 1979.

Vickers, G. Motivation theory—A cybernetic contribution. *Behavioral Science*, 1973, *18*, 242–249.

Wicker, A. W. Processes which mediate behavior-environment congruence. *Behavioral Science*, 1972, *17*, 265–277.

4. Personality and Social Behavior

HANS J. EYSENCK
University of London

INTRODUCTION

Traditionally, the determinants of social behavior are analyzed in two major categories. The first is the social situation; a type of behavior that individuals can be expected to show is obviously circumscribed by the situation in which they find themselves. When attacked by enemies, you can show heroism or cowardice; when in a group with other people, you can be sociable or unsociable; when someone is trying to persuade you to do something, you can be suggestible or nonsuggestible, and so forth. The situation determines the dimension along which your behavior may lie; the dimension cowardice-heroism does not apply to the type of situation calling for sociability-nonsociability, or suggestibility-nonsuggestibility. In this sense, what is sometimes called situationism obviously describes an important aspect of social behavior; the situation determines the kinds of behavior relevant to it.

Once we define the dimensions relevant to the situation, we notice that reactions can be varied. This is implicit in the notion that we are dealing with a continuum. When attacked, some people behave in a heroic fashion, others in a cowardly one; the situation, while defining the continuum of relevant reaction, does not define the particular reactions shown by different people.

This necessitates the second type of variable needed for a total description of the social interactions involved—personality. The variability of people in identical situations necessitates the concept of personality and its scientific study. This need was brought out by the ninety-nine-year-old Greek philosopher Theophrastus, when he asked the question that inspired his book *Characters:* "Why is it that while all Greece lies under the same sky and all the Greeks are educated alike, it has befallen us to have characters variously constituted?" Individual differences in reaction to identical situations are a most prominent part of the general picture and demand an explanation.

Descriptively, such an explanation has usually been furnished in terms of traits. From time immemorial, the person in the street, as well as the philosopher and the psychologist, have identified such traits as sociability, impulsiveness, activity, and persistence. These traits do little more than define the observed continua established by different types of situations. They do not furnish us with an explanation of why a person is sociable, or suggestible, or persistent. Many critics have pointed out that this practice may be tautological (Lundin 1961). We observe people behaving in a sociable or nonsociable manner and ascribe their behavior to a trait of sociability; we observe people behaving in a persistent or nonpersistent manner and ascribe this behavior to a trait of persistence. Lundin likened this practice to that of the early instinct theorists who ascribed behavior to a given instinct; as he pointed out, the instinct is derived from the behavior and cannot therefore be used to explain the behavior in question.

This type of objection has two answers. First, description must precede explanation. We must know what is to be explained before we can proceed to frame causal hypotheses. Trait descriptions are meant to be descriptions of differences in behavior along a certain dimension; they are not meant to give a causal explanation of why this behavior occurs. Such a causal explanation must, of course, follow, but the descriptive phase is important and cannot be aborted.

This point is reinforced by the second one, which is logically connected with the first. Positing traits is easy, but it is not enough. A descriptive study is needed. Such a study can easily show that the postulated trait does not exist or that instead of one trait there are several, quite unconnected ones. An experimental and statistical method for solving the question of no-trait, one trait, or many is needed. Such a statistical method is available in the correlational and factor analytical methodologies elaborated by statisticians and psychologists since their beginnings in the work of Galton and Pearson (Mackenzie 1981). The fact that empirical work along these lines has brought out many surprises and much discussion illustrates that we are not dealing with a tautology but with an experimental problem that must be dealt with along empirical lines. A few examples may illustrate this point.

One example is the early work of Hartshorne and May (1928, 1929) and Hartshorne and Shuttleworth (1930) on deceit, service and self-control, and the organization of character. These studies were carried out to test the hypothesis that trans-situational consistency existed in behavior and could be used to uphold the notion of traits and personality in general. Thorndike (1903) had put forward the revolutionary view that "there are no broad, general traits of personality, no general consistent forms of conduct, which, if they existed, would make for consistency of behavior and stability of personality, but only independent and specific stimulus-response bonds or habits (28)." Thus, we have a position that the hypothetical traits such as sociability, persistence, and impulsiveness do not exist; the question is clearly not to be answered by arguing that the assumption of trait existence is tautological.

Hartshorne and May concluded on the basis of testing many children in many experimental situations, that there was no support for the theory that such personality traits as honesty-deceitfulness existed in the sense of transcending individual situations; their conclusion was one of complete response specificity. Eysenck (1970), reanalyzing their results, found their conclusion did not follow from their own data; different situations showed uniformly positive intercorrelations, and situations could be combined into batteries of tests having very high reliabilities and validities, approaching those found in intelligence tests. A battery of nine tests of deceitful behavior, for instance, was found to have a reliability of .72 and a predictive validity of .85. Tests of socially approved behavior, such as cooperation, had similarly high reliabilities and validities, and all types of tests correlated highly with external ratings made by teachers.

The Hartshorne and May studies are still occasionally cited as proof that Thorndike was right and that trans-situational traits do not exist; such critics cannot be familiar with the statistical appendices to the Hartshorne and May books, which contain all the material necessary to refute their own conclusions.

As an example of the question of one or two traits, consider a paper by Eysenck (1956) concerned with whether sociability (or social shyness, as Guilford named it in his personality system) was a unitary factor, as postulated by Guilford on the basis of factor analysis. Arguing from content analysis and a consideration of previous correlational studies, Eysenck postulated that social shyness could be due to two different causes, giving rise to two independent factors. One cause of social shyness probably related to neuroticism was fear of other people, anxiety in their presence, and worry about their intentions and powers. The other cause, probably related to introversion, was a feeling of disinterest in being with other people, a preference for being by oneself, and a general dislike of boisterous parties.

As a test of these two alternative hypotheses, Eysenck correlated the various items in the Guilford scale of social shyness with measures of extroversion and neuroticism and showed that approximatly half the items correlated highly with E, but not with N, while the other half correlated highly with N but not with E. Analysis of the content of the items showed that those correlating with N indicated fear of other people, whereas those correlating negatively with E indicated not caring to be with other people. Here again, then, is clarification of an important debate regarding the description of sociable versus nonsociable behavior; the results could not have been predicted on the basis of common sense, and the outcome is not tautological.

Given the traits are not tautological postulates in a descriptive system of personality, we must add a further important consideration—the empirical question of intercorrelations between traits. When we talk about such traits as sociability, impulsiveness, and activity, we assume they are independent; but this assumption may not be justified and demands an empirical answer. Eysenck (1947, 1957, 1967, 1981e) based his system of personality description on the major factors or dimensions that emerge when many traits are intercorrelated and the resulting matrix of intercorrelations factor analyzed. Many such analyses have been published. Royce's (1973) major survey suggests that the three factors emerging again and again from these analyses coincide essentially with the three factors that emerged from my work (Eysenck and Eysenck 1969, 1976). I will therefore introduce them under the names I have used; other investigators have used other terms, of course.

The three factors are extroversion versus introversion, neuroticism versus stability, and psychoticism versus superego functioning. Traditionally, these three factors are referred to in terms of single letters— E, N, and P. Note that there is nothing tautological about these three factors' emerging again and again from the descriptive literature. This empirical finding was not foreseen by most investigators whose work Royce summarized. We thus emerge with a descriptive hierarchical system at the top level of which are the three concepts of P, E, and N, each based on the observed intercorrelations among a variety of traits. Each trait, in turn, is defined in terms of the intercorrelations among a number of specific situational responses made by people and either observed in real-life situations, rated by people who know the probands well, or self-rated on personality questionnaires. Ample evidence shows that these three methods of description yield similar results (Eysenck and Eysenck 1969).

CROSS-CULTURAL COMPARISONS

The importance of cross-cultural comparisons is that if the three major type factors were found only in a particular type of culture or society, say the Western, and not in Asian or African cultures, then the generality of personality description would be extremely restricted and no fundamental importance would attach to it. If, on the other hand, it could be shown that the same personality dimensions emerged independently in many cultures, then a more general importance could be claimed for the concepts involved.

In thus making cross-cultural comparisons, three major and different questions are involved, and much of the literature unfortunately confounds these questions to a degree that makes the results unacceptable. The first question is: "Is it possible to postulate that the same factors isolated in culture 1 (in this case, England) can be found in culture 2?" Eysenck and Eysenck (1981) tried to answer this question by using the following paradigm.

Identical questions (suitably translated into the language of culture 2) are administered to groups of at least 500 male and 500 female adults and/or juvenile members of the two cultures, preferably constituting a reasonably random sample of population. Product-moment item intercorrelations are then calculated, and factor analysis followed by oblique rotation of factors carried out. Indices of factor comparison are calculated to indicate the degree to which the two sets of factors resemble each other; rather arbitrarily, a minimum correlation of .95, and preferably a correlation of .98, is required before the factors are considered sufficiently similar or identical to accept that both countries share the same factor structure for personality description.

Many such comparisons have been carried out involving the European countries of Greece, Yugoslavia, and France; Asian areas of Japan, India, and Hong Kong; African countries such as Nigeria. Both adults and children were used in these studies, and the universal finding was that similar or identical factors do emerge in these various countries, when compared with the original analyses done in England (Eysenck and Eysenck 1981). We can thus conclude that there is sufficient generality to the factors in question to state with some finality that descriptively human beings in the cultures studied vary in their behavior in terms of the same major dimensions. This is an important fundamental finding for any theory of personality.

The other two questions raised by transcultural studies are less important in this context. The first question concerns the elaboration of a questionnaire applicable to any given country. Although the factors are identical, one or two items usually show differential factor loadings and must be omitted in using the questionnaire as a measuring tool in culture 2. This requires writing a new weight matrix but does not produce any particular difficulties, other than that the two countries cannot be compared meaningfully in terms of the old weight matrix, as is the almost universal custom in most published researches. The third problem, then, is to calculate a third weight matrix relating only to items with similar loadings for the two countries in question. This new weight matrix enables us to find scores on which to base a true or proper comparison.

Note that the descriptive value of the major dimensions of personality extends also to the animal world, where studies have been conducted on the social behavior of rhesus monkeys and rats by a variety of investigators interested mainly in the N and E dimensions. The work of Alfano and Traina (1971), Broadhurst (1975), Chamove et al.

(1972), Eysenck and Broadhurst (1946), Freixanet (1980), Pallarés (1978), Sevilla (1975), Sevilla and Garau (1978), and Tohema et al. (1981) are evidence that deductions made from the general theory can be verified in the animal field. This finding is important since the hypothesis that the major causal factors underlying these descriptive variables are biological in nature suggests that animals also should show behavior patterns similar to those observed in human beings.

GENETIC DETERMINANTS

Factors or dimensions of personality so general as to transcend cultural boundaries are likely to have some fundamental biological basis (Eysenck 1967), and thus it becomes important to seek genetic determination of individual differences in personality. Many studies have been performed, usually using MZ twins brought up in isolation (Shields 1962), or comparisons between MZ and DZ twins (Loehlin and Nichols 1976; Eaves and Eysenck 1975, 1976a, 1976b, 1977; Eaves et al. 1977a, 1977b), and reviews of the literature have been published by Eysenck (1976c) and Fulker (1981). The methods used have been path analysis and the methods of biometrical genetical analysis associated with the Birmingham School. It is important to realize that recent advances in the analysis of twin data and also in the analysis of data involving adopted children and intrafamilial relations (Eysenck, 1981a) mean that many traditional objections to estimates of heritability are no longer tenable.

First, universally, there is considerable heritability to different traits and dimensions of personality. When measurement error is eliminated statistically, genetic factors account for approximately three-quarters to two-thirds of the total variance; thus, personality is almost as heritable as intelligence (Eysenck 1979b). Intelligence heritability involves not only additive genetic variance but also such factors as dominance and assortative mating; personality heritability, however, depends entirely on additive genetic factors, and no evidence exists for dominance or assortative mating.

The environmental variance also contains important differences. Thus, for intelligence, between-family environmental variance is about twice as important as within-family environmental variance; for personality, almost the total burden of environmental variation is borne by within-family factors, with little or nothing for between-family environmental factors. We thus know a lot about the genetic architecture of personality (Fulker 1981); and what we know demonstrates conclusively that additive genetic factors play an important role in the genesis of individual differences in P, E, and N, as well as of the various traits, the intercorrelations between which are responsible for postulating these type factors.

THE SITUATIONIST CRITIQUE

In view of the evidence reviewed concerning the importance of factors P, E, and N, the evidence for cross-cultural replicability of the same factors, and the strong genetic determination of individual differences along these three dimensions, it seems a task of supererogation to discuss criticisms by Mischel (1968, 1977, 1979) and others of the whole conception of traits and personality. M.W. Eysenck and H. J. Eysenck's (1980) detailed critique of Mischel will not be repeated here. Before considering the causal factors in determining personality differences, we will state that the distinction made by Mischel and his followers between situational determinants and personality determinants in social behavior is purely artificial, as indicated at the beginning of this chapter. Implicit in the postulation of a trait is the postulation of a social situation appropriate for evoking that trait; it is meaningless to talk about sociability as a trait without postulating a social situation in which differences in sociability can become apparent. Thus, we are always dealing with an interactionist type of theory, that is, a theory taking into account both situations and personality traits (Magnusson and Endler 1977).

Another point, discussed below, is the importance of predicting and controlling parameter values; most personality researches published in recent years have failed to consider the range of stimulus values within which a given correlation would be expected to appear; yet the well-known inverse-U relation between drive and performance suggests that in many cases choice of stimulus values would crucially determine the size and even direction of the correlations found. Neglect of such vital variables makes many published researches appear of doubtful value in deciding the importance of personality for predicting human conduct and behavior (Eysenck 1981b, 1981c).

CAUSAL FACTORS DETERMINING INDIVIDUAL DIFFERENCES

After a first attempt to use Hull's concepts of inhibition and excitation for this purpose (Eysenck 1957), Eysenck (1967), finding these less than completely successful, turned to such physiological concepts as cortical arousal and limbic system activation to account for differences in E and N, respectively.

The theory in question, illustrated in Figure 4-1, shows the visceral brain (limbic system) as responsible for differences in N and the reticular formation-cortex arousal loop as responsible for individual differences in E. The theory states, in brief, that high resting levels of arousal are characteristic of introverts and responsible for introverted behavior patterns, whereas low levels of cortical arousal are characteristic of extroverts and responsible for extroverted behavior patterns (Eysenck 1981e). Overresponsiveness and underresponsiveness of the limbic system, respectively, are made responsible for high and low N types of behavior. The biological determination of differences in P is less clearly documented but seems related to hormonal secretions, particularly of androgen in one form or another (Eysenck and Eysenck 1976).

Verifying such a wide-ranging hypothesis is difficult. However, Stelmack (1981), in his review of the psychophysiology of extroversion and neuroticism, showed that much evidence favors the hypothesis, as do many anomalies relating particularly to changes in parameters. Parameter values and how the theory can predict them will be discussed later; here, let us note that the evidence on the whole favors the theory and that we have a beginning for a causal theory of personality. Alternative physiological hypotheses to those ofered by Eysenck and accounting for the same descriptive factors are discussed by Gray (1981) and Powell (1979).

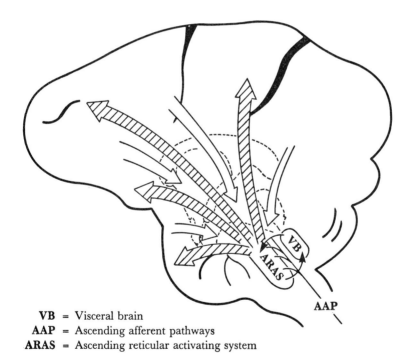

VB = Visceral brain
AAP = Ascending afferent pathways
ARAS = Ascending reticular activating system

Figure 4–1. Diagrammatic Representation of the Interaction between the Limbic System (visceral brain) and the Reticular-Cortical Arousal System. (Source: From H. J. Eysenck, *The Biological Basis of Personality*, 1967. Courtesy of Charles C Thomas, Publisher, Springfield, Illinois.)

Psychophysiological tests are the most direct for testing causal theory; psychological laboratory tests also test many deductions that can be made from the theory. Most deductions that have been made and tested (Eysenck 1967, 1976b, 1981e) have been verified, thus supporting the theory. Of importance in looking at these deductions is that parameter values are important and that these parameter values in turn can be predicted from the general theory.

Of particular importance is the Pavlovian concept of transmarginal inhibition (extinction with reinforcement). This concept predicts a curvilinear regression of the dependent variable (such as conditioning) on the independent variable (strength of stimulation, strength of unconditioned stimulus, etc.). Pavlov's law of strength indicates that conditioning becomes stronger as the strength of the unconditioned stimulus increases; however, there is an optimal point beyond which increases in the strength of the unconditioned stimulus produce paradoxical or transmarginal or protective inhibition (Pavlov uses these terms interchangeably) and further increases in the strength of the unconditioned stimulus produce decrements in the strength of the conditioned reaction.

This curvilinear regression has become well-known in several different guises—the Yerkes-Dodson Law, or the inverted-U relation between drive and response. It is relevant to deductions from Eysenck's personality theory, because according to that theory individuals differ *ab initio* in the strength of their cortical arousal system, or in the strength of their automatic (emotional) reaction to anxiety-producing stimuli. Thus, persons high on introversion and high on neuroticism would be expected to show an optimal point on the curve earlier (i.e., with weaker stimuli), and ambiverts earlier than extroverts or low N scorers. Note here the link between the concepts of extroversion and the strong nervous system, first introduced by Pavlov; he used "extinction with reinforcement" as the best available measure for distinguishing between dogs characterized by a strong or weak nervous system (Eysenck 1981b).

The hypothesis that the incidence of transmarginal inhibition would occur at a lower level of UCS intensity in introverts and extroverts was tested by Eysenck and Levey (1972). Figures 4-2 and 4-3 show the rate of eyelid conditioning for introverts and extroverts, respectively, under conditions theoretically favoring the former (see Figure 4-2) or the latter (see Figure 2-3). Note that introverts are clearly superior to extroverts under the former conditions, and extroverts to introverts under the latter, as demanded by the theory. There is little doubt that for rate of conditioning, transmarginal inhibition occurs earlier in the case of introverts than in the case of extroverts.

Frigon (1976) tested the same hypothesis using the electroencephalographic variant of extinction with reinforcement. Testing each sub-

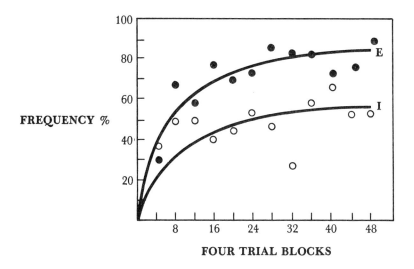

FOUR TRIAL BLOCKS

Figure 4-2. Rate of Eyelid Conditioning for Introverts and Extroverts under Conditions of Partial Reinforcement, Weak UCS, and Short CS-UCS Interval. (Source: From H. J. Eysenck, *The Biological Basis of Personality*, 1967. Courtesy of Charles C Thomas, Publisher, Springfield, Illinois.)

ject in four quadrants produced by high and low E and N scores, respectively, he concluded that "the analysis of variance of CR magnitudes showed that, in the 'extinction with reinforcement' condition, the duration of the conditioned desynchronization progressively decreases for introverts and remains stable for extraverts. It is clear from the results that introverts are more cortically aroused than extraverts when both are exposed to objectively identical physical stimulation before proceeding with the series of rapid representations of the CS. The EEG CR is unaffected in extraverts by the building up of excitation in the nerve cells during 'extinction with reinforcement' while introverts show a CR decrease. This is taken as an indication of weakness of the nervous system in introverts and strength of nervous system in extraverts" (473).

Eysenck (1981b, 1981c) offers many other examples of the curvilinear regression between drive (arousal) and performance, including work on perception (Shigehisa and Symons 1973); intensity modulation (augmenting and reducing) as shown in averaged evoked potentials (Zuckerman et al. 1974); salivary secretion as a function of taste bud stimulation by lemon juice (Eysenck and Eysenck 1967; S. B. G. Eysenck and H. J. Eysenck 1967); the effect of smoking on CNVs of introverts and extroverts respectively (Eysenck and O'Connor, 1979;

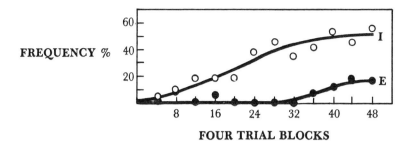

Figure 4-3. Rate of Eyelid Conditioning for Introverts and Extroverts under Conditions of Partial Reinforcement, Weak UCS, and Short CS-UCS Interval. (Source: From H. J. Eysenck, *The Biological Basis of Personality*, 1967. Courtesy of Charles C Thomas, Publisher, Springfield, Illinois.)

O'Connor 1980), and so on. (This last study is an example of the relationship between psychopharmacology and personality, which also frequently demonstrates this curvilinear regression and has been discussed in some detail by Eysenck (1981d). These few examples must suffice to illustrate the wide range of the principle involved and its importance for the experimental study of personality.

BIOLOGICAL FOUNDATIONS OF PERSONALITY AND SOCIAL BEHAVIOR

Clearly, a person with an overactive limbic system will tend to react more strongly than do most people to emotional stimuli, will take longer to return to a normal baseline, and will condition more strongly to emotional UCS because of the increased strength of the stimuli involved. However, in the case of extroversion, the links are not as obvious; a short discussion may be useful.

The first and most obvious link would be to cognitive functioning, such as attentional behavior, vigilance, and the consolidation of the memory trace. The large literature on human memory (M. W. Eysenck 1977) discusses how extroverts and introverts differ, particularly in the retrieval of memories. Vigilance, according to the arousal theory, should be significantly greater in introverts than in extroverts. Many studies have verified this relationship (Eysenck 1967). Although too obvious to require much comment, as M. W. Eysenck (1977) has shown, some resulting connections are more complex than might have first been thought and require considerable integration with various laws of experimental psychology, such as Walker's theorem.

One major way in which a direct connection can be made between the habitual arousal level of the cortex and social behavior, other than along cognitive lines, is through Pavlovian conditioning. Conditioning is improved by arousal, and hence introverts would be expected to condition better than extroverts if they are on the ascending limb of the inverse-U model relating arousal to performance. We have seen that this is so, as many studies illustrate (Jones et al. 1980).

This link is important in the writer's theories linking sex and personality (Eysenck 1976a), crime and personality (Eysenck 1977b), psychopathic behavior and personality (Eysenck and Eysenck 1978), and neurosis and personality (Eysenck 1977a; Eysenck and Rachman 1956), for example; these links will be discussed in detail below. Here, note that if Pavlovian conditioning is important in mediating certain types of social influence, then individual differences in conditioning and extinction related to the arousal level of the cortex, and hence to extroversion/introversion, must also be relevant and important.

A third link, related directly to motivational factors, appears in diagrammatic form in Figure 4-4, from Eysenck (1963). It shows the relationship between level of stimulation, on the abscissa, and hedonic tone, on the ordinate. (Stimulation, for the sake of the argument, is here defined in terms of sensory intensity, but what Berlyne has called "collative properties" could also be substituted for level of stimulation, as argued elsewhere [Eysenck 1981c].)

As the center curve shows, the average person dislikes both very low stimulation (sensory deprivation) and very high stimulation (pain); he or she prefers an intermediate level of stimulation, as shown by the optimum level (O.L.$_p$). Introverts show a curve displaced to the left, extroverts a curve displaced toward the right, because the high arousal level of the former tends to raise the experienced level of stimulation, while the low arousal level of the latter lowers it. Thus, the optimum level for introverts (O.L.$_I$) is also displaced to the left, that of extroverts (O.L.$_E$) to the right. For a given level of stimulation, say A, the stimulation is felt as pleasant for introverts, unpleasant for extroverts, and indifferent for the ambiverts. At point B, everything is reversed; stimulation at that point is pleasant for extroverts and unpleasant for introverts.

Certain obvious deductions, relevant to ordinary life experiences and also testable in the laboratory, can be made from Figure 4-4. We would thus expect introverts to be more tolerant of sensory deprivation, extroverts to be more tolerant of painful stimulation; evidence strongly suggests that this is so (Eysenck 1967, 1981e). The theory also suggests that extroverts would be what Zuckerman (1979) calls "sensation-seekers"—they would seek to raise their arousal level from an unsatisfactorily low amount to something closer to their optimum level (O.L.$_E$). Introverts would show the opposite tendency, sensation avoid-

POPULATION

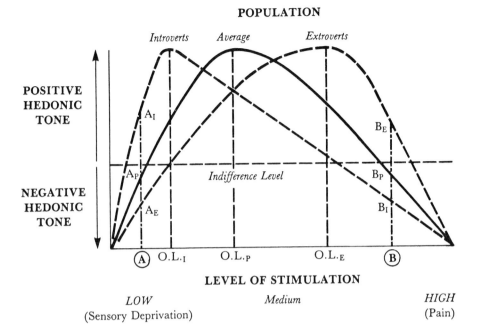

Figure 4-4. Hedonic Tone as a Function of Level of Sensory Stimulation for Extroverts, Ambiverts, and Introverts. (Source: From H. J. Eysenck, *The Biological Basis of Personality*, 1967. Courtesy of Charles C Thomas, Publisher, Springfield, Illinois.)

ing, and lower the degree of sensory input to maintain their optimum level of arousal ($O.L._I$), which is much lower than that of extroverts.

An experimental study illustrated this difference. One at a time, in a silent, dark laboratory extroverts and introverts were asked to push a button; their operant frequency was determined before the contingencies were introduced. These contingencies were that more frequent pushing of the button would produce three seconds' worth of bright lights and loud jazz music played on a juke box. The operant level of introverts and extroverts was equal; but when the operant conditioning was introduced, extroverts pushed the button more frequently, thus assuring an adequate supply of sensory stimulation, whereas introverts decreased the frequency of button pushing, in order to safeguard against this too strong sensory stimulation.

In a reversal of the experimental procedure with another group, the subjects were tested in a brightly lit and noisy condition, where pushing the button more frequently would produce darkness and silence; under these conditions, introverts pushed the button more frequently than before and extroverts pushed less frequently. It does not take much imagination to see how such an experiment could be extended to account for extroverts' liking the bright lights and loud disco music provided in places of amusement and bars, whereas introverts would shy away from such places (Weisen 1965).

EXAMPLES OF PERSONALITY DIFFERENCES
AND SOCIAL BEHAVIOR

Neurosis

One central application of this work is relating personality to neurosis (particularly the dysthymic neuroses) and antisocial behavior, hysteria, and criminality (Eysenck 1976a, 1977a, 1977b). The writer's theory of neurosis implicates Pavlovian conditioning as the main factor, suggesting that all major neurosis symptoms are either conditioned emotional responses or behavior reactions to these CRs (Eysenck 1979a). On the other hand, antisocial, hysterical, and psychopathic reactions are believed to occur due to a lack of conditioning of socially desirable behaviors (Eysenck 1977b, 1980). The expectation from these hypotheses is that introverts would be more likely to produce neurotic reactions, extroverts to produce antisocial and hysterical ones, and high neuroticism would be an important factor for both types of reaction, by adding autonomic drive to the habits formed in either direction, and, according to Hull, multiplying drive by habit to produce performance (behavior). The evidence, while not conclusive, favors the hypothesis; many differences along the predicted lines have been observed in English-speaking countries and also in countries behind the Iron Curtain (such as Hungary), and in Third World countries (such as India) (Eysenck 1977b). Obviously, personality is not the only factor making for neurotic or antisocial behavior, but it is implicated as one factor in the causal chain that should not be disregarded.

Sexual Behavior

Sexual behavior is another obvious example because two lines of deduction lead to similar consequences. One line leads, via sensation-seeking, to a prediction that extroverts seek sexual stimulation more strongly than do introverts; the other line leads via the conditioning of socially desirable reactions to the conclusion that introverts resist temptation more readily than do extroverts. Basing himself on these types of deduction, Eysenck (1976a) made the following predictions:

1. Extroverts will have intercourse at a younger age than introverts.
2. Extroverts will have intercourse more frequently than introverts.
3. Extroverts will have intercourse with more different partners.
4. Extroverts will have intercourse in more different positions than introverts.
5. Extroverts will indulge in more varied sexual behavior outside intercourse.
6. Extroverts will indulge in longer precoital love play than introverts.

The evidence on all these points is reasonably strong. A study of a large sample of German students (Giese and Schmidt 1968) reveals that extroverts masturbate less, pet to orgasm more, have coitus more frequently, have coitus at a younger age, adopt more different positions in coitus, indulge longer in precoital love play, and practice fellatio and cunnilingus more frequently. On some of these items, differences are greater for men than for women; this is expected on the grounds that in our society, men set the pace in sexual relationships, so their personality is expressed more clearly in the procedures adopted.

Two studies reported by Zuckerman et al. (1972) and Zuckerman (personal communication) used the Zuckerman sensation-seeking scales, which are related to extroversion. The correlations between sensation-seeking scales and sexual behavior were all positive and significant. The correlations are with the Zuckerman sexual experience scale, listing types of sexual behavior the individual either had or had not experienced, ranging from kissing and breast fondling to fellatio and cunnilingus. He also asked questions about the number of sexual partners each individual had had.

The prediction was that all scales would correlate positively with the number of heterosexual activities endorsed and the number of heterosexual partners. The scale involving heterosexual activity was administered to two separate populations, that involving heterosexual partners only to one. All correlations are positive, as expected, both for males and females, and they bear out the prediction. For instance, thrill and adventure-seeking correlates .44 with heterosexual activities[1] and .47 with the number of heterosexual partners. We can tentatively conclude that empirical findings bear out the predicted relationship between sex and personality.

Learning and Performance

This work on the relationship between personality (particularly extroversion) and sexual behavior may hint why sociability is such a fundamental aspect of extroversion. The most likely link here is probably the arousing effect of social interaction; such factors as the simple presence of people, gazing at others, talking to them, or interacting with them in other ways have been shown to produce powerful arousing effects. Zajonc (1965) surveyed many studies on social facilitation that integrate well with the major lessons learned from work on learning and memory (M. W. Eysenck 1977; Eysenck 1973). According to the inverted-U relationship between arousal and performance, easy tasks are facilitated by arousal, difficult ones made harder. Zajonc reviews studies in which learning and performance are studied under nonsocial conditions (i.e., without anyone present) and under social conditions (i.e., with other persons present). As early as 1924, Allport postulated that "the sights and sounds of others doing the same thing" augmented ongoing responses; this augmentation, however, was proposed to occur only for overt motor responses. "Intellectual or implicit responses of thought are hampered rather than facilitated by the presence of others," he thought. This conclusion might be interpreted as an early adumbration of the application of the Yerkes-Dodson Law to the effects of social stimulation. Later work was more specific.

Zajonc, summing up several later investigations, stated, "it would appear that the emission of well-learned responses is facilitated by the presence of spectators while the acquisition of new responses is impaired. To put the statement in conventional psychological language, performance is facilitated and learning is impaired by the presence of spectators." He refined this statement by having recourse to a theoretical statement rather like Spence's general theory (Eysenck 1973)—if the dominant responses in a situation are the correct ones, social facilitation will occur. If the dominant responses are incorrect, social arousal will strengthen these incorrect responses, thus making learning more difficult. These experiments all deal with the presence of spectators, that is, with other people who take no active part in the experiment. Other studies have dealt with the participation of others in a variety of tasks.

Zajonc (1965) also summarizes a series of well-known studies by Allport and Dashiell using the co-action paradigm—situations in which the subject acts either in the presence of others also active in the same task, or else not so active. Allport's subjects worked either in separate cubicles or sitting around a common table, and many different tasks were studied; the outcome of his work, and that of others, fits into a general theoretical statement such as that in the previous paragraph.

Zajonc continued his survey by considering work on animals, which is too far removed from the interest here to be summarized; he did suggest that it also fit into a general theoretical statement of the Spence type. We can thus say that social interaction has an arousing effect on learning and performance, that this effect is in line with work previously surveyed on the effects of arousal, and that it seems to follow that underaroused, extroverted people should be more likely to seek out personal contacts than would overaroused, introverted people. Thus, the trait of sociability, which is central to most conceptualizations of extroversion, can be seen as a direct consequence of arousal differences between extroverts and introverts.

Work done after Zajonc has supported his views (e.g., Zajonc and Sales 1966; Carment 1970a, 1970b; Matlin and Zajonc 1969; Martens 1969a, 1969b; Hunt and Hillery 1973; Cottrell, Rittle, and Wack 1967; Innes and Young 1975; Geen 1973, 1974; Desportes 1976). However, certain theoretical criticisms of the hypothesis say the mere presence of an audience produces these effects. Some investigators agree (e.g., Chapman 1973, 1974); most, however, have argued that the subject must experience apprehension at being evaluated by the audience (e.g., Cottrell et al. 1968; Henchy and Glass 1968; Sasfy and Okum 1974). As Cottrell et al. (1968, 1972) stated, the presence of others would therefore appear to be a stimulus eliciting a learned drive associated with anxiety over being judged.

This argument is consistent with traditional explanations of social facilitation in lower animals, most of which emphasize some aspect of the behavior of conspecifics and not their mere physical presence. Weiss and Miller (1971) discussed these theoretical points at some length, also raising the question of incentive motivation—whether the secondary drive in the social motivation situation could also be based on primary appetitive states (e.g., expectation of praise rather than of criticism). A discussion of these issues ranges too far outside the topic.

From the view of arousal produced by association with people, the question of whether the mere presence or expectations associated with their presence is causal is of secondary importance. The addition of some r_g - s_g mechanism to the mere presence paradigm would not invalidate (and might strengthen) arguments about introvert-extrovert differences. Social interaction effects have been linked with introversion-extroversion in several papers, the most important of which have been reprinted in Eysenck's (1971) set of *Readings in Extraversion-Introversion*. Unfortunately, most papers studying the interaction of personality and social facilitation used anxiety as the personality variable preferred (Berkey and Hoppe 1972; Cox 1966, 1968; Ganzer 1968; Pederson 1970). Difficulties arise in interpreting anxiety, which is a mixture of introversion and neuroticism; it is difficult if not impossible to relate observed effects to one or the other of the two component traits of anxiety.

Educational Psychology

The causal model of personality thus explains the kind of behavior prominent in the descriptive model and also some relations among personality and sexual, criminal, neurotic, and social behavior. If personality is as important a factor in human behavior as I believe, then in experimental, social, industrial, educational, and abnormal psychology the interaction between personality factors and the main independent variables would contribute greatly to the total variance. Failing to consider personality factors would throw much of this variance into the error term (Eysenck 1967). Much evidence has been given elsewhere (Eysenck 1981e) of the truth of this assertion in these various fields. Here, we will look only at some examples from educational psychology; Eysenck (1978) has given a more detailed review of this particular field, and Wilson (1981) of the wider field of social behavior.

Consider the differences between the so-called discovery method and the method of traditional direct instruction. Such comparisons as have been carried out to study the relative superiority of one or the other have usually failed to disclose any marked differences. Leith (1974) examined the possibility that the greater readiness of extroverts to become bored by routines but likely to respond to stimulus variation, and of introverts to be disturbed by changes of set but able to maintain attentiveness to a highly prompted task, would result in a methods-by-personality interaction. Teaching materials for a genetics course (for naïve students) were carefully prepared to give equal amounts of learning and transfer in randomly chosen groups of students; the materials were so chosen as to cover a range of personal discovery, tolerance for uncertainty and error-making, as well as a difference that may be described as plunging into the deep end or stepping into the shallow end of the pool.

Two hundred students were tested one week and again five weeks after the end of the course, with a series of largely transfer items. Non-anxious subjects were better learners than were anxious subjects. The major finding was a significant interaction effect between personality and method, as illustrated in Figure 4-5.

On both testing occasions, introverts and extroverts learned equally well on the average; thus, there is no overall superiority of one method over the other. But extroverts learned much better than did introverts with the discovery method, whereas introverts learned better than did extroverts with the direct teaching (reception) method. For the second test, the difference in score between extroverts and introverts is 30 vs. 18; that is, extroverts do almost twice as well as introverts! This is a tremendous difference; the difference for reception learning is greater for the one-week period. This experiment clearly illustrates the danger of comparing different methods of teaching without measuring personality at the same time and looking for different reactions of different personality types to the methods of teaching under examination.

As another example of the interaction between personality, achievement, and conditions of learning and testing, consider Leith's (1972a)

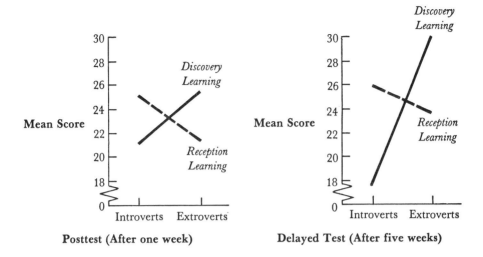

Figure 4-5. Interaction of Strategies of Instruction (reception versus discovery) with Extroversion on Two Occasions of Testing Achievement and Problem Solving. (Source: G. O. Leith, Individual differences in learning: Interactions of personality and teaching methods. In *Personality and Academic Progress*, Conference proceeding. London: Association of Educational Psychologists, 1974. Used by permission.)

experiment on 106 children who were given an intelligence test, tests of extroversion and neuroticism, and three verbal creativity tests. Half the children were given the creativity tests in a relaxed atmosphere; the other half were given the creativity tests, in a moderately stressful manner (induced by instructions to do their best and not delay and by statements about the relation of the tests to academic ability). Extroverts and nonanxious children did better under reduced stress; introverts and anxious children under stress. The results appear in Figure 4-6; note that personality interacts significantly with conditions in a manner predicted by Leith from the arousal theory of personality (Eysenck 1967).

Another area showing marked personality interaction phenomena is paired learning—learning in a situation where two learners are paired with each other. Consider first Leith's (1974) study in which pairing was on the basis of anxiety; neuroticism, pairs being either similar in score on this variable, or opposite—anxious, the other stable. Table 4-1 shows the main results; note that extraordinary improvements over the same pairings are shown by the unlike pairings. Opposite anxiety pairs showed nearly a 100 percent superiority over same anxiety pairs

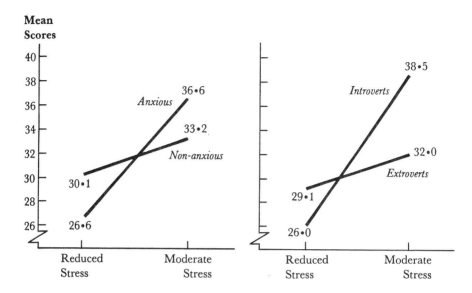

Figure 4-6. Interaction of Treatment (stress vs. nonstress) and Personality; Effects Are Shown Separately for Anxiety and Introversion-Extroversion. (Source: G. O. Leith, The relationship between intelligence, personality, and creativity under two conditions of stress. *British Journal of Educational Psychology*, 1972, *42*, 240–247. Used by permission of Scottish Academic Press [Journals] Limited.)

on the transfer test! (The pairs were also subdivided according to heterogeneity or homogeneity in ability; the figures in brackets refer to the heterogeneous pairs.)

Table 4-2 shows the results of a similar experiment, using extroversion-introversion instead of anxiety-neuroticism. Note that when working individually, introverts were significantly superior; this superiority vanished when the students worked in pairs. Homogeneous pairs here worked better than did heterogeneous pairs, regardless of whether the pair was made up of two extroverts or two introverts. These results open up fascinating vistas of both research and educational practice.

Pairing heterogeneous children, one anxiously and the other not, is one way to combat the negative effects of anxiety; another way is suggested in an experiment by Trown and Leith (1975). Nearly 500 boys and girls took part in the experiment contrasting the effects of supportive and of explorative strategies in mathematics teaching in four elementary schools; the mean age of the children was ten years, six months.

TABLE 4–1
Comparisons of Achievements and Behavior of Same
and Different Anxiety Level Pairs

Opposite anxiety pairs	Achieved	74% (32%)	More on the posttest than same anxiety pairs
Opposite anxiety pairs	Achieved	98% (113%)	More on the transfer-test than same anxiety pairs
Opposite anxiety pairs	Spent	59% (36%)	More time in showing solidarity, raising other's status, giving help, and rewarding than same anxiety pairs
Opposite anxiety pairs	Spent	112% (132%)	More time asking for orientation, information, confirmation, than same anxiety pairs
Opposite anxiety pairs	Spent	11% (20%)	Less time in disagreeing, passively rejecting, withholding help than same anxiety pairs
Opposite anxiety pairs	Spent	49% (25%)	Less time in showing antagonism, deflating other, asserting self than same anxiety pairs

(Heterogeneous ability pairs in parentheses, homogeneous ability pairs with no parentheses.)

Source: Leith, G. O. Individual differences in learning: Interactions of personality and teaching methods. In *Personality and Academic Progress*. (Conference proceedings. London: Association of Educational Psychologists, 1974. Used by permission.

In the case of the supportive strategy, the sequence employed over each of the twelve sections of learning material was that of teacher-provided statement of organizing principle, followed by related pupil activity with mathematical models and subsequent teacher restatement of principle. Such statements were both spoken and written on the blackboard. The same activities with models were used in the exploratory strategy, but this time at the beginning of each section of the learning

TABLE 4-2
Achievements of Students Learning in Homogeneous or
Heterogeneous Personality Pairs or as Individuals

Personality	Homogeneous pairs	Heterogeneous pairs	Individuals
Introverts	32.2	27.3	30.0
Extroverts	30.6	27.7	25.4
Significance of differences (1-tailed)	N.S.	N.S.	p<.01

Homogeneous vs. heterogeneous pairs: p<.01
Homogeneous pairs vs. individuals: p<.025.

Source: Leith, G. O. Individual differences in learning: Interactions of personality and teaching methods. In *Personality and Academic Progress.* Conference proceedings. London: Association of Educational Psychologists, 1974. Used by permission.

sequence. Each teacher statement of principle was delayed until pupils had been given the opportunity to perceive the relationship themselves and had been encouraged to attempt an appropriate generalization.

Results appear in Table 4-3. Anxiety level distinguished between those who were able to profit greatly from the learner-centered exploratory approach and those whom it clearly handicapped. The teacher-centered supportive strategy, on the other hand, was almost equally effective at each level of anxiety. Overall differences (i.e., neglecting the personality interaction) between the strategies were minimal; thus, neglecting the personality dimensions would have led to the erroneous conclusion that strategies were identical in their effects. Note that this experiment contained an ability effect (in the expected direction) but no ability-treatment interaction.

The experiment's results, as the authors emphasize, are germane to an evaluation of the Nuffield mathematics scheme, suggesting that this may improve the performance of some (nonanxious) children and worsen the performance of other (anxious) children. Such a conclusion cannot, of course, be based on the results of one experiment and cannot be extrapolated to other subjects; but the conclusion does suggest the importance of proper experimental investigation of interaction effects.

TABLE 4-3
Strategy-Anxiety Interaction (by Sex)
Mean Scores for Retained Learning

	Boys (N per cell = 40)		Girls (N per cell = 40)		All pupils (N per cell = 80)	
	Low anx.	High anx.	Low anx.	High anx.	Low anx.	High anx.
Supportive strategy	15.98	15.26	16.63	17.73	16.30	16.49
Exploratory strategy	20.30	12.33	18.30	14.25	19.30	13.29

Source: Trown, E. A., and Leith, G. O. Decision rules for teaching strategy in primary schools: Personality-treatment interaction. *British Journal of Educational Psychology*, 1975, *45*. Used by permission of Scottish Academic Press (Journals) Limited.

These and other examples given by Eysenck (1978) and Wilson (1981) illustrate that main effects in applied work are usually weak or nonexistent; interaction effects, however, particularly when predicted on the basis of a relevant theory, are important and of great practical relevance. Cronbach and Snow (1977) report many failures to find interaction effects with ability, to some extent also with personality; but in the latter case, this occurs because many investigators have tried inappropriate methods based on feeble or nonexistent theories; only by applying the best available theories to making predictions can we hope to obtain significant results.

CONCLUSION

This conclusion agrees with Cronbach's (1957) famous talk about "the two disciplines of scientific psychology"—experimental psychology, of the traditional kind, on the one hand, and the psychometric study of individual differences, on the other. He emphasized that each discipline usually works in isolation, without attending to what the other is doing, and that consequently both are fatally weakened in their attempts to establish a scientific psychology. Only by collaboration can we establish such a desired objective; in this interchange each can make useful contributions to the efforts of the other.

A proper theory of personality can suggest the testing of interactions that would rescue much variance from the error term; conversely, experimental psychology can contribute to the work of the personality psychologist by suggesting causal factors responsible for the descriptive findings of the latter. Insofar as Mischel, in criticizing trait concepts and personality theories generally, has in mind the rather arbitrary administration of multiphasic personality inventories constructed in an equally arbitrary manner, without benefit of proper correlational and factor analytic methods, and without theoretical sophistication, he is right in condemning such work and pointing out its relative failure to produce reasonable, acceptable, and replicable results. Such objurgations do not, however, apply to the proper construction and use of personality theories, both for the theoretical and the applied fields.

We can end this discussion by indicating the similarity between physics and psychology, as far as the interaction between functional laws and individuality of reaction is concerned. Figure 4-7, in the left diagram, shows Hooke's Law of Elasticity: Stress = k × Strain, where k is the constant (the modulus of elasticity) that depends on the nature of the material and type of stress used to produce a strain. This constant k (the stress/strain ratio), called Young's Modulus, is illustrated (with certain simplifications) in the figure. A and B are two metals differing in elasticity; they are stressed by increasing loads, and the elongation corresponding to each load plotted on the abscissa. Note that identical loads give rise to quite divergent elongations, α and β.

The right diagram illustrates a similar analysis of human behavior in an experimental situation productive of emotion. Again, the stress (independent variable) is plotted on the ordinate and the strain (dependent variable) on the abscissa; A and B represent an emotionally stable and emotionally unstable individual, or group of individuals, respectively. Identical stress θ_1 gives rise to different strains α and β. It

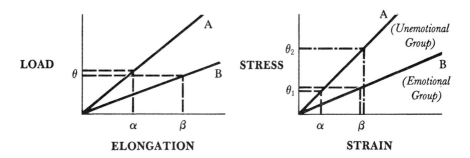

Figure 4-7. Hooke's Law (A) as Applied to the Measurement of Emotionality (B). (Source: H. J. Eysenck, The measurement of emotion: Psychological parameters and methods. In L. Levi (ed.), *Emotions: Their Parameters and Measurement*, p. 442. Copyright © 1975, Raven Press, New York. Used by permission.)

would require stress θ_2 to make the strain in A individuals equal to that produced by θ_1 in B individuals.

Differences between θ_1 and θ_2 are the kinds of differences traditionally studied by experimental psychologists; differences between A and B are the kinds of differences traditionally studied by personality psychologists, who believe in the importance of constitutional factors, and by clinical psychologists. Physicists do not attempt to choose between these two sets of variables or to study them in isolation; it seems equally futile for psychologists to do so (Eysenck 1975).

ENDNOTE

1. Divergent thinking, a cognitive ability, is related to personality through the extraverted temperament, as Spearman (1927) hypothesized. Leith (1972b) and others found evidence favoring this view and also supported Hudson's (1966) finding linking divergent thinking with preference for arts subjects and convergent thinking with preference for science subjects.

REFERENCES

Alfano, L., & Traina, F. Studio del comportamento del ratto: Intercorrelazioni di misure in diverse condizioni sperimentali. *Bulletino de Psicologia Applicata*, 1971, *103*, 93–104.

Allport, F. H. *Social psychology*. Boston: Houghton Mifflin, 1924.

Berkey, A. S., & Hoppe, R. A. The combined effect of audience and anxiety on paired associates learning. *Psychonomic Science*, 1972, *29*, 351–353.

Broadhurst, P. L. The Maudsley reactive and non-reactive strains of rats: A survey. *Behavioral Genetics*, 1975, *5*, 299–319.

Carment, D. W. Rate of simple motor responding as a function of coaction, competition and sex of the participants. *Psychonomic Science*, 1970, *19*, 340–341. (a)

Carment, D. W. Rate of simple motor responding as a function of differential outcomes and the actual and implied presence of a coactor. *Psychonomic Science*, 1970, *20*, 115–116. (b)

Chamove, A. S., Eysenck, H. J., & Harlow, H. F. Personality in monkeys: Factor analysis of rhesus social behaviour. *Quarterly Journal of Experimental Psychology*, 1972, *24*, 496–504.

Chapman, A. J. Social facilitation of laughter in children. *Journal of Experimental Social Psychology*, 1973, *9*, 528–541.

Chapman, A. J. An electromyographic study of social facilitation: A test of the "mere presence" hypothesis. *British Journal of Psychology*, 1974, *65*, 123-128.

Cottrell, N. B. Social facilitation. In C. G. McClintock (Ed.), *Experimental social psychology.* New York: Holt, Rinehart & Winston, 1972.

Cottrell, N. B., Rittle, R. H., & Wack, D. C. The presence of an audience and test type (competitional or non-competitional) as joint determinants of performance in paired-associate learning. *Journal of Personality*, 1967, *35*, 423-434.

Cottrell, N. B., Wack, D. L., Sekerak, G. J., & Rittle, R. H. Social facilitation of dominant responses by the presence of an audience and the mere presence of others. *Journal of Personality and Social Psychology*, 1968, *9*, 245-250.

Cox, F. N. Some effects of test anxiety and presence or absence of other persons on boys' performance on a repetitive motor task. *Journal of Experimental Child Psychology*, 1966, *3*, 100-112.

Cox, F. N. Some relationships between test anxiety presence or absence of male persons and boys' performance on a repetitive motor task. *Journal of Experimental Child Psychology*, 1968, *5*, 1-12.

Cronbach, L. J. The two disciplines of scientific psychology. *American Psychologist*, 1957, *12*, 671-684.

Cronbach, L. J. & Snow, R. E. *Aptitudes and instructional methods: A handbook for research on interactions.* New York: Irvington, 1977.

Desportes, J. P. *Les effets de la présence de l'expérimenteur dans les sciences du comportement.* Paris: Editions du Centre National de la Recherche Scientifique, 1976.

Eaves, L., & Eysenck, H. J. The nature of extraversion: A genetical analysis. *Journal of Personality and Social Psychology*, 1975, *32*, 102-112.

Eaves, L., & Eysenck, H. J. Genetic and environmental components of inconsistency and unrepeatability in twins' responses to neuroticism questionnaire. *Behavior Genetics*, 1976, *6*, 145-160. (a)

Eaves, L., & Eysenck, H. J. Genotype × age interaction for neuroticism, *Behavior Genetics*, 1976, *6*, 359-362. (b)

Eaves, L., & Eysenck, H. J. Genotype-environmental model for psychoticism. *Advances in Behaviour Research & Therapy*, 1977, *1*, 5-26.

Eaves, L. J., Last, K., Martin, N. G., & Jinks, J. L. A progressive approach to non-additivity and genotype-environmental covariance in the analysis of human differences. *British Journal of Mathematical and Statistical Psychology*, 1977, *30*, 1-42. (a)

Eaves, L. J., Martin, N. G., & Eysenck, S. B. G. An application of the analysis of covariance structures to the psychogenetical study of impulsiveness. *British Journal of Mathematical and Statistical Psychology*, 1977, *30*, 185-197. (b)

Eysenck, H. J. *Dimensions of personality*. London: Routledge & Kegan Paul, 1947.

Eysenck, H. J. The questionnaire measurement of neuroticism and extraversion. *Rivista di Psicologia*, 1956, *50*, 113-140.

Eysenck, H. J. *The Dynamics of anxiety and hysteria*. London: Routledge & Kegan Paul, 1957.

Eysenck, H. J. (Ed.). *Experiments with drugs*. London: Pergamon Press, 1963.

Eysenck, H. J. *The biological basis of personality*. Springfield, Ill.: C. C Thomas, 1967.

Eysenck, H. J. *The structure of human personality*, 3rd ed. London: Methuen, 1970.

Eysenck, H. J. (Ed.). *Readings in extraversion-introversion*, 3 vols. London: Staples, 1971.

Eysenck, H. J. Personality, learning and "anxiety." In H. J. Eysenck, (Ed.), *Handbook of abnormal psychology*, 2nd ed. London: Pitman, 1973.

Eysenck, H. J. The measurement of emotion: Psychological parameters and methods. In L. Levi (Ed.), *Emotions in their parameters and measurement*, 439-467. New York: Raven Press, 1975.

Eysenck, H. J. *Sex and personality*. London: Open Books, 1976. (a)

Eysenck, H. J. *The measurement of personality*. Lancaster: Medical & Technical Publishers, 1976. (b)

Eysenck, H. J. Genetic factors in personality development. In A. R. Kaplan (Ed.), *Human behavior genetics*, 198-229. Springfield, Ill.: C. C. Thomas, 1976. (c)

Eysenck, H. J. *You and neurosis*. London: Temple Smith, 1977. (a)

Eysenck, H. J. *Crime and personality*, 3rd ed. London: Routledge & Kegan Paul, 1977. (b)

Eysenck, H. J. The development of personality and its relation to learning. In S. Murray-Smith (Ed.), *Melbourne studies in education*, pp. 134-181. Melbourne: University Press, 1978.

Eysenck, H. J. The conditioning model of neurosis. *The Behavioral and Brain Sciences*, 1979, *2*, 155-199. (a)

Eysenck, H. J. *The Structure and measurement of intelligence*. London: Springer, 1979. (b)

Eysenck, H. J. Personality, psychopathy and criminality. In *Lo psicopatico delinquente*. Milan: A. Guiffre, 1980.

Eysenck, H. J. Pavlovian concepts and personality dimensions: The nature of modern typology. In G. Mangan (Ed.), *Essays in honour of V. D. Nebylitsyn*. London: Pergamon Press, 1981. (b)

Eysenck, H. J. Arousal, intrinsic motivation, and personality. In H. I. Day (Ed.), *Advances in intrinsic motivation and aesthetics.* New York: Plenum, 1981. (c)

Eysenck, H. J. Psychopharmacology and personality. In W. Janke (Ed.), *Symposium on personality and response variability to psychotropic drugs.* London: Pergamon Press, 1981. (d)

Eysenck, H. J. (Ed.). *A model for personality.* London: Springer, 1981. (e)

Eysenck, H. J., & Broadhurst, P. L. Introduction, part II: Experiments with animals. In H. J. Eysenck (Ed.), *Experiments in motivation.* London: Pergamon Press, 1964.

Eysenck, H. J., & Eysenck, S. B. G. On the unitary nature of extraversion. *Acta Psychologica,* 1967, *26,* 383–390.

Eysenck, H. J., & Eysenck, S. B. G. *Personality structure and measurement.* London: Routledge & Kegan Paul, 1969.

Eysenck, H. J., & Eysenck, S. B. G. *Psychoticism as a dimension of personality.* London: Hodder & Stoughton, 1976.

Eysenck, H. J., & Eysenck, S. B. G. Psychopathy, personality and genetics. In *Psychopathic behaviour,* R. D. Hare & D. Shalling, (Eds.), London: John Wiley & Sons, 1978.

Eysenck, H. J., & Eysenck, S. B. G. Culture and personality abnormalities. In I. Al-Issa (Ed.), *Culture and psychopathology.* New York; University Park Press, 1981.

Eysenck, H. J., & Levey, A. Conditioning, introversion-extraversion and the strength of the nervous system. In V. D. Nebylitsyn & J. A. Gray (Eds.), *Biological bases of individual behaviour.* London: Academic Press, 1972.

Eysenck, H. J., & O'Connor, K. Smoking, arousal and personality. In A. Redmond & C. Izard (Eds.), *Electro-physiological effects of nicotine.* Amsterdam: Elsevier/North Holland, 1979.

Eysenck, H. J., & Rachman, S. J. *The cause and cures of neurosis.* London: Routledge and Kegan Paul, 1965.

Eysenck, M. W. *Human memory.* London: Pergamon, 1971.

Eysenck, M. W., & Eysenck, H. J. Mischel and the concept of personality. *British Journal of Psychology,* 1980, *71,* 191–204.

Eysenck, S. B. G., & Eysenck, H. J. Physiological reactivity to sensory stimulation as a measure of personality. *Psychological Reports,* 1967, *20,* 45–46.

Freixanet, M. G. Validacion de medidas conductuales en el test de campo abierto. *Revista de Psicologia General y Aplicada,* 1980, *35,* 447–455.

Frigon, J. Extraversion, neuroticism and strength of the nervous system. *British Journal of Psychology,* 1976, *67,* 467–474.

Fulker, D. W. The genetic and environmental architecture of psychoticism, extraversion and neuroticism. In H. J. Eysenck (Ed.), *A model for personality.* New York: Springer, 1981.

Ganzer, V. J. Effects of audience presence and test anxiety on learning and retention in a serial learning situation. *Journal of Personality and Social Psychology,* 1986, *8,* 194-199.

Geen, R. G. Effects of being observed in short- and long-term recall. *Journal of Experimental Psychology,* 1973, *100,* 395-398.

Geen, R. G. Effects of evaluation apprehension on memory over intervals of varying length. *Journal of Experimental Psychology,* 1974, *102,* 908-910.

Giese H., & Schmidt, A. *Studenten sexualität.* Hamburg: Rowohlt, 1968.

Gray, J. Alternative theories of personality. In H. J. Eysenck (Ed.), *A model of personality.* London: Springer, 1981.

Hartshorne, H., & May, M. A. *Studies in deceit.* New York: Macmillan, 1928.

Hartshorne, H., & May, M. A. *Studies in service and self-control.* New York: Macmillan, 1929.

Hartshorne, H., & Shuttleworth, F. K. *Studies in the organization of character.* New York: Macmillan, 1930.

Henchy, P. J., & Glass, D. C. Evaluation apprehension and the social facilitation of dominant and subordinate responses. *Journal of Personality and Social Psychology,* 1968, *10,* 446-454.

Hudson, L. *Contrary imaginations.* London: Methuen, 1966.

Hunt, P. J., & Hillery, J. M. Social facilitation in a coaction setting: an examination of the effects over learning trials. *Journal of Experimental Social Psychology,* 1973, *9,* 563-571.

Innes, J. M., & Young, R. F. The effect of presence of an audience, evaluation apprehension and objective self-awareness on learning. *Journal of Experimental Social Psychology,* 1975, *11,* 35-52.

Jones, J., Eysenck, H. J., Martin, I., & Levey, A. B. Personality and the topography of the conditioned eyelid response. *Personality and Individual Differences,* 1980, *2,* 61-83.

Leith, G. O. The relationships between intelligence, personality and creativity under two conditions of stress. *British Journal of Educational Psychology,* 1972, *42,* 240-247.

Leith, G. O. Personality, intellectual style and study background. *Afdeling onderzoek en ontarikkeling von wetenschappelijk onderwijs.* Rijksuniversiteit Utrecht, 1972. (b)

Leith, G. O. Individual differences in learning: Interactions of personality and teaching methods. In *Personality and academic progress,*

Conference Proceedings, pp. 14–25. London: Association of Educational Psychologists, 1974.

Loehlin, J. C., & Nichols, R. C. *Heredity, Environment and Personality.* London: University of Texas Press, 1976.

Lundin, R. W. *Personality: An experimental approach.* New York: Macmillan, 1961.

Mackenzie, D. A. *Statistics in Britain: 1865–1930.* Edinburgh: Edinburgh University Press, 1981.

Magnusson, D., & Endler, N. S. (Eds.). *Personality at the crossroads: Current issues in interactional psychology.* Hillsdale, N.J.: Lawrence Erlbaum Associates, 1977.

Martens, R. Effect of an audience on learning and performance of a complex motor skill. *Journal of Personality and Social Psychology,* 1969, *12,* 252–260. (a)

Martens, R. Palmar sweating and the presence of an audience. *Journal of Experimental Social Psychology,* 1969, *5,* 371–374. (b)

Matlin, M. V., & Zajonc, R. B. Social facilitation of word associations. *Journal of Personality and Social Psychology,* 1969, *10,* 435–460.

Mischel, W. *Personality and Assessment.* London: Wiley, 1968.

Mischel, W. The interaction of person and situation. In D. Magnusson & N. S. Endler (Eds.), *Personality at the crossroads: Current issues in interactional psychology.* Hillsdale, N.J.: Lawrence Erlbaum Associates, 1977.

Mischel, W. On the interface of cognition and personality: Beyond the person-situation debate. *American Psychologist,* 1979, *34,* 740–754.

O'Connor, K. The contingent negative variation and individual differences in smoking behaviour. *Personality and Individual Differences,* 1980, *1,* 57–72.

Pallarés, A. T. *Intensitate de L'estimul incondicionat i differencies individuals, en condicionament D'evitacio "shuttle."* Barcelona: Publicaciones de la Universidad Autonoma de Barcelona, 1978.

Pederson, A. M. Effects of test anxiety and coacting groups on learning and performance. *Perceptual & Motor Skills,* 1970, *30,* 55–62.

Powell, G. *Brain and personality.* London: Praeger, 1979.

Royce, J. R. The conceptual framework for a multi-factor theory of individuality. In J. R. Royce (Ed.), *Multivariate analysis and psychological theory,* pp. 305–407. London: Academic Press, 1973.

Sasfy, J., & Okum, M. Form of evaluation and audience expertness and joint determinants of audience effects. *Journal of Experimental Social Psychology,* 1974, *10,* 461–467.

Sevilla, L. G. Extincio de RF50, inhibicio i personalitat en rates mascles

Wistar. *Temas Monograficos de Psicologia, Departamento de Psicologia Universidad Autonoma de Barcelona,* 1975, No. 1, 1–56.

Sevilla, L. G., & Garau, A. Extraversion y deambulacion de la rata en el camp abierto. *Revista Latinoamericana de Psicologia,* 1978, *10,* 211–226.

Shigehisa, T., & Symons, J. R. Reliability of auditory responses under increasing intensity of visual stimulation in relation to personality. *British Journal of Psychology,* 1973, *64,* 375–381.

Spearman, C. *The abilities of man.* London: Macmillan, 1927.

Stelmack, R. N. The psychophysiology of extraversion and neuroticism. In H. J. Eysenck (Ed.), *A model for personality.* London: Springer, 1981.

Thorndike, E. L. *Educational psychology.* New York: Teachers College, 1903.

Tohema, A., Garcia-Sevilla, L., & Garau, A. *Studies on an analogue of extraversion in the rat.* Unpublished manuscript, Departamento de Psicologia, Universidad Autonoma de Barcelona, 1981.

Trown, E. A., & Leith, G. O. Decision rules for teaching strategies in primary schools: Personality-treatment interaction. *British Journal of Educational Psychology,* 1975, *45,* 130–140.

Weisen, A. Differential reinforcing effects of onset and offset of stimulation on the operant behavior of normals, neurotics and psychopaths. Unpublished Ph.D. thesis, University of Florida, 1965.

Weiss, R. G., & Miller, F. G. The drive theory of social facilitation. *Psychological Review,* 1971, *78,* 44–57.

Wilson, G. Personality and social behaviour. In H. J. Eysenck (Ed.), *A model for personality.* London: Springer, 1981.

Zajonc, R. B. Social facilitation. *Science,* 1965, *149,* 269–274.

Zajonc, R. B., & Sales, S. M. Social facilitation of dominant and subordinate responses. *Journal of Experimental Social Psychology,* 1966, *2,* 160–168.

Zuckerman, M. *Sensation seeking.* Hillsdale, N.J.: Lawrence Erlbaum Associates, 1979.

Zuckerman, M., Bone, R. N., Neary, R., Mangelsdurff, P., & Brustman, B. What is the sensation seeker? Personality trait and experience correlates of the sensation-seeking scales. *Journal of Consulting and Clinical Psychology,* 1972, *39,* 308–321.

Zuckerman, M., Murtaugh, T., & Siegal, J. Sensation seeking and cortical augmenting-reducing. *Psychophysiology,* 1974, *11,* 535–542.

5. The Definition of the Situation: A Review*

ROBERT A. STEBBINS
University of Calgary

INTRODUCTION

The concept *definition of the situation* has served for more than sixty years in social psychological theory, even though its importance through the decades has not been uniform. Until recently, it was the exclusive domain of sociologists. It has also been misinterpreted during its lifetime, although not as badly as other sociological concepts.

The different uses of the concept of definition of the situation indicate the need to establish the one to be used here. Definition of the situation is the overall meaning of the immediate situation for each individual participating in it, as established through conscious interpretation and synthesis of its relevant personal, social, physical, and temporal considerations and through its relevant preformed cognitive structures that people carry with them from situation to situation. The meaning or definition of a situation must be established before goal-directed behavior can occur. That meaning is a subjective state of mind; it intervenes between perception of what is happening and purposive action (or inaction) carried out with reference to what is perceived.[1]

Only the concept of the definition of the situation is discussed here and not its cousin, the social situation. The latter is considered only to the extent that individuals defining a situation subjectively structure the situation itself. But situational analysis can be, and often has been, an objective undertaking ignoring individual definitions of the situation being studied, including the personal structuring of it. Or, the focus may be on situated interaction, which may take the definitions of the participants as given, rather than as an object of study. Excluded also are conceptions in sociology, psychology, and anthropology dealing with a part of the overall meaning of, or process of establishing that meaning in, situations. Meadows's (1974) comprehensive review indicates there are a number of these.

*I am grateful to Arthur W. Frank III for his careful and thoughtful critique of this chapter.

THE HISTORY OF A CONCEPT

There are three identifiable periods in the development of the concept of the definition of the situation, none of which, at present, have terminated. The first period, the symbolic interactionist period, began in 1918. The ethnomethodological period started in 1968. The social psychological period has been a consistent influence in this field only since 1972, although related developments can be traced as far back as the early 1940s.

The Symbolic Interactionist Foundation

Given the length of the symbolic interactionist period, it is no surprise that several approaches to the development of a theory of the definition of the situation have emerged. They are discussed here as the personality, motivational, dramaturgical, and reality construction approaches.

Historically, the definition of the situation, as a theoretical concept, has predominantly been the concern of American sociologists, especially those interested in symbolic interactionism. The term *definition of the situation* was coined by Thomas and Znaniecki (1918–1920) in their five-volume study, *The Polish Peasant in Europe and America*, wherein they described the breakdown of the traditional Polish peasant community after its transplantation to the United States by emigrating Poles. Actual adjustments to this condition were made in various social situations in America by means of individual definitions of them based on personal attitudes and wishes. This study and the one in which the often quoted phrase, "If men define situations as real, they are real in their consequences," appears (Thomas and Thomas 1928, 572), established the idea of the definition of the situation as a working conceptual tool in American sociology in general, and in its symbolic interactionist branch in particular.

The Polish Peasant contained many observations that now stand as key propositions in the theory of the definition of the situation. It described the basic sequence of stages of definining a situation: perception, definition, and behavior. Several types of dispositions often activated during this process were explored, including the four wishes and various personality traits and attitudes. Thomas and Znaniecki saw the significance of the distinction between situations as subjectively perceived and objectively there. They also treated the defining of situations as a more or less conscious activity, as do their symbolic interactionist colleagues today, and pointed out that many definitions crystallize at the cultural level into ready-made interpretations of particular recurrent events. The process of preliminary reflection was said to be important, even in selecting and applying cultural definitions to routine situations, but especially in defining unusual situations. However common or different the setting to be defined, all settings and thus all definitions of them are unique; the human and nonhuman elements comprising each one never combine in exactly the same way.

Thomas, sometimes with the help of his wife, continued to fill out this rudimentary statement for the next nineteen years, culminating in his response to Blumer's (1939) critique of the 1918 classic. In *Old World Traits Transplanted* (1921), Thomas et al. noted that while we are forming a new definition of the situation, goal-directed action is frozen and our emotional and physical reactions become "random" (Thomas et al., 1921, 262). In a later work, he established the philosophical foundation for studying the definition of the situation by observing that a sense of individualism is inherent in defining situations and determining subsequent behavior, though it is never complete. This stance is still the one most symbolic interactionists embrace today. In the language of the determinism-free-will debate he espoused a "soft determinism" (Matza 1964, chapt. 1).[2]

In a 1928 paper, Thomas's strong psychological orientation led him to conclude that habit is a definition of a certain type of situation and that being aware of defining situations is only present when new stimuli challenge established habits (Thomas 1928, 153). These observations contradict his earlier position and do not coincide with the modern symbolic interactionist view of the degree of awareness present in the defining process (Stebbins 1975, 31–32).

Znaniecki also continued to build on the foundation laid in 1918. His final statement, in *Cultural Sciences* (1952, 242-260), contains the most detailed presentation of the process and product of the definition of the situation up to that time. He was less equivocal on the subject of reflection than was his collaborator:

> Such a conception of a situation, reached by the agent after reflection, has been termed *definition of the situation*. . . . The common aspect of these definitions is that they all require reflection as an ideational activity, which may or may not be connected with realistic activities. People can act without defining situations, and they can define situations without acting. (1952, 243)[3]

Znaniecki underscored the importance of purpose or goal when defining situations. He also introduced three new types of definitions: prospective, retrospective, and vicarious. Prospective refers to situations that definers believe they will actually or possibly face in the future. Retrospective refers to situations previously defined. Vicarious denotes our interpretations of others' situations, whether past, present, or future.

Despite these contributions, the idea of the definition of the situation was never as central to Znaniecki's thought as it was to Thomas's.

From approximately 1930 until his death in 1958, Znaniecki was more interested in developing his functional theory, in which the definition of the situation and other social psychological processes were subsumed under the concept of system (Martindale 1960, 467–469). He eventually withdrew completely from social psychology to pursue his macro-sociological interests.

Thomas's theoretical work on definition of the situation (and Znaniecki's, for that matter) was part of a theory of social personality (Janowitz 1966, xi). It remained for Mills (1940) to set in motion the relocation of the study of the definition of the situation to the field of motivation, which is where most of today's scholars explicitly or implicitly place it. Drawing on the earlier work of Burke, Mead, and Dewey, Mills observed that a motive, imputed or avowed,

> tends to be one which is to the actor and to the other members of a situation an unquestioned answer to questions concerning social and lingual conduct. . . . Motives are acceptable justifications for present, future, or past programs or acts. (1940, 906)

Mills, however, was more concerned with the general problem of motivation than with the specific concept of the definition of the situation. Thomas and Znaniecki are scarcely mentioned, and their central idea is ignored.

The next major contribution to the burgeoning theory of the definition of the situation came in 1942 with the publication of MacIver's theoretical tour de force, *Social Causation.* He renamed his version of the definition of the situation the "dynamic assessment" even while acknowledging its similarity to the ideas of Thomas and Znaniecki (1942, 372, *n*.1). One of MacIver's most enduring additions to the theory was to fill in some details about how social forms emerge from converging definitions of situations by many different individuals, thereby anticipating work done more than twenty years later by the students of reality construction. The group convergence or collective definition of the situation underlies group activities, institutional arrangements, folkways, and social behavior in general. Such phenomena as crime rates, statutes, social movements, changes in mores, modes of living, social divisions of labor, business cycles, and levels of unemployment are ultimately traceable to the meaning people ascribe to certain events (MacIver 1942, 300–313).

In other words, the dynamic assessment or definition of the situation can be seen as a causal agent that produces social change:

> A dynamic assessment weighs alternatives not yet actualized, sets what would be the consequences if this course were taken over against what would be the consequences if that course were taken. It is in this regard a causal judgment. (1942, 292)

Later in the book he stated:

> The primary contrast between social causation and the causation re-
> vealed in physical and in biological phenomena is that the former in-
> volves the socio-psychological nexus. (1942, 371)

> For the interpretation of social phenomena we are concerned not with
> the individual assessment as such but with the modes and processes of
> interindividual assessment, as they emerge in historical events, statistical
> facts, social trends and movements of various kinds, institutions . . .
> and the various unpurposed resultants of social behavior. Back of all of
> these lies the converging and conflicting assessments generated within
> the social situation. (1942, 374)

Later that decade, Merton proposed a variation on MacIver's group
assessment theme. Working directly from the Thomas theorem, "If men
define situations as real, they are real in their consequences," Merton
(1957, 421–436) pointed out that, under certain conditions, individual
definitions of a situation, even though objectively false, can make the
originally false perception come true. He illustrated the self-fulfilling
prophecy with the effects of a rumor on the solvency of a local bank.[4]

The next theoretical development came from Foote, who completed the link between motivation and definition of the situation
started more than a decade earlier by Mills. With the following well-
known passage, he launched what has come to be known as the sociological theory of motivation:

> In a sentence, we take motivation to refer to the degree to which a
> human being, as a participant in the ongoing social process in which he
> necessarily finds himself, defines a problematic situation as calling for
> performance of a particular act, with more or less anticipated consum-
> mations and consequences, and thereby his organism releases the energy
> appropriate to performing it. (1951, 15)

Foote also added the proposition that our relevant social identities are
among the major predispositions activated by the events at hand. Because they are enduring, these identities foster continuity in our definitions of successive situations.[5]

Goffman was the first in this line of theorists to identify and explore the dramaturgical side of defining situations. People express their
definitions before an audience of situated others through such devices
as impression management, front- and backstage behavior, role playing,
and everyday presentations of self called performances. Much of Goffman's work in this area, however, dealt with "expressions given off,"
which are mostly nonverbal and unintentional (1959, 4). His work deviated from the theoretical mainstream as it had developed to that time,
for symbolic interactionist interest had been centered predominantly
on the awareness level of the defining process.

Goffman also examined the collective definition of the situation, labeled the *working consensus.* It is the "single overall definition . . . which involves not so much a real agreement as to what exists but rather a real agreement as to whose claims concerning what issues will be temporarily honored" (1959, 9-10). With such an interest, Goffman can also be classified with another group of symbolic interactionists who study the definition of the situation—the reality constructionists.

In a pair of articles and a book, Stebbins (1967, 1969, 1975) organized the preceding ideas into a motivational theory of the definition of the situation. He dealt with the failure of these men to define and describe, in other than a general way, the subsidiary concept of situation. We start subjectively structuring the situation the moment we enter it, the structuring proceeding according to a purpose or "action orientation" we have in mind. Here, we personally and selectively create our own subjective view of that situation. This must be done before it can be defined and before goal-directed action can take place there. The action orientation helps set temporal, social, and physical boundaries of the setting.

Stebbins also reinstated the indispensable notion of predisposition, thrown out earlier by Foote, as an umbrella concept for the various personality and cultural factors influencing the defining process. The modern conceptualization of predisposition as described by Campbell (1963) and Newcomb et al. (1965, 40-46, 67-73) eliminated Foote's objections with the idea. Campbell limited his statement strictly to acquired states, which endure and remain dormant until activated by situational stimuli. These activated products of past experience impinge on our awareness, equip us with specific, usually habitual views of the world, and guide behavior in the present. Stebbins also identified some important situational factors that bear on definitions of the situation.

In the 1969 paper, Stebbins tackled the problem, only cursorily explored to this point, of how much active defining of situations actually occurs. Only a little active defining in habitual personal or cultural definitions occurs, other than to determine that the present circumstances call for a particular habitual or cultural definition. By contrast, unique personal definitions require a significant amount of active defining in the form of improvisation since no standard habitual or cultural meaning readily fits the immediate situation.

The 1969 paper also presents the most detailed statement yet of the basic sequence of stages of defining the situation. The description of stages leaves no doubt that the study of the definition of the situation is a generalizing enterprise, not an idiographic one, as suggested by earlier theorists, who tended to concentrate on case studies.

1. Typical actors in a given identity enter a typical setting with a particular action orientation in mind.

2. Certain aspects of these surroundings, some of which relate to the orientations, activate or awaken some of the predisposition the actors characteristically carry with them.

3. The aspects of the surroundings, the orientations, and the activated predispositions, when considered together, initiate further selection of a cultural or habitual definition or further construction of a unique one.

4. This definition guides subsequent goal directed action in the situation, at least until reinterpretation occurs. (Stebbins 1969, 196)

This paper also dealt with the problem of researching definitions of situations by presenting thirteen operational statements within the phases of (1) identifying the ongoing events and (2) selecting a cultural or habitual definition or construction of a unique one.

The report on teachers' definitions of classroom situations includes a discussion on the amounts of reflection needed to define routine as opposed to unusual situations (Stebbins 1975, 22-26). Some unusual situations trap the actor in the cruel paradox that he or she must act quickly but sensibly, which requires time to create an effective plan of action to deal with the events of the moment. Other unusual situations allow time to think before action is necessary.

The problematic nature of some social situations continues to attract symbolic interactionists. Lofland (1976, 33-37) wrote that many events in daily life are ambiguous or subject to competing definitions. This occurs when there is extensive heterogeneity or hierarchy among the people in a situation; when there is an extensive amount, range, or complexity of equipment in it; when large or numerous spaces are involved; and when the situation is temporally long.

Ball's (1972) discussion of the personal consistency assumption adds to the theory. It is taken for granted in daily life that there is uniformity in the ways we define similar situations over time, in the ways categories of actors define them, and in the ways we define them with respect to particular interactants. Ball also noted that, through a sort of hypothesis testing, people learn how others see the situation; definitions are tentatively tried out on them and accepted, rejected, or modified on the basis of their reactions. Depending on how unusual the situation is, negotiation may occur as individual participants try to persuade the others that their version of what is happening is most accurate or suitable.

In the end, the theory of the definition of the situation, as Mills and Foote suggested, is, among other things, a sociological theory of motivation (Stebbins 1975, 32-35). This theory avoids the mechanistic assumptions in the model of mainstream psychology, while it stresses the subjectivity believed to precede much of human action. It certainly helps solve the research problem addressed in the study of motivation: "to account for the *patterning, timing, and direction of behavior*, especially for persistent movement toward a goal" (Shibutani 1961, 181).[6]

Perinbanayagam (1974) clearly explicated the dramaturgical component in the definition of situations and reviewed contributions to this approach of earlier thinkers, notably Goffman. For dramaturgical sociologists, life is theater and people are like playwrights in that they use communicative techniques to express their definitions of situations to others in the same setting. That is, they dramatize their values, intentions, moods, and beliefs as they interact with others doing the same. This approach concentrates on the theaterlike aspects of our everyday interchanges, not on the metaphorical aspects of life as drama. Drama is make-believe; dramaturgical communication is real.

The dramaturgical, motivational, and personality approaches to the definition of the situation are mainly concerned with explaining the behavior of situated individuals. The reality construction approach picks up where these three approaches leave off. It is concerned with how the definitions of already behaving, or interacting, individuals coalesce into a collectively recognized understanding of what is going on and how individual and collective definitions spawn new social forms and modifications of existing ones.

Berger and Luckmann (1966, 51) suggested that "habitualization" as a standardized predefinition of the situation is a necessary precondition in the institutionalization of any social form. Stebbins (1974) holds that people define commonly perceived changes in their social and physical environment. Over time and through interaction within each definer's social circle, these definitions coalesce into a consensually held view of what has happened. Eventually, these collective definitions spread to other social circles through the social network ties that enable the original definers of the change to associate with those in other parts of the community.[7]

Berger and Kellner (1970) emphasized the taken-for-granted quality of cultural definitions in reality construction. Individuals move through many routine stituations in the course of everyday living. Here, they apply standard definitions that, however, require continual validation. This validation is accomplished in social interaction with others in the setting, especially significant others:

> The plausibility and stability of the world, as socially defined, is dependent upon the strength and continuity of significant relationships in which conversation about this world can be continually carried on. . . . The reality of the world is sustained through conversation with significant others. (1970, 53)

Once the notion took root that the definition of the situation, individual and collective, can also be viewed as a form of reality construction, the stage was set for introducing a new level of analysis. Reality construction rests on consensus, which, in turn, asks how any given consensus emerges in a social situation. The answer leads, among other places, to an examination of the cultural structures human beings bring to the situations they define. The consciousness bias of the symbolic interactionists acted as a decoy, drawing them away from the study of these matters, despite their involvement with such concepts as habit, cultural definition, and personal consistency.

The Ethnomethodological Correction

The label *ethnomethodologist* is used here, for lack of a better one, to identify scholars who have shown a direct interest in the definition of the situation from a cultural structure perspective, in distinction to the consciousness perspective of the symbolic interactionists. Definition of the situation as a concept has always been more peripheral to ethnomethodology than to symbolic interactionism. Still, the former had only barely begun to develop when McHugh undertook his study of defining situations. Though it contained a certain symbolic interactionist flavor, it fundamentally examined selected aspects of the assumed side of the organization of meaning in routine interaction; an emphasis that squares with the general program of ethnomethodology (c.f., Wootton 1975, 59).

One of ethnomethodology's tasks is to identify the taken-for-granted rules of everyday life and how they are practiced or used there:

> I shall do this by immediately asserting that rules (norms, values) are a means by which society and definition can be said to coexist, because rules inhabit both collective conscience and the member's definition. Rules are socially organized in the most encompassing sense of the term. (McHugh 1968, 13)

McHugh was particularly interested in rules that are necessary for order. He called these "constitutive rules," or rules that people are unaware of but that still help them define situations in their daily routine.

McHugh (1968, chapt. 3) developed an analytic framework based on two key concepts: emergence and relativity. Emergence is a temporal process wherein, through memory, past events are said to influence our definition of present situations, present situations are influenced by inferences about the future, and future situations will be used to reconstruct our definitions of the past. The ideal closely resembles Znaniecki's prospective and retrospective definitions. Relativity refers to the absence of an ultimate reality. Rather, multiple realities are made obvious through their relationships across the boundaries of space.

Time and space are ways of describing how we construct definitions of the countless situations we enter.

In chapter 4, McHugh lists the properties of emergence and relativity. By means of the process of emergence, individuals discover through time certain patterns in their situations and hence in their definitions of them. McHugh discusses the properties of theme, elaboration (the situated expression of themes), fit (how an actual instance corresponds to theme), authorship (personal interpretation of signs and behaviors), and revelation (the interpretation of signs and behaviors with reference to each other). Relativity rests on the process of role taking, of discerning others' standpoints in the same situation. Its properties are typicality (representativeness of behavior), likelihood (probability of behavior occurring), causal texture (cause of behavior), technical efficiency (effectiveness in reaching desired ends), moral requiredness (right and wrong, evaluation), and substantive congruency (accuracy of others' definitions of the situation).[8]

Goffman also eventually repudiated the consciousness bias of symbolic interactionism. Like McHugh, he searched for sets of constitutive rules or interdependent practices he called "frames." Behind every definition of the situation lies a frame that, even though the individual is unaware of it, shapes his or her behavioral response to the events of the immediate present.

> I assume that definitions of a situation are built up in accordance with principles of organization which govern events—at least social ones—and our subjective involvement in them; frame is the word I use to refer to such of these basic elements as I am able to identify. . . . My phrase "frame analysis" is a slogan to refer to the examination in these terms of the organization of experience. (Goffman 1974, 10–11)

Goffman thus abandoned his earlier interest in the dramaturgy of defining situations for a program of frame analysis of the rules of cognition and communication that underlie the construction of our many social worlds. He is now concerned less with actual situations or types of situations than with the structure of frames that are essentially unaffected by the events of everyday life. The rules of frame are analogous to the syntactical structures in language.

McHugh retained a degree of affiliation with the symbolic interactionist approach to the defining of situations by incorporating such notions as role taking and typification (identification) into his framework.[9] Goffman, however, has cleanly broken with symbolic interactionism. Gonos (1977) pointed out that Goffman rejects, as a proper focus of research, the subjective side of defining situations. Role taking, or *Verstehen*, for example, only facilitates our grasp of the affective and cognitive states of others in the setting, not the rules by which they unwittingly guide their behavior. Meaning, on the one hand, is the starting point for situational analysis for a symbolic interactionist; behavior follows meaning. Goffman, on the other hand, holds that inner states, including meaning, follow behavior that, in turn, is predicated on a cultural system of categories and rules governing the creation and communication of meaning (Gonos 1977, 863).

The concept of self, or of personality as used by Thomas and Znaniecki, is also rejected in Goffman's frame analysis. In Gonos's words:

> A structuralist analysis, such as Goffman's, assumes a different starting point than that of interactionism. . . . We can say that it does not "start with" social actors, but with the socially given frame that exists prior to these individuals, who are called upon to give it life. . . . Individual selves do not exist except for a tenuous social reality that certain frames bestow upon them. (Gonos 1977, 865)

Interactionists, such as MacIver, Merton, and Stebbins, discussed the capacities of individuals, alone and collectively, for building and changing institutionalized forms or structures, starting with their own creative thoughts and actions. In Goffman's frame analysis, individuals are conceived of as vehicles for continuing previously formed structures. Human beings are "resources," in Goffman's *Frame Analysis* terminology, who manifest the hidden rules and categories.

The symbolic interactionists and those classified here as ethnomethodologists still share at least one intellectual concern: the description and construction of social reality. McHugh's and Goffman's analyses, as well as those of the symbolic interactionists, have a common starting point: the Thomas theorem, "If men define situations as real, they are real in their consequences" (Meadows 1974, 44; Frank 1979, 185-188). Ethnomethodologists are interested in the cultural structuring of the kind of social reality referred to under the symbolic interactionist approach as the cultural definition. That is the social reality of much of routine life.

Symbolic interactionists are attracted to the side of reality construction of which we are more or less aware—to the perception of others, to role taking, to the selecting or devising of a situationally appropriate plan of action, to the justification of actions, to their dramaturgical expression, and to negotiating definitions of reality in search of a working consensus. The symbolic interactionist approach is most useful for analyzing situations ambiguous or complicated by competing standard definitions; a significant degree of active reflection is required here (Lofland 1976, 33-37; Stebbins 1975, 16, 22-25, 100-102). But these troublesome aspects seem to pervade many routine situations to a significant degree; they are not limited to the unusual events of life.

The Social Psychological Synthesis

Situation as a theoretical concept has had, at best, a marginal existence in psychological social psychology.[10] Credit for giving it the modicum of visibility it has gained goes to psychologists who have maintained contact with sociology. For example, Newcomb et al. (1965, 68–69) described how stored dispositions or attitudes, when joined by situational forces, shape behavior within a given setting. Miller (1968, 647) extensively reviewed studies dealing with one aspect or another of the situation as it affects the behavior of people within it. But these writings deal with situations, not with the defining of them. Until recently, only Lewin, through his concept of "life space," came close to the idea of definition of situation as shaped by the symbolic interactionists.

Cartwright summed up Lewin's notion of life space in his Foreword to a collection of the latter's papers:

> The most fundamental construct for Lewin is, of course, that of "field." All behavior (including action, thinking, wishing, striving, valuing, achieving, etc.) is conceived as a change of some state of a field in a given unit of time. . . . The life space [i.e., field] is defined so that at any given time it includes all facts that have existence and excludes those that do not have existence *for the individual or group under study* [italics in original]. . . . Lewin chose to attribute existence to anything having demonstrable effects. In individual psychology, the environment and the person as consciously perceived by the person are ordinarily included in the life space. But, in addition, unconscious states are also included to the extent that by direct observation or inference the scientist can determine that they have effects. (Lewin 1951, xi–xii)

This auspicious start for a psychological treatment of the definition of the situation foundered and died, however. Instead, other parts of Lewin's theories captured his students' attention, leading eventually to the rise of group dynamics and contemporary experimental social psychology. The few who remained interested in his psychological ecology (notably Barker and Wright) concentrated on the objective aspects of the behavior setting and its boundaries, to the exclusion of its subjective meaning.

Even though the term *situation* appeared in more social psychology textbooks during the 1960s than previously, the turning point in recognizing the significance of situational meaning was Harré and Secord's (1972) book, *The Explanation of Social Behaviour*. They abandoned positivist psychology to work from their own paradigm, which stressed the importance of "mechanisms" that generate behavior—a scientific pursuit they dubbed *ethogeny*. "The main process involved in them," they posited, "is self-direction according to the meaning ascribed to the situation" or to an "episode" within the situation (1972, 9).

The meaning of an episode is found, in part, in the actors' accounts of their behavior there, as conveyed through everyday language. Various types of episodes exist and can be identified by their beginning and end, though they are difficult to classify since they lack explicit rules. Meaning also comes from rules, where they exist. Rules are prescriptions for behavior of which individuals are aware. They guide their behavior in episodes.

A role consists of a set of rules to be followed by a particular category of individual. Individuals also dramaturgically and consciously control the style as well as the actions of their episodic behavior. Language is one power individuals bring to episodes. Another is their set of short-term capacities, or states of affective readiness, to act. Liabilities complement powers by blocking or circumventing exercise of the latter. Commonsense or human nature terms, such as *coward*, label these powers and liabilities in everyday life. Each social self is a cluster of powers and liabilities.

Harre and Secord's works played a major role in provoking what Backman (1979) believes is a paradigmatic revolution in experimental social psychology. In 1975, the British Psychological Society sponsored a workshop at Oxford University on new developments in social psychological methods. A subsequent published anthology organized according to the themes of the workshop (Ginsburg 1979) indicate that a number of psychological social psychologists are heading toward a synthesis of the ethnomethodological and symbolic interactionist approaches to the definition of the situation. Argyle (1979), for example, noted that, to obtain a full account of a situation, one must examine seven separate but interdependent components: elements of behavior used, goals or motives of the participants, rules, tasks, roles, physical setting and equipment, and cognitive concepts and skills. One must pay attention in such an analysis not only to the situation, but also to its constituent episodes, which are the most critical units to scrutinize. Defining and identifying episodes remains a problem in this approach; they were loosely defined by Harre and Secord (1972, 154) as: "*any* sequence of happenings . . . which has some principle of unity."

Early ethogenics, with its emphasis on conscious linguistic accounts of behavior, roles and rules, intentional dramaturgical control, and the like, had more in common with symbolic interaction than with ethnomethodology. Harré (1977) since redressed this imbalance by promoting account analysis as the essence of ethogenics. Here, he merged with the structuralism of a latter-day group of ethnomethodologists who call themselves conversational analysts.

Account analysis is neither very fancy nor strange. It is the analysis of both the social force and explanatory content of the speech produced by social actors as a guide to the structure of the cognitive resources required for the genesis of intelligible and warrantable social action by those actors. . . . Regarding it [action] as part of [an ongoing] structure makes it intelligible. If it is to be warranted it must be at the right place in that structure for an item of that kind. (1977, 284)

A common assumption that binds the work of Harré and Secord, Argyle, and others of the ethogenic school to that of Goffman and the conversational analysts is that, to use Harré's terminology, we carry around preformed structures or templates leading to situated behavioral or product structures. As in structural linguistics, the subject is unaware of this process. Yet, Harré and his associates also attend to episodes, sequences of episodes, and situations, which could be labeled *emergent structures*, because they are recognizable collective products of interacting individuals defining a shared situation. Here, the ethogenists' interests converge with those of such reality constructionists as Berger, Luckmann, and Kellner.

These psychological social psychologists are engaged in a major effort to synthesize all that preceded them dealing with the definition of the situation in psychology, ethnomethodology, and symbolic interaction. Furnham's recent work and the contents of this collection attest to the scope of this endeavor. Furnham and Argyle (1981) produced the most extensive inventory yet of the elements of the social situation.

These elements are arranged within three sets of features: physical, temporal, and psychological. The first set subsumes the boundaries of, the props used in, the modifiers found in (e.g., color, noise, light), and the spatial arrangements of situations. These last three incorporate the contributions of environmental psychology and proxemics into the study of the definition of the situation.

The second set of features refers to the duration and progression of events (episodes) and actions within the situation. The third, by means of the concept of rules, encompasses the ethogenic ideas of Harré and Secord and those of Goffman and the conversational analysts. It also includes goals, social roles, and constructs, or cognitive sets that help make sense of the world in which we live. The latter closely resembles the notion of predisposition used in the symbolic interactionist theory of the definition of the situation. Furnham's model for the interaction of these elements indicates that he is presently more interested in the personal structuring of the situation and how this might change than in the actual process of defining it, although there is some overlap.

STUDYING THE DEFINITION OF THE SITUATION

The interdisciplinary character of today's research on the definition of the situation has resulted in a methodological picture more complex than the life history approach taken by Thomas and Znaniecki more than sixty years ago. Their data were gathered in unstructured interviews, which remains an important procedure today. Waller (1932) was the first to use the method of participant observation to study this process, which he did in schoolrooms. For the next twenty-five years, however, symbolic interactionists did little more than theorize about the definition of the situation. Systematic contact with the empirical world was reestablished with Goffman's (1959) dramaturgical field study. Goffman's work at this point in his career, though theoretically significant, was methodologically no different from that of his predecessors.

The same can be said for most empirical work by Stebbins (1971, 1975) and Stebbins and Flynn (1975), the only other symbolic interactionists to study the definition of the situation directly. As part of an earlier theoretical paper, however, Stebbins (1969) reported one of the first attempts to experiment on defining situations. Structured questionnaires, rating scales, and the Kuhn-McPartland Twenty Statements Test were used to gather data on how students in a university classroom defined a secretly manipulated interruption by two outsiders of lectures on a controversial topic. Data collection was guided by the thirteen operationalizations presented in the same paper.

A year earlier, McHugh (1968) published the results of a similar project, hoping to demonstrate the importance of relativity and emergence as requisites to orderly interaction. In addition to the use of an anomie scale and a simple structured response procedure, he experimentally introduced disruption or anomie into a laboratory situation to determine if relativity and emergence would disappear under that condition. For the most part, they did not. His experiment and Stebbins's dealt with unusual situations.

McHugh's experiment was a laboratory adaptation of the field procedure recommended by Garfinkle for disrupting social worlds to discover their underlying social rules. Today, role breaking and role interruption are mainly studied by field observation. Argyle (1979, 26–28) further suggested interviewing mobile individuals or newcomers to a particular group or subculture as a way of identifying assumed rules. Or, standardized questionnaires might be given to its members to develop a list of important proscriptive and prescriptive rules for each situation and set of situations. This procedure facilitates identifying a hierarchy of classes of situations and sets of rules that apply at various levels of generality. Another way to discover assumed rules is to study the sanctions for breaking them. Multidimensional scaling has been used for this purpose.

Raw data for rule analysis can be gathered by direct observation, voice and video recordings, or film. Role playing has been an effective procedure, as has the autobiography. The repertory grid, another useful instrument, inventories the repertoire and properties of a person's constructs (see articles in Ginsburg 1979, chaps. 6, 8, 9). Content analysis is often used to describe conversations.

THE DEFINITION OF THE SITUATION IN EXPLANATION

The ethnomethodological and social psychological periods in the development of the theory of the definition of the situation have brought not only an expansion of research techniques but also a more prominent explanatory role for its core concept. Historically, the definition of the situation has played three theoretical roles in the research process: (1) as a post hoc explanation; (2) as an organizing principle for previously collected data; (3) as an object of study. Notwithstanding direct examination of the idea by Thomas, Znaniecki, Goffman, and Stebbins, its use during the symbolic interactionist period has been largely confined to the first role. Holsti's (1970) research exemplified this tendency. In studying the 1914 international crisis, he found that the variation in perception of hostility among foreign policy leaders could be accounted for by their definitions of that situation.

Waller's (1932) research on classrooms illustrated the use of the concept of the definition of the situation as an organizing principle. It is the main theme in chapter 18, where he traces the consequences for education of conflicting definitions of schoolroom events by teachers and pupils. From this perspective, he examined discipline, sportsmanship, property, academic performance, and other topics.

Most research treating definitions of situations as objects of research has been exploratory. Its primary aims have been to describe the properties and processes of types of definitions and to determine the place of those types within some broader social scientific theory. In the past, one rarely found the definition of the situation as a main concept in one or more hypotheses to be tested in a controlled research design. In this sense, it has seldom been an object of study (for exceptions, see Gorden 1951; McHugh 1968).[11]

Direct experimentation on the definition of the situation is most likely to remain the province of the psychological social psychologists. They have already made a start, though such research is typically done in the name of the meaning of the situation; the term *definition of the situation* is not used. Indeed, experimentation will probably be one important way these psychologists distinguish their efforts in this field from those of the ethnomethodologists and the symbolic interactionists. Even here, however, their work is likely to retain a substantial exploratory flavor as they join their colleagues in other disciplines in the difficult task of shaping the definition of the situation as a theoretical concept and describing its many empirical manifestations.

CONCLUSIONS

Despite extensive developments since 1918, Thomas and Znaniecki would still recognize the present theory of the definition of the situation. The position that any definition is more or less conscious is still held by most symbolic interactionists and psychologists. The assertion that some definitions are cultural and thus ready-made jibes with the ethogenic-ethnomethodological stance that preformed structures are being applied to recurrent situations. Thomas's later assertion that the definitions of many situations are habitual also appears to fit their perspective. The individualism in the Thomas and Znaniecki statements survives today in the writings of the symbolic interactionists and the psychological social psychologists. Still, theirs is a soft determinism, which tacitly recognizes the role of preformed structures in human behavior. Of note, too, is the fit of Znaniecki's retrospective and prospective definitions with McHugh's emergence and with De Waele and Harré's (1979) autobiographical method, which they use to identify internal structures.

Thus, there is considerable continuity of thought from the founding fathers to the present. But the group of scholars who coined the term *definition of the situation* and laid much of its theoretical foundation now appear content to leave further theorizing and research to the ethnomethodologists and social psychologists. Perhaps this situation will change. For the moment, however, symbolic interactionists are content with treating the definition of the situation as part of their conceptual heritage and, as such, no longer in need of additional refinement. In this venerated role, it serves as a handy post hoc explanation and organizing principle for data collected for purposes. For the time being, then, advances in this area will come from psychological social psychology and ethnomethodology, where new approaches to the problem of explaining the meaning of situated events have sprung from contact with fresh theoretical and methodological perspectives.

ENDNOTES

1. The sequence of perception, definition, and action is discussed more extensively in earlier works by the author (Stebbins 1975, 5-17; 1969; 1967).

2. The liberal or laissez-faire position of definition of the situation theory and symbolic interactionism has earned this line of thought the scorn of at least one neo-Marxist sociologist who holds that it is ac-

tually reactionary. It is ignorant of social class forces. It fosters class oppression, instead of opposing it (Grabiner 1975).

3. Also see p. 246.

4. This essay was originally published in 1949.

5. Use of the term *predisposition* here is mine, not Foote's. He rejected the idea as it was defined in his day. Present use is based on a subsequent reconceptualization discussed later in this essay.

6. Sociologists have written on various aspects of motivation, all of which can be incorporated into the theory of the definition of the situation and its thirteen operational statements (Stebbins 1975, 18–19). For example, see works by Franks (1974) on competence; Scott and Lyman (1968), Schutz (1967, 69–71), and Weigert (1975) on accounts; and Blum and McHugh (1971) on the social ascription of motives.

7. See Stebbins (1974, 115) for discussion of the view that Berger and Luckmann's habitualization is actually a consequence of institutionalization rather than an antecedent of it.

8. McHugh's interest in the causes of behavior from an ethnomethodological standpoint is one he unwittingly shares with the attribution theorists of experimental social psychology. The relationship between attribution theory and the definition of the situation is examined elsewhere (Stebbins 1979).

9. At least one author has interpreted McHugh's work as a symbolic interactionist endeavor (Hewitt 1976, 105–127).

10. Psychological social psychology refers to social psychology as developed by those trained in psychology departments (House 1977). Among them are the experimental social psychologists.

11. Although McHugh (1968) did not explicitly state a hypothesis, one can easily be inferred. Stebbins's (1969) experiment was exploratory and hence without predictions of any sort.

REFERENCES

Argyle, M. Sequences in social behaviour as a function of the situation. In G. P. Ginsburg (Ed.), *Emerging strategies in social psychological research.* New York: John Wiley, 1979.

Backman, C. W. Epilogue: A new paradigm? In G. P. Ginsburg (Ed.), *Emerging strategies in social psychological research.* New York: John Wiley, 1979.

Ball, D. W. The definition of the situation: Some theoretical and methodological consequences of taking W. I. Thomas seriously. *Journal for the Theory of Social Behaviour*, 1972, 2, 61–82.

152 / *Robert A. Stebbins*

Berger, P. L., & Kellner, H. Marriage and the construction of reality. In H. P. Dreitzel (Ed.), *Recent sociology, No. 2*. New York: Macmillan, 1970.

Berger, P. L., & Luckmann, T. *The social construction of reality*. Garden City, N.Y.: Doubleday, 1966.

Blum, A. F., & McHugh, P. The social ascription of motives. *American Sociological Review*, 1971, *36*, 98–109.

Blumer, H. *An appraisal of Thomas Znaniecki's the Polish peasant in Europe and America*. New York: Social Science Research Council, 1939.

Campbell, D. T. Social attitudes and other acquired behavioral dispositions. In S. Koch (Ed.), *Psychology: A study of a science* (Vol. 6). New York: McGraw-Hill, 1963.

De Waele, J. P., & Harré, R. Autobiography as a psychological method. In G. P. Ginsburg (Ed.), *Emerging strategies in social psychological research*. New York: John Wiley, 1979.

Foote, N. N. Identification as the basis for a theory of motivation. *American Sociological Review*, 1951, *16*, 14–21.

Frank, A. W. III. Reality construction in interaction. *Annual Review of Sociology* (Vol. 5). Palo Alto, Calif.: Annual Review, Inc., 1979.

Franks, D. D. Current conceptions of competency motivation and self-validations. In D. Field (Ed.), *Social psychology for sociologists*. New York: John Wiley, 1974.

Furnham, A., & Argyle, M. (Eds.). *The psychology of social situations*. Oxford: Pergamon, 1981.

Ginsburg, G. P. (Ed.). *Emerging strategies in social psychological research*. New York: John Wiley, 1979.

Goffman, E. *The presentation of self in everyday life*. Garden City, N. Y.: Doubleday, 1959.

Goffman, E. *Frame analysis*. New York: Harper, 1974.

Gonos, G. Situation versus frame: The interactionist and the structuralist analyses of everyday life. *American Sociological Review*, 1977, *42*, 854–867.

Gorden, R. L. Interaction between attitude and the definition of the situation in the expression of opinion. *American Sociological Review*, 1951, *17*, 50–58.

Grabiner, G. The situational sociologies. *The insurgent sociologist*, 1975, *5*, 80–81.

Harré, R. The ethogenic approach: Theory and practice. In L. Berkowitz (Ed.), *Advances in experimental social psychology* (Vol. 10). New York: Academic Press, 1977.

Harré, R., & Secord, P. F. *The explanation of social behaviour*. Totowa, N. J.: Littlefield, Adams, 1972.

Hewitt, J. P. *Self and society.* Boston: Allyn and Bacon, 1976.

Holsti, O. R. Individual differences in definition of the situation. *Journal of Conflict Resolution*, 1970, *14*, 303–310.

House, J. S. The three faces of social psychology. *Sociometry*, 1977, *40*, 161–177.

Janowitz, M. Introduction. In W. I. Thomas, *On social organization and social personality.* Chicago: University of Chicago Press, 1966.

Lewin, K. *Field theory in social science.* New York: Harper, 1951.

Lofland, J. *Doing social life: The qualitative study of human interaction in natural settings.* New York: John Wiley, 1976.

MacIver, R. M. *Social causation.* New York: Harper, 1942.

Martindale, D. *The nature and types of sociological theory.* Boston: Houghton Mifflin, 1960.

Matza, D. *Delinquency and drift.* New York: John Wiley, 1964.

McHugh, P. *Defining the situation.* Indianapolis: Bobbs-Merrill, 1968.

Meadows, P. Situational theory: Perspective constructions of social reality. Paper presented at the Annual Meeting of the American Sociological Association, Montreal, August 1974.

Merton, R. K. *Social theory and social structure*, rev. ed. New York: Free Press, 1957.

Miller, D. R. The study of social relationships: Situation, identity, and social interaction. In S. Koch (Ed.), *Psychology: A study of a science* (Vol. 5). New York: McGraw-Hill, 1963.

Mills, C. W. Situated actions and vocabularies of motives. *American Sociological Review*, 1940, *5*, 904–913.

Newcomb, T. M., Turner, R. H., & Converse, P. E. *Social psychology.* New York: Holt, Rinehart & Winston, 1965.

Perinbanayagam, R. S. The definition of the situation: An analysis of the ethnomethodological and dramaturgical view. *Sociological Quarterly*, 1974, *15*, 521–541.

Schutz, A. *Collected paper I: The problem of social reality*, M. Natanson (Ed.). The Hague: Martinus Nijhoff, 1967.

Scott, M. B., & Lyman, S. M. Accounts. *American Sociological Review*, 1968, *33*, 46–62.

Shibutani, T. *Society and personality.* Englewood Cliffs, N.J.: Prentice-Hall, 1961.

Stebbins, R. A. A theory of the definition of the situation. *Canadian Review of Sociology and Anthropology*, 1967, *4*, 148–164.

Stebbins, R. A. Studying the definition of the situation: Theory and field research strategies. *Canadian Review of Sociology and Anthropology*, 1969, *6*, 193–211.

Stebbins, R. A. The meaning of disorderly behavior: Teacher definitions of a classroom situation. *Sociology of Education*, 1971, *44*, 217–236.

Stebbins, R. A. Formalization: Notes on a theory of the rise and change of social forms. *International Journal of Contemporary Sociology*, 1974. *11*, 105–119.

Stebbins. R. A. *Teachers and meaning: Definition of classroom situations*, Leiden: E. J. Brill, 1975.

Stebbins, R. A. Attribution, labelling, and definition of the situation. *SASP Newsletter*, 1979, *5*, 7–9.

Stebbins, R. A., and Flynn, C. Police definitions of the situation. *Canadian Journal of Criminology and Corrections*, 1975, *17*, 334–353.

Thomas, W. I. The configurations of personality. In C. M. Child et al., *The unconscious: A symposium.* New York: Alfred A. Knopf, 1928.

Thomas, W. I., Park, R. E., & Miller, H. A. *Old world traits transplanted.* New York: Harper & Bros., 1921.

Thomas, W. I., & Thomas, D. S. *The child in America.* New York: Alfred A. Knopf, 1928.

Thomas, W. I., & Znaniecki, F. *The Polish peasant in Europe and America*, 5 vols. Boston: Richard G. Badger, 1918–1920.

Waller, W. *The sociology of teaching.* New York: John Wiley, 1932.

Weigert, A. J. Alfred Schutz on a theory of motivation. *Pacific Sociological Review*, 1975, *18*, 83–102.

Wootton, A. *Dilemmas of discourse.* London: George Allen & Unwin, 1975.

Znaniecki, F. *Cultural sciences.* Urbana, Ill.: University of Illinois Press, 1952.

6. *Understanding Episodes*

ROM HARRÉ
University of Oxford

THEORY

Analytic Models

This essay uses the notions of model and analogy since I prefer to emphasize the neglected iconic aspects of conceptual thinking. However, everything that I have to say could be put in terms of conceptual systems and semantic relations.

To deal with the problematic character of the world as it is presented to us, it is necessary to approach that world with some analytical tools in mind. The world as it is presented is complex and differentiable in many ways.

Physical scientists were the first to learn that the world they were investigating did not present itself to them as facts. To identify patterns from which laws of nature might be formulated, the seamless web of reality had to be analyzed, emphasizing some aspects and ignoring others. This happened in different ways. Sometimes the emphasis on certain aspects of physical reality has come from an underlying metaphysical theory more or less directly. For instance, the shift from qualitative to quantitative chemistry was a direct consequence of the development of a metaphysics for chemistry in terms of atomic clusters and individual atomic elements. Sometimes the metaphysical issues and assumptions are only indirectly related to the chosen methods of analysis.

A striking example of the use of an independent analytical model is Boyle's investigation of the properties of gases. Boyle wanted to demonstrate the falsehood of the theological proposition that nature as animated by God abhorred a vacuum. He had to establish that air could fill a vacuum naturally by its material properties. This led him to choose a particular analytical model for investigating air—air as a spring. This model led him to trap a quantity of air in a tube to see how it behaved under differing pressures. He literally made an air spring.

To treat human actions as intentional is an example of the role of metaphysics in science; to treat them as orderly and ritualistic is an example of the effect of adopting an analytical model. To do episode analysis properly, our analytical models should be explicitly acknowledged. In much of the old-style—particularly, American—work, analytical models were being used but were not examined. In most cases we can see that these models were local common-sense understandings of the social world and thus were very ethnocentric. Only by making the analytical models explicit is it possible to identify their historically located properties, such as, for example, their connection with a taken-for-granted political position. Ethogenic analysis uses a cluster of hierarchically organized analytical models having the following form: the most general is that of dramatic performance. This form enables us to make such analytical distinctions as that among scene, actor, and action. These distinctions can be further refined. For example, in refining the notion of action, models can be introduced ad lib for a specific analytical purpose. Two models have proved particularly powerful—the problem-solving model and the liturgical model. Many others also exist, each with its advantages and each of which must be carefully circumscribed by an explicit exploration of its limitations.

An analogy has positive, negative, and natural aspects. The concepts derived on the basis of it are similitudes and metaphors. In practice, the distinction between simile and metaphor is important. Only metaphor expands our vocabulary through conceptual novelty (Boyd 1979). By using analytical models, nonrandom patterns in the complex web of social reality can be identified and a terminology developed to describe them. This terminology is related to the method by which the models have been disentangled and to the exact status of the analytical models deployed.

Explanatory Models

Nothing follows from successfully using an analytical model to explain the social patterns in question. A dramaturgical model, however successful, does not predetermine whether we are looking at a pattern whose origin is genetic, or in the acquisition of early habits, or in social conventions, or in explicit rule-following by conscious agents. Analyzing and explaining action are logically independent activities. The concepts used in the one do not predetermine those that must be used with others. However, in formulating explanatory theories, the use of models and analogies is of equal importance to their use in analysis.

The reason for the appearance of models and analogies in the explanatory phase of theory construction is obvious. It derives from the fact that the processes responsible for the production of action and the active agents that are the source of observable activity generally cannot be examined by the same empirical methods and models as used in the analysis phase of a scientific program. The initial step in theory-construction is to imagine a possible productive process that is (1) within the bounds of plausibility, and (2) capable of producing a close analogue of the patterned events revealed by using analytical models. An explanatory theory, then, must refer to a hypothetical process of production functionally analogous to the real but unknown process in that its behavior stimulates the problematic patterns of experience it was introduced to explain. So, for example, if we think of the basic form of social action as the conduct of conscious actors following explicit rules and use that as the source of our explanatory models, we then will give an account of the production of patterns of actions in terms of some form of rule-following. But this is an analogy relationship.

In exploring the positive, negative, and neutral aspects of the analogy, we may eliminate the notion of consciousness when we formulate the explanatory theory. The notion of rule, too, will be transformed in shifting the application from the source model, where it has a literal application, to the explanatory theory, where it may be metaphor. In general, ethogenic methodology has been directed toward developing and testing analytical models rather than explanatory theories. The action-theory for which von Cranach and others are responsible seems a coordinate kind of approach using an explanatory model much like the analytical models the ethogenic method has so far developed. (See von Cranach and Harré 1982.)

Theories of Competence (of Resources of Knowledge and Belief) and Theories of Performance (of the Production of Action)

The most general form of a nonbehaviorist psychology requires that the various human actions be construed as founded on culturally distinct systems of belief. The processes by which people come to do these things are modes of reasoning rather than operations of causal mechanisms. They fall under such criteria as are provided by the rules of logic revealed in conceptual analysis of relevant talk. Ethogenic methodology using both analytical models and the analysis of accounts is concerned wholly with theories of competence; that is, with resources for social action embodied in a corpus of knowledge and belief. Account analysis is not a methodology for developing theories of performance.

A competence theory can take many different forms. One must distinguish between competence theories that are taxonomies of belief and theories that take a generative form. The latter purport to be able to derive most of a particular form's content of social competence from a few general principles, in some axiomatic or quasiaxiomatic (generative) way.

In the early days of ethogenic analysis, Clarke and Harré were convinced that the success, as it then seemed, of generative grammar in the hands of the M.I.T. school was an encouragement to suppose that a similar sort of treatment could be developed for social rules. However, the more empirical work that has been done, the clearer it is that no such generative system is possible.

This conclusion suggests that the mode of organizing social knowledge and the methods by which it is brought into relation to action are not like those the generative theory of grammar implies for organizing and using linguistic knowledge. In short, a theory of competence reflects that skill in social action is learned by most people through picking up independent and distinctive systems and conventions, each of which is adjusted to a particular range of situations and persons. The problem for the theorist is to choose the most satisfactory method of classification so the particular items so classified are readily recoverable.

The Location of Resources

Today's philosophers are concerned with the problem of the ultimate viability of the traditional Cartesian metaphysics that assimilates the distinction between inner and outer with that between the subjective and the objective. Since the second phase of Wittgenstein's philosophy became well known, philosophers have increasingly tended to abandon any attempt to decide the issue of whether the mental is inner-subjective or outer-subjective—the issue between mentalism and behaviorism. The distinction on which the debate concerning other minds has been grounded is itself an error. Abandoning the distinction, however, leaves unanswered the question of how to locate the mental.

A beginning could be made by using a two-dimensional space for locating psychological processes, attributes, and states. One dimension could represent whether the psychological attribute or process is found in individuals or in collectives. The other dimension could represent display—whether a psychological attribute, such as rationality, is a feature of public or private discourse. Treating these axes as orthogonal provides a two-dimensional space in which to locate various allegedly psychological entities (see Figure 6–1).

This essay is interested in the location of such alleged psychological entities as beliefs and rules for interpreting the behavior of other people. It seems that if we distinguish between items of knowledge and belief and corpora of knowledge and belief, we can locate items in individuals and corpora in collectives. Thus, for example, the totality of knowledge required to perform some category of social activity, such as prosecuting a war or conducting a symphony, is not located in any one individual, though each individual in the collective has a fragment of the whole. Individually located knowledge can be publicly displayed, such as when the only witness to an accident gives evidence in court. But knowledge publicly displayed on maps in subways is no one's (or

PSYCHOLOGICAL SPACE

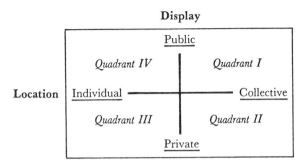

Figure 6–1. Psychological Space

everyone's) knowledge. Using a two-dimensional plane helps locate a number of troubling psychological attributes, states, phenomena, and processes that the attempt to think within the Cartesian distinction fails to deal with adequately.

Powerful arguments suggest that emotions are as much generated by social public processes and embody social structural relations as they are created by individual and private feelings (Silver and Sabini 1978). It also seems reasonable to pursue the idea that much cognitive processing is social/public rather than individual/private. In particular, the requirements summed up in the demand that discourse be rational are essentially public and socially maintained ways of presenting oneself as a social being of worth. In a recent exchange in the *Psychological Review*, Tajfel, protesting the attempt to reduce social psychology to individual psychology, missed this important mark, since he seemed to think that cognitive processing and reasoning are essentially individual and probably private.

Four Kinds of Episodes

Using the four-quadrant space defined by the two orthogonal axes of location and display as a system of classification yields four main kinds of episodes. In Quadrant I are episodes in which both the knowledge and the cognitive processes for applying it are public-collective. In Quadrant III are episodes in which an individual draws in an idiosyncratic way on ideas of action known only to himself or herself. The common room of a mental hospital for seriously disturbed patients could exemplify Quadrant III. Quadrant II defines a type of episode in which the private actions of an individual are fully under the influence of collective rules and interpretations, perhaps through a breviary (saying mass when alone, for example).

Among the most interesting episodes are those defined in Quadrant IV. A group of people is confronted with one or more of its members acting according to social beliefs they do not share. By coming to share these beliefs, new social rules and conventions are engendered. By classifying the actions of the maverick as insane, the collective refuses to change its social belief system.

The case cited by Brenner (1982) is classified as an episode of Quadrant IV type. In the case, the maverick response to the question "What are you studying?" in the public-collective context of a modern university is, "I'm studying alchemy." This kind of response suggests some personal cognitive scheme, but the public-collective context does not provide for it to have sense.

Unfolding episodes of types defined for Quadrants I and II is predetermined by the collective (who have relatively stable belief systems); but there can be no certainty how episodes typical of quadrants III and IV will develop. Bizarre private beliefs can develop into anything from poetry to paranoia, even though these classifications are public and collective and presuppose an action in an event of type Quadrant IV.

METHOD

This section on ethogenic method emphasizes certain features not fully appreciated by some commentators on ethogenic psychology, particularly the use of accounts.

Model-Controlled Ethnography

As mentioned in the theoretical section, the facts of social life do not speak for themselves. The social world, as we experience it, is a complicated entity, and its processes pass with a swiftness that only the socially competent who have reduced much of their action to habit are likely to find comfortable. Under these circumstances, general philosophy of science tells us that analytical models are indispensable for revealing the structures, or rather some of the structures, of ordered pattern in the worlds of our experience. The difference between the ethogenic and an anthropological use of an analytical model lies only in the explicit formulation of the analytical model in the ethogenic method. Anthropologists bring analytical models to their ethnographic studies, too. But anthropological method does not (and certainly has not) required their explicit formulation.

A striking difference between the effect of using different analytical models is exemplified in the cultural patterns identified among the Trobrianders by Malinowski (1922) relative to a typical male view of a society and those identified by Weiner (1976) deploying a female view of society. Weiner had Malinowski's perceptions at hand, so her picture of Trobriand society is much richer and more satisfactory than his. We can understand the differences between their ethnographies in terms of the analytical models they used on the society and its social practices. Similar examples of the availability of patterns relative to the taken-for-granted cognitive sets or analytical models of ethnographers have appeared in recent Japanese ethology, where complex behavior patterns among female monkeys were visible only to women ethologists.

Faced with some piece of data such as a transcript or a video recording, the ethogenically oriented social psychologist tries out a variety of analytical models, seeking one producing the most order in the material. By using the basic dramaturgical model, scenes and settings can be identified. Further use of this model helps distinguish a group of people who are like an audience from those who are the active participants. How normative control is exercised must be seen as an analogue of direction, while attention to the unfolding action is like a drama director's attention to role-positions, costume, and the plot.

Proceeding with an imposed conceptual system, the next level in the hierarchy of analytical models would identify events in terms of an agonistic or game model in which the participants' actions appear as competitive engagement according to rule. The results of a model-controlled ethnographic investigation stand as hypotheses as to the structure, meanings, and forms of order present in the events. The first test of such hypotheses is to contrast them with the folk understandings of the events in question. At this stage of the investigation, no a priori priority can be given to one or the other.

Account Analysis

Those of us who spend time with people in their natural settings are struck by the enormous amount of talking they do. The first step in dealing with social talk analytically is to separate phatic speech from other forms of talk. Phatic speech seems to function to maintain social order without advancing social action. For instance, to read "You must come up and see me sometime" as phatic talk excludes the rejoinder "When?" The function of phatic talk is to maintain civility and sociability without commitment to further specific interactions. Social action is provided for, but not required by, such talk. The preliminary elimination of phatic elements leaves us with substantial talk.

Substantial talk functions in social life in a wide variety of ways. This section focuses on only three. Substantial social talk is first seen as rhetorical, as involved in generating a particular interpretation of the social activity as substantiating an impression of the characters of those who engage in it. Recent students of scientific talk have noticed the rhetorical role of logical concepts in that talk, since logic seems to play little role in the genesis of scientific discourse. They are there, as some scientists are willing to acknowledge, as part of the apparatus of self-presentation, just as tough talk helps children appear as football hooligans. At most, logic forms argumentative bases, providing for a rejoinder to a possible form of criticism (Knorr-Cetina 1982).

That being acknowledged, some preliminary hypotheses such as those just offered on the role of logical concepts in discourse can be used to peel off the purely rhetorical aspects of talk. We are left with two further uses of accounts. We must distinguish accounts forming part of the action itself, in particular those involved in disambiguating problematic events in social life. Marsh et al. (1978) noticed that football fans used their accounts to reinterpret the ritualistic display of aggression as real violence. Accounts are also used to introduce normative material into the discourse to warrant or sanction actions in the form in which they have been disambiguated. In short, accounts displays both rules and conventions of interpretation of action and the forms of ideal action.

We now have two sets of hypotheses—the first derived from the model-controlled ethnography, and the second derived from the three-phase analysis of accounts. What are these hypotheses about? The theoretical section argued that account analysis should not be mistakenly thought of as a kind of performance methodology. For methods of studying performance, we must look to the action theory of von Cranach and others.

Account analysis and model-controlled ethnography aim at identifying systems of knowledge and belief. The hypotheses arising from the joint use of ethnographic and account analysis are attempts at representing the knowledge and belief required to perform the actions necessary for a certain type of episode in that society. What sort of knowledge and belief? In my view, we have hypotheses as to the social, that is, public-collective, systems of knowledge and belief. In short, accounts present us with the rules of ideal action. The next step is to ask why that action in that milieu, under those rules, was ideal.

A fourth phase of account analysis seems called for; that is, we now need to ask whether another level of understanding is in accounts, some grasp of the social force of the action. Are there folk-sociological theories? At first, it seems implausible to expect such a level of knowledge displayed in accounts.

However, recent work suggested that such knowledge is routinely displayed if the slightest encouragement is given to express it. Kreckel's (1981) seminal work showed how easy it is to acquire extremely detailed, highly sophisticated analysis of action at this level provided the right social relations have been achieved with the participants. From the theoretical point of view, the level we are now talking of is the level of social act; that is, what moves in what social world achieve what?

Harré's work on violence (Marsh et al. 1978) showed that a high level of understanding is available and is frequently routinely deployed by the actors themselves. Nisbett's attempts to denigrate self-knowledge are based on bad methodology (Nisbett & Wilson 1977).

An interesting research matter would be to follow up the kind of studies that Moscovici (1952) did on *représentations sociales* to see how folk-social theorizing embodies ethological, Marxist, and Freudian theories that were, at some earlier period, the province of professional psychologists and sociologists.

Coding the Representation

The result of these analyses consists of two sets of hypotheses that should be able to be shown as isomorphic representations of a common belief-system and, in principle, mutually translatable one into the other. If matching by translation can be achieved, then anthropological explanation and the folk understanding depend on only one system of belief. Where the isomorphism is good, functional analyses purporting to displace folk-accounts can be excluded by Ockham's Razor. This essay considers only such cases. The problem of dealing with a disparity between folk resources and ethnographers' reconstructions requires a separate work.

Presuming, then, that as in the more successful recent uses of ethogenic methods, the coordination or mutual translation of the two texts can be achieved, what is the status of the object so produced? To answer that, we must solve a problem about the translation rules coordinating the texts.

By what right do we assert a synonymy between two terms, one of which derives from the outsider's ethnography, however amateur, and the other from the insider's system of interpretation serving as the semantic rules for vocabulary for the social presentation of accounts? Here we have the familiar scientific technique of boot-strapping. By presuming the propriety of intuitively supported translations, we can test the degree of fit by other means. The answer to that question must be given in terms of the testing methodology, which will be introduced in the next section. It will become clear that by using the analysis-synthesis methodology we can achieve scientific advances impossible on the hypothesis-prediction scheme, in that only the former will resolve the problem of how to test hypotheses of synonymy.

A further point must be made about the status of the work thus far described. The upshot of an ethnographic ethogenic investigation is an array of statements (sentences) that are a verbal representation of a system of belief for use in some public activity. It should not be inferred from the necessity of such a form of representation, for the purposes of public action and public communication, that in *rerum natura*, so to speak, knowledge and belief exist as sentences, whether encoded in the mind of the one or the many. An ordered array of such sentences is still a sentential object and is only one among many possible social resources needed for disambiguating and warranting the actions of real life.

The coding procedure runs as follows. The socially distinguishable situation (scene and setting, together with their social meanings and the persons appropriate to them) is the leading taxonomic concept to be classified relative to scenes, settings, and situations. The rules of action-interpretation and of ideal action response are the means by which action is disambiguated and warranted in each specific social milieu. Ethogenics and action-theory can be backed by the hypothesis that when a performance is studied by some action-theoretic methods of von Cranach et al., it will turn out that the means-ends structures, the basic elements in their performance-theory, consist of items from the coded results of the ethogenic investigation of systems of social knowledge and belief. This hypothesis binds together the analytical and explanatory models in ethogenic theory. It is an empirical hypothesis and may be false.

The Connection to the Work of Schutz and Luckmann

Schutz and Luckmann (1973) argued for the general thesis that a corpus of knowledge is differentiated because of the social structure of the collective where it is located. In a truly social social-psychology, this principle must be drawn in. Classifying items of knowledge and belief around the distinctive social situations for which they are relevant should lead to a set of clusters of cognitive items. These items could be arranged in a matrix, with the representation of each distinctive situation-type serving as the leading element of each row. The detailed structure of the matrix of social competence might be expected to differ from person to person even within a fairly tightly knit social group. Further, if social knowledge is a corpus of knowledge like any other, then Schutz and Luckmann's thesis suggests that an ethogenic analysis of the cognitive processes involved in an episode, whether unique or one of a kind, should be supplemented.

One might try to find out how the collective theorizes about itself, what are its exemplary tales, its symbolic ritual practices, and so on. Hypotheses about its microsocial structure should emerge from these studies. The final step in episode analysis could be represented by the following equation:

Individual matrices of social knowledge × social structure of the collective = ideal matrix of social knowledge for that collective.

Testing of Hypotheses

In the natural sciences, hypotheses are tested by two major methods. Philosophers have recently concentrated on the hypothesis-prediction scheme codified in the deductive nomological theory of scientific explanations preferred by the logical empiricists. According to the theory, a hypothesis is tested by using it to make predictions with the help of specified initial conditions and then experimenting to see if the prediction is verified or falsified. The methodology of that way of proceeding is well known through the work of Popper, whose conjectures and refutations methodology can be seen as a critical development of logical positivism. However, it is not the only way hypotheses are tested.

An alternative testing methodology common in chemistry now, thanks to computer simulation, appears in other branches of science. This methodology seems particularly appropriate in cases where an important aspect of the entities studied is their structure. In many cases, the parts of a natural being preserve their identity only when connected into a structure. In chemistry, a structured science, one way to test the analysis of an organic compound is by attempting to synthesize the substance previously analyzed, or some close analogue of it, by chemical means. If a synthesis can be successfully achieved, then the analysis is so far verified.

Linguists have used a similar method. One way to test the adequacy of a grammatical theory is to use that grammar to try to generate all and only the grammatically acceptable sentences of language. Of course, fragments of the hypothesis-prediction test schema are involved in analysis-synthesis tests, but the latter cannot be reduced to the former. An analysis/synthesis test for the satisfactoriness of a set of hypotheses represented in the cognitive matrices referred to in the last section would be to use those hypotheses as explicit rules of action and fully formulated rules of interpretation to reconstruct fragments of social life in the appropriate situations. Remember, one is here testing only an analogue of the real process used by real actors to generate action. The implications of conscious attention in the phrase *explicit rules of action* should be eliminated and the notion of rule taken metaphorically. Just as grammarians depend on native speakers' intuitions of testing the products of their reconstructions, so an ethogenic psychologist might draw on the intuitions of native actors as to the propriety of the action created by a cast of players explicitly following the rules. This kind of simulation can take a variety of forms. Ginsburg (1979) discussed ways in which dramatic reconstruction and role-playing can test various aspects of hypotheses about the form and content of social knowledge that competent actors require.

The test for the depth of an analysis of an episode is the plausibility of the synthesis of an episode of the same social category.

REFERENCES

Boyd, R. Metaphor and theory change. In A. Orthony (Ed.), *Metaphor and thought.* Cambridge: Cambridge University Press, 1979.

Brenner, M. Actor's powers. In M. von Cranach and R. Harré (Eds.), *The analysis of action.* Cambridge: Cambridge University Press, 1982.

Ginsburg, G. *Emerging strategies in social psychological research.* Chichester: Wiley, 1979.

Knorr-Cetina, K. *The manufacture of knowledge.* Oxford: Pergamon Press, 1981.

Kreckel, M. *Communicative acts and shared knowledge in natural discourse.* London: Academic Press, 1981.

Malinowski, B. *Argonauts of the Western Pacific.* London: Routledge, 1922.

Marsh, P., Rosser, E., & Harré, R. *The rules of disorder.* London: Routledge & Kegan, Paul, 1978.

Moscovici, S. *La psychoanalyse, son image et sa publique.* Paris: Presse Universitaire de France, 1952.

Nisbett, R., & Wilson, T. Telling more than we can know: Verbal reports on mental processes. *Psychological Review,* 1977, *84,* 231–259.

Schutz, A., & Luckmann, T. *The structures of the life world.* London: Heinemann, 1973.

Silver, M., & Sabini, J. The social construction of envy. *Journal for the Theory of Social Behaviour,* 1978, *8,* 313–332.

von Cranach, M., & Harré, R. *The analysis of action.* Cambridge: Cambridge University Press, 1982.

Weiner, A. *Women of virtue, men of renown.* Austin: University of Texas Press, 1976.

III

Applications: Clinical, Community, Environmental, and Linguistic Psychology

7. *Social Fit and Misfit: An Interactional Account of Social Difficulty*

PETER TROWER
University of Leicester

INTRODUCTION

The relationship between social difficulty and psychiatric disorder is well documented in the psychological and psychiatric literature, much of which has recently focused on social skill deficiency (Hersen 1979). Despite a number of advances, considerable dissatisfaction with assessment has been expressed (Bellack 1979) and there is a need for advances in this area.

One problem of some current assessment methods is they follow the traditional diagnostic approach of focusing on the individual or diagnostic group and looking for personality types or psychiatric disorder types. For example, many questionnaires purport to measure social anxiety, assertiveness, and so on, and new personality factors such as shyness have been identified (Crozier 1979). Many of the main clinical groups, such as schizophrenics and depressives, have had their social skill profiles drawn.

The main objection here is to an undue emphasis on the person, alias patient, since personal variables, no matter how well based on behavioral sampling or rigorous psychometrics, account for only part of the variance. Misattribution of all the variance to the person can only lead to a distorted assessment and faulty treatment objectives.

Recent developments in social and clinical psychology based on the interactionist model (Endler and Magnusson 1975) insist that adequate assessment must consider three sources of variance: person variables, situation variables, and the interaction of the two. This approach has certain problems, such as mechanistic implications, but it provides a more comprehensive model within which to conceptualize clinical assessment. For example, certain patients such as social phobics may exhibit stable and characteristic patterns of avoidance behavior and anxiety symptoms across time and situations; it is equally to be expected that certain situations characteristically elicit avoidance behavior patterns and anxiety, such as appearing before an audience, from phobics and also from most people.

The focus of assessment, therefore, should be on problem situations as well as on problem persons. The prediction would be that problem situations would have the greatest scope for social failure, whereas problem persons would have the greatest tendency to fail. Putting the two together would produce an almost inevitable result. Some people may lack skills; equally, some situations require highly complex skills and are difficult for most people. Again, the combination results in a much higher probability of failure than when the reverse is true—a competent person in a nondemanding situation. Interaction effects clearly can range widely between these extremes.

One way to conceptualize these interactions is in terms of fit. Effective P x S interaction occurs when there is positive fit between P and S, such that there is congruence between the two in terms of skills required, rules followed, and so on. The person's ability to bring about positive fit—either by adapting his or her behavior or by modifying the situation—is the measure of social competence. Ineffective P X S interaction occurs where there is a failure to fit between P and S such that the congruence among skills, rules, goals, and so on is lacking.

This chapter first presents some findings on the patterns of social difficulty attributable to persons on the one hand and situations on the other. It then offers a speculative theory of P x S fit to help explain these other findings. The next section examines the social difficulty reported in thirty common situations by two patient samples (the Elms and Littlemore) and in two nonpatient groups (students and nurses). (Some of the data appear in previously published studies.)

SURVEYS OF SOCIAL DIFFICULTY

The Patient Samples

In the Elms survey, ninety-two consecutively referred or re-referred patients to the Elms Clinic, Banbury (England), with diagnoses of neuroses or personality disorder were given a battery of tests, were interviewed, and participated in a social interaction test. Most of the thirty-five women in the sample were diagnosed as reactive depression; the fifty-seven men were almost equally divided among depression, anxiety states, and personality disorders. The survey, designed to investigate the nature and extent of social inadequacy, found twenty-seven percent of the patients to be inadequate on behavioral, social, and personality criteria. The results are reported in Bryant, Trower, Yardley, Urbieta, and Letemendia (1976).

This chapter reports results for one measure, the Social Situations Questionnaire (Trower, Bryant, and Argyle 1978), which asks for the amount of social difficulty (anxiety or discomfort experienced) in thirty common social situations and tasks. Social difficulty is expressed as a score ranging from 0 (no difficulty) through 1 (slight), 2 (moderate), 3 (great), and 4 (avoidance, if possible). The situations range from walking down the street to such focused interactions as getting to know someone. The questionnaire was found to have validity in significantly discriminating the patients independently judged as normally skilled from those judged as unskilled (mean score = 25.82, 52.57 respectively; t = 3.16; $d.f.$ = 38; $p < 0.01$). The questionnaire was also found to have split half reliability in terms of Cronbach's Alpha coefficient (Alpha = .82).

In the Littlemore sample (Oxford, England), the thirty-eight patients were referred for inclusion in an outcome study comparing two types of behavioral treatment—social skills training and systematic desensitization—across two types of social problem—social phobia and social skill deficiency (Trower, Yardley, Bryant, and Shaw 1978). In other words, the patients fell into two equal-sized groups—socially phobic and socially unskilled. All patients completed the Social Situations Questionnaire. This sample served to some extent to replicate the Elms sample, though its composition differed in that the patients were a group selected specifically for having social problems, compared to the Elms patients, who were a random sample.

The Nonpatient Samples

In the student survey, a random sample of 228 Oxford University undergraduates completed the Social Situations Questionnaire (Bryant and Trower 1974). This was a postal survey, and no other measures were taken.

The nurse sample was a random sample of thirty-eight female, white, South African nurses working in a hospital in Natal (Furnham 1983). This sample, although not ideal for present purposes, is chosen in the absence of any other comparable nonpsychiatric group with whom we may draw comparisons with the student and patient samples. (Furnham's [1983] study compared three cultural groups—the European group discussed here, plus an African group and an Indian group. We shall not consider these two groups but will confine the discussion to social difficulty in one cultural group.) The nurses also completed an extended version of the Social Situations Questionnaire. Only twenty-nine of the original situations are used; the item "going into pubs" was dropped because women in South Africa are not legally allowed into pubs or bars.

Results

Problem persons. Looking first at the nonpatient samples, we find that within a possible range of scores 0–4, the average situation score for the students is .59 (*sd* .32) (i.e., well below slight difficulty); that of the South African nurses is .68 (*sd* .41), a difference just significant statistically (*t* = 2.059; *d.f.* 28, *p* < .05). Two situations particularly distinguished the two groups: the students ranked going to dances and discos in the top one or two (women one, men two), with a mean of 1.27 (see Table 7-1), but the nurses placed this item twelfth, with a mean of .75. Conversely, the nurses placed meeting strangers third most difficult ($\bar{x}$ = 1.27), compared with the students at thirteenth position ($\bar{x}$ = .68).

The average situation score for the Elms patients is 1.35 (*sd* 1.36) (between slight and moderate difficulty), a score significantly higher than the students' (*t* = 20.71, *d.f.* 29, *p* < .0001) and the nurses' (*t* = 15.54, *d.f.* 28, *p* < .0001). In terms of spread of difficulty across situations, some patients found all twenty-nine situations moderately difficult or worse whereas students found three-quarters of the situations moderately difficult or worse.

For the two subgroups of skilled and unskilled patients, the unskilled sample had a significantly higher mean score (1.94, *sd* 1.06—or just under moderate difficulty) than the skilled group (.94, *sd* .85) at just under slight difficulty (*t* = 9.8; *d.f.* 29; *p* < .0001). Twenty-two percent of the unskilled patients had average scores above 3 (great difficulty), but only 3 percent of the skilled group did so. The worst situation for both groups was "taking the initiative in conversation." Unskilled patients reported great difficulty in this situation ($\bar{x}$ = 3.0) compared with the skilled patients' middle to moderate ($\bar{x}$ = 1.66). This difference was verified in a behavior test—a ten-minute conversation with a stranger—in which the unskilled patients emitted significantly less conversation and less nonverbal behavior than did the skilled group (Bryant et al. 1976).

The skilled and unskilled patients gave the same top rank order to taking the initiative in conversation, but they differed markedly in their rankings of other situations (see Table 7-1). The situations most differentiating the two groups were going out with someone of the opposite sex, which the unskilled group ranked third ($\bar{x}$ = 1.5), and the skilled ranked sixteenth ($\bar{x}$ = .93); and going to pubs, which the skilled group found third most difficult situation ($\bar{x}$ = 1.5), and the unskilled second easiest (ranked twenty-ninth, $\bar{x}$ = .91). Finally, the unskilled group ranked approaching others as second most difficult ($\bar{x}$ = 2.83), whereas the skilled group ranked this sixth ($\bar{x}$ = 1.26). Since the unskilled group had a preponderance of single men and the skilled group of women, gender role expectations may account for some of these differences.

Do these results suggest that averagely skilled psychiatric patients cope well with social situations? Comparison with the nonpatient groups does not support an affirmative answer, since the difference in mean scores was highly significant (*t* = 9.39; *d.f.* 29; *p* < .001). The

TABLE 7–1

Mean Scores of Difficulty and Assigned Rank Order Positions
for Two Patient Groups and Two Nonpatient Groups

Mean Rank No.	Situation	Mean Score	Little-more Patients	Elms Patients	Students	Nurses
1.	Approaching others	1.76	1.	1.5	2	3.5
2.	Room full of people	1.6	4.5	1.5	6.5	1
3.	Taking initiative in conversation	1.59	3	3	4	5.5
4.	Going to dances	1.5	6	4	1	12
5.	People you don't know well	1.48	11.5	9.5	3	2
6.	Meeting strangers	1.47	7	5	13	3.5
7.	Going to parties	1.43	2	7	5	10
8.	Talking about self	1.4	9	12	10	5.5
9.	People looking at you	1.36	15.5	6	11	7
10.	Being with group of opposite sex	1.32	4.5	9.5	8	16
11.	Getting to know in depth	1.31	8	8	12	10
12.	Going out with opposite sex	1.2	11.5	15	9	14
13.	Making decisions	1.18	20	13	6.5	8
14.	Going into pubs	1.11	21	16	22	–
15.	Making friends	1.09	14	14	15	17
16.	Disagreeing with others	1.08	10	20	19.5	15
17.	Entertaining people at home	1.07	15.5	11	19.5	19
18.	Looking at people in eyes	1.04	17	17	14	19
19.	Being with group of same sex	0.98	13	19	22	19
20.	Being with younger people	0.97	23	21.5	17	13
21.	People close to you	0.92	24	24	16	10
22.	Mixing at work	0.9	22	18	18	21
23.	Being with mixed group	0.89	18.9	21.5	22	23.5

TABLE 7-1 *(cont.)*

Mean Rank No.	Situation	Mean Score	Little-more Patients	Elms Patients	Students	Nurses
24.	Going into restaurants	0.83	18.5	23	26	26
25.	Being with older people	0.63	2.55	28	24	22
26.	Going on public transport	0.59	27	25	29	23.5
27.	Being with only one other	0.55	25.5	29	25	25
28.	Going into shops	0.48	29	27	27	27
29.5.	Walking down the street	0.41	30	26	30	28
29.5.	Being with friends	0.41	28	30	28	29

skilled patients scored worst on most situations, but the only situation with a markedly different ranking was being with people you don't know well, ranked third and second by students and nurses, but only ninth by the skilled patients.

So far, then, general differences exist between groups in intensity of difficulty, but there do not seem to be many strong differences in the pattern of difficulties across situations. However, the domain of patients with high social difficulties is not as homogeneous as the Elms data so far presented might imply. Social difficulty can be due to high anxiety (of other symptoms) or social deficiency or both. Elsewhere (Argyle, Bryant, and Trower 1974; Trower et al. 1978), we have advanced and tested the notion of two types of social failure with different etiologies—primary failure due to inadequate social skills, and secondary failure due to some other cause, such as disruptive anxiety.

In the Littlemore sample, two groups represent these types—socially unskilled patients (primary failure) and socially phobic (secondary failure). We might expect these two groups to be similar in experiencing high levels of social difficulty (both being referred for social problems) but showing a different pattern of difficulty across situations. For example, the unskilled group would have more difficulty in tasks requiring high social exposure.

First, the Littlemore sample as a whole showed a general mean somewhat worse than the Elms sample as a whole ($\bar{x}$ = 1.71, 1.36 respectively; t = 6.9; $d.f.$ 29; $p < .02$) but similar to the Elms unskilled group. When subdivided into social unskilled and socially phobic, the difference between the subsamples was also significant ($\bar{x}$ = 1.85), 1.56 respectively; t = 2.7; *d.f.* 29; $p < .02$), but the correlations were relatively close and both relatively high, as expected. However, the correlation between the Littlemore subsamples was fairly low (r = .55), suggesting a different pattern of difficulties.

Indeed, although similar in general difficulty, these two groups were strikingly different in their responses to different situations. These differences are reported in Table 7-2. Table 7-2 shows the unskilled group experiencing significantly greater difficulty in seven situations and tasks, the greatest rank order difference being getting to know someone in depth and approaching others. Other difficulties are also situations involving acquaintanceship. Only one situation discriminates in the other direction—the skilled phobics rank "going into restaurants and cafés" as the worse situation, the unskilled as one of the least difficult.

Given these differences, principal components analyses were carried out in the expectation that the components for the two groups would differ in structure. The results of these analyses appear in Table 7-3. For the phobic group, the first component accounted for 31 percent of the variance and identified on its positive pole situations that speculatively might be said to characterize public exposure situations, particularly carrying out some activity (e.g., eating) in front of strangers. At its negative pole, it picks socially safe and undemanding situations. For the unskilled group, the first component loads at the positive end on acquaintanceship tasks, which can be said to demand social skills; the situations on the negative pole are also socially safe and undemanding.

Problem situations. If difficulties are attributable to characteristics of individuals or groups, then we should find differences between these individuals and groups consistently across situations. These kinds of data have been examined above. If difficulties are attributable to inherent properties of situations, then we should find differences between situations operating across persons. The question some researchers pose, then, is which situations, if any, are inherently difficult for everyone?

We first computed the correlations in reported difficulty between the groups in thirty situations. The students and nurses correlated highly (r = .82), suggesting common experiences between them. The patients in the Elms and Littlemore samples also correlated well (r = .86). However, the correlations between nonpatients and patients were also surprisingly high. (Littlemore students, r = .85; Elms students, r = .84; Littlemore nurses, r = .73; Elms nurses, r = .82.) It is interesting to note that Furnham (1983) also found a highly significant relationship among his three racial groups using Kendall's coefficient of concordance (W = .44; p < .0001).

This pattern suggested strong commonalities across groups. The rank orders for groups and a mean rank were calculated and given with

TABLE 7–2
Mean Scores of Difficulty and Rank Order Position for
Socially Unskilled and Socially Phobic Patients.
Situations Ranked as for Table 1.

Mean Rank No.	Situations	Phobic Group $\bar{x}$ score	Rank	Unskilled Group $\bar{x}$ score	Rank
1.	Approaching others	1.94	7.5	3.22	1
2.	Room full of people	2.39	2.5	2.11	14
3.	Taking initiative in conversation	2.06	5	2.50	3.5
4.	Going to dances	2.17	4	2.28	8.5
5.	People you don't know well	1.78	11	2.22	10.5
6.	Meeting strangers	1.94	7.5	2.44	6
7.	Going to parties	2.39	2.5	2.22	10.5
8.	Talking about self	1.83	10	2.28	8.5
9.	People looking at you	1.67	13.5	1.94	13.5
10.	Being with group of opposite sex	2.00	6	2.50	3.5
11.	Getting to know in depth	1.44	18	2.83	2
12.	Going out with opposite sex	1.56	16	2.44	6
13.	Making decisions	1.17	24	2.17	12.5
14.	Going into pubs	1.67	13.5	1.44	22
15.	Making friends	1.22	22.5	2.44	6
16.	Disagreeing with others	1.89	9	2.17	12.5
17.	Entertaining people at home	1.67	13.5	1.94	13.5
18.	Looking at people in eyes	1.44	18	2.00	17
19.	Being with group of same sex	1.67	13.5	2.06	15.5
20.	Being with younger people	1.22	22.5	1.72	20
21.	People close to you	1.44	18	1.11	24
22.	Mixing at work	1.39	20	1.67	21
23.	Being with mixed group	1.33	21	2.06	15.5
24.	Going into restaurants	2.5	1	0.89	26
25.	Being with older people	1.06	25	1.06	25
26.	Going on public transport	1.00	26	0.78	27.5

27.	Being with only one other	0.94	27.5	1.17	23
28.	Going into shops	0.72	29	0.67	29
29.5	Walking down the street	0.5	30	0.50	30
29.5	Being with friends	0.94	27.5	0.78	27.5

their situation means in Table 7-1. Here can be seen a strong pattern at the top and bottom of the situation hierarchy. The top-ranked situations—approaching others, going into a roomful of people, taking the initiative in conversation, going to dances, meeting strangers, and so on—are mainly of the getting acquainted variety and also involve public exposure to relative strangers. Such a picture was also reported by Bryant et al. (1974) in a principal components analysis of the students' responses.

Before considering the factors responsible for high difficulty in persons and situations, we should deal with one apparent contradiction. On one hand, we appear to have differences between groups, in particular, between the socially unskilled and socially phobic groups; yet we now report striking similarities across groups and differences between situations. In fact, this contradiction is easily resolved within the person/situation interaction model, in that each model accounts for a proportion of the variance. The unskilled and phobic patients showed marked differences in reaction to eight situations, but there were no significant differences on any of the other twenty-two situations. The contradiction only crops up when adopting a personologist position or a situationist position, where the investigator is led to account for the variance in one direction.

SPECULATIONS ON A MODEL OF SOCIAL DIFFICULTY

Social difficulty has been described earlier as a function of problem persons, problem situations, and their interaction; some data have been presented to illustrate this difficulty. Some speculative dimensions will now be suggested to help explain these and other findings. For ease of argument, we begin with situation dimensions.

Situation Dimensions

What dimensions of situations can we identify as rendering them problematic? When we slice the total variance cake, as in analysis of variance, the size of the slice due to the situation will, of course, vary depending on the characteristics or structure of the situation. At one extreme are highly structured situations with comprehensive, manda-

TABLE 7–3
Summary of Results of Principal Components Analyses of
Social Difficulty Responses of Two Patient Groups
in 30 Situations

Socially Phobic Group Component 1 (31%)		Socially Unskilled Group Component 1 (43%)	
Situation	Loading	Situation	Loading
1. Going into cafes	4.65	1. Approaching others	6.14
2. Going to parties	4.40	2. Getting to know in depth	4.15
3. Room full of people	3.70	3. Group, opposite sex	2.87
4. Going to dances	3.61	4. Taking initiative	2.90
5. Meeting strangers	2.24	5. Going out, opposite sex	2.87
. . .		. . .	
26. Being with older people	-2.17	26. Going into cafes	-4.19
27. Being with friends	-2.53	27. Being with friends	-4.46
28. Being with one person	-2.82	28. Going into shops	-5.14
29. Going into shops	-3.26	29. Going on buses	-5.33
30. Walking down street	-4.48	30. Walking down street	-5.87
Component 2 (15%)		Component 2 (10%)	
1. People looking at you	3.40	1. Going to dances	2.74
2. Disagreeing	3.32	2. Going to parties	2.35
3. Talking about self	2.77	3. Going out, opposite sex	2.23
. . .		. . .	
28. Going on buses	-2.51	28. Room full of people	-2.31
29. Going into cafes	-2.56	29. People looking at you	-2.88
30. Going to parties	-2.27	30. Looking at people	-3.58

tory, and explicit rules and scripts that constrain most of the behavior within them. At the other extreme are situations with little structure, few rules, and little constraint. Examples are a wedding versus behavior in one's private apartment (Price and Bouffard 1974).

The level of structure can be beneficial or problematic, depending on the dimensional components described below. Highly structured situations will be beneficial if they help individuals know better what to do appropriately and acceptably and if they constrain antisocial behaviors, but they will be problematic if they are difficult to learn, teach antisocial rules, restrict the learning of informal skills, or coerce persons into institutional or submissive behavior. Low structured situations have advantages and disadvantages for opposite reasons, of course.

A few clinical studies have compared the constraining effect of situations or settings on persons. A good recent study by Strain and Ezzell (1978) measured the disruptive and inappropriate behavior of disturbed adolescents across three situations that they said varied on a continuum of structure and expected behavioral performance: a classroom instruction period; an afternoon rap, which was a review period; and Transactional Analysis. Results showed strong situation effects in that there was more D/I behavior in the least structured situation, and so on.

Let us now look in more detail at the dimensional components dictating the extent and nature of structure of situations:

1. Scripted vs. unscripted. Situations have rules, roles, pieces, and so on, and in this sense are analogous to games (Argyle 1976). These rules and roles are organized to facilitate the situation's purpose or goal and are designed to enable people to cooperate jointly to achieve social solutions. Highly structured situations also have what Schank and Abelson (1977) termed *scripts* to refer to standardized roles, props, and sequences of actions; an example is the restaurant script. Obviously, the more scripted the situation, the more it proscribes and prescribes (i.e., constrains) behavior within it. Argyle, Graham, Campbell, and White (1979) found that work situations and formal social situations (such as going to the doctor's, a tutorial, a sherry party, or a play) had more rules than other situations (such as shopping with a friend, chatting in a laundromat).

   Another way of distinguishing is to say that some rules (constitutive rules [Collett 1977]) define the situation and are not negotiable (such as weddings and other ceremonies), whereas other rules are negotiable within limits. Generally, scripts make interaction easier, since they inform the person what to do. However, scripted situations may be more difficult if the script is inaccessible, complex, and carries heavy sanctions if deviated from, or requires antisocial or negative behavior.

   Unscripted situations have advantages in that they have less potential for rule-breaking and can be better dealt with by means of face-saving devices, allow for more spontaneity, expression of personality, negotiation of goals, and so on. However, unscripted situations can be more difficult because of the lack of clear directives and greater potential for negative or ambiguous behavior of other persons.

2. Explicit vs. implicit rules. Scripts and the rules generating them vary in their accessibility. Explicit rules are easily available; marrying couples, for example, are coached in the procedures of the wedding, just as actors are coached before appearing on stage. Such formal situations are more likely to have explicit scripts. Implicit rules, on the other hand, are less sharply drawn and less obvious. There are less overt and more covert cues or markers (see Giles, Scherer, and Taylor [1979] for a review of one class of markers) to required behavior, perhaps in the form less of directions or signs than of linguistic and nonverbal implications and tacit suggestions. Several authors have pointed out that nonverbal communication is an implicit language of innuendo, its ambiguity serving an important social function. Labov and Fanshel (1977) write: "Speakers need a form of communication which is *deniable*. It is advantageous for them to express hostility, challenge the competence of others, or express friendliness and affection in a way that can be denied if they are explicitly held to account for it (46)."

Implicit rules and cues are obviously more difficult to detect and decode accurately (Shea and Rosenfeld 1976) and more likely to raise anxiety about (a) behaving in the wrong way, and (b) the possibility for negative messages being embedded in ambiguous cues.

3. Situations have hierarchies of rules, the more fundamental ones being more important and the consequences of breaking them more serious. This fact helps explain why some demands of the situation account for more variance in behavior than do others—important rules would constrain behavior more. We found this in a study of Littlemore Hospital, where it was more serious not to talk enough in a first encounter than, for example, not to smile long enough. Some elements were bound more by rules of the situation (talking, looking), others more by rules of the person (smiling, gesturing, posture shifting).

Not only do situations probably have hierarchical rule structures within them, but some situations also have intrinsically more important rules than others, just as some laws are more important than others. It may be easier to follow the script in formal situations, but it may be more serious to deviate from the script than in informal, more flexible situations where face-saving and other mitigating devices are more easily available.

4. High vs. low skill repertoires. Some situations are more difficult because they are more demanding of skill repertoires. Low
structured and unfamiliar situations can be like this because behavior options are open, predictability is low, and they therefore require participants to have a variety of skill strategies.
Even highly structured, explicitly cued situations can be difficult if they are complex because of the variety of rules and
roles (such as bargaining with one party vs several with different interests, or hosting a small group of same-sex peers vs a
large mixed group of different classes, races, sexes, and statuses).

5. Public vs. private goals. The structure of situations varies
depending on their goals. A distinction is commonly made
between task-oriented and social-oriented situations; this
chapter focuses on the latter. One distinction is between situations designed to encourage first-time encounters and those designed for people already well acquainted. The more public
situations helping bring strangers together include dances,
discos, parties, conferences; they are held on neutral (or neu-
tralized) territory. More private situations are designed for
familiar interactions where relationships are established; they
include clubs, homes, and some institutions. Of course, both
types can cater to a mix of familiar/unfamiliar interactions.
However, there are special rules for doing this—unexpected visitors are often unwelcome at home and should give notice while
cliques of friends at parties can be criticized for not mixing.

In the more public context, situation rules and rules of
etiquette and self-presentation are in the foreground, while
the expression of personality, attitudes, and emotions is re-
pressed. In familiar settings, the reverse tends to be true; idiosyncratic rule structures, shaped by personalities of participants,
tend to take over and stabilize, as in the family setting. Unfamiliar situations would seem to be more difficult, since the
behavior of strangers is less predictable than known others
(strangers may not adhere to the rules and so on) and participants must discover new rules and face the risk of behaving
incorrectly. However, familiar situations also pose serious problems; for example, being too predictable, lacking novelty, and
being boring or even depressing. Novelty may be a person need,
which these situations intrinsically lack. Rules, even if implicit,
are well known because of familiarity and are likely to be
constraining.

6. Specific vs. general. Situations can vary on a dimension of
specificity-generality, at one end being unique, at the other

being common. Few people would know how to conduct themselves with the Jones family, but most would know what to do
in an interview, even though both situations can be quite stable
over time. More difficulties would be experienced, of course, in
unique situations on this dimension.

7. Selective vs. unselective. Situations can be selective or unselective. Such public places as dance halls and bus stops are unselective; the Royal Society and other exclusive clubs are selective.
Problems arise in both, since rules of approach operate in the
former, rules of entry in the latter, and anxieties about proper
conduct of approach may arise.

8. Some situations and situation roles provoke objective self-
awareness, such as in first encounters or in the role of interviewee, because they involve self-presentation, scrutinizing by
others, and possible loss of face.
   A related role difference is whether a person is required to
be active, take responsibility, and make decisions for which he
or she is answerable; or passive and without such responsibility,
such as host vs being guest, participant vs spectator.

We have discussed some properties of situations that make them
difficult or easy for participants. However, some situations are not only
difficult but also abnormal. A normal situation presumably elicits behavior acceptable to the wider society and facilitates achieving socially
acceptable and positively enhancing goals. A neurotic situation, then,
elicits abnormal (that is, antisocial or sick) behavior, extreme emotions,
and negative attitudes (stress, depression, hostility, and so on) that fail
to facilitate achievement of its set goals or even the opposite of set
goals or that facilitate antisocial or harmful goals. One can imagine a
Milgram obedience situation here.

Now, if at least some of these dimensions cover at least some of the
situations (some of the time), how do they explain the problematic
situations described earlier? Here, we had a number of similar social
tasks: meeting strangers, approaching others, keeping a conversation
going. They form a coherent cluster that is high on informality; they do
not have rigid structures or scripts and, therefore, the security these
would give; they have definite, though flexible, rules of conduct; but
these rules are more implicit than explicit and may be difficult to detect: there are no notices of how to ask a person to dance or talk to a
stranger, but there are right and wrong ways of doing it. There are unfamiliar situations and there is uncertainty about others' reactions; they
are likely to provoke self-awareness due to the demand for self-presentation and active participation. However, it may be argued whether
these problem situations are also abnormal and, if so, whether they

could be improved. I argue they are not abnormal, they are well-fitted to facilitating the goal of interaction between strangers and exploration of friendship possibilities, and our task should be to make their structure better known so they can be more easily used to increase their number, perhaps by establishing patient clubs and social groups so social isolates can more easily have access to other people.

However, are these the only problematic situations? If we want to find truly abnormal situations, we can look, as others have done, to where the most abnormal forms of behavior can be found. Two examples are institutions, in particular psychiatric and penal, and homes, particularly the homes of schizophrenics.

The most dramatic experimental demonstration of institutional effects is the study by Haney, Banks, and Zimbardo (1973) on a simulated prison. Within days of the start of the experiment, prisoners displayed a syndrome of passivity, dependency, depression, and helplessness, while guards displayed power, status, and group identification.

Much has been written on the institutionalizing effect of long-stay hospitalization on schizophrenics, where practically all forms of social behavior disappear and asocial behavior patterns are extremely stable over time. Sanson-Fisher, Poole, and Thompson (1979) made a detailed study of behavior patterns within a general hospital psychiatric unit—a progressive research-oriented unit catering to short-stay acute patients and described as a model setting. However, it was found that the staff spent a majority of time interacting with patients. Patients spent about half of their time in solitary behaviors. There was a territorial separation of the two groups in different areas of the unit. Apparently, most of the staff agreed that the unit did not meet the stated therapeutic goals of the unit; it can be argued that the setting and its rules worked against such an objective.

In a review, Wills (1978) found that therapists generally have negative attitudes toward patients who are uncooperative, (i.e., resistant to influence), and that in psychiatric hospitals in particular staff expectations for conformity are more stringent than in most other settings. We may argue for a clear case of an abnormal or neurotic setting, in which abnormal behavior is reinforced and the de facto goals are clearly antitherapeutic. If this is so, then we have a clear case for changing these situations.

Another clearly abnormal setting is the typical schizophreniform family. A number of studies in different parts of the world show that the most powerful predictor of schizophrenic relapse is the home environment, where significant others are either critical, disapproving, sarcastic, and/or angry towards the patient, or are overconcerned, overprotective, and solicitous, (Brown, Birley, and Wing 1972; Vaughn and Leff 1976; Liberman, Wallace, Vaughn, and Snyder 1979). Both the family and institution would score high on controlling the behavior of certain persons, where P variance is at a minimum, and where rules are idiosyncratic, coercive, and well known.

Person Dimensions

Just as a proportion of the total variance in behavior can be attributed to the situation and its rules, so a reciprocal proportion can be attributed to persons or personalities within them. At one extreme, persons may be highly consistent in their behavior across time and situations, always producing much the same behavioral profile; or they may be consistent across situations but not time, depending on their changing moods, purposes, and skills. At the other extreme, persons may be inconsistent in so far as they change their behavior radically according to whatever situation they are in. Problems exist at both extremes. The highly consistent person may fail to adapt to important situation requirements, breaking rules and being penalized or rejected.

Many studies confirm that certain patient types exhibit characteristic behavior patterns, with the implication that patients behave that way across situations. Some studies have more directly tested the consistency hypothesis, however. Moos (1968, 1969) showed patients varied less than staff in their reported reactions to different situations and also varied less on behavioral measures. Trower (1980) showed unskilled patients varied less across phases of one situation (getting acquainted) on virtually all elements of behavior measured.

While it is adaptive to vary according to the situation, this process can also be taken too far; thus, at the other extreme, we have highly inconsistent individuals who may overaccommodate, fail to assert themselves, yield too easily, and thereby fail to achieve personal goals and satisfaction of desires. Unassertive, socially anxious but skilled individuals may fit this description; it would be interesting to test this empirically.

Let us now consider some dimensional components of persona that may underlie consistency and variability in behavior and may explain the structure of problem persons.

1. Restricted vs elaborated skill repertoires. People vary in their possession of social knowledge and rules that guide perception and conduct. Mischel (1973) uses the concept cognitive and behavioral construction competencies to refer to these capabilities. At the more general level, these competencies are represented by beliefs, stereotypes, and other cognitive schemas or rule systems that help organize and select information about the environment and guide subsequent action.

     There are clearly a variety of types of schemas—for situations (Schank and Abelson 1977), for persons (Mischel 1973), and for self (Markus 1977). Since people do not generate anew every sequence of behavior they perform, they must also possess, at a more specific level, repertoires of scripts (Schank and Abelson 1977) or component skills (Trower 1980) specifying exact actions and sequences and functioning in a more or less automated or mindless way (Langer 1978) for familiar situations and bits of interaction. Guided by general schemas, the skilled individual is assumed to draw on his or her repertoire of scripts—choosing, organizing, abandoning, and reorganizing them in accordance with changes in the situation, reappraisal of the personalities of others, and changes in plans. Such a skilled individual, therefore, would possess a large repertoire of schemas and scripts and show flexibility in their use.

Problems would arise if an individual possessed a small repertoire and showed rigidity in their use. Having restricted repertoire, he or she would be less likely to know what to do in many situations and by default simply fall back on the script known best. Due to certain cognitive processes discussed later and in Trower (1981), certain types of psychiatric patient do develop very few and very rigid schemas and scripts and consequently exhibit the consistent behavior patterns referred to. Of course, the process of flexibility can be taken too far; a person may skillfully follow appropriate scripts but would choose those serving the goals of others rather than self (i.e., to be unassertive).

2. Appropriate vs. inappropriate situation schemas. Within his or her repertoire, a person must, of course, have appropriate situation scripts shared by others and must be able to select the right situation. However, due to certain learning histories, some persons have idiosyncratic scripts and schemas. Such persons perceive situations in idiosyncratic ways, giving rise to well-known problems of systematic biasing.

Obviously, people are more prone to behave inappropriately if they perceptually distort social markers. Messe, Stollak, Larson, and Michaels (1979) found that both positive and negative distorters behaved less adaptively than did accurate perceivers across different social contexts. It is also true that people perceiving situations as similar will behave similarly within them, as Magnusson and Ekehammer (1978) showed. Persons will vary in their discriminative skills; those showing less discrimination may perform more similarly across situations, giving rise to response consistency found in psychiatric patients.

3. Appropriate vs. inappropriate self and other person schemas. People with low self-esteem presumably possess evaluatively

poor self-schemas such that they believe they are, or may become, inadequate personalities, introverts, social failures, and in other ways worthless. It is equally to be expected that many people have evaluatively poor schemas for others—that others are hostile, hateful, rejecting, and so on.

Research on clinical populations indicates such individuals guide their conduct in such a way and conduct themselves inadequately or depressively (Dryden 1981) or, in order to avoid becoming worthless, conduct themselves according to such rules as "I must behave humbly or people will reject me" (Alden and Safran 1978). This behavior will be detrimental in so far as it produces negative reactions from others (Trower 1981). Both rational emotive therapy (Ellis 1962) and cognitive therapy (Beck 1976) assess neurotic problems in terms of such beliefs.

4. External vs. internal monitoring. People vary in the extent to which they monitor cues in situations or their own internal beliefs and feelings. Snyder (1974, 1979) found evidence of a dispositional tendency of high versus low self-monitoring, which is a way of saying some are external (situation) monitors and others are internal monitors. Internal monitors are prone to miss or distort social cues and to be guided in perception and performance by their self-beliefs and internal cues, giving rise to greater cross-situational consistency in behavior. Internally guided individuals are the counterpart to the highly scripted situations.

5. High vs. low self-consciousness. Individuals differ in their tendencies to be self-conscious in social situations; that is, in the tendency to direct attention to themselves as social objects (Fenigstein, Scheier, and Buss 1975). This process is independent of self-monitoring (Fenigstein 1979).

The disposition to self-consciousness carries with it certain characteristic cognitive processing phenomena, such as self-attribution of the cause of negative outcomes (self-blame) (Fenigstein 1979). When self-concepts are negative, self-consciousness clearly exacerbates self-criticism and associated anxiety, discomfort, and embarrassment and effectively disrupts rather than facilitates performance (Brockner and Hulton 1978).

7. Demanding vs. nondemanding goals and standards. Individuals vary in their wants and needs; to satisfy them, they must seek and enter situations providing the appropriate social goals. One person's goals may be found only in intrinsically difficult situations; another's may be more easily accessible. For example,

young people generally have to enter first-encounter or dating situations if they are to establish friendship outside the home.

Such problems can recur later in life following bereavement of spouse, divorce, children leaving home, or because of change of work, or unemployment. However, individuals also differ in the standards they set themselves in the form of social success (important or numerous friendships) or unrealistically high levels of social competence, or promotion, for example. In these cases, the chances of failure increase in proportion to the difficulty of the goals or standards they desire.

7. High vs. low outcome expectancies. Whatever goals and competencies the person may have, the person chooses to act or not act in a particular way depending on personal expectancies of achieving certain outcomes (Mischel 1973) or on self-efficacy expectations (Bandura 1977). Certain patients are known to have expectations of noncontingency (Abramson, Seligman, and Teasdale 1978) or no control (Wortman and Brehm 1975). (See also Carver, Blaney, and Scheier 1979). Some authors, following Rotter (1954), also consider levels of subjective expectancy to be personality trait, though this is a debatable issue. In any event, a person will be less likely to learn skills or achieve goals if he or she has low expectations of positive outcomes, which, in turn, lead to withdrawal.

Other person dimensions not listed include cognitive complexity, field dependence-independence, and so on; we shall not attempt such an exhaustive list here. In summary, unskilled patients have more difficulty in more situations than other groups perhaps because they have restricted skill repertoires, possess inappropriate situation and person (self and other) schemas, are internal monitors, high in self-consciousness, and have demanding or unrealistic goals and standards. We have no direct evidence of this since we do not take the appropriate measures—a task for the future. However, an explanation purely in terms of social skills no longer seems adequate for several reasons discussed elsewhere (Trower 1981).

Interaction Fit

We predict that problem situations would have the greatest scope for social failure, whereas problem persons would have the greatest tendency to fail. Putting the two together would produce an even more predictable result—that problem persons would have greatest difficulty in just the same situations that most people do—only more so. This is what we found. As we saw earlier, the situations ranked highest for difficulty by most groups involved actively seeking contact with relative strangers. This was also true for psychiatric patients, particularly socially inadequate patients. However, students, for example, ranked these situations slight to moderate difficulty, whereas the socially inadequate patients ranked them great difficulty or avoidance if possible. In other words, the profile is not different, it is more accentuated.

How can we best conceptualize these difficulties? One way to describe them is in terms of a simple model of P × S fit—characteristics of persons fail to fit matching characteristics of situations they enter. Here are some examples:

1. Persons with restricted skill repertoires enter situations requiring elaborated skill performances (e.g., fast-changing, informal situations). This category includes rigid script-following in flexible script-requiring situations.

2. Persons selecting the wrong situation or person scripts enter highly scripted situations requiring strict conformity to the rules. This most obviously happens in formal situations but can also occur in informal (e.g., first encounter) situations, where a person fails to conform to such rules as disclosure reciprocity.

3. Persons who are internal monitors enter situations with implicit rules. In other words, the person poor at monitoring cues will have greatest problems in situations where cues are difficult to detect.

4. Persons with high self-conscious dispositions enter situations tending to elicit self-consciousness.

5. Persons with low efficacy expectations enter situations demanding high skill performances.

Many combinations can be considered. There are also complex interactions between the dimensions within persons (e.g., self-consciousness exacerbates negative self-schemas, unrealistic standards produce even lower efficacy expectations), within situations (e.g., high scriptedness and implicit rules makes for greater difficulty), and between persons and situations.

A model of P × S fit implies an ideal of persons and situations fitting together on salient characteristics. Problems arise when there are failures of fit, as in the examples above. First, then, the dichotomy exists between person-situation fit and misfit. Person-situation fit means complementarity between the dimensions we have considered (and others) so there is mutual conformity to one set of rules, scripts, and goals. Person-situation misfit implies failure of complementarity on dimensional characteristics such that at least two sets of rules, scripts, and goals are mutually incompatible, such as where a player tries to play football in a game of cricket, or a participant treats an informal peer encounter as if it were an interview, or a group member tries to exchange gossip with the chairman during a formal meeting; these situations result in an overt clash of interests and possible breakdown in the interaction.

Second, however, a more subtle dichotomy exists between positive and negative fit. Although both involve complementarity of characteristics and conformity to a common activity, the former results in positive, the latter in negative, outcomes.

Consider the three possibilities of fit: (1) where the situation fits the person (P[s]) (for example, where a person takes the initiative in establishing scripts and goals, that is, structures a low-scripted situation); (2) where the person fits the situation (S[p]) (that is, the person conforms to a high-scripted, formal situation); and (3) where a compromise is negotiated based on the needs of the person and requirements of the situation and needs of others (PS). The fit can be positive—skillful manipulation of the situation, willing conformity to the situation or agreeable compromise. Persons achieve their goals, rules are not broken.

However, the fit can be negative. In (1), the persons may alter the situation (P[s]) by forcing others to comply but generating hostility and rejection (e.g., the overdisclosing depressive who gets compliance by means of guilt [Dryden 1981]). In (2), a person may entirely conform to the situation (and others) but in doing so sacrifices personal needs and goals. In (3), an accommodation may be agreed, intensely disliked by others, but complied with in order to secure some other payoff.

In dealing with positive and negative fit, we have moved from a mechanistic version of the P × S model, in which the two components interact as if they were independent entities, to a dynamic version of the model, in which P and S have a mutual two-way influence, such that P changes S and vice versa (Endler and Edwards 1978). We may thus have a continuous process of a positive or a negative cycle of events. To show more clearly the effects of negative fit of the first type—S fits P—consider a hypothetical case, Joe Smith, in a hypothetical situation, a party.

Joe is a young, single, heterosexual male, has a history of isolation and poor social skills, and is depressed. To understand his problem, we reconstruct a problem interaction at a recent party he attended. We find his poor cue recognition skills (internal monitoring) interact with this type of situation's low cue salience (implicit rules) and unfamiliarity, so he fails to detect cues—a feedback problem. His high self-conscious proneness interacts with the situation's self-conscious eliciting properties, triggering off internal monitoring of negative self-beliefs (e.g., he is disliked) and negative perceptual stereotypes (e.g., people are hostile and critical). Thus guided by internal schemas, he behaves consistently and unresponsively to the situation. He behaves defensively, that is, he is cold, untalkative, and sullen—a style appropriate within his cognitive schema. By doing so, he alters the situation, particularly the responses of others.

Here we see how person characteristics interact with situation characteristics to produce negative fit of the type P(s). Negative fit, produced by Joe's own actions, takes the form of rejection, communicated indirectly perhaps by the overly formal behavior by others. For Joe, this behavior confirms his original negative belief. The pattern will repeat itself in a continuous self-fulfilling prophecy—he produces the effects he predicts (Trower 1981). The effect for Joe is depression. Joe is not aware of course of the process; he attributes it down to his social inadequacy or the world's hostility.

Now consider negative fit of the second type—P fits S—in which Joe Smith enters a different type of setting where relationships have been established, such as home or institutions. Because of his familiarity with the situation, Joe knows the rules and is highly sensitized to them. He perceives the situation as highly scripted with severe penalties for breaking the rules; given his poor self-esteem, he fears negative evaluation and, therefore, conforms. He also has low expectations of effectively changing the situation to obtain his own goals and abandons all efforts to do so. He may end up feeling coerced, submissive, and frustrated.

Of course, individuals differ in their tendencies to conform to the situation or to bring about changes in the situation to suit their own purposes. However, for successfully functioning individuals, there tends to be a progression from first encounter situations, where P fits S, to established interactions, where S fits P or a compromise is negotiated. For example, a stranger will follow etiquette rules and other formalities when entering a setting for the first time, repressing personality tendencies until he or she comprehends the group's special rules. Later, however, the person will exert his or her personality and seek personal own goals, thus switching his or her strategy to the second or third type of fit—emerging perhaps as a new leader or reaching a new accommodation with the others.

The socially unskilled, however, such as Joe Smith, may follow the reverse pattern, inadvertently producing the S fits P type fit in first encounters, but finding himself in the P fits S type of interactions as the situation becomes an established one. He thus suffers on all scores—he fails in friendship-forming situations by being a negative influence, and he fails in familiar setting by overconforming. The experience of many such personality disorders, of course, reflects this pattern. Evidence shows such patients have few, if any, friends and have little social life (Bryant et al. 1976). At the same time, they remain at home into their twenties, thirties, and later, in institutions for much of their lives.

CONCLUSION

This chapter began with the criticism that some current assessment methods in the social skills domain may have taken a wrong turn in focusing on the individual; following a powerful medical tradition in diagnosis. This approach invites us to attribute causes of the patient's abnormal social behavior entirely to the individual—his or her disposition or illness—who must therefore be treated for it. This position is untenable most clearly in cases where the situation plays an overwhelming role in shaping behavior.

The chapter then developed a model based on the interactional approach, in which the problem—and its solution—lay in the dynamic interaction, or fit, between characteristics of the person and the situation. Positive fit represented the ideal; misfit and negative fit represented forms of social failure.

The first steps toward an analysis of misfit and negative fit entails assessing key characteristics both of the individual patient and the situation he or she inhabits. The chapter listed seven dimensional descriptive components of persons and situations that are prime candidates for such assessment. Several assessment measures for the dimensions listed (Mischel 1981) already exist, and the author and others are carrying this work further. Possessing such information will enable the therapist to identify the type of negative fit in which the patient is trapped and the key components which the therapist will have to modify to bring about change. For such an inherently difficult and complex area as social skills training, nothing less comprehensive is likely to produce planned benefit.

REFERENCES

Abramson, L. Y., Seligman, M. E. P., & Teasdale, J. D. Learned helplessness in humans: Critique and reformulation. *Journal of Abnormal Psychology*, 1978, *87*, 49-74.

Alden, L., & Safran, J. Irrational beliefs and nonassertive behavior. *Cognitive Therapy and Research*, 1978, *2*, 357-364.

Argyle, M. Personality and social behaviour. In R. Harré (Ed.), *Personality*. Oxford: Blackwell, 1976.

Argyle, M., Bryant, B., & Trower, P. Social skills training and psychotherapy. *Psychological Medicine*, 1974, *4*, 435-443.

Argyle, M., Graham, J. A., Campbell, A., & White, P. The rules of different situations. *New Zealand Psychologist*, 1979, *8*, 13-22.

Bandura, A. *Social learning theory.* Englewood Cliffs, N.J.: Prentice-Hall, 1977.

Beck, A. T. *Cognitive therapy and the emotional disorders.* New York: International Universities Press, 1976.

Bellack, A. S. A critical appraisal of strategies for assessing social skill. *Behavioral Assessment*, 1979, *1*, 157-176.

Brockner, J., & Hulton, A. J. B. How to reverse the vicious circle of low self-esteem: The importance of attentional focus. *Journal of Experimental Social Psychology*, 1978, *14*, 564-578.

Brown, G., Birley, J. L. T., & Wing, J. K. Influence of family life on the course of schizophrenia. *British Journal of Psychiatry*, 1972, *121*, 241-258.

Bryant, B. M., & Trower, P. Social difficulty in a student sample. *British Journal of Educational Psychology*, 1974, *44*, 13-21.

Bryant, B., Trower, P., Yardley, K., Urbieta, H., & Letemendia, F. J. J. A survey of social inadequacy among psychiatric outpatients. *Psychological Medicine*, 1976, *6*, 101-112.

Carver, C. S., Blaney, P. H., & Scheier, M. Reassertion and giving up: The interactive role of self-directed attention and outcome expectancy. *Journal of Personality and Social Psychology*, 1979, *38*, 1859-1870.

Collett, P. The rules of conduct. In P. Collett (Ed.)., *Social rules and social behaviour.* Oxford: Blackwell, 1977.

Crozier, W. R. Shyness as a dimension of personality. *British Journal of Social and Clinical Psychology*, 1979, *18*, 121-128.

Dryden, W. The relationships of depressed persons. In R. Gilmour and S. Duck (Eds.), *Personal relationships in disorder.* London: Academic Press, 1981.

Ellis, A. *Reason and emotion in psychotherapy.* New York: Lyle Stewart, 1962. (Paperback edition: New York: Citadel Press, 1977.)

Endler, N. S., & Edwards, J. Person by treatment interactions in personality research. In L. Pervin and M. Lewis, (Eds.) *Perspectives in interactional psychology.* New York: Plenum, 1978.

Endler, N. S., & Magnusson, D. (Eds.). *Interactional psychology and personality.* Washington, D.C.: Hemisphere Publishing Corp., 1975.

Fenigstein, A. Self-consciousness, self-attention and social interaction. *Journal of Personality and Social Psychology*, 1979, *37*, 75-86.

Fenigstein, A., Scheier, M. F., & Buss, A. H. Public and private self-consciousness: Assessment and theory. *Journal of Consulting and Clinical Psychology*, 1975, *87*, 49-74.

Furnham, A. Social difficulty in three cultures. *International Journal of Psychology*, 1983, *18*, 215-228.

Giles, H., Scherer, K. R., & Taylor, D. M. Speech markers in social interaction. In K. R. Scherer and H. Giles (Eds.), *Social markers in speech.* Cambridge: Cambridge University Press, 1979.

Haney, C., Banks, C., & Zimbardo, P. Interpersonal dynamics in a simulated prison. *International Journal of Criminology and Penology*, 1973, *1*, 69-97.

Hersen, M. Modification of skill deficits in psychiatric patients. In A. S. Bellack & M. Hersen (Eds.), *Research and practice in social skills training.* New York and London: Plenum Press, 1979.

Labov, W., & Fanshel, D. *Therapeutic discourse.* New York: Academic Press, 1977.

Langer, E. J. Rethinking the role of thought in social interaction. In J. H. Harvey, W. J. Ickes, & R. F. Kidd (Eds.), *New directions in attribution research* (Vol. II). Hillside, N.J.: Lawrence Erlbaum Associates, 1978.

Liberman, R. P., Wallace, C. J., Vaughn, C. E., & Snyder, K. L. Paper presented at the Conference on Psychotherapy of Schizophrenia: Current Status and New Directions. New Haven, Ct.: Yale University, April 1979.

Magnusson, D., & Ekehammer, B. Similar situations, similar behaviours?: A study of intraindividual congruence between situation perception and situation reactions. *Journal of Research in Personality*, 1978, *12*, 41-48.

Markus, H. Self-schemata and processing information about the self. *Journal of Personality and Social Psychology*, 1977, *35*, 63-78.

Messe, L. A., Stollak, G. E., Larson, R. W., and Michaels, G. Y. Interpersonal consequences of person perception processes in two social contexts. *Journal of Personality and Social Psychology*, 1979, *37*, 369-379.

Mischel, W. Towards a cognitive social learning reconceptualization of personality. *Psychological Review*, 1973, *80*, 252-283.

Mischel, W. A cognitive social learning approach to assessment. In T. V. Merluzzi, C. R. Glass, and M. Genest (Eds.), *Cognitive assessment.* New York: Guilford Press, 1981.

Moos, R. H. Situational analysis of a therapeutic community milieu. *Journal of Abnormal Psychology*, 1968, *73*, 49-61.

Moos, R. H. Sources of variance in response to questionnaires and in behaviour. *Journal of Abnormal Psychology*, 1969, *74*, 405-412.

Price, R. H., & Bouffard, D. L. Behavioral appropriateness and situational constraint as dimensions of social behavior. *Journal of Personality and Social Psychology*, 1974, *30*, 579–586.

Rotter, J. B. *Social learning and clinical psychology:* Englewood Cliffs, N.J.: Prentice-Hall, 1954.

Sanson-Fisher, R. W., Poole, A. D., & Thompson, V. Behaviour patterns within a general hospital psychiatric unit: An observational study. *Behavior Research and Therapy*, 1979, *17*, 317–332.

Schank, R. C., and Abelson, R. P. *Scripts, plans, goals and understanding*. Hillsdale, N. J.: Lawrence Erlbaum Associates, 1977.

Shea, M., & Rosenfeld, H. M. Functional employment of nonverbal social reinforcers in dyadic learning. *Journal of Personality and Social Psychology*. 1976, *34*, 228–239.

Snyder, M. Self-monitoring of expressive behaviour. *Journal of Personality and Social Psychology*, 1974, *30*, 526–537.

Snyder, M. Self-monitoring processes. In L. Berkowitz (Ed.), *Advances in experimental social psychology* (Vol. 12). New York: Academic Press, 1979.

Strain, P. S., & Ezzell, D. The sequence and distribution of behavioral disordered adolescents' disruptive/inappropriate behaviors. *Behavior Modification*, 1978, *2*, 403–425.

Trower, P. Situational analysis of the components and processes of behavior of socially skilled and unskilled patients. *Journal of Consulting and Clinical Psychology*, 1980, *48*, 327–339.

Trower, P. Social skill disorder: Mechanisms of failure. In R. Gilmour and S. Duck (Eds.), *Personal relationships in disorder*. London: Academic Press, 1981.

Trower, P., Bryant, B. M., & Argyle, M. *Social skills and mental health*. London: Methuen, 1978.

Trower, P., Yardley, K., Bryant, B. M., & Shaw, P. The treatment of social failure: A comparison of anxiety-reduction and skills-acquisition procedures on two social problems. *Behavior Modification*, 1978, *2*, 41–60.

Vaughn, C. E., & Leff, J. P. The influence of family and social factors on the course of psychiatric illness. *British Journal of Psychiatry*, 1976, *129*, 125–137.

Wills, T. A. Perceptions of clients by professional helpers. *Psychological Bulletin*, 1978, *85*, 968–1000.

Wortman, C. B., & Brehm, J. W. Responses to uncontrollable outcomes: An integration of reactance theory and the learned helplessness model. In L. Berkowitz (Ed.), *Advances in experimental social psychology*. New York: Academic Press, 1975.

8. Cooperation Dilemmas

RICHARD PRICE
University of Michigan

INTRODUCTION

This chapter discusses the role of situational theory in understanding certain social problems. Broadly speaking, situational theory seeks explanations for behavior in the social environment, rather than exclusively in the characteristics of individuals. This tradition in social science has a relatively long history and in recent years has experienced something of a resurgence.

Note that the phrase *social problems* does not suggest that social problems can be solved in the same sense that mathematical problems can be solved. As Sarason (1978) suggested, it may be more accurate to speak of "problem changing" than of problem solving when discussing social problems.

Nevertheless, one contribution situational theory can make in the arena of social problem solving is heuristic. Heuristics help us discover or learn and can guide further investigation of a problem. For example, Argyle (1982) creatively used the concept *games* as one heuristic for studying social situations. He showed that by isolating the elements of situations as games, one can illuminate aspects of situations that might otherwise be ignored; and by changing the elements or their arrangement, one can debug problem situations.

This chapter also examines another situational heuristic in some detail. These situations, cooperation dilemmas, have also been called "social traps" by Platt (1973). They include the commons dilemma described by Hardin (1968) in his article "The Tragedy of the Commons."

This situational heuristic helps illuminate a class of social problems increasingly salient in our lives. In addition, it deals with questions of individual versus collective interest, cooperation and competition, and the rights and responsibilities of individuals and communities. These themes have not received adequate emphasis in much of the behavioral science research conducted from a situational perspective. The study of cooperation dilemmas can suggest, if not solutions, then at least different ways of coping with them.

ALTERNATIVE FORMULATIONS

Cooperation dilemmas have been discussed in terms of several theoretical frameworks. A brief survey of three such frameworks will illuminate the dimensions of such dilemma situations.

Commons Dilemma

To begin, consider an example first described by Hardin (1968) as the commons dilemma and later discussed in detail by Hardin and Baden (1977). The commons dilemma metaphor is based on the use of common grazing land typical of New England villages during colonial times. These public grasslands existed in villages, where villagers grazed cows. Such a social arrangement, Hardin noted, worked reasonably well until individual farmers realized they could profit more by enlarging their herds and grazing them on the public land. As each farmer increased his herd, however, the total number of cattle increased and grass became increasingly scarce, until finally the commons were destroyed. Thus, individual owners seeking individual gains ultimately experienced a collective loss. The dilemma in this situation is clear: the individual engages in a behavior or activity to his or her initial individual short-term advantage but damaging to the group as a whole in the long run.

Hardin and others (Dawes 1980; Edney 1980) argued that the dilemma is a prototype situation for a variety of current social problems, including: (1) individual decisions about child bearing that produce a long-run population problem; (2) individual decisions about the use of automobiles that ultimately pollute our "commons" in the form of our air supply; and (3) the individual exploitation of the oceans that ultimately depletes this resource. The key in this instance is a conflict between short-term individual interests and advantage on the one hand, and long-term collective interest on the other.

Reinforcement-Oriented Formulations

Hardin's paradigm is metaphorical: Platt (1973) called this type of situation a *social trap* and interpreted it in reinforcement terms. Platt's formulation is generally Skinnerian and can be depicted as follows. A stimulus or situation (S) elicits a behavior (B), which, in turn, produces a result or reinforcement (R). This sequence of events can be divided into actions of the organism (behaviors) and actions or inputs from the environment. In this formulation, the initial stimulus situation and the result or reinforcement are both *situations.*

Following Platt's formulation, the *social trap* or *dilemma* depends on the incongruity between the personal short-term outcomes for a given behavior and the group long-term consequences of the behavior.

Thus, a social trap occurs when there is opposition between a short-term individual reinforcement for a particular behavior and a long-term consequence for the group.

Borrowing from Platt's notation and elaborating it, the social trap situation can be written as follows:

$$B$$

$$S \quad \overset{+\ldots\ldots-}{\underset{\text{Rsp} \qquad \text{Rgl}}{}}$$

Thus, the individually rewarding immediate profits lead the farmer to increase the size of his herd. The long-term negative consequence for the group, as well as for the individual, is the deletion of the common grazing ground.

Platt also suggested a second kind of social trap situation, a *counter trap* or *fence*, where the negative short-term individual consequences of a behavior reduce the probability of its being performed again and thus block a long-term positive consequence for the group. Again, following and elaborating on Platt's notation, a formulation for *social fences* is as follows:

$$B$$

$$S \quad \overset{-\ldots//\ldots+}{\underset{\text{Rsp} \qquad \text{Rgl}}{}}$$

Even though the reinforcement approach is familiar, particularly to psychologists, its simplicity may obscure as much as it reveals about cooperation dilemmas. As Edney (1980) notes, this formulation offers no role for values, individual differences in social orientation, or cognitive processes. What the individual brings to such dilemma situations may be as important as the pattern of reinforcement in understanding how they unfold or are resolved.

Game Theory Approaches

Dawes (1980) summarized the literature on *dilemma games* in which a game theoretical perspective and methodology is used to understand cooperation dilemmas. Dawes argued that a game is simply a system of payoffs depending on the combination of choices made by the players. In dilemma games, each player makes one of two choices—either for social defection or social cooperation. The payoff to each player depends on his or her choice and on the number of players in the game also making one of the two choices. A moment's reflection shows that, in this case, many defecting choices result in a *tragedy of the commons*, whereas large proportions of participants engaging in cooperative behavior produce the optimal result for the group.

However, Dawes pointed out that the game theory approach to cooperation dilemmas does not focus exclusively on concrete payoffs associated with social cooperation or social defection. He noted that most of us engage in a wide variety of positive social behaviors even though we recognize rationally that the payoff for engaging in them is essentially zero. Dawes observed:

> Many of us would not rob a bank, even if we knew that we could get away with it, and even if we could be assured that none of our friends or neighbors would know. Many of us give money to public television or the United Fund, even though we know that our paltry contribution will make no difference in terms of the services rendered. Most of us take the trouble to vote even though we know that the probability that an election will be decided by a single ballot is effectively zero. And some couples desiring a large family do in fact limit its size not out of desire, but out of a belief that it is not moral to have too many children.
>
> All these behaviors involve rejecting a payoff that is larger for one that is smaller. The potential bank robbers could be wealthy, the contributors could save their money, the voters could save themselves inconvenience, and the couples who want children could have them. The point is that people making these decisions have *utilities* that determine their behavior, utilities associated with aspects of their behavior other than the external payoffs they would receive. (175)

The importance of Dawes's observation should be obvious—he suggested the economic view of people who in every circumstance maximize economic gain is untenable. Most social acts require we set aside immediate short-term gains for uncertain long-term goals or ideals. The fact that we do so cannot be understood on purely selfish grounds. Utilities govern our behavior in such dilemmas and are made up of personal values, morals, or feelings of responsibility that are weighed in the decision to engage in social cooperation or social defection.

In reviewing research on dilemma games, Dawes made several additional important observations. First, he noted cooperation dilemma games of the sort discussed here differ in important ways from the two-person prisoners dilemma game that received so much attention in social psychological research. First, social cooperation or social defection has its impact entirely on the other player in a two-person game, whereas in cooperation dilemmas the impact of defecting behavior is spread out over a number of players. Second, in many cases, the defecting behavior in social dilemmas is often anonymous. Finally, in two-person games, each person can directly punish the other for defection, but in the case of social dilemmas, the outcome is more uncertain for any player. Dawes thus concluded that *n-person dilemma games* are more appropriate simulations of the cooperation dilemmas considered in this chapter.

Dawes also acknowledged "n-person dilemma games are lousy *simulations* of the social dilemmas with which most of us are concerned. . . . Findings about how small groups of subjects behave in contrived situations cannot be generalized to statements about how to save the world. . . . What must be assumed is that the psychological and social factors that lead to defection or cooperation in small-scale dilemmas are roughly the same as those that influence behavior in large dilemmas" (188–189). Dawes pointed out that this assumption should be based on broader theoretical notions about what leads people to cooperate or defect in general, and that the proper use of games is not to simulate the explicit nature of the cooperation dilemma itself but to use the game as an opportunity to investigate variables outside the structure of the game.

Dawes thought carefully about the specific nature and limitations of the game theoretical approach to understanding cooperation dilemmas. His position makes no unreasonable claims for the game's theoretical approach, recognizes both advantages as well as their limitations, and emphasizes the concept of *utility* as a framework for understanding motivations for engaging in social cooperation or defection.

SOME PROBLEMS WITH CONTEMPORARY RESEARCH ON SETTINGS AND SITUATIONS

An earlier paper (Price 1982) argued that much of the research on situations suffered from several problems: (1) uncertainty about how situations should be sampled and the resulting doubtful ecological validity of the research; (2) heavy reliance on the study of cognitive or verbal representations of situations, rather than a study of situations themselves; (3) a lack of a clear temporal or longitudinal orientation to the study of situations when they obviously evolve over time; (4) a tendency to ignore a situation's institutional or historical context even though the context gives it much of its meaning; and (5) not enough application of our thinking about situational variables to contemporary social problems. It is interesting to ask how the cooperation dilemma paradigm fares when examined in the light of these criticisms.

A decision rule for sampling situations and a judgment about the ecological validity of our research require some theoretical assumptions about what is of interest and what are the essential elements. If the goal is to develop a rule for sampling situations involving cooperation dilemmas, we need a set of parameters that will allow us to decide, at least in a preliminary way, whether a particular situation has the essential properties of a cooperation dilemma. A tentative list might include the following six elements:

1. an individual who is a member of some collectivity or group
2. an actual or potential resource to which individuals have actual or potential access
3. a class of individual decisions relevant to the resource
4. outcomes for individual decisions enacted in relation to the resource
5. outcomes in the available level of the resource itself
6. a temporal element that allows the tracking of the situation over time.

The cooperation dilemma formulation does not rule out either the study of cognitive representations of situations or the study of situations in vivo. It does, however, allow us to generate a set of correspondence rules between simulations or other theoretical or empirical representations of such situations and the actual situations as they unfold in the behavioral environment. Such a set of correspondence rules based on the elements listed above allows us to make judgments about the adequacy of any simulation or laboratory representation of actual situations.

The paradigm also points out an important role for cognitive representations in the study of situations. Perceptions or expectations regarding short- and long-term gains for individuals as they engage in behavior relevant to a common resource pool is important to understand in predicting behavior. This view is consistent with Jessor's (1982) findings that variables measuring the perceived environment can account for large proportions of the variance in behavior and cannot, therefore, be ignored.

In the case of cooperation dilemmas, a temporal or longitudinal aspect is implicit. The paradigm suggests observing reciprocal behavior and its outcome over time as it affects a commonly held actual or potential resource.

The cooperation dilemma also directs our attention to the situation's physical or social environment. It may include, as Craik (1982) suggested, technical, organizational, and policy considerations and individual perceptions of these contextual variables as part of the cognitive framework of the people interacting in the situation.

The human significance of the situations that can be studied in the cooperation dilemma paradigm need not be defended. The examples offered speak for themselves. The advantage of this situational formulation is that it casts in bold relief a number of themes at the core of the social enterprise, not the least of which is the inherent tension between individual and collective interest.

COOPERATION DILEMMAS IN THE COMMUNITY CONTEXT

Dilemmas of the sort described thus far range from the dramatic to the prosaic. They are ubiquitous in community life. One example was offered by Schelling (1971) in his article "The Ecology of Micromotives." Platt (1973) called this "the case of the missing hero." As Platt noted:

> Consider the situation, a summer Sunday evening, when thousands of cars coming back from a Cape Cod weekend on a two-lane road and a mattress falls unnoticed from the top of a station wagon and lies in the northbound lane. All of the cars behind, being uncertain, go around the mattress, waiting for the cars in the southbound lane to go by, and the result is a traffic jam that backs up for miles.
>
> Now who moves the mattress? The answer is, generally, no one. People far back in the line do not know what the trouble is and cannot help, and the drivers close to the mattress are thinking only of how to get around it quickly—and after they have spent so long in line, they are damned if they will spend another several minutes, perhaps endangering themselves, to stop to move the thing. Those who have gone past, of course, no longer have any incentive for moving it. . . .
>
> In such a situation, it is true that sometimes a hero does come forward. Once, when I told an Englishman this story, he said, "Hah! That's only a problem for *Americans!* If there had been a single Englishman in that line, he would have gotten out and moved the mattress, because we are trained in childhood to take leadership in a case like that." (644)

Leaving aside the question of cross-cultural comparisons, the mattress problem nicely illustrates the character of the dilemma situation. The anticipated negative short-term consequences of making an individual effort to move the mattress reduce the probability of individual behavior that will have longer-term positive consequences for the group.

A second more dramatic neighborhood example is the infamous case of Kitty Genovese in New York City. Kitty Genovese was raped and killed while more than thirty neighbors watched from their apartment windows—not one called the police. An understandable public outcry followed this event, and yet, it, too, fits the paradigm of a social fence. As Platt noted, "It is clear that there is a certain individual barrier against calling the police. Not only must you tear yourself away from the spectacle, but you face the probability of having to testify in court and even a chance of being hunted down by the murderer or his friends. Each observer may have felt a strong prick of social conscience at the time, but simply hoped that someone else would make the troublesome phone call first" (641).

The cooperation dilemma formulation helps illuminate certain situational aspects of a variety of social problems that otherwise would seem idiosyncratic and unrelated. Consider another example. In a recent series of studies, Garbarino (1980) attempted to examine social environments that produce higher or lower risks for child abuse and neglect.

He and his colleagues did a comparative study of neighborhoods to examine what in the neighborhood and what interactions placed children at higher or lower risk for child abuse and neglect. The researchers carefully selected neighborhoods on the basis of census tract data matched for socioeconomic status. Both relatively poor neighborhoods selected differed in one important way. One was lower in its overall rate of child abuse and neglect than the other neighborhood, based on the general prevalence of child abuse and neglect in the comparable areas. The other high-risk neighborhood, even though it had a similar socioeconomic status, had a higher than average incidence of child abuse and neglect.

Garbarino then did ethnographic studies of the two neighborhoods to examine the ways in which they differed. He found that the high-risk neighborhood was comprised of families locked into competition for scarce social resources. The parents in this neighborhood typically sought an advantage by getting all they could from others while giving as little as they possibly could. They were ambivalent about neighborly exchanges. They also experienced a sense of "drain" in coping with everyday problems so that additional effort to help others "cost" them more. The low-risk neighborhood, on the other hand, consisted of parents who were relatively free from this experience of drain. They were able to engage in reciprocal neighborly exchanges of help and support, including child care, without fear of exploitation (Garbarino 1980).

Cast in terms of this discussion, the high-risk neighborhood is one at risk, not only for child abuse and neglect; it is also more likely to experience a variety of cooperation dilemmas. In this neighborhood, the perceived short-term gains for individual behavior are high and the perceived cost associated with other helping behaviors may be greater. Thus, perhaps, high-risk neighborhoods, in this case, are neighborhoods in which: a) the actual availability of helping resources is lower; b) the expectation for reciprocity is lower; and c) because of an experience of "drain," the willingness to give mutual aid in a reciprocal relationship is also lower.

It is interesting to speculate on what is required to avoid cooperation dilemmas in the context of neighborhood helping. If one considers a community's or a neighborhood's willingness to help as a resource pool that must be replenished regularly in order to draw on it, then initial efforts to help are required to build trust and reciprocity, and restraints on individual exploitation of the pool must be established.

COPING STRATEGIES

Earlier, this chapter suggested that the cooperation dilemma paradigm could be a useful situational heuristic for understanding a range of social problems involving individual behavior in relation to the group. The same formulation can provide hypotheses about possible ways of coping with such dilemmas.

Reward Structure

One set of suggestions involves shifting the reinforcement contingencies for individual behaviors (Platt 1973), for example, changing the delay between initial short-term behavior and its long-term negative consequences. This can be done symbolically by pointing out the long-term negative consequences both for the individual and for the group of social defection. Shifting reinforcement contingencies can also be done by restructuring the situation so counter-reinforcers encourage behaviors that are for the long-term collective good. These counter-reinforcers can also discourage behaviors that are for the short-term individual advantage and the long-term costs for the group. Providing socially sanctioned rewards for individual behavior that is for the long-term good can provide such counter-reinforcers.

Rothman, Erlich, and Teresa (1976), reviewing the literature on voluntary participation in communities, suggested strategies for increasing individual rewards for participation. They classified rewards as instrumental, interim-anticipatory, social interpersonal, and symbolic. They suggested guidelines for implementing efforts that will maximize such rewards.

One can also reward behaviors that compete with the individual trap-producing behavior. The most obvious and widely used solution has been to shift the control of reinforcement contingencies to a superordinate authority with social sanctions to apply reinforcement contingencies. Thus, fish and game commissions, government regulatory agencies, and other official bodies apply both negative reinforcement for individual exploitative behavior and incentives for behavior in the long-term common good. They are the instruments of social policy with which we are all familiar.

Any approach suggesting that the reinforcement structure of the dilemma situation be altered faces serious practical problems. In many cases, it is unclear who controls such rewards or how feasible their restructuring actually is. Furthermore, it is ironic that most proposals for reinforcement restructuring assume the unilateral control of rewards that is unattainable and constitutes the essence of the dilemma in the first place.

Education

A second approach to the problem involves developing an enhanced situation recognition capability. As Platt noted, the easiest way to diffuse an impending dilemma is to tell everyone about it. As simple as this sounds, it is often difficult since it requires recognizing the development of a dilemma before it occurs. However, getting a "metapicture" of the situation and its consequences, including the competitive processes involved and their outcome, can help. This process suggests that public education efforts that help individuals recognize the long-term costs of their behavior can reduce dilemmas.

Developing the capacity to recognize emerging cooperation dilemmas is important for community leaders. As individuals who could be made sensitive to the collective costs of social defection, community leaders are in a favorable position to point out their dangers and suggest alternative behavior to avoid social defection.

Another option is offered by Edney (1979 a, b), who suggested that continuous and reliable information about the level of resources available and other people's resource behavior may also affect individual behavior. This, however, may be a double-edged sword since information about other people's behavior in their own interests rather than in the common good may lead other people to become locked into a competitive pattern of behavior.

Research

Using the cooperation dilemma as a situational heuristic also offers the possibility that simulations can be brought into the laboratory to incorporate the main features of the dilemma and allow systematic testing of hypotheses about the variables controlling individual cooperative behavior. For example, Cass and Edney (1978), using a computer simulation of a commons dilemma, varied the rate at which common resources regenerated. They also contrasted conditions in which experiment participants harvested resources from a common field or from a territory of their own that was a subdivision of the common territory. They found that dividing the common territory into private territories had a beneficial effect on the harvest rate and resulted in less resource depletion. Thus, this laboratory experiment, in effect, divided the common property into individual territories where individual incentives for careful harvesting had more direct positive and negative consequences for the individual.

Laboratory simulations and games also can help in the search for solutions to the commons dilemma by providing simulations of dilemmas for which the participants must generate their own solutions. Edney (1979b) described the *Nuts Game*, in which groups of individuals are presented with a shallow dish containing ten small machine nuts. They are told only that each individual must get as many nuts as possible and that at the end of each ten-second period, the nuts will be replenished by doubling the number remaining in the dish. Despite many ecological disasters in which the resource was immediately depleted, some groups developed unique solutions to the problem, imposing a variety of constraints on each person's harvesting behavior.

Another approach to searching for solutions to cooperation dilemmas can be to engage in comparative community and ethological studies to discover how various community groups, organizations, or entire communities have developed unique solutions to particular types of dilemmas, the hypothesis being that a number of regularly occurring dilemmas have been avoided by solutions developed in particular cultural contexts. Thus, comparative social studies provide a potentially rich source of information about strategies for coping with cooperation dilemmas. Furthermore, in some cultural contexts these solutions have become institutionalized as traditions because of their long-term survival value for the group.

Another advantage of searching for culturally unique solutions to such dilemmas is that many solutions to social problems are rejected despite their apparent logic because of a poor fit with the cultural context into which they were introduced. Thus, in order to insure the adoption of a coping strategy for dealing with a dilemma, sensitivity to the cultural context of the group may be critical.

SOCIAL PROBLEM SOLVING AND COOPERATION DILEMMAS

The thesis of this chapter is that a situational perspective on social problems can help in the arena of social problem solving. The cooperation dilemma paradigm can provide a useful heuristic for conceptualizing a range of social problems and strategies for coping with them that involve relationships between individual and collective behavior.

As Sarason (1978) made clear, social problems cannot be solved in the same sense that arithmetic problems can be solved; many social problems are not solvable in any final sense. They are, instead, dilemmas that must be solved again and again. He also argued that these social problems contain many value dilemmas. Furthermore, attempts to analyze and cope with them require taking a value stance about the nature of individual and collective good.

Analyses and attempts to cope with such problems probably will produce changes in the locus of the problem and its dynamics rather than solutions in any final sense. This is no reason to abandon attempts to cope with social problems; it is, however, a good reason to be modest about the outcomes of our attempts. Perhaps, in the long run, one characteristic of humanity is the willingness to try to invent new coping strategies in the interest of the collective good when short-term individual interests seem so compelling.

As Thomas (1981) recently remarked:

> We live today in a world densely populated by human beings living in close communication with each other all over the surface of the planet. Viewed from a certain distance the earth has the look of a single society, a community, the swarming of an intensely social species trying to figure out ways to become successfully interdependent. (3)

Our success in that enterprise will surely depend on our ingenuity in dealing with the ubiquitous dilemmas of cooperation.

REFERENCES

Argyle, M. The experimental study of the basic features of situations. In D. Magnusson (Ed.), *The situation: An interactional perspective.* Hillsdale, N.J.: Lawrence Erlbaum Associates, 1982.

Cass, R., & Edney, J. J. The commons dilemma: A simulation testing the effects of resource visibility and territorial division. *Human Ecology*, 1978, *6*, 371–386.

Craik, K. H. Environmental assessment and situational analysis. In D. Magnusson (Ed.), *The situation: An interactional perspective.* Hillsdale, N.J.: Lawrence Erlbaum Associates, 1982.

Dawes, R. M. Social dilemmas. *Annual Review of Psychology*, 1980, *31*, 169–193.

Edney, J. Free riders in route to disaster. *Psychology Today*, 1979, *13*, 80–102. (a)

Edney, J. J. The nuts game: A concise commons dilemma analog. *Environmental Psychology and Nonverbal Behavior*, 1979, *3*, 252–254. (b)

Edney, J. J. The commons problem: Alternative perspectives. *American Psychologist*, 1980, *35*, 131–150.

Garbarino, J. Preventing child maltreatment. In R. H. Price, J. Monahan, R. Ketterer, & B. Bader (Eds.), *Annual review of community mental health prevention.* Beverly Hills, Calif.: Sage Publications, 1980.

Hardin, G. The tragedy of the commons. *Science*, 1968, *162*, 1243–1248.

Hardin, G., & Baden, J. *Managing the commons.* San Francisco: W. H. Freeman, 1977.

Jessor, R. The perceived environment and the study of adolescent problem behavior. In D. Magnusson (Ed.), *The situation: An interactional prespective.* Hillsdale, N.J.: Lawrence Erlbaum Associates, 1982.

Platt, J. Social traps. *American Psychologist*, 1973, *28*, 641–651.

Price, R. H. Risky situations. In D. Magnusson (Ed.), *The situation: An interactional perspective.* Hillsdale, N.J.: Lawrence Erlbaum Associates, 1982.

Rothman, J., Erlich, J. L., & Teresa, J. G. *Promoting innovation and change in organizations and communities.* New York: Wiley, 1976.

Sarason, S. B. The nature of problem solving in social action. *American Psychologist*, 1978, *33*, 370-380.

Schelling, T. The ecology of micromotives. *Public Interest*, 1971, *25*, 61-98.

Thomas, L. Unacceptable damage. *New York Review of Books*, September 24, 1981, 3.

9. Putting Situations in Their Place*

DAVID CANTER
University of Surrey

A ROLE FOR THE PHYSICAL CONTEXT

We take for granted in our daily lives that human beings have a physical existence and require such environmental resources as space, heat, and light for their social interactions and individual activities. The scale of resources society assigns to the physical environment is illustrated, for example, by the fact that in most countries the building industry, which provides these facilities, is usually a major industry. Furthermore, we expect any account of the social activities in a little-known culture, either a popular account through the media or a learned one from an anthropologist, to provide some information on the physical environment, architecture, and objects of that culture.

The well-established discipline of archaeology, which studies social processes, is heavily based on a culture's physical artifacts—its deserted monuments, pottery shards, ground plans, and the like. Yet it would be hard to demonstrate that archaeology is less scientific than psychology or that its insights into the human condition are less valid. History books and museums, weekly magazines and daily papers, novels and films all describe and explain the physical context in which human activities occur. For example, in the opening paragraph of *Time Regained*, Proust (1957) describes in detail the curtains in the room in which his central character finds himself, contrasting them with the decorations in other rooms he has known. Yet Proust's interests and purposes in writing are as abstract as those of any psychologist. He is not concerned simply with external objectivity, but with human experience and the social interactions of which it is composed.

The reasons for changing and developing the physical surroundings, as well as for describing the physical context of human activities, go beyond the merely functional. In other words, the role the physical environment plays in human experience, how it contributes to social interactions and ways of life, is a dominant reason for popular concern with it. To survive, human beings must be warm and dry and have a place to sleep; it is also clear that for at least the last 10,000 years, and possibly longer (Preziosi 1979), these minimum functional require-ments have been overlaid by many other roles, both psychological and social, for the physical surroundings.

As part of the attempt to understand the role physical environ-ment plays in social behavior the cross-disciplinary subdiscipline of environmental psychology has, in recent years, brought together psychologists, geographers, sociologists, architects, planners, and others (see Canter and Craik 1981 and Russell and Ward 1982 for recent reviews). It is surprising that the emergence of environmental psychology is such a recent development but possibly more surpris-ing that its links to activities in other areas of social psychology have been so tenuous (as Spencer 1981a discussed). The time is ripe for developing more effective links between the social and the environ-mental perspectives within psychology, so both can benefit from, as well as contribute to, understanding the significance of our phys-ical surroundings. Thus, this chapter explores some bridges made possible by recent developments in both social and environmental psychology.

Until recently, despite the high probability of the social psycho-logical significance of the physical surroundings, as revealed by both popular accounts and other social sciences (see, for example, Michelson 1970; Knox 1975; Jackle et al. 1976; Rapoport 1977), neither social psychology nor most other areas of psychology successfully accom-modated what Margulis (1980) called "the objective physical environ-ment" into their theoretical formulation. Margulis argued, for example, in reviewing learning theory, personality theory, social psychological theory, and perceptual theory, that "in general the objective environ-ment in psychological theory has a null status." He argued that until recently, even perceptual theory presented a view of perception that "mirrored the internal world of values." So that "psychologists, as a rule, have favoured points of view that stress what is inside the head, not what the head is inside of."

Even within environmental psychology, authors noted that the physical surroundings are often given only a minimal role in the issues studied. The symposium at the APA convention from which Margulis is quoted explored this weakness in environmental psychology. Archea (1977), in discussing privacy studies, made the same point: "The en-vironment presented in this literature tends to lack enduring properties which set it apart from the behaviour to which it is presumably re-lated" (117). It is against this background that social psychologists have directed little attention to the role of the physical surroundings (Spencer 1981b).

The Sins of the Forefathers

How, then, did social scientists get into this situation in which many around us appear to notice a physical environment but we have difficulty talking about it? Can the emerging situational approach help us out of this situation?

One answer suggests that, almost like the biblical curse, the sins of the forefathers are being visited on their grandchildren. This curse, stemming from the laboratory tradition, has been transmitted to many environmental psychologists who have tried to shake off that tradition; there is a danger that it is finding its way into studies of situations.

When psychologists in general, and social psychologists in particular, embraced the experimental laboratory approach, they also adopted the view that the laboratory is a neutral setting, playing no part in the processes to be studied. Within the laboratory framework, the actual laboratory itself—its size, shape, color, location, and so on— is deemed to play no role in the experimental processes. Thus, the literature of laboratory psychology did not develop a language for describing (or a set of ways of thinking about) the physical setting's role in the processes being studied.

By the time psychologists concerned with the environment dragged their studies out of the laboratory (if not into the open air, at least to the office down the corridor), a set of problems and a language of study had been developed for discussing psychological issues. The new breed were stuck with attitudes, personalities, perceptions and the like, both literally and conceptually. They were stuck with thinking of the environment as another set of variables to be manipulated or controlled, variables they thought happened to be difficult to deal with in the laboratory.

There thus first emerged ecological psychologists, led by Barker (1968). Environmental psychologists such as Craik (1970) and Proshansky (1970) then tried to understand human activities in their naturally occurring contexts and the role the environment might play in those activities; but they had to draw heavily on conceptual tools from the disciplines from which they were trying to break away.

Barker (1965) observed children's behavior, profoundly aware of the artificiality of the operant traditions then current. Within the accepted behavorist perspective on the nature of scientific psychology, he studied what children did in their natural habitats. The experimenter thus had a minimal effect on what was being studied. Barker believed any overt interaction between psychologist and subject, such as asking questions, would contaminate results. Barker and his colleagues (1978), as a consequence, restricted their activities to observing behavior in situ. Yet they were apparently unaware that this fear of contamination from unwanted interactions had driven psychologists into the laboratory in the first place. Thus, Barker, his associates, and students shared with laboratory-based psychologists a narrow focus on what was to be studied and on tactics considered appropriate for such studies.

Of course, not all of Barker's students or their students were so orthodox. Recent developments in the approach have introduced questionnaire and other procedures less focused on observations (Wicker 1979; Bechtel 1982). Even with these developments, however, Barker's ecological psychology still remains isolated from broader ecological perspectives within the social sciences at large (see, e.g., Richerson and McEvoy 1976) because its conceptual tools are so restricted to the behaviorist tradition.

Unlike Barker, Craik (1976) was motivated to environmental concerns by what he saw as the strengths of existing approaches within psychology and their potential for use in the untried realm of the physical surroundings. In particular, he saw the study of the environment as a development in personality measurement and developed scales for carrying out environmental assessment and inventories for distinguishing between people in their environmental responses. Craik (1981) described environmental psychology as "the invasion of an array of relatively distinct and mature research traditions, currently viable within scientific psychology, into the domain of person-environment relations." Although Craik's formulations went beyond Barker's by including the subject's descriptions of their environmental experiences, he still focused on "what is inside the head, not what the head is inside of."

Neither Barker nor Craik's influential writings nor the writings of many other early environmental psychologists (cf. Stokols 1978) described actual physical settings. Proshansky (1970) made the important contribution of pointing to the need actually to map places and the behavior within them if they were to be understood. The book of readings he and his colleagues produced was one of the first to include plans and axonometric drawings of buildings as well as photographs of actual settings. But this innovation, although frequently quoted, has yet to be fully integrated into the mainstream of environmental psychology research. For example, the epitome of Proshansky's approach as demonstrated in the detailed study carried out by his colleagues finds only few parallels in other research (Richer 1979; Canter 1972; Hart 1979).

A number of people active in environmental psychology for some time have questioned the initial bases of their activities. Sommer (1974), for example, questioned the practical value of the notion of "personal space." Wohlwill (1973) asked whether the environment is in the head. Only a few psychologists looked directly at the role the physical environment in all its shapes and forms plays in human experience. This has meant that the applicability gap perceived to exist between designers and researchers is still an issue for discussion (Hill 1979) and that some psychologists are not convinced that environmental psychology has any future (Taylor 1980).

The consequence of this state in environmental psychology is now beginning to leave its mark as other developments in psychology turn to this new field for assistance. A number of developments within social psychology now encourage textbook writers to include at least a section on environmental psychology. Yet it is understandable that their view of environmental psychology, based almost inevitably on its early faltering steps, should be so uninspiring. Thus, recently Argyle et al. (1981) characterized environmental psychologists as having "a behaviouristic approach to experimentation," as being "closely aligned to the pure social learning theory position, which holds that individual difference variables are a function of the environment" and are underplaying "the role of the subject, both in selecting, avoiding, negotiating or defining social situations" (23). These weaknesses are true of some work of some environmental psychologists, but this is not their fault. They have drawn on the same sources as other psychologists and fallen into the same traps.

The reason these pitfalls are so important here is that if social psychologists buy back from environmental psychologists the concepts and procedures they bought from social and experimental psychologists a generation earlier, the same problems are likely to be recycled under a different label. Thus, in their recent overview of social situations, Argyle and his colleagues make the confusion of devoting a chapter to "environmental setting." The opening sentence of that chapter refers to the physical environment as a "feature of situations." They thus get caught in the confusion referred to earlier, of dealing with the physical environment as another set of variables to be considered in a situation, rather than recognizing that human beings inevitably have a physical presence and that the physical must therefore be an integral component of any situation, not simply a cause of, or an effect produced by behavior.

Of course, the integral, systemic nature of the physical environment's contribution is implicit in the assertion by Argyle and his colleagues that transactions with the surroundings are stimulated as much by the individual as by the surroundings. This was also argued by Proshansky and his colleagues (1970) and enshrined in the book *Environmental Interaction* in which Canter and Stringer (1975) developed a similar argument. Furthermore, by pointing out, as Argyle et al. did, that the physical surroundings often reflect the goals of the users of those settings, they showed that human actions must play a more fundamentally causal role than the physical variables themselves. By emphasizing human agency rather than responses to environmental stimuli, the starting point for any activity is looked for in the actions of people.

But again the process is set in motion whereby the physical nature of our existence is lost sight of and processes within the individual again become superordinate.

The problem here is a profound philosophical one that has, like most problems in philosophy, been debated at least since Plato's time. In essence, if a dualist distinction is proposed between the physical and the psychological aspects of reality, then it is difficult to show how or where these dual realms of existence can affect each other. Any causal link between subjective and objective reality requires their coming into contact with each other. But how can they do that if they are distinct aspects of existence? On the other hand, if we take our own experience as paramount, recognizing the physical world as a product of our own perceptions and cognitions, then it is difficult to accept that modifications of those surroundings can be of any substantial consequence.

This summary of the epistemological questions central to exploring the psychological significance of the physical environment does not begin to do justice to the subtleties and complexities of more than 2,000 years of philosophical debate and the vast libraries exploring these themes. The reader wishing a further understanding of this debate should read a classic introductory text such as Russell (1927) or a more recent review such as Ayer (1982), or Pirsig's more popular account (1974), or even the script of *Jumpers* (Stoppard 1972). Within the area of environmental research, Hillier and Leaman (1973) and more recently Teymur (1981) argued in some detail that the lack of philosophical clarity makes the bridge between psychology and the physical environment so difficult to build.

The importance of this debate can be gauged from two conflicting facts. On the one hand, as noted, most societies assign a lot of their resources to shaping the physical surroundings. Many different professional groups, architecture, interior design, planning, and so on, have been established to create and manage these physical resources. On the other hand, the few psychologists concerned with the human consequences of the physical surroundings have had difficulty in establishing any clear, direct causal effects of the physical environment on behavior. This has been true since the days of the Hawthorne investigations (Roethlisberger and Dickson 1939).

Of course, preferences and differences in evaluative descriptions of environments can be readily established (e.g., Nasar 1981; Espe 1981), and studies of differences between groups in their reactions to the surroundings are frequently published (e.g., Webley 1981; Schroeder 1981). However, reports of the direct effects of the physical environment on human behavior are rare, and those published tend to be in the psychological domain (e.g., Hawkins 1981; Rohles and Munson 1981). This lack of support for a dualist perspective is also found when attempts are made to act on the findings of studies of the physical surroundings. As Bechtel (1980) has shown from a major review of environmental evaluations, they do not connect with the issues confronting decision makers and rarely lead to implementation.

There is thus growing evidence that as long as the human and the physical are treated as separate realms of discourse and brought together only at a notional level through general models of interaction, psychologists will continue to be caught in the various cul-de-sacs of dualism. They will continue to attempt to get out of these awkward situations by studies focusing on the human components, preferences, individual differences, conceptualizations, expectations, and the like, without connecting directly with the physical aspects of experience and with a consequent weakness of potential for application. These difficulties exist in any psychology still struggling with the remnants of the dualist framework of stimulus and response. It follows that they are central to the attempts of social and environmental psychologists to incorporate the physical surroundings into their theoretical formulations.

THE CONCEPT OF PLACE

A brief review of the recent history of our understanding of the environment's role in social behavior provides four points on which to build the foundations of bridges between social and environmental psychology.

1. There is a prima facie case for the relevance of the physical surroundings to social behavior.
2. Both social and environmental psychology have had difficulty accommodating physical variables directly into their theoretical formulations.
3. The difficulty of integrating physical variables into environmentally oriented studies has its roots in part in the experimental laboratory tradition and the epistemological dualism typically assumed within that tradition.
4. As Argyle et al. (1981) pointed out, many environmental studies, especially in North America, have been in the behaviorist tradition. People's goals, objectives, or reasons for being in any particular location are not normally considered.

Following from these four points, I propose to identify units of environmental experience for which some people use the term *place*.

The first detailed formulation of *place* as a technical term describing an approach to located action was detailed in Canter (1977). This approach has many general parallels to the writings of Tuan (1977) and

Relph (1979) and other geographers (e.g., Buttimer and Seamon 1980; Seamon 1979), but there are some important differences in emphasis. The most fruitful way to think of places in a psychological framework is as a quanta of experience. As in physics, the smallest units of energy normally available are quanta of energy, and all energy can usually be released only in multiples of these quanta; it is proposed there are similarities in human experience. We think of ourselves as being in one place or another. A distinct locational component to experience is always present.

However, an immediate caution is necessary—the parallels with physics are not precise. The molecules of chemistry have some properties this theory assigns to places. In other words, components of places can readily combine with each other to form new quanta of experience. Similarly, attention can be directed to larger or smaller place scales. We can focus our experience on big molecules or small ones; a city can be a place psychologically just as much as a corner of a room can.

Places, then, are the major building blocks for understanding human actions in their naturally occurring context. Both behavior settings and situations occur within places. One place may house many of Barker's behavioral settings or Argyle's situations, at the same or different times. It must be emphasized, though, that places are part of experience. They cannot be specified independently of the people experiencing them. The central postulates are that people always situate their actions in a specifiable place and that the nature of the place so specified is an important ingredient in understanding human actions and experience. One goal for any science of situated human action is classifying the places in which those actions occur.

How, then, are we to describe and classify places? Again, a clue can be found in chemistry. Consider the analogy of elements and how they are classified and described. Distinct elements can, of course, be named for their special properties (for example, hydrogen was so named by Lavoisier because it was seen as a maker of water). In the same way, if we have evidence for their distinctness we can specify places such as bedrooms, park benches, hospitals, or inner cities. Like the early chemists, we may often confuse similar places and not distinguish different ones in our labeling. But descriptions are the key to any future improvement of labeling.

In chemistry, the growth in understanding of the nature of atomic weight as a crucial descriptor of elements helped stabilize the classification system. For places, it is proposed that three sets of properties are the key to their distinctness. Taken together, these sets describe much of what is psychologically significant about a place. They are not variables to be dealt with independently and intercorrelated but aspects of places to be explored.

The three constituents of places are:

1. The activities understood to occur at a location and the reasons for them.
2. The evaluative conceptualizations that are held of the occurrence of those activities.
3. The physical properties of the place as they are evaluated in relation to the activities.

Let me emphasize again that places can be readily distinguished from behavior settings and situations. Unlike behavior settings, places a) are not created by the investigator on the basis of observing behavior and b) have distinct evaluative and physical components. Unlike situations, at least as identified by Argyle and his colleagues (1981), places have a distinct enduring existence as well as being inevitably intertwined with the location's physical properties.

Some of the best examples of place descriptions are in the work of novelists rather than scientists. Reference has been made to Proust; at the other end of the writing spectrum, a delightful example of a place description is in the closing chapter of Milne's *The House at Pooh Corner.*

> They walked on, thinking of This and That, and by-and-by they came to an enchanted place on the very top of the Forest called Galleons Lap, which is sixty-something trees in a circle; and Christopher Robin knew that it was enchanted because nobody had ever been able to count whether it was sixty-three or sixty-four, not even when he tied a piece of string round each tree after he had counted it. Being enchanted, its floor was not like the floor of the Forest, gorse and bracken and heather, but close-set grass, quiet and smooth and green. It was the only place in the Forest where you could sit down carelessly, without getting up again almost at once and looking for somewhere else. Sitting there you could see the whole world spread out until it reached the sky, and whatever there was all the world over was with them in Galleons Lap. (Milne 1928, 169–172)

An analysis of Milne's description of Galleons Lap shows that:

1. It gives pointers to the direct experience of the place's structure and location. The position of Galleons Lap in the forest, the texture of the floor, and even the experience of so many trees that a six-year-old cannot possibly hope to count them accurately all highlight the setting's physical aspects characterizing the experience of it.
2. It provides reference to the activities associated with the place. It is a comfortable place to sit during a walk in the forest and to contemplate the world.

3. It gives an account of the feelings and conceptions associated with the place. It is enchanted and quiet and a place where "all the world over" is with you.

These constituents have been isolated for identification under three broad headings here, but the experience of the place clearly is a unique blend of them all. Galleons Lap as a place can be seen as a system containing the physical location "at the very top of the Forest," which is thought of as being "enchanted" and where it is possible to indulge in the activity of "sitting down carelessly." For study and analysis, it is necessary to divide the places' components into their constituent parts, but the essence of the argument is that they are always components of an integrated system.

It is thus always possible, in literature, at least, to re-create one, or possibly two, components of a place from others specified. For example, Drabble's (1979) book on landscape in literature is about the conceptions and evaluations associated with particular ways of describing landscapes and how these conceptions in their turn are a function of the uses of and culturally embedded approaches to thinking about and experiencing landscape.

Girouard (1978), an architectural historian, shows that the physical form of English country houses and their changes from the sixteenth century to the present can only be understood as part of changes in the pattern of activities in the house and the changing symbolic qualities important to associate with those activities. For example, Girouard argues that one of the strongest influences leading to design changes in English country houses was the increasing gap between the upper and lower strata in society, accentuated by the disappearance of the intermediate ranks who no longer needed to put themselves under the protection of the great by entering their service.

The large baronial halls of medieval times, in which all members of a vast household ate together, gave way to quarters associated with each social stratum in the household. The location, style, and furnishing of each section of the house responded as much to what went on in those places as to what was believed to be the appropriate symbolic representation of their place in the household. The size and pretensions of the houses overall were "an accurate index of the ambitions—or lack of them—of their owners."

Thus, together with the changes in the society's structure and in people's expectations of their physical surroundings are parallel changes in the physical forms housing social behavior. But note that the parallels between the physical components of the English country house and its behavioral components would not be possible, at any time, were it not for the distinct roles existing in a household and the social norms and rules guiding who does what where. The influence of role differences and guiding rules is not limited to historic houses. Ellis (1982), for instance, showed that these social processes can be found in controlling the use of public spaces on council housing (publicly owned) estates. They provide a basis for understanding how places come into being and change.

PLACE ROLES AND RULES

Literary and historical illustrations, by their nature, do not provide any specific indications as to what psychological processes generate and maintain the experience of places. Some powerful roots in psychological theory do clarify how places form units of experience.

The notion that people can cope with their life experiences insofar as they can develop an articulated structure for conceptualizing those experiences has origins in Mead (1967) and has since been elaborated by many authors (e.g., Brittan 1973). For psychologists, the stimulus of Kelly's (1955) Personal Construct Theory provided the impetus for harnessing this model to explain social behavior. Quarter of a century after Kelly's major publication, it is still instructive to read. His statement of the communality and sociality corollaries of his theory gives direct understanding of how the personal experience of places can still be part of something as public and socially shared as the physical environment.

In his communality corollary, Kelly states that the similarity of the psychological processes of any two people is a function of how similar their construction of experience is. It follows that if two people expect the same relationships between physical and social events (construing their experience of these events in a similar way), then the meaning to them of that combination of events will be similar. The sociality corollary emphasizes that the possibility of one person's playing a role in the social processes of any other person derives from the first person's ability to construe the construction processes of the other person.

Thus, two people must realize that they expect the same associations between physical and social events for them to be able to use a place in relation to each other. If a lecturer sits at the back of the lecture hall anticipating that the students will sit on their desks and face him, then until they share an understanding of his conceptualization of the place they will not be able to use it appropriately. It follows from the sociality corollary that places are shared aspects of experience. They are components of our conceptual systems deriving validity from their similarity to those of other people who experience the same places. This is how it is possible for places to be part of public discourse and awareness yet essentially components of individual, personal conceptual systems.

Although personal construct theory provides a useful starting point for understanding places, it still relies on the relatively primitive mechanisms of people recognizing associations between the constituents of places in order to build up a conceptualization of those places. Primitive though it is, this lays the framework for a powerful self-fulfilling prophecy. To use any place, an individual must be aware of the pattern of activities that might be expected in that location and of how satisfactory those activities are likely to be. The person is thus likely to use the place in accordance with those expectations, thereby creating the basis for others to recognize and support the expectations the individual had. However, if this were the only mechanism available for developing conceptualizations and the related actions of places, then our experience would be hard and painfully won and would not be subject to the changes that are apparent.

The elaboration of these primitive processes comes fruitfully from another aspect of Kelly's theory that evolved within the framework of the ethogenic approach as espoused by Harré (1979).

This approach recognizes the significance of people's goals, or purposes. Two consequences of taking a goal orientation have implications for understanding place experience, as they do for studying situations in general. One is that the people's roles in any setting will influence how they conceptualize that setting. The other consequence is that systems of social rules will be drawn on and transmitted so the use of places can be an effective part of the society's fabric. Whether an open area is regarded as a public path or a private garden is in part determined by the accepted rules governing that place and the ease with which the people who experience that place can recognize or learn those rules (cf. Ellis 1982).

The Stability of Place Rules

The existence of socially negotiated expectations of what happens in places leads to the predictions that relatively stable rules of place use can be identified, that these rules will relate to the place users' interpretation of the physical clues a place provides of its use. Such predictions are, of course, open to empirical test. Furthermore, only through empirical investigation can the particular existing place rules be identified and classified.

With the enhanced hindsight this view of place provides, we see that many empirical studies often presented under the heading personal space are, in fact, demonstrations of the rules associated with particular places. Much relevant empirical evidence in the pioneering reports of such studies by Sommer (1969) noted how regularly the sequence of seat selection at library tables was governed by rules of maximizing distance and minimizing potential eye contact. Other studies, such as Delong's (1970) account of seating in a committee room, also shows place rules clearly in operation. Rosengren and DeVault's (1963) fascinating account of how a mother-to-be in a maternity hospital is treated differently as she moves closer to the delivery room also clearly shows how consistent rules of social interaction relate directly to physical location and its associated design and layout.

However, these studies, evolving within the social psychological framework, pay little attention to the salient features of the physical surroundings in which the behavior being studied actually occurs. We are told little of the location, shape, or size of the library tables, or of the physical details in many other studies of personal space. Even Altman (1975), in his later summary of these and related studies, with an eye to the significance of the physical surroundings, finds it difficult to indicate how the surroundings actually contribute to the development and reflection of role differences and the establishment of rules of place. Intriguing studies by Sommer et al. (1981) have begun to rectify this weakness. He noted how the physical structure and organization of food shopping facilities, notably supermarkets and farmer's markets, create a context where different social interaction patterns are expected both among customers and between customers and the sales people.

These empirical studies reveal the existence of a rich set of place rules, but research is needed to address this issue more directly. Such research need not be only anthropological; various forms of field experiment are also possible. One example of such a study going further to show how the rules of a place can be established and modified in relation to physical form can be drawn from a study presented in detail in Canter and Kenny (1975, 152-154).

In that study, students were invited into a lecture room in which chairs were arranged in rows. As the students entered, a lecturer standing at the front of the room, with his back near the wall, gave them a questionnaire and asked them to sit down and take part in an experiment. A second group of students were invited in to the room; this time, the lecturer was standing near the front row of desks. In both cases, the students sat at about the same distance from where the lecturer was standing. They sat further back in the lecture room when he was standing near the front rows of seats than when he was standing a few feet away from those seats. Many readers have experienced the phenomenon especially with students in their first year at college. They use the room layout to distance themselves both physically and metaphorically from what they presumably find as a threatening prospect for formal interaction.

Particularly interesting about this study of student seat selection, beyond the distancing mechanism, was that the investigator went on to explore the consequences of altering the room's furniture arrangement. The study was repeated with the chairs arranged in a semi-circle. In this case, the lecturer's location did not have any measurable effect on the seats the group chose. In other words, the mechanism seemingly operating here was that what students believed would occur in the room led them to apply an appropriate set of rules to guide their use of space, in accordance with what they wished to achieve in the room. When they thought the activity was a formal one in which they could, in a sense, get away from the lecturer, they tried to optimize their distance from him. When they saw from the layout of the furniture that a more informal interaction was expected, they used different principles to choose seats.

Note that the change in the physical structure did not directly effect behavior. A more subtle role must be conceived for the physical surroundings than as a mere stimulus. The most interesting findings here are how the interaction between the use of the space by a person in one role group and the layout of that space is related to the use of the space by other role groups.

Unfortunately, like so many intriguing studies in psychology, no replications have been published. Other parallel studies in different contexts suggest themselves. For example, how does a customer act if a bank manager calls him or her into the office (or to his or her desk) as opposed to getting up to lead the customer over. How do rowdy crowds behave in response to different types of movement of groups of police officers when areas have been demarcated for different groups as opposed to when they have not?

The Reliability of Place Rules

One reason for following through on the place approach to situations is to establish a level of analysis of the contexts of human action consistent and stable enough to allow classification. Beyond the evidence that the rules for actions in places are stable, it is necessary to show they do not change except in relation to properties of the use of places themselves. This proposition can have remarkable implications, many of a practical consequence. The strongest example can be derived from looking at what happens in a building on fire. Even in extreme circumstances, well-established place-related rules continued to operate (cf. studies reviewed in Canter 1980).

The most dramatic example is the fire at the Kentucky Supper Club in which more than a hundred people died (Best 1977). While this fire was in progress, waitresses showed patrons out of the building. Later interviews revealed that many waitresses only showed out people sitting at their stations. Patrons unlucky enough to be at a table where the waitress was trapped by smoke sat as smoke filled the room, while people at the next table had been shown out by their waitress.

At a more general level, studies by Canter et al. (1980) of behavior in fires revealed a consistent difference in the sequence of actions of husbands when compared with wives. Typically, the husband attempts to fight or investigate the fire, whereas the wife is more likely to inform others and get away from the fire. These different patterns clearly relate to the different role/rule structures within the average household. They have the consequence that if anybody is likely to get hurt in a fire through inappropriate actions, it is the husband rather than the wife. On the other hand, studies in hospitals, where the nursing staff is predominantly female, do not reveal a sex bias in the activities carried out in a fire. Differences relate closely to a person's position in the hierarchy and how that hierarchy normally functions in relation to locations within the hospital.

The Contribution of the Physical Component of Places

The role/rule perspective on places and their experience explains why it is difficult to establish direct and simple effects of the physical environment on behavior. If the physical component reflects, facilitates, or inhibits the evolution of rules for the differential pattern of place uses by varying role groups, then changes in the role structure or developments in the rule system would produce different patterns of place use in the same places. But this does not mean that the physical form of place is irrelevant. The reverse is true; it always plays a role in the definition and evolution of a place. Transposing role/rule relationships to new physical forms is likely to start a process resulting in a different pattern of role/rule relationships.

It follows that challenges to the researcher are to a) identify consistent place-related rules, b) classify the varieties of places commonly occurring and c) establish the roles that the components of places play in developing place use and place experience. We now turn to the first of these challenges, taking as an example a commonly experienced place—the home.

PLACES IN THE HOME

In considering the home, one question is whether the unit of place experience described as a home can be shown to have in it a patterned structure of place use reflecting the various rules constituting living in a house or apartment. Canter and Lee's (1974) study provides a useful basis for this exploration. It used data from Japanese high-rise apartments and thus is of interest because the identification of rules is often easier for a culture obviously different from that of the researcher.

The perception of patterns in a foreign setting is less likely to be dulled by familiarity.

Japanese Houses

Western visitors are often told that Japanese households are completely flexible—beds can be taken from cupboards and rolled out on floors; low, portable dining tables can be moved into a corner. Thus, no rules as to which space be used for what purpose seem to apply. As Nishihara (1967) argues:

> The notion of continuous and uninterrupted spatial flow pervades even the storage spaces, which are treated much as the actual living spaces.... Since these interiors conform to a number of needs they actually serve no function at all. When a bed is needed, the Japanese bring it in, and when a table is required, they bring that in too. In other words the Japanese house is functionally flexible.

This view is antithetical to the theory of place use outlined above, so Canter and Lee's (1974) study is instructive. This study used plans of 120 Japanese apartments, with the furniture in the apartment recorded on the plans. By content analyzing the furniture, it was possible to see which pieces of furniture were likely to be found together in the same room across the plans.

In effect, two stages in the process are being explored. The first stage assumes that people buy furniture and arrange it in their rooms in accordance with the activities they wish to occur in that room. The second stage assumes that to facilitate activities within a household, it is necessary to avoid housing conflicting activities by designating separate places for incompatible activities. Thus, by looking at the types of furniture grouping it is possible to identify what sorts of conflicts are being avoided and to find out what place rules exist. Put another way, the study allows the listing of patterns of objectives people have in their house; the goals or range of intentions they are striving toward when they move into and furnish a house. This study of Japanese furniture shows, in effect, an archaeological account of the relationships between the activities in the home.

An MDS analysis of the data showed first that some pieces of furniture are more general or possibly flexible in their use. Such furniture as a large Japanese cushion or charcoal brazier have high correlations across all rooms, on average, with all other pieces of furniture, showing that they are not special to any particular locations in the house. On the other hand, some furniture is more specific in its use and more likely to be found in only one location—such as a dining table or a bed. This finding gives a first clue to underlying principles of space use in a Japanese household. Some activities are considered general, open-ended, and compatible with other activities. In contrast, some furniture seems specific in the activities associated with it.

This concept of an activity's specificity has many implications for looking at situations. Some situations have clear rules; other situations have only loose, general rules. It seems probable that people learn to cope with these different sorts of situations in different ways.

Looking at the more specific situations, using room labels for simplicity, a living room, kitchen, bedroom, study, and dining room emerge from the results. It is possible also to recognize a distinction within the kitchen of a utility room and a cooking facility. In the study area, desk-related activities can be distinguished from activities more related to recreation and music.

Nishihara's statements are therefore not found to have empirical support when modern Japanese apartments are used to generate data. His ideas are thus either an abstraction based on general ways of thinking about Japanese domestic life or relate only to special houses used by the rich (or poor) in the past, or both. Also note that although the actual furniture in Japanese houses differs from that in the West, the structure of activities it reveals is recognizable. Can similar patterns be established with studies carried out in Britain? To answer this question, a number of studies have been conducted.

The Structure of Living Room Situations

Tagg (1974) asked undergraduates in Scotland what activities they did in which room in their house. He obtained a similar structure to that found in Japan. In a more recent study, Kimura (1982) looked at English houses. In particular, he became interested in the curious British institution of the living room. He approached 100 households in the Guildford area, gave them a list of activities, and asked how frequently they were likely to occur in their own living rooms. Using the same procedure as for the Japanese data, Kimura found a clear distinction between general activities likely to occur in most living rooms and thus seemingly compatible with other activities and more specific activities likely to differentiate between living rooms. He thus found evidence for a pattern of place rules being used. It was possible to distinguish living rooms on the basis of whether they were more likely to house such activities as eating, or studying, or listening to stereo, or cleaning, or making things.

A generalized schematic representation based on the MDS analyses referred to is presented in Figure 9-1. The basis of this representation is that the closer together any two activities are in the diagram, the more likely are they to occur in the same locations; that is, the more compatible are their place rules. The diagram's circular structure is a product of the essentially qualitative distinction between the activities

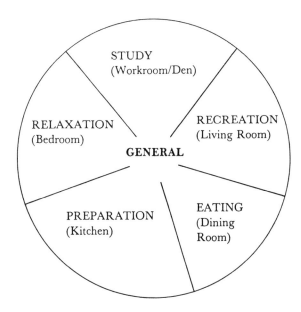

Figure 9-1. Schematic Representation of Domestic Activities and Their Place Compatibilities, Derived from MDS Analyses

rather than a distinction based on quantitative dimensions. Figure 9-1 thus parallels such representations as Munsell's color system (see, e.g., Boyce 1981, 12) in which hues of colors form a circle going through blue, purple, red, yellow, green, and back to blue. In Munsell's circular representation, the direction from the center of the circle to its periphery represents increase in chroma, the grey combination of all colors being at the center and the most colorful colors at the edge. In the schematic representation of activity compatibilities in Figure 9-1, the general activities that can occur anywhere are at the center and the highly place specific activities are around the circumference of the circle.

The schematic summary of the ways in which activities are distinguished from each other by rules relating to where they are likely to occur has interesting implications for which combinations of activities are most feasible. Activities close together in the diagram are potentially more place compatible than are those further apart. For example, certain arrangements can be easily accommodated—the living/dining room; the study/living room; the study/bedroom. The further away any two situations are from each other in this model, the more likely they are to be difficult to coalesce. It can thus be hypothesized that sleeping and eating or studying and cooking in the same space are more likely to be problematic. These hypotheses are open to direct empirical test.

The schematic diagram has other uses, especially when seen as a summary model of a social system. For example, does the nature of the general activities in the center change across cultures? Are there special patterns of coping when the notionally incompatible activities are forced together? How do participants' understanding of the physical structure of place-specific activities shape their use of spaces? One problem now is to find situations in which the model does not hold; these are likely to be situations governed by different rule structures.

THE STRUCTURE OF BUILDING INTERPRETATIONS

Similarities between the structure of place rules have been found for living rooms, apartments, and houses. The question therefore follows whether differences at the scale of the buildings within a city also relate to a general conceptual structure, and secondly, whether this structure bears any relationship to that found for domestic experiences. It can be argued that buildings, like rooms in a house, can accommodate combinations of some activities more readily than others. A school may not be expected to house activities associated with blocks of apartments, whereas it might be expected that offices and factories were similar to each other. One important issue emerging here is whether building designs represent the range of compatibilities of activities the buildings accommodate. Do architects make a university look more like an office block than a school because they are referring to a structured relationship between the rules governing the use of those places?

One direct way to study this is to show people pictures of buildings and to ask them what the buildings are and then to derive correlations from the resulting agreements and disagreements. In other words, illustrations typically thought to represent similar types of buildings can be placed together in some multidimensional space. Young (1978) carried out such a study in Britain, with a number of refinements; complementary yet independent studies were carried out by Groat (1982) in California and by Krampen (1979) in Germany. These studies reveal an organized, structured relationships between what buildings look like and the types of activities and institutions those buildings are expected to house. In effect, these studies show that a building's physical form can indicate the type of role/rule structures governing the patterns of behavior in the building.

A clear illustration of how the interpretation of buildings has a coherent structure can be derived from Young's (1978) study. He asked people to produce drawings representing each of six typical types of buildings. He then showed these drawings to another group and asked them to guess which types of buildings they were. Each drawing was scored on the basis of the accuracy with which people recognized its creator's intentions. The scores were used to produce an MDS configuration, as shown in Figure 9-2. In Figure 9-2, sketches of representative drawings have been placed at points in the two-dimensional, computer-generated space. In the original computer printout, every drawing was represented by a number. However, the results are more obvious when a sample of the numbers are represented by drawings. As in other MDS diagrams, the closer together any two drawings are, the more similar are they. In this case, the more similar are the assignment of building types to them by the respondents.

Figure 9-2 thus reveals a pattern of expectation of the situations that buildings may house. The pattern is reflected in the physical form those buildings take. Like the domestic activities in Figure 9-1, a qualitative order is also apparent in Figure 9-2, from houses to offices to factories to schools to churches and back to houses. Young used only these six building types in his study so it is an open question as to the location of such other places as hospitals, shops, traffic terminals, and so on. Note, however, that in using the same six building types in Germany, Krampen (1979) produced a similar structure. The only difference was that schools were closer to offices than to factories, presumably indicating something about cross-national differences in attitudes to education.

A question for future research is whether the structure emerging from the studies of buildings bears any relationships to the patterns found for room activities. Two general hypotheses underlie this question:

1. Does the central focus of each pattern of activities in a place relate to each component of the overall structure of building types?

2. Does the pattern of building types reflect, or parallel, the pattern of activities in the home?

Support for each hypothesis would have wide-ranging implications for both theory and practice.

THE EXPERIENCE OF PLACE

Activities and physical description are only two components of places. A third component can be described as the feelings a person has about a place. The most direct way this can be articulated is to ask a person how satisfactory a place is, the extent to which he or she is attracted toward it. Despite the limitations to what people can put into words, either due to their ability to verbalize their reactions or their willingness to publicize private feelings, using language to describe places is such a developed activity in our culture (as revealed by earlier reference to Proust, Drabble, and Milne), that asking people about their delight or distaste with particular places is often the most fruitful starting point

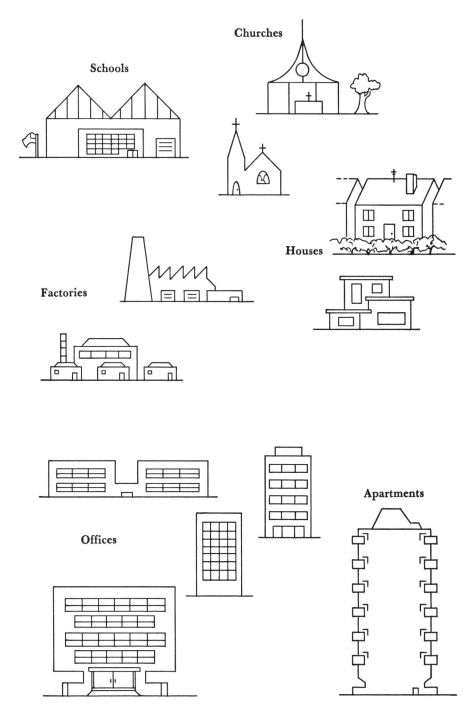

Figure 9–2. Representation of MDS Analysis of Building Types (after Young 1978)

for exploring the success or failure of place uses or place forms. But even if a nondirective, less interventionist approach is taken to place evaluation, as in Bechtel's (1982) ecological explorations, or the studies of room furniture discussed earlier, the affective component of place experience is still implicit.

Place satisfaction provides a valuable key to understanding the structures described so far. The patterns of rules existing for places are rules created to enable people to live a pleasant, acceptable, comfortable existence. If the rules did not facilitiate the satisfactory use of a place, they would not persist. We therefore need to know more about the structure of satisfactions people have with their places because these attitudes are a guide to the motivations leading people to enter into the sorts of informal social negotiations and contracts that make place rules possible. In a sense, any discussion of the social psychological principles making up the structure of people's experiences of places must be complemented by the individual motivational components that provide the organizations of the objectives or intentions people have in using places.

A number of studies carried out within the framework considered here (Kenny and Canter 1981; Canter and Rees 1982) indicated the consistency with which people use the physical surroundings to help them achieve their objectives within that situation. Also consistent is that the core objectives characterizing an individual's interaction pattern in any place are distinct from one place to another. Focal processes thus seem central to place satisfaction. For example, in housing, the general pleasantness and welcomingness of the house frequently enshrined in the quality of the living room appears to be crucial (Canter and Rees 1982). Other facilities, such as the heating system or the amount of space for parking, are ancillary to this core construct. If, on the other hand, a hospital is considered, it is found that the patient-nurse contact, particularly at the bedside, forms the central core for a nurse's satisfaction with a hospital ward (Kenny and Canter 1981).

A second recurrent finding is that the structure of the facilities ancillary to this central core is at least threefold, dealing with:

1. Social issues; in other words, contacts with other people or displays made for public consumption

2. Issues to do with the amount of space available; and to do with

3. Services provided, not necessarily based in one location; the fabric or infrastructure making the place possible.

These aspects of satisfaction with a place imply a model of people as both social and having a physical existence. They must be accommodated in a certain size space with particular properties and a particular environment created by the services. There is thus an implication that people are motivated both by their social existence and their existence as physical objects.

Roles and Satisfaction

If it is accepted that people are part of a social context in which they are trying to achieve acceptable levels of satisfaction by interacting with other people in particular places, then it is clear that their roles in those places and how they interact within them will differ from person to person. It is therefore feasible that the type of satisfaction they will have with a place will differ according to their role in that place.

The term *role* is potentially ambiguous. I have attempted to clarify it by writing about an environmental role (Canter 1977)—the pattern of interactions a person has in any particular place. Elsewhere, I summarized a number of studies clearly showing that the pattern of interactions a person has in a place will relate to his or her place satisfaction (Canter 1979). One study, for example, illustrated the similarity and differences between different male inhabitants of a school who were asked to evaluate that school (Gerngros-Haas 1982). Her results showed that the school parts to which the individual has access or his responsibilities within the school distinguish him from others in terms of his evaluation. Indeed, the more difference between people in their environmental role, the more likely they are to have differing satisfactions with their settings.

What, then, are the implications of role differences in satisfaction for the structures of rules in different places? One type of answer can be drawn from a study by Canter and Walker (1978). In England, Walker interviewed all people involved in creating a public housing estate, asking them what their major concerns about the housing estate were. She then examined the similarities and differences among individuals on the basis of their concerns. Some people were concerned with the building's administration, some with the building fabric itself, and some with it as an aspect of the suburb's housing requirements. People also differed in terms of how much interaction they had with the actual building. Clearly, the rules they emphasized about the housing facility's creation differed because of their different types of interaction with the entity being produced. The whole notion of *housing* meant something different to each role group.

BRIDGING SOCIAL AND ENVIRONMENTAL PSYCHOLOGY

In summary, this chapter argued that both environmental psychology and social psychology have suffered from an inability to accommodate effectively the physical surroundings in their formulations. The developing importance within social psychology of the study of situations, when taken together with the models of place experience presented here, probably provides fruitful bases for developing bridges between social and environmental psychology and, in so doing, provides a more effective role for the physical components of place within social and environmental models.

The experience of place has been characterized as having three integrated components: activities, evaluations, and physical form. The system of experiences of any given place brings these components into interaction with each other because of the rules people recognize for the use of places. These rules are both a function of the role a person has in any given place and are motivated by a person's desire to achieve role-related objectives. The extent to which people feel able to do this is indicated by their evaluation of a place.

The framework outlined here, then, draws attention to the interrelationships between:

1. Rule-guided place use

2. The roles people have in those places

3. Place evaluations

4. The structured meanings of the physical forms of places.

Much empirical and theoretical work must be done to elaborate fully and to clarify this framework, but the consistencies to which it has already pointed are encouraging. To conclude, this chapter considers the basis this framework provides for integrating developments in social and environmental psychology.

Social Skills and Place Experience

Before considering some of the more general theoretical bridges now possible, a more specific link to understanding social skills is of interest. Argyle et al. (1981), in particular, argued that understanding situations has much to offer to social skills training. He makes it clear that being able to perform social skills effectively involves recognizing a particular situation's structure and the roles within it.

One difficulty with a strictly situational approach is that the variability and changes characteristic of situations have led to an inability to provide an acceptable classification scheme for situations. Thus, much social skill training has focused on particular and specific events, such as how to be assertive when told to work during a lunch break, or how to apply for a job on the telephone (cf. Wilkinson and Canter 1982), or how to greet people. Of course, our understanding of social skills has developed rapidly over the last few years, as Trower discussed in chapter 7. Until some superordinate categorization is available of the contexts in which social skills occur, there is the risk that people's training to cope in one place will not necessarily transfer to other places.

It is therefore tempting to ask if the overall structures of places illustrated in Figures 9-1 and 9-2 might provide the basis for classifying the broad types of social skills people must master to survive in society. Indeed, have social skills trainers tended to concentrate on living room skills at the expense of bedroom skills? Or, at a larger scale, have domestic social skills been emphasized to the detriment of social skills in offices or factories?

In raising these questions, it must be emphasized that the integrated systemic nature of our place experience precludes the notion that people are different types of beings in different places. Analogous social and psychological processes run through all place experience. But even at an elementary level, it is apparent that a person's ability to comprehend a place's social structure from its physical form and the location of people within it, as well as to recognize the role possibilities provided by how the space is used, contributes directly to the person's skill in performing effectively in that place.

This chapter suggests two more specific sets of hypotheses beyond the general guidance that might be taken from a place perspective. First, if the qualitative relationships represented in Figures 9-1 and 9-2 are valid, then is the transfer of social skills more effective if the places between which the transfer is made are qualitatively similar? For example, are people who are socially effective in a domestic setting more likely to be effective in an office than in a school? Secondly, are people's skills general or place specific?

Two subsidiary questions arise here. One is whether the development of skills grows from one specific place, such as the home, slowly encompassing all the types of place of which a person gains experience (moving around the periphery of Figure 9-2, say), or whether people develop a general level of social skill that becomes differentiated over time (starting from the middle of the circle). The second subsidiary question is whether there is a radical difference in gaining a command of general social skills (at the center of Figures 9-1 and 9-2) when compared to how people gain a command of place-specific social skills.

Whatever the answers to these questions, and whether the place perspective is shown to be valuable in helping us understand social skills and develop ways of training people in them, it is clear that exploring the possibilities for such links will result in a clarification of both social skills and the psychology of place.

Some Bridges

As recent books have revealed, many students of personality differences now accept that much of human behavior can be explained only if the interaction between a person and the situation in which he or she finds himself or herself is also considered; the P X S debate (Forgas 1979; Ginsburg 1979; Harvey 1981; Krasner 1980; Magnusson 1981). That this development is facilitating the broader uptake of an environmental perspective is shown directly in chapters in these books by researchers recognized in environmental psychology (e.g., Craik 1981; Stokols and Shumaker 1981). This chapter is therefore one of a growing number of bridges and it is therefore probably valuable, finally, to identify the links that the place perspective outlined here appear to offer for future research.

1. *The social texture of places.* In his overview of emerging strategies in social psychology, Ginsburg (1979) emphasized the "meanings of actions, events and settings." Harré (1979) brings this closer to the place perspective by discussing the "social texture of space and time." There thus appears to be a growing acceptance that our experience of the physical world is characterized by the assignment of meanings to locations. These meanings incorporate expectations about role-rule relationships and the resulting pattern of activities. It is also clear that to operate within these places, we must be able to recognize the place rules and roles guiding patterns of place use.

Future research could explore what is expected of different classes of places and how understanding different physical forms contributes to what is expected of various role performances. Further, if the setting appears at odds with the patterns of behavior anticipated for other reasons, what coping strategies do people adopt for dealing with these discrepancies? Stokols's (1979) congruence analysis of stress showed some theoretical developments that may help answer this question.

2. *Place cognition.* Harvey (1981) saw the integration of environmental concepts into many areas of psychology as inextricably linked to understanding cognitive processes. This viewpoint can be supported directly from the environmental psychology literature by how environmental cognition studies played a predominant role in the field's development (Russell and Ward 1982). The place framework adds impetus to this development by highlighting the contribution an understanding of physical form and location makes to understanding the social behavior that physical form houses. If a place always has a social as well as a physical component in cognition, then the student of place experience cannot afford to ignore developments in either social or cognitive psychology.

3. *Place and situation prototypes.* More specifically, the suggestion that places form units of experience has interesting parallels in Nancy Cantor's (Cantor 1982) argument that most people understand behavior by drawing on a categorical structure of situations. In essence, her

argument, drawn from cognitive models in psychology, is that people use prototypes of situations to the extent that a list of consensual situation prototypes can be presented. This suggests two questions in our current framework. Are there identifiable consensual place prototypes? If so, how do they relate to situational prototypes? The question of the structural relationships in each prototype group and between groups is also of interest.

The importance of answering these questions can be gauged from the paradox that she recognizes of people being able to articulate situational prototypes but not appearing to draw on them directly when interpreting others' behavior. Perhaps by changing the level of analysis from situations to places, both in terms of prototypes and evaluated patterns of space use, a coherent perspective complementing her "person-oriented" resolution of the paradox can evolve.

4. *Places and social episodes.* When focusing on behavior patterns in a place, the significance of the sequence and structure of those patterns (their episodic nature) becomes paramount. Forgas (1979) mapped out the issues to consider to understand social episodes. He recognized directly that certain "physical components of the environment have a disproportionally important role in the definition and regulation of the interaction episodes occurring within that milieu" (46). He also saw the environment's symbolic meaning as a major mechanism by which it plays its role. However, he virtually restricted his conceptualization of the physical environment to "physical props and furnishings." He moved from what he called "global environments," such as drug stores or residential treatment institutions, at one scale to white coats or chair arrangements at the other. As a consequence, he incorporated the organizational environment either as the contribution to social episodes from the global scale or as symbolic markers giving information about who is allowed to sit where.

The examples of social episodes in buildings on fire illustrate how Forgas's valuable insights can be extended. It was argued that in a home or a hospital, the pattern of rules as to who should do what where, together with the related demarcation of roles, gave rise to and were facilitated by consistent patterns of place use. Thus, during a fire, the social episodes were a direct product of the existing patterns of place behavior. We must know more, of course, about how place rules and social episodes complement each other. The question of whether different types of place tend to house episodes with different structure is also raised.

In some types of place, the appropriate physical form of a place may directly parallel the structure of its characteristic social episodes. For example, as seen in Rosengren and DeVault's (1963) consideration of an obstetrics hospital, which characteristically houses episodes having a distinct sequential order, it may be that understanding how the physical layout represents and facilitates this sequence helps us understand the stages in the social episodes occurring there.

This overview of a few directions in which bridges between environmental and social psychology can be built by using the place perspective shows that much must be done. Perhaps the strongest motivations for carrying out these tasks are that the curious distinction between environmental and social concerns will cease to exist and that some other divisions in the psychological literature, such as between the social and cognitive areas, may also be challenged.

REFERENCES

Altman, I. *The environment and social behavior.* Monterey, Calif.: Brooks/Cole, 1975.

Archea, J. The place of architectural factors in behavioral theories of privacy. *Journal of Social Issues,* 1977, *33*, 116–137.

Argyle, M., Furnham, A., & Graham, J. A. *Social situations.* Cambridge: Cambridge University Press, 1981.

Ayer, A. J. *Philosophy in the twentieth century.* London: Weidenfeld and Nicholson, 1982.

Barker, R. G. Explorations in ecological psychology. *American Psychologist,* 1965, *20*, 1–14.

Barker, R. B. *Ecological psychology.* Stanford, Calif.: Stanford University Press, 1968.

Barker, R. G., & Associates. *Habitats, environments and human behavior.* London: Jossey-Bass, 1978.

Bechtel, R. B. Contributions of ecological psychology to the evaluation of environments. *International Review of Applied Psychology,* 1980, *31*, 153–168.

Best, R. L. *The Beverley Hills Supper Club Fire.* Washington, D.C.: National Bureau of Standards, 1977.

Boyce, P. R. *Human factors in lighting.* London: Applied Science Publishers, 1981.

Brittan, A. *Meaning and situation.* London: Routledge and Kegan Paul, 1973.

Buttimer, A., & Seamon, D. (Eds.). *The human experience of space and place.* New York: St. Martin's Press, 1980.

Canter, D. Royal Hospital for Sick Children: A psychological analysis. *The Architects' Journal,* 1972, *156*, 525–564.

Canter, D. *The psychology of place.* London: Architectural Press, 1977.

Canter, D. Y à t-il des lois d'interaction environmentales? In J. Simon (Ed.), *Proceedings of 4th IAAP at Louvain-la-Neuve.* Louvain: University Catholic, 1979.

Canter, D., Breaux, J., & Sime, J. *Domestic, multiple occupancy and hospital fires.* In D. Canter (Ed.). Chichester: Wiley, 1980.

Canter, D., & Canter, S. (Eds.). *Designing for therapeutic environments.* Chichester: Wiley, 1979.

Canter, D., & Craik, K. H. Environmental psychology. *Journal of Environmental Psychology*, 1981, *1*, 1–11.

Canter, D., & Kenny, C. The spatial environment. In D. Canter and P. Stringer (Eds.)., *Environmental interaction.* London: Surrey University Press, 1975.

Canter, D., & Lee, K. H. A non-reactive study of room usage in modern Japanese apartments. In D. Canter & T. Lee (Eds.), *Psychology and the built environment.* London: Architectural Press, 1974.

Canter, D., & Rees, K. A multivariate model of housing satisfaction. *International Review of Applied Psychology* 1982, *31*, 185–208.

Canter, D., & Stringer, P. *Environmental interaction.* London: Surrey University Press, 1975.

Cantor, N. Perceptions of situations: Situation prototypes and person-situation prototypes. In D. Magnusson (Ed.), *Toward a psychology of situations: An interactional perspective.* Hillsdale, N.J.: Lawrence Erlbaum Associates, 1982.

Craik, K. H. Environmental psychology. In K. H. Craik et al. (Eds.), *New directions in psychology.* New York: Holt, Rinehart and Winston, 1970.

Craik, K. The personality research paradigm in environmental psychology. In S. Wapner, B. Kaplan, & S. Cohen (Ed.), *Experiencing the Environment.* New York: Plenum, 1976.

Craik, K. H. Environmental assessment and situational analysis. In D. Magnusson (Ed.), *The situation: An interactional perspective.* Hillsdale, N.J.: Lawrence Erlbaum Associates, 1981.

Delong, A. J. Dominance—territorial relations in a small group. *Environment and Behaviour*, 1970, *2*, 179–191.

Drabble, M. *A writer's Britain.* London: Thames and Hudson, 1979.

Ellis, P. Shared outdoor space and shared meaning. *International Review of Applied Psychology*, 1982, *31*, 209–222.

Espe, H. Differences in the perception of national socialist and classicist architecture. *Journal of Environmental Psychology*, 1981, *1*, 33–42.

Forgas, J. P. *Social episodes: The study of interaction routines.* London: Academic Press, 1979.

Ginsburg, G. P. (Ed.). *Emerging strategies in social psychological research.* Chichester, Eng.: Wiley, 1979.

Girouard, M. *Life in the English country house: A social and architectural history.* London: Yale University Press, 1978.

Groat, L. Meaning of post-modern architecture: An examination using the multiple sorting task. *Journal of Environmental Psychology,* 1982, *2,* 3–22.

Harré, R. *Social being.* Oxford: Blackwell, 1979.

Hart, R. *Children's experience of place: A developmental study.* New York: Irvington Press, 1979.

Harvey, J. H. (Ed.). *Cognition, social behavior, and the environment.* Hillsdale, N.J.: Lawrence Erlbaum Associates, 1981.

Hawkins, L. H. The influence of air ions, temperature and humidity on subjective well-being and comfort. *Journal of Environmental Psychology,* 1981, *1,* 279–292.

Hill, M. R. Misunderstanding the goals of science: Myths, reconciliation, and an example. In A. D. Seidel & S. Danford (Eds.), *EDRA 10 proceedings.* Washington, D.C.: EDRA, 1979.

Hillier, W. R. G., & Leaman, A. The man-environment paradigm and its paradoxes. *Architectural Design,* August 1973.

Jakle, J. A., Brunn, S., & Roseman, C. C. *Human spatial behavior: A social geography.* North Scituate, Mass.: Duxbury, 1976.

Kelly, G. A. *The psychology of personal constructs.* New York: Norton, 1955.

Kenny, C., & Canter, D. A facet structure of nurses' evaluations of ward designs. *Journal of Occupational Psychology,* 1981, *54,* 93–108.

Kimura, M. A cross-cultural comparison of living room use and evaluation. Surrey University: Ph.D. Thesis (unpublished), 1982.

Knox, P. L. *Social well-being: A spatial perspective.* London: Oxford University Press, 1975.

Krampen, M. *Meaning in the urban environment.* London: Pion, 1979.

Krasner, L. (Ed.). *Environmental design and human behavior: A psychology of the individual in society.* New York: Pergamon, 1980.

Magnusson, D. (Ed.). *Towards a psychology of situations.* Hillsdale, N.J.: Lawrence Erlbaum Associates, 1981.

Margulis, S. T. An overview of the status of the objective physical environment in psychological theory. Paper presented to APA Convention, Montreal, September 4, in the Symposium *The Status of the Objective, Physical Environment in Environmental Psychology,* 1980.

Mead, G. M. *Mind, self and society.* Chicago: University of Chicago Press, 1967.

Michelson, W. *Man and his urban environment.* Reading, Mass.: Addison-Wesley, 1970.

Milne, A. A. *The house at Pooh Corner.* London: Methuen, 1928.

Nasar, J. L. Visual preferences of elderly public housing residents: Residential street scenes. *Journal of Environmental Psychology,* 1981, *1*, 303–314.

Nishihara, K. *Japanese houses: Patterns for living.* Tokyo: Japan Publications, 1967.

Pirsig, R. M. *Zen and the art of motorcycle maintenance: An enquiry into values.* London: Bodeley Head, 1974.

Proshansky, H. M., Ittelson, W. H., & Rivlin, L. G. (Eds.). *Environmental psychology: Man and his physical setting.* New York: Holt, Rinehart and Winston, 1970.

Proust, M. *Time regained.* London: Chatto and Windus, 1957.

Rapoport, A. *Human aspects of urban form.* Oxford: Pergamon, 1977.

Relph, J. *Place and placelessness.* London: Pion, 1979.

Richer, J. Physical environments for autistic children—four case studies. In D. Canter & S. Canter (Eds.), *Designing for therapeutic environments.* Chichester: Wiley, 1979.

Richerson, P. J., & McEvoy, J. III. (Eds.). *Human ecology: An environmental approach.* North Scituate, Mass: Duxbury, 1976.

Roethlisberger, F. J., & Dickson, W. J. *Management and the worker.* Cambridge, Mass: Harvard University Press, 1939.

Rohles, F. H., & Munson, D. M. Sleep and the sleep environment temperature. *Journal of Environmental Psychology,* 1981, *1*, 207–214.

Rosengren, W. R., & DeVaults, S. The sociology of time and in an obstetrical hospital. In E. Freidson, (Ed.), *The hospital in modern society.* London: The Free Press of Glencoe, 1963.

Russell, B. *Outline of philosophy.* London: Allen and Unwin, 1927.

Russell, J. A., & Ward, L. M. Environmental psychology. *Annual Review of Psychology,* 1982, *33*, 651–688.

Schroeder, H. The effect of perceived conflict on evaluations of natural resource management goals. *Journal of Environmental Psychology,* 1981, *1*, 61–72.

Seamon, D. *A geography of the lifeworld: Movement, rest and encounter.* London: Croom Helm, 1979.

Sommer, R. *Personal space: The behavioral basis of design.* Englewood Cliffs, N.J.: Prentice-Hall, 1969.

Sommer, R. Looking back at personal space. In J. Lang, C. Burnette, W. Moleski, & D. Vachon (Eds.), *Designing for human behavior.* Stroudsburg, Pa.: Dowden, Hutchinson and Ross, 1974.

Sommer, R., Herrick, J., & Sommer, T. R. The behavioural ecology of supermarkets and farmers' markets. *Journal of Environmental Psychology,* 1981, *1*, 13–19.

Spencer, C. Physical determinism and environmental cognition: Two major themes of early environmental psychology which served to keep it apart from social psychology. Paper presented to the colloquium on *The Position of Environmental Psychology in Relation to Social Psychology*, Paris, June 1981. (a)

Spencer, C. The new social psychology and its relation to environmental psychology. *Journal of Environmental Psychology*, 1981, *1*, 329–336. (b)

Stokols, D. Environmental psychology. *Annual Review of Psychology*, 1978, *29*, 253–295.

Stokols, D. A congruence analysis of stress. In I. Sarason & C. Spielberger (Eds.), *Stress and anxiety* (Vol. 6). Washington, D.C.: Hemisphere Press, 1979.

Stokols, D., & Shumaker, S. A. People in place: A transactional view of settings. In J. H. Harvey (Ed.), *Cognition, social behavior and the environment*. Hillsdale, N.J.: Lawrence Erlbaum Associates, 1981.

Stoppard, T. *Jumpers*. London: Faber and Faber, 1972.

Tagg, S. K. The subjective meanings of rooms: Some analyses and investigations. In D. Canter & T. R. Lee (Eds.), *Psychology and the built environment*. London: Architectural Press, 1974.

Taylor, R. B. Is environmental psychology dying? *Population and Environmental Psychology Newsletter*, 1980, *1*, 14–15.

Teymur, N. *Environmental discourse*. London: ?uestion Press, 1981.

Tuan, Y. *Space and place: The perspective of experience*. Minneapolis: University of Minnesota Press, 1977.

Webley, P. Sex differences in home range and cognitive maps in eight-year-old children. *Journal of Environmental Psychology*, 1981, *1*, 293–302.

Wicker, A. W. *An introduction to ecological psychology*. Monterey, Calif.: Brooks/Cole, 1979.

Wilkinson, J., & Canter, S. *Social skills training manual*. Chichester, Eng.: Wiley, 1982.

Wohlwill, J. F. The environment is not in the head. In W. F. E. Preiser (Ed.), *EDRA 4*. Stroudsburg, Pa.: Dowden, Hutchinson and Ross, 1973.

Young, D. *The interpretation of form: Meanings and ambiguities in contemporary architecture*. University of Surrey: M.Sc. thesis (unpublished), 1978.

10. Cognitive Structures, Speech, and Social Situations: Two Integrative Models [1]

HOWARD GILES
University of Bristol

and MILES HEWSTONE
Maison des Sciences de l'Homme

INTRODUCTION

To a large extent, the history of sociolinguistics has been the study of variations in speech in different social contexts (e.g., Labov 1970). This theme is still important to many researchers today (e.g., St. Clair and Giles 1980; Furnham 1982; Herrmann 1982). Central to this emphasis on situational features is that speakers can select from a plurality of linguistic possibilities; that is, a speech repertoire is available to them (Gumperz 1964; Ervin-Tripp 1964). Possessing such a speech repertoire enables speakers to select different languages or dialects for producing essentially the same message, alternative forms of the same lexical item; a range of syntactic forms varying in complexity for the same phrase or clause; and/or a different accent, pitch range, speech rate, and intonation pattern for the same set of utterances. As Hymes (1972, 38) stated:

> No normal person, and no normal community, is limited to a single way
> of speaking, to an unchanging monotony that would preclude indica-
> tion of respect, insolence, mock seriousness, humor. . . .

This chapter briefly reviews some early contributions of sociolinguists and some more recent work of social psychologists showing how speech is determined by objective characteristics of the situation in which it is spoken. However, the aim is not simply to describe and evaluate previous work but to develop the study of speech along with some contemporary research in social psychology on intergroup relations on the one hand and the perceived structure of social situations on the other. This integrative approach allows us to move toward a more dynamic conception of the interrelationships between speech and social situations.

By developing notions formulated earlier (Smith, Giles, and Hewstone 1980), this chapter proposes models not only of how speech is (in the terminology of the experimental method) a dependent variable of an individual's subjective definition of a situation, but also of the conditions under which speech can function as an independent variable actively defining and redefining the nature of a situation for the participants involved.

PREVIOUS APPROACHES TO SPEECH AND SOCIAL SITUATIONS

One early influential landmark in the sociolinguistic literature is the concept of *diglossia* (Ferguson 1959), relating to the use of two languages or dialects in bilingual or bidialectal societies each serving different functions with different status connotations. The L(low) variety is most often confined to areas such as the home, everyday activities, and friendship, and the H(high) variety is often acquired later in the socialization process and reserved for the areas of education and administration. Consider Paraguayans' use of Spanish when speaking in the more formal contexts of public life and their shift to Guarani within the privacy of the home, or the use of Classical Arabic in certain Middle Eastern cultures for formal speech and the use of more colloquial Arabic varieties when formality is not required (see Figure 10-1).

Since it diglossia was introduced and researched, two broad patterns have emerged. The first development involved the closer specification of the classes of situations or social domains that would elicit either High or Low varieties of speech. Fishman (1972) proposed five general social domains: the family, neighborhood, religion, education, and employment. He noted that for the bilingual Mexican-American in the United States, Spanish might be used in the context of the family, neighborhood, or religion, but English would be used on the job or in the classroom. An important feature of his analysis was that given the two varieties and their fulfilling of these separate functions in the various domains cited, their linguistic structures will represent this disparity and not be equivalent (cf. Argyle, Furnham, and Graham 1981). Thus, for instance, informal grammatical structures and lexical items associated with the kitchen could be found only in Spanish for these Mexican-Americans, but not in their use of English.

The second development emerging from diglossia research involves extending the concept to include not only unrelated varieties (such as standard language vs. vernacular or colonial vs. native language) but also functionally differentiated varieties that may occur (Fishman 1972). For this reason, Platt (1977) invoked the notion of *polyglossia* as a simple dichotomy into High and Low varieties as grossly insufficient in many multilingual societies. For instance, the ethnic Chinese in

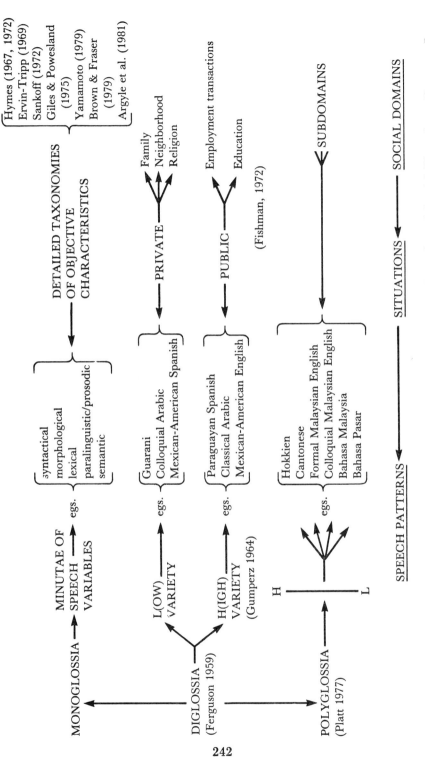

Figure 10-1. Developments in the "Objective Taxonomy" Approach to Speech and Social Situations (Source: *Language Sciences*, Vol. 4, No. 2, 1982. Used by permission.)

Malaysia have a speech repertoire including six varieties for use in particular domains or even subdomains, including Hokkien, Cantonese, formal Malaysian English, colloquial Malaysian English, the official standard Malay (Bahasa Malaysia), and Bazaar Malay (Bahasa Pasar).

More recent developments (see Figure 10-1) have been concerned with elaborating both previous trends and examining them in monolingual communities (Ervin-Tripp 1969), so taxonomies now emerge of how more specific objective characteristics of social situations (e.g.,the age of the person addressed) affect specifiable speech patterns (e.g., even the minutiae of vowel and consonant variants). The first to receive widespread acceptance was that of Hymes (1967; 1972), although his taxonomy concentrated attention on three components: setting (locating the interaction), participants (the specific characteristics of the interactants), and ends or purposes (the extended objectives). Specific features of subsequent taxonomies deserve mention.

For instance, Ervin-Tripp (1969) and Yamamoto (1979) provided situational hierarchies with a view to formulating rules for social grammars specifying the particular speech patterns appropriate for certain situations. Giles and Powesland (1975) stressed the salience of the characteristics of the person addressed over other situational variables. Brown and Fraser (1979) and Argyle et al. (1981) opted for the preeminence of the interaction's purpose in determining the speech patterns produced. They suggested, "purpose is the motor which sets the chassis of setting and participants going" (39). This model merits closer examination. It is the most comprehensive to date and archetypal of the objective taxonomy approach and also considers speakers as actors in a dynamic social relationship rather than as static individuals. This dynamic aspect is lacking in such previous models as Hyme's taxonomy. This criticism has not gone unnoticed in the literature (Fielding and Fraser 1978).

The Brown and Fraser Model

As seen in Figure 10-2, Brown and Fraser divide their taxonomy of situations into two components of scene and participants. Scene is further subdivided into setting and purpose and then into finer distinctions. Participants is subdivided into individual and relational characteristics, also followed by finer discriminations.

From the voluminous literature on this issue, it would be more instructive at this time to recapitulate some speech correlates associated with these objective features of the situation.[2]

Regarding scenes as a whole, Brown and Fraser noted, as have others, that the dimension of formality vs. informality can account for much variance (Joos 1962; cf. Irvine 1979 for a critical examination of language and formality). Research has shown that the more formal the

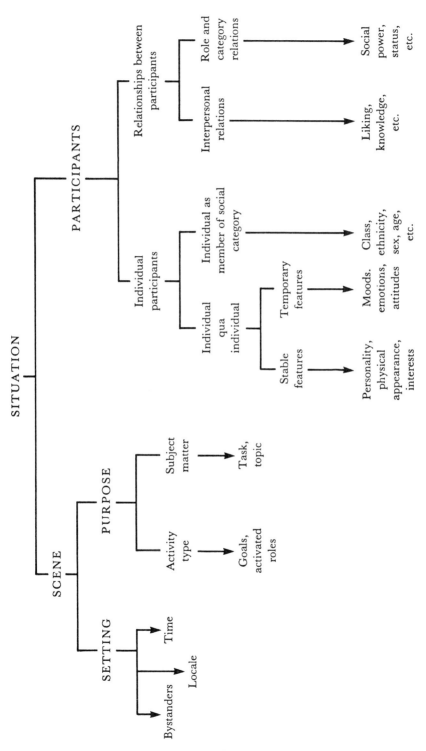

Figure 10-2. Components of Situation (Source: After Brown & Fraser, 1979, p. 35: from *Language Sciences*, Vol. 14, No. 2, Used by permission.)

244

situation, the more prestigious the pronunciation patterns adopted and the more nominal the speech style as manifest in lengthy, syntactically complex utterances; many filled hesitations; and many nouns, adjectives, and prepositions. More exotic examples indicate that the social composition of the interaction and its physical and temporal locations have important consequences for linguistic use in specific characteristics of scene. For instance, in a particular Aboriginal language, a distinctive mother-in-law code is spoken whenever the implied relative is present (bystander effect). Some Polynesian societies avoid the king's name or anything approaching the sound of it in the confines of his kingdom (locale effect). In Morocco, a different Arabic word denoting *needle* is rendered in the morning from the one used for the rest of the day (time effect).

In the purpose of the scene, different large-scale activity types have their own particular speech styles. The activity type of casual chatting, for example, has a more verbal style (as manifest in short, syntactically simple utterances, and the frequent use of verbs, pronouns, and adverbs) than the activity type of lecturing, which is more nominal. Naturally, the subject matter of the activity type has important speech correlates. For example, the more emotionally arousing the topic discussed, the more likely the speaker will adopt colloquial and nonstandard pronunciation patterns, a faster speech rate, and more disfluencies.

In the second major component of situations—participants—speech correlates have been found in connection with their stable characteristics, transitory states, and social category memberships. For instance, extroverts talk louder and pause less than do introverts; depressives are verbally less productive and talk more softly with fewer high overtones than do normals; and males use a different pitch range from females. The relationships between participants, whether interpersonal, role, or category, also affect the speech patterns evoked. Thus, participants who like each other display more verbal productivity and self-disclosure; they also display less silent pausing than people not so attracted.

Occupational and social roles can be reflected in asymmetrical patterns of address, as in the case of students calling their teacher *sir* or *Miss* and receiving their last name in return. Similarly, the power and status relationship holding between different social groups, whether between the sexes, social classes, ethnic groups, or generations, may induce group members in the subordinate position to opt for the commonly termed *restrictive code* and its supposed grammatical simplicities when interacting with members of the dominant group.

Brown and Fraser's (1979) important point is that speakers' speech patterns may not be a function of their individual or social groups' characteristics, as is often assumed. Rather, speech patterns can reflect the social relationships between speakers and their interlocutors in different scenes (Brown and Levinson 1979). In other words, if the power or affective relationship between two speakers is changed, the ensuing patterns will be modified in response.

A superficial examination of the Brown and Fraser model suggests that it is just another, albeit more sophisticated, descriptive taxonomy of the objective characteristics determining certain speech patterns. However, three features of their analysis mitigate against this appraisal and merit systematic investigation if we are to propose a theoretical leap in reformulating their model. First, Brown and Fraser are implicitly aware that within a situation a speaker may act, and be seen to act, either as an individual qua individual or as an examplar of a particular social category (Hewstone and Giles 1984). Second, they acknowledge, as have many sociolinguists (e.g., Hymes 1972), that "any understanding of the nature of the scene, *as viewed by the participants*, is essential in order to detect and interpret many of the markers that appear in their speech" (Brown and Fraser 1979, 54; our italics). This line of reasoning merits further research (cf. Bradac 1982). Such a subjective approach has a substantial body of research attending it under the rubrics of ethnomethodology, symbolic interactionism, and phenomenological sociology. More research is needed on how these methodological approaches can best be used in studying language use. Third, they underline the notion that "codes are not simply passively marking but are in large part creating the situation" (Brown and Fraser 1979, 48).

This chapter discusses these important issues and explores their implications as the basis for developing a number of testable propositions. It is first necessary, however, to consider some relevant research by social psychologists on intergroup relations and the perceived structure of social situations. These findings provide a basis for the theoretical framework in this chapter.

RELEVANT CONTEMPORARY
SOCIAL PSYCHOLOGICAL RESEARCH

Intergroup Relations

Until recently, there has been an individualistic empirical and theoretical bias in the social psychology of intergroup relations in the sense that intraindividual and interindividual factors have been transported into the intergroup arena in an attempt to elucidate the underlying processes (Moscovici 1972; Sampson 1977; Steiner 1974; Tajfel 1972). For example, the notions of authoritarianism, frustration-aggression, and belief dissimilarity have been used to examine intergroup discrimination and prejudice (for critiques, cf. Billig 1976; Brown and Turner 1981). Recent research, however, has shown not only that these factors cannot account for intergroup discriminations under minimal categorization conditions (that is, when individuals are allocated membership into two distinct categories where resources are not scarce for either group), but also that processes of a different order, such as social identification and social identity, operate at the intergroup level (Billig and Tajfel 1973; Tajfel 1978).

To elaborate, consider the extremes of two types of interaction discussed by Tajfel and Turner (1979, 34):

> At one extreme is the interaction between two or more individuals which is *fully* determined by their interpersonal relationships and individual characteristics and not at all affected by various social groups or categories to which they respectively belong. The other extreme consists of interactions between two or more individuals (or groups of individuals) which are *fully* determined by their respective memberships of various social groups or categories, and are not at all affected by the inter-individual personal relationships between the people involved.

These two extremes are considered as lying at either end of a bipolar continuum labeled interindividual and intergroup encounters, respectively (Brown and Turner 1981; Tajfel 1974). It has been argued that the more members of a group conceive of an encounter as being towards the intergroup pole [3]

> . . . the more uniformity will they show in their behavior towards members of the relevant outgroups . . . [and] . . . the more they will tend to treat members of the outgroup as undifferentiated items in a unified social category rather than in terms of their individual characteristics. (Tajfel and Turner 1979, 36)

Tajfel and his co-workers developed a theory for understanding behavior at the intergroup end of the continuum (Tajfel 1978; Turner and Giles 1981). In essence, their theory suggests that when individuals identify with a social group, they desire to derive satisfaction from their membership; that is, they wish to possess a positive rather than a negative group identity. Realizing the affect associated with ingroup identity comes through making intergroup comparisons between the position of one's own group and that of the other on certain valued dimensions, such as power, resources, or capabilities. Much theory and the empirical research deriving from it is concerned with understanding the conditions necessary and strategies used to achieve a positive ingroup identity by psychological differentiation in valued directions from outgroups.

Because speech style can be an important dimension of identity for many social groupings, particularly age, class, and ethnic categories (Giles 1977; Giles and Saint-Jacques 1979), it is necessary to consider further the interindividual and intergroup continuum with regard to its potential speech correlates. At this juncture, it would be useful to refer to work on speech accommodation theory, our preferred basis for understanding the processes underlying an individual's shift in speech style from one person to another (Giles and Powesland 1975; Street and Giles 1983; Thakerar, Giles, and Cheshire 1982). An important proposition of this theory is that a speaker possessing strong ingroup loyalty and defining an interaction in intergroup terms will wish to assume a positive social identity. One strategy toward achieving this positive social identity might involve linguistic differentiation from the outgroup member (Giles 1978; Taylor and Royer 1980).

This process of "psycholinguistic distinctiveness" (Giles, Bourhis, and Taylor 1977) could be manifest by code-switching to one's ingroup language or emphasizing the ingroup dialect by broadening one's accent or adopting ingroup slang and discourse structures (Giles 1979). In short, under conditions of positive group identity, the more a situation is defined in intergroup terms, the more speech divergence is promoted (Bourhis and Giles 1977; Bourhis et al. 1979; Lambert 1979; Ryan 1979), the format of which would depend on a variety of intergroup variables. Included among these would be the perceived status relations between the two groups (Tajfel 1978) and the speaker's cognitive representations of the degree to which sociostructural factors were in the group's favor (Bourhis, Giles, and Rosenthal 1981; Kramarae 1981). Of additional importance would be the extent to which the speaker identified with other meaningful social categories having positive group identities in which the individual has high within-group status (Giles and Johnson 1981).

Until now, this discussion has emphasized the influence of interpersonal-intergroup perceptions of the situation on encoding speech variables; however, decoding processes may also be affected (cf. Bourhis et al. 1975; Doise et al. 1976; Genesee and Bourhis 1982). For example, perceiving a situation in intergroup terms or an individual as a category member may have repercussions on the attributions made about that situation or individual (Hewstone and Jaspars 1982; Jaspars and Hewstone 1982). Hewstone (1983) argued that, given the demonstrable significance of language at both interpersonal and intergroup levels, linguistic cues provide potent sources for developing attributions (Giles, Scherer, and Taylor 1979).

Social Situations

Social psychology has recently seen an explosion of work on the perceived structure of social situations (see Argyle, Furnham, and Graham 1981). This interest in defining the situation has also been evident in the work of symbolic interactionists (see St. Clair 1982). As O'Keefe and Delia (in press) point out, however, symbolic interactionists have failed to recognize the importance of individual psychological structure.

We acknowledge this fact and now examine some contemporary social psychological research on the structure of social situations.

One approach to analyzing social situations, adopted by Argyle, Furnham, and Graham (1981), develops from the central hypothesis that situations enable people to attain goals. Thus, an analysis of the perceived goal structure of social situations is desirable. Lists of goals for a particular situation are obtained. Each goal then is rated for its importance in each situation and role. Principal components analysis (PCA) or some similar type of multivariate analysis is used to reveal the structure of the goals. These two methods, importance ratings by individuals and then PCA, indicate which goal is relevant for a particular role in a particular situation.

Although the approach by Argyle et al. (see also Argyle 1976) for the analysis of situations is arguably the most encompassing (examining the structure of the situation in terms of behavior, rules, structural and motivational themes, roles, pieces, and concepts), this chapter concentrates on research on the fundamental dimensions underlying people's perceptions of interpersonal relations and communication. The reason for this orientation is that much work in this domain has not been systematically related to speech behavior (see Forgas 1979). The goal structure approach might make a significant contribution to this area, but we mention it here as an option for the future.

Typifying the dimensional approach, Wish and Kaplan (1977) asked subjects to evaluate a series of hypothetical communication episodes involving both role relationships (e.g., bitter enemies) and situational contexts (e.g., exchanging views about a politician they both dislike). Multidimensional scaling (MDS) analyses of the data revealed that subjects cognitively represented the episodes on five dimensions: cooperative-competitive, intense-superficial, formal-informal, dominant-equal, task oriented–non-task oriented (cf. Wish, Deutsch, and Kaplan 1976).

In another study (Wish 1975), in which the hypothetical episodes to be evaluated explicitly included the raters themselves (e.g., you and a co-worker attempting to work out a compromise when your goals are strongly opposed), the same five dimensions emerged. Both studies found that the nature of the role relationship affected formality and dominance, whereas the situational context affected the dimensions of cooperation, intensity, and task-relatedness.

In another study, subjects were asked to view a series of 1½ minute videotape recordings involving different scenes with husband-wife, lawyer-client, strangers, and so on. Even when real communication episodes were observed, the same dimensions accounted for subjects' definitions of the situations (Wish 1978).

Wish's (1978) findings reveal that different subgroups attach different emphasis to the five dimensions. Thus, for instance, left-wing students placed more weight on the dominance-equality dimension than did students of other sociopolitical persuasions.

The importance of subcultural differences emerges strongly from the related research of Forgas (1978), who asked different sections of the community to evaluate, again on bipolar scales, social episodes with which they were familiar. Again using multidimensional scaling techniques, he found that different status groups within an institution placed different weights on the same dimensions they used for defining the same social episodes. Thus, within an academic university department, the teaching faculty tended to judge situations more in terms of the dimensions of involvement; research students preferred the socioemotional dimension; and technical and other staff relied most on the anxiety dimension (cf. Forgas et al. 1979).

Forgas (1976) also found that certain groups have more complex construals of episodes than do others; for example, undergraduate students used three dimensions whereas housewives used two for construing the same social situations. Moreover, even when different subgroups adopt common dimensions for construal, they may use different ends of the same continua. In this vein, Forgas (1979, 282) commented that "while 'socializing with friends' appears to be natural, self-selected entertainment, for housewifes it may be a more demanding, formal and organized affair, involving an element of self-presentation."

Also, different subgroups (e.g., two college rugby teams) cognitively cluster the same social situations in different ways (cf. Argyle and Little 1972). For instance, a more cohesive rugby team construed sports and other informal gatherings as highly similar, whereas a team that trained together less regularly differentiated sport from other social activities (see Forgas 1980).

Overall, Forgas's work in Britain has shown that people use the same dimensions for construing social situations found by Wish in the United States. Of equal importance here is the set of findings suggesting that different individuals can use different dimensions for construing the same situation. In addition, the dimensions used by different people may vary in complexity; and even when different individuals use common dimensions, they can place different weights on them and can see the same episodes at opposite poles of the same dimension.

Rosenberg and Sedlak (1972) pointed out that a dimensional structure based on group data may not be the most accurate description of the structure of the individuals comprising the group. Logistical problems are involved in analyzing the configurations of each individual, however. Individual differences MDS (e.g., Carroll and Chang's 1970 INDSCAL) prove useful here. This model examines both a Euclidean representation of the structure as perceived by the whole group (the group space) and a representation of each individual's space. Forgas and Wish used this analysis in several studies. We argue here that the gain in statistical rigor offered by such an approach offsets the loss in idiographic accuracy.[4]

No objective classification of situations such as presented by Brown and Fraser (1979) is sufficient to understand different individuals' subjective definitions of the same social episodes. This is why current studies in sociolinguistics, which are limited to the objective classifications of codes, cannot deal with the negotiation of social reality, the concept of emergence in symbolic interactionism, and other aspects of social interaction. For example, objectively describing a social situation as a formal interview on a serious topic with a 90-year-old black woman may have little predictive value about her likely speech patterns if she defines the interview informally, considers the subject matter irrelevant and trivial, and feels "white" and 50 years old. In other words, speech is sometimes likely to depend more on how speakers cognitively represent their characteristics and subjectively define the scene than on any objective classification.

The final issue about work on the perception of social situations is that individuals may have been forced to use these five dimensions because that was the only possible response in the research situation (see Eiser 1975 and Hewstone 1983 for a discussion of response language in social judgment research). It may be that they would have used other dimensions if they had been available. Whatever the importance of this criticism, we should be wary of asserting that individuals always perceive situations in these terms, or that such perceptions always guide their behavior.

Langer (1978) made a similar criticism of attribution theory studies. She acknowledged that people can perceive the world in cause-effect terms but suggested that research should be directed toward ascertaining when they do so and how often. Langer criticized explicitly cognitive models of social interaction, arguing that "most of the time people are not consciously seeking explanations or trying to assess their cognitive processes" (38).

We accept this point and do not maintain that these dimensions are important in all social situations. Indeed, in many routine interactions, people probably only need to process minimal cues in order to engage a script to interact successfully in the situations (see Roloff and Berger 1983). Yet it would be interesting to know in what kinds of situations individuals use or ignore these cognitive structures, or even whether they are conscious of them at all (cf. Berger 1980).

THE THEORETICAL FRAMEWORK

Toward a Model of Speech as a Dependent Variable of Social Situations

By integrating central notions from the two previous areas of interindividual/intergroup distinctions and the five subjective dimensions, we can provide a more cognitive model for understanding situational determinants of speech. The five bipolar dimensions arising from Wish's work in particular provide thirty-two logical possibilities for defining a social episode. Each possibility could be considered in either interindividual or intergroup terms. Here we have selected four typical ways of defining a social situation according to these dimensions. These appear as A1 to D1 in Table 10-1.

The situations A to D are examples of concrete situations described by objective characteristics likely leading to those subjective definitions for many individuals. Wish (1978) discovered certain linguistic attributes of communication episodes that cue observers' definitions of the situation; for instance, "interactors rated as task oriented frequently made strong requests such as for commitment, compliance, or acceptance of a proposition" (Wish 1978, 376-377).

Conversely, however, little information exists on what speech to expect under which situational definitions (cf. Price and Bouffard 1974). This should be an empirical priority for future development in this field. Nevertheless, previous research from the objective taxonomy approach provides implicit hypotheses regarding what likely speech will ensue on a variety of linguistic levels for certain situations. These situations appear as patterns A2 to D2 in Table 10-1. When a situation is defined (as in A1) in terms of cooperation, informality, nonintensity, equality, nontask orientation, one can predict speech patterns similar to those appearing in A2.

Returning to the nomenclature of diglossia and in relation to the work of Levinson (1978), these speech forms in traditional value terms can be termed *low* varieties (cf. Argyle et al. 1981; Brown and Fraser 1979, 46). However, if the same situation is also defined in intergroup terms as in C1 (interestingly enough, future research will likely uncover important additional subjective *intergroup* dimensions), it is possible to predict an attenuation of at least certain ingroup speech markers or convergence to occur simultaneously.[5] On the other hand, when a situation is defined in terms of competition, formality, intensity, nonequality, and task orientation, as in B1, it is possible to predict high speech forms, illustrated in B2. However, if the encounter is defined in intergroup terms, as in D1, a prediction can be made about the linguistic accentuation of ingroup speech markers or divergence to occur as well (cf. Giles, Scherer, and Taylor 1979).

We are thus suggesting that any objective situation, such as A, can be perceived by different people under different circumstances in many ways; that is, not only as A1 in this particular case, but as B1 or C1 or even D1, and so on. These cognitive structures often influence individuals' speech outputs more than the situation's supposed objective attributes.

It is an empirical question as to how often situations' objective and subjective characteristics do not overlap to a large degree. Our stance is

TABLE 10-1
Toward a Model of Speech as a Dependent Variable of Social Situations

	A	B	C	D
Objective Characteristics of Certain Typical Social Situation (eg. A–D)	Friends chatting during coffee break	Prosecuting and defense lawyers in law court	Welsh and English rugby supporters in pub after International with mutually satisfactory result	Trade Union and Management negotiation crisis
Possible Cognitive Structures of Social Situations by Participants	**A1** Interindividual encounter Cooperative Informal Relaxed Equal Not task-related	**B1** Interindividual encounter Competitive Formal Tense Not equal Task-related	**C1** Intergroup encounter Cooperative Informal Relaxed Equal Not task-related	**D1** Intergroup encounter Competitive Formal Tense Not equal Task-related
Potential Speech Patterns	**A2** Low linguistic diversity "Restricted" code Verbal style nonstandard pronunciations imprecise enunciations 1st name (& informal address forms)	**B2** High linguistic diversity "Elaborated" code Nominal style standard pronunciations precise enunciations Title +/or last name address forms	**C2** Low linguistic diversity "Restricted" code Verbal style nonstandard pronunciations imprecise enunciations 1st name (& informal address forms) Plus attenuation of ingroup speech markers (speech convergence)	**D2** High linguistic diversity "Elaborated" code Nominal style standard pronunciations precise enunciations Title +/or last address forms Plus accentuation of ingroup speech markers (speech divergence)

Source: *Language Sciences*, Vol. 4, No. 2, 1982. Used by permission.

based on the notion that enough lack of overlap exists for the objective taxonomy approach to be theoretically inadequate to account for the relationships between speech and situation. We propose that perceptions of situation often are more potent determinants of repertoire selection and shifting than are objective attributes of these same contexts. We thus need an extensive empirical research program to elucidate precisely under what conditions this happens, and why. We hasten to add that we are not so shortsighted as to wish merely to replace an objective classification with a subjective one. Hence, we have carefully pointed out that subjective construals of situations may sometimes have little, if any, determining effects on speech output. For instance, even if the cognitive structures relating to situational perceptions are contrary in essence to the objective characteristics of context (e.g., an interviewee finds an interviewer's questions naïve and inappropriate yet desperately requires a job), perceived normative pressures relating to the latter may override the former cognitive structures anyway (cf. Ajzen and Fishbein 1980).

Relatedly, part of a situation's subjective meaning is often based on an appraisal of its presumed objective characteristics. Furthermore, other factors such as speakers' interactional goals and desires for particular modes of self-presentation may dictate language behaviors more than either subjective or objective definitions of the situation. Ultimately, then, we must move toward a theoretical model that considers the interactive influence of subjective, objective, normative, self-presentational, and goal-oriented factors in understanding the relationships between speech and situation. (See Smith, Giles, and Hewstone 1983 for a fuller discussion of these complexities.)

Toward a Model of Speech as an Independent Variable of Social Situations

For the most part, speech and social situations have been discussed dichotomously. The discussion has relegated speech variables to the role of covariates of social categories and situation. To avoid circularity in explanation, social variables should theoretically be operationalized along strictly nonlinguistic lines. Whether this can, in fact, be achieved is not only doubtful but also central to the perspective of this chapter.

Speech, far from playing the universal role of a pale reflection of underlying social reality, is, as Brown and Fraser (1979) pointed out, a central and defining facet of reality (Berger and Luckman 1967). On this issue, Smith, Giles, and Hewstone (1980, 285) pointed out:

> . . . our assignment of an interlocutor to a certain SES or ethnic category, or our definition of a social situation as informal or technical, can on many occasions be based exclusively on our interpretations of the

other's speech. To exclude language *a priori* from a definition of social variables is to run the risk of employing concepts that are impoverished from the perspective of participants and observers of interaction.

In many social situations, participants look to each other's speech as a means of social comparison (Festinger 1954; Suls and Miller 1977) to determine how the other is construing the interaction that can be an important guideline to situational definition (see also Lind and O'Barr 1979). In other words, speech not only acts (in the terminology of the experimental method) as a dependent variable of situational definitions, but it can also function actively as an independent variable by providing participants with cues on how to structure their definitions of those situations cognitively (cf. Taylor and Giles 1979). As Giles, Scherer, and Taylor (1979, 355) commented:

> A meeting in an informal, unconstrained situation may become defined as an opportunity for idle chatter, ingratiation, a chance to engage in sensitive business matters, or as a means of appearing to others that one is socially active. Which one of these the situation evolves into may sometimes depend on the participants, the speech markers they employ, and the extent to which these are perceived, reciprocated and jointly acted upon.

However, as several scholars indicated recently, the social input to conversation is not constant and assumptions about role and status relationships vary as the conversation progresses. These changes are signalled through speech itself (Argyle 1980; Clarke 1975; Gumperz 1977; Rommetveit 1974). For instance, an important feature of the symbolic interactionist tradition (Blumer 1969; Mead 1934) is concerned with how people approach each other with fixed meanings based on preliminary definitions of the situation and how they mutually influence each other as the interaction progresses, with the resulting meanings often being the products of compromise and accommodation (Hewitt 1976; Manis and Meltzer 1967; St. Clair 1980). Ethnomethodologists have also been concerned with studying conversations as cooperative endeavors (Garfinkel 1972), and Berger (1979) developed a theory of communicative behavior for elucidating how and at what stage during the course of a relationship participants will change their verbal strategies in order to proceed to a new level of knowledge, understanding, and explanation of the other participants and their behavior in the situation (see also Berger and Bradac 1982).

The common grounds of these approaches are that they conceptualize behavior in a dynamic manner and that the meaning of communication is socially negotiated (see Schenkein 1978; Scotton 1980). A need therefore arises to develop a model of speech functioning not only as a static independent variable for initially defining social situations, but for redefining them as well. Such a model might attend to the following issues:

> When will speech influence the initial definition of the situation? Who will take the initiative, activate which cognitive structures and by means of which speech patterns? When and how will a redefinition of the social situation be attempted? Under what conditions will speech be *the* salient cue to situational definition and redefinition?

The following propositions are an initial attempt to address these questions with a focus on the relative status of participants as one albeit obviously not the only, important parameter influencing communicative behavior (see Berger et al. 1977).

> *Proposition I:* Speech can act as an initial definer of situations under at least two conditions.
> A. When normative demands for appropriate behavior are ambiguous, nonexistent, or not available.

Scotton (1979) pointed to such a situation in East Africa, where norms regarding the use of certain languages over others are unclear for multilingual speakers. As she stated, ". . . on what basis is one to say, for example, that a conversation with a neighbor is necessarily less formal, less public, or more personal than a conversation with a shopkeeper?" (Scotton 1979, 78). In this cultural context, and undoubtedly in others, speakers often avoid committing themselves and refuse to define the situation by opting for a safe choice of language. They achieve this neutrality by constantly code switching between lingua franca. Here, Swahili and English provide the codes for this neutrality (Scotton 1976). In other situations, speakers opt for one mode of speech, such as English, to define the situation formally or perhaps to develop a more cultured perspective on the proceedings at hand.

> B. When two or more sets of social norms are deemed appropriate

Society often provides explicit norms, but it does not always provide a hierarchy of them to aid behavior. Thus, for example, Genesee and Bourhis (1982) pointed to the dilemma of language choice facing French Canadian clerks, salesmen, and shop assistants when serving English Canadians in Quebec. Traditional, historical, and economic dominance of English, together with the situational norm implying the customer is always correct, suggest the use of the client's mother tongue, English. At the same time, however, emerging sociocultural norms, as reflected in the passing of Bill 101 making French the only official language in the province, invite the use of French. The use of speech style in these circumstances, then, dictates with which norms the participants wish to operate. Given the importance of appropriate norms, their violation might be expected to be particularly important for defining the situation.

> *Proposition II:* Situational definitions by speech will more likely occur, and ultimately be accepted, if initiated by the highest status participant (cf. Brown and Gilman 1960).

This would be manifest by speech similar to type B2 in Table 10–1 from the higher status speaker (or to type D2 if the situation is perceived as an intergroup encounter) to create cognitive structures in the lower status other of a formal, dominant, task-related social atmosphere conducive to legitimizing the former's relative superiority. If relative status between participants is unclear at the interaction's initial phase (e.g., between two experts from different disciplines at a conference), then relative prestige must be negotiated between them before one can legitimately define the situation. Moreover, if status negotiations are anticipated as, or found to be, unresolved or mutually unacceptable, both parties will want to define the interaction in terms of cognitive structures of cooperation, equality, and nonintensity (see A1 and C1), which would be manifest by speech similar to type A2—or to type C2 if the encounter is perceived in intergroup terms.

Good (1979) discussed some speech strategies used to maintain casualness and equality during an interaction. These strategies include requests rather than commands and the use of contradictions or reassuring remarks rather than agreement when the other has made self-effacing statements. Both strategies facilitate what Good calls the parity principle in conversations. Thus, speech acts not only as a definer of situations but also as a maintainer of them. Needless to say, other dimensions of status will operate in different contexts, including ethnic and class, as well as in situations relating to task performance and sex roles (Leet-Pelligrini 1980).

> *Proposition III:* Attempted redefinitions of the social situation by speech will more likely occur under at least four conditions.
> A. When a high status person's authority or competence has been unquestionably established and he or she feels comfortable and secure.

This would be manifest by the higher status speaker shifting speech toward type A2, or toward C2 if the encounter is perceived in intergroup terms, to create cognitive structures in the recipients of an informal, relaxed atmosphere wherein social cohesion could be better fostered (see A1 and C1). This proposition is reflected in the teaching profession's maxim that respect and authority should be established for at least a term in the classroom before the teacher can safely resort to a more casual approach with students (see first-in maxim, Scotton 1980).

    B. When a high status person's authority or status has been questioned and/or threatened (Tajfel 1974; Turner and Brown 1978) or the perceived goals of interaction have been considered unfulfilled.

This would be manifest by the higher status speaker's resorting to stronger or more frequent expressions of speech similar to type B2, or D2 if the situation is perceived as an intergroup encounter, to promote dominance and/or task-relatedness (see B1 and D1) in the cognitive structures of the lower status individuals and perhaps to shift the conversation into a more serious frame of reference.

    C. When a lower status person has considered his or her inferiority to be unfair and potentially changeable (Tajfel 1974; Turner and Brown 1978).

This would be manifest by the lower status speaker's shifting his or her speech towards type A2, including in this instance accentuating ingroup speech markers if the situation is perceived in intergroup terms, to make unacceptable the other's cognitive structuring of the situation along status and dominance lines (i.e., to construe it now as in A1). Bourhis (1979, 131–134) pointed out that such speakers may not simply try to redefine just cognitive structuring of the social situation itself through speech strategies but may also use language to expand the range of social situations in which their own choice of speech variety is perceived as being the prerogative. Ultimately, any newly acquired equality could be directed into higher status by changing the nature of the task to one in which the previously lower status speaker was now the undisputed leader (Miller and Steinberg 1975). As Brown and Fraser (1979, 53–54) commented:

> Hierarchical social status is . . . contextually relative in certain respects, or at least the domains in which status expressions are relevant vary contextually, so that a doctor consulting a lawyer on a legal question might well express deference in formulating her query, whereas the lawyer when consulting the doctor about his heart condition would be the one to express deference.

    D. When a person has found (or actively made) his or her interlocutor cognitively or behaviorally more predictable (Berger 1979; Berger and Bradac 1982).

This would be manifest by the person's shifting his or her speech toward type A2, or toward type C2 if the encounter is perceived in intergroup terms, to induce cognitive structures in the recipient of either A1 or C1, thereby permitting more intimate discourse to ensue.

> *Proposition IV:* Speech will assume more salience as the cue to defining a social situation subjectively as well as redefining it when physical and social constraints are obstacles to definition and redefinition by other means.

Therefore, if participants desire to promote cooperation and informality, but cannot change dress style or physical distance between them (e.g., telephone conversations, seating arrangements at committee meetings), then speech will become the prime vehicle for situational constructions. However, we suggest that speech cues have qualities making them a more desirable means for achieving a successful redefinition than do other potential environmental changes. This is evident in Brown and Fraser's (1979) notion that speech changes once introduced often have ambiguous social meanings.

For instance, a Welsh person's broadening his or her Celtic brogue could signal the desire to become more familiar with another or alternatively the desire to emphasize national, or even class, identity (cf. Giles, Scherer, and Taylor 1979, 363–364; Taylor and Giles 1979, 232–233). The range of possibilities likely for attributing shifts in speech style, then, allows speakers a more covert means of subtly changing situational definitions in a more socially acceptable manner than by other strategies.

CONCLUSION

Perhaps we have been overly ambitious in attempting to cover so much ground in so limited a space. It has not been possible to do justice to the models reviewed, and we trust that by our omissions we have not misrepresented the work cited.

This chapter has tried to illustrate some deficiencies in sociolinguistic accounts of the relations between speech and situations, particularly in terms of warning of the dangers of using only static, objective taxonomies of situations for understanding speech variations. We have also attempted to suggest how theory and data from social psychology might help correct the previous limitations.

As stressed in other contexts (e.g., Robinson, Giles, and Smith 1980; Beebe and Giles 1983), we do not see social psychology as a panacea for deficiencies in the study of language and society. Rather, we view a social psychological perspective as an important complement to established approaches. Even the recent burgeoning of social cognition research in social psychology does not provide any ready answers to how speakers decide what to say and how to say it or how listeners form impressions of others on the basis of speech styles (cf. Giles and Ryan 1982). In this sense, inter- or even multidisciplinary work of the type advocated implicitly here may be significant for the future development of theoretical models in social psychology.

At the same time, we have attempted to produce a cognitive model focusing on the mediating role of speakers' own cognitive representations of the situation as one of the important set of forces determining speech variation. We regard this as a concrete direction to consider empirically with the proposal to elaborate the model ultimately with respect to the objective taxonomy approach, speakers' motivational tendencies, goals, and social norms (see Smith, Giles, and Hewstone 1983). We also formulated an embryonic model for considering speech as an active independent variable, not only in defining, maintaining, and redefining social situations, but also in sometimes avoiding situational definitions, which will hopefully help us understand how individuals create as well as respond to social situations. In this sense, we view speech and situation as interdependent, operating simultaneously as reflecting a speaker's cognitive representation of the situation and also as potentially defining the situation for other participants (see Smith, Giles, and Hewstone 1980 for further details).

We thus hope that the social psychological constructs and theory outlined here will be of value for methodological, empirical, and theoretical advances in the interrelationships between speech and social situations, an area of core significance historically to sociolinguistics and the language sciences.

ENDNOTES

1. We are grateful to Charles Berger, Richard Bourhis, Guy Fielding, Richard Hudson, Robert St. Clair, Carol Scotton, and Philip Smith for their useful comments on earlier drafts of this paper. Dr. Hewstone acknowledges with gratitude the financial support of the Leverhulme Trust.

2. The reader is referred to Brown and Fraser, as well as to other chapters in Scherer and Giles (1979), for further details of findings and references in the overview of research on speech and situations.

3. It is more useful to consider these two types of interaction as comprising two separate, orthogonal continua in the sense that an individual may define a situation as being high or low in interindividual and intergroup terms simultaneously (see Stephenson 1981). The importance of this distinction is that an individual may consider a situation

as high in both interindividual and intergroup terms (e.g., an occasion when a person is undecided about whether his or her interlocutor is a typical representative of an outgroup) and also as low in both these respects (e.g., an occasion when an individual is inattentive, distracted, fatigued, drugged, etc.). The four quadrants, then, comprising this two-dimensional space would lend themselves to different patterns of interactive behavior that should be manifest linguistically.

4. These options, however, raise a serious methodological issue—whether to opt for idiographic (individual-based) or nomothetic (aggregate-based) measures of cognitive structure. Examples of idiographic measures are Kelly's (1955) Personal Construct Theory and case studies of implicit personality theory (see Rosenberg and Jones 1972; Rosenberg and Sedlak 1972). The advantage of these techniques is that they may achieve a better fit with an individual's actual cognitive system, although comparing across persons is difficult (but not impossible; see Fransella and Bannister 1977). The nomothetic techniques (e.g., Osgood, Suci, and Tannenbaum's [1957] semantic differential approach to the measurement of meaning; Norman's [1963] taxonomy of personality characteristics) have more generality but may ignore significant individual differences. It is beyond the scope of this chapter to evaluate these alternatives; the reader is referred to Rosenberg and Sedlak (1972).

5. For a more detailed discussion of greater complexities inherent in the presumed relationship between speech convergence/divergence and intergroup perceptions, see Giles, Bourhis, and Taylor (1977), Giles (1978; 1979), and Giles and Johnson (1981).

REFERENCES

Ajzen, I., & Fishbein, M. *Understanding attitudes and predicting social behavior.* Englewood Cliffs, N.J.: Prentice-Hall, 1980.

Argyle, M. *Personality and social behavior.* In R. Harré (Ed.), *Personality.* Oxford: Blackwell, 1976.

Argyle, M. Language and social interaction. In H. Giles, W. P. Robinson, & P. M. Smith (Eds.), *Language: Social psychological perspectives.* Oxford: Pergamon, 1980.

Argyle, M., Furnham, A., & Graham, J. *Social situations.* Cambridge: Cambridge University Press, 1981.

Argyle, M., & Little, B. Do personality traits apply to social behavior? *Journal of the Theory of Social Behavior,* 1972, 2, 1–35.

Beebe, L., & Giles, H. Speech accommodation theories: A discussion in terms of second language acquisition. *International Journal of the Sociology of Language,* 1983, 46.

Berger, C. R. Beyond initial interaction: Uncertainty, understanding and the development of interpersonal relationships. In H. Giles & R. N. St. Clair (Eds.), *Language and social psychology.* Oxford: Blackwell, 1979.

Berger, C. R. Self-consciousness and the study of interpersonal interaction: Approaches and issues. In H. Giles, W. P. Robinson, & P. M. Smith (Eds.), *Language: Social psychological perspectives.* Oxford: Pergamon, 1980.

Berger, C. R., & Bradac, J. J. *Language and social knowledge: Uncertainty in interpersonal relationships.* London: Edward Arnold, 1982.

Berger, J., Fisek, M. H., Norman, R. Z., & Zelditch, M., Jr. *Status characteristics and social interaction: An expectancy-states approach.* New York: Elsevier, 1977.

Berger, P. L., & Luckmann, T. *The social construction of reality.* London: Allen Lane, 1967.

Billig, M. *The social psychology of intergroup relations.* London: Academic Press, 1976.

Billig, M., & Tajfel, H. Social categorization and similarity in intergroup behavior. *European Journal of Social Psychology*, 1973, *3*, 27-52.

Blumer, B. *Symbolic interactionism: Perspective and method.* Englewood Cliffs, N.J.: Prentice-Hall, 1969.

Bourhis, R. Y. Language in ethnic interaction: A social psychological approach. In H. Giles & B. Saint-Jacques (Eds.), *Language and ethnic relations.* Oxford: Pergamon, 1979.

Bourhis, R. Y., & Giles, H. The language of intergroup distinctiveness. In H. Giles (Ed.), *Language, ethnicity and intergroup relations.* London: Academic Press, 1977.

Bourhis, R. Y., Giles, H., & Lambert, W. E. Social consequences of accommodating one's speech style: A cross-national investigation. *International Journal of the Sociology of Language*, 1975, *6*, 55-72.

Bourhis, R. Y., Giles, H., Leyens, J. P., & Tajfel, H. Psycholinguistic distinctiveness: Language divergence in Belgium. In H. Giles & R. N. St. Clair (Eds.), *Language and social psychology.* Oxford: Blackwell, 1979.

Bourhis, R. Y., Giles, H., & Rosenthal, D. Notes on the construction of a "subjective vitality" questionnaire for ethnolinguistic groups. *Journal of Multicultural and Multilingual Development*, 1981, *2*, 145-155.

Bradac, J. J. A rose by another name: Attitudinal consequences of lexical variation. In E. B. Ryan & H. Giles (Eds.), *Attitudes towards language variation: Social and applied contexts.* London: Edward Arnold, 1982.

Brown, P., & Fraser, C. Speech as a marker of situation. In K. R. Scherer & H. Giles (Eds.), *Social markers in speech.* Cambridge: Cambridge University Press, 1979.

Brown, P., & Levinson, S. Social structure, groups and interaction. In K. R. Scherer & H. Giles (Eds.), *Social markers in speech.* Cambridge: Cambridge University Press, 1979.

Brown, R., & Gilman, A. The pronouns of power and solidarity. In T. Sebeok (Ed.), *Style in language.* Cambridge, Mass.: Technology Press, 1960.

Brown, R. J., & Turner, J. C. Interpersonal and intergroup behavior. In J. C. Turner & H. Giles (Eds.), *Intergroup behavior.* Oxford: Blackwell, 1981.

Carroll, J., & Chang, J. J. Analysis of individual differences in multidimensional scaling via an N-way generalization of Eckhart-Young decomposition. *Psychometrika,* 1970, *35,* 283-319.

Clarke, D. D. The use and recognition of sequential structure in dialogue. *British Journal of Social and Clinical Psychology,* 1975, *14,* 333-340.

Doise, W., Sinclair, A., & Bourhis, R. Y. Evaluation of accent convergence and divergence in cooperative and competitive intergroup situations. *British Journal of Social and Clinical Psychology,* 1976, *15,* 247-252.

Eiser, J. R. Attitudes and the use of evaluative language: A two-way process. *Journal for the Theory of Social Behavior,* 1975, *5,* 235-248.

Ervin-Tripp, S. M. An analysis of the interaction of language, topic and listener. *American Anthropologist,* 1964, *66,* 86-102.

Ervin-Tripp, S. M. Sociolinguistics. In L. Berkowitz (Ed.), *Advances in experimental social psychology* (Vol. 4). New York: Academic Press, 1969.

Ferguson, C. A. Diglossia. *Word,* 1959, *15,* 325-340.

Festinger, L. A theory of social comparison processes. *Human Relations,* 1954, *7,* 117-140.

Fielding, G., & Fraser, C. Language and interpersonal relations. In I. Markova (Ed.), *Language and social context.* London: Wiley, 1978.

Fishman, J. A. The relationship between micro- and macro-sociolinguistics in the study of who speaks what language to whom and when. In J. B. Pride & J. Holmes (Eds.), *Sociolinguistics.* Harmondsworth: Penguin, 1972.

Forgas, J. P. The perception of social episodes: Categorical and dimensional representations in two different social milieus. *Journal of Personality and Social Psychology,* 1976, *33,* 199-209.

Forgas, J. P. Social episodes and social structure in an academic setting: The social environment of an intact group. *Journal of Experimental Social Psychology*, 1978, *14*, 434–448.

Forgas, J. P. Multidimensional scaling of social episodes: A new method in social psychology. In G. P. Ginsburg (Ed.), *Emerging strategies in social psychology.* London: Wiley, 1979.

Forgas, J. P. *Social episodes: The study of interaction routines.* London: Academic Press, 1980.

Forgas, J. P., Argyle, M., & Ginsberg, G. Social episodes and person perception: The fluctuating structure of an academic group. *Journal of Social Psychology*, 1979, *109*, 207–222.

Fransella, F., & Bannister, D. *A manual for the repertory grid technique.* London: Academic Press, 1977.

Furnham, A. The message, the context and the medium. *Language and Communication*, 1982, *2*, 33–47.

Garfinkel, H. Studies of the routine grounds of everyday activities. In D. Sudnow (Ed.), *Studies in social interaction.* New York: Free Press, 1972.

Genesee, F., & Bourhis, R. Y. Sociolinguistic and social psychological factors in cross-cultural communication. *Journal of Language and Social Psychology.* 1982.

Giles, H. *Language, ethnicity and intergroup relations.* London: Academic Press, 1977.

Giles, H. Linguistic differentiation in ethnic groups. In H. Tajfel (Ed.), *Differentiation between social groups.* London: Academic Press, 1978.

Giles, H. Ethnicity markers in speech. In K. R. Scherer & H. Giles (Eds.), *Social markers in speech.* Cambridge: Cambridge University Press, 1979.

Giles, H., Bourhis, R. Y., & Taylor, D. M. Towards a theory of language in ethnic group relations. In H. Giles (Ed.), *Language, ethnicity and intergroup relations.* London: Academic Press, 1977.

Giles, H., & Johnson, P. The role of language in inter-ethnic behavior. In J. C. Turner & H. Giles (Eds.), *Intergroup behavior.* Oxford: Blackwell, 1981.

Giles, H., & Powesland, P. F. *Speech style and social evaluation.* London: Academic Press, 1975.

Giles, H., & Ryan, E. B. Prolegomena for developing a social psychological theory of language attitudes. In E. B. Ryan & H. Giles (Eds.), *Attitudes toward language variation: Social and applied contexts.* London: Edward Arnold, 1982.

Giles, H., & Saint-Jacques, B. (Eds.). *Language and ethnic relations.* Oxford: Pergamon, 1979.

Giles, H., Scherer, K. R., & Taylor, D. M. Speech markers in social interaction. In K. R. Scherer & H. Giles (Eds.), *Social markers in speech.* Cambridge: Cambridge University Press, 1979.

Good, C. Language as social activity: Negotiating conversation. *Journal of Pragmatics,* 1979, *3,* 151-167.

Gumperz, J. J. Linguistic and social interaction in two communities. *American Anthropologist,* 1964, *66,* 137-153.

Gumperz, J. J. Sociocultural knowledge in conversational inference. In M. Saville-Troike (Ed.), *Georgetown 28th Round Table on languages and linguistics monograph series.* Washington, D.C.: Georgetown University Press, 1977.

Herrmann, T. Language and situation: The *Pars Pro Toto* principle. In C. Fraser & K. R. Scherer (Eds.), *Advances in the social psychology of language.* Cambridge: Cambridge University Press, 1982.

Hewitt, J. P. *Self and society: A symbolic interactionist social psychology.* Boston: Allyn and Bacon, 1976.

Hewstone, M. The role of language in attribution processes. In J. Jaspars, F. Fincham, & M. Hewstone (Eds.), *Attribution theory and research: Conceptual, developmental and social dimensions.* London: Academic Press, 1983.

Hewstone, M., & Giles, H. Intergroup conflict. In A. Gale & A. Chapman (Eds.), *Psychology and social problems: An introduction to applied psychology.* Chichester: Wiley, 1984.

Hewstone, M., & Jaspars, J. Intergroup relations and attribution processes. In H. Tajfel (Ed.), *Social identity and intergroup behavior.* Cambridge: Cambridge University Press, 1982.

Hymes, D. Models of the interaction of language and social setting. *Journal of Social Issues,* 1967, *23,* 8-28.

Hymes, D. Models of the interaction of language and social life. In J. J. Gumperz & D. Hymes (Eds.), *Directions in sociolinguistics: The ethnography of communication.* New York: Holt, Rinehart and Winston, 1972.

Irvine, J. Formality and informality in speech events. *American Anthropologist,* 1979, *81,* 773-790.

Jaspars, J., & Hewstone, M. Cross-cultural interaction, social attribution and intergroup relations. In S. Bochner (Ed.), *Cultures in contact: Studies in cross-cultural interaction.* Oxford: Pergamon, 1982.

Joos, M. The five clocks. *International Journal of American Linguistics,* 1962, *28,* Part 5.

Kelly, G. A. *The psychology of personal constructs,* 2 vols. New York: Norton, 1955.

Kramarae, C. *Women and men speaking.* Rowley, Mass.: Newbury House, 1981.

Labov, W. The study of language in its social context. *Studium Generale*, 1970, *23*, 66–84.

Lambert, W. E. Language as a factor in intergroup relations. In H. Giles & R. N. St. Clair (Eds.), *Language and social psychology*. Oxford: Blackwell, 1979.

Langer, E. J. Rethinking the role of thought in social interaction. In J. H. Harvey, W. J. Ickes, & R. F. Kidd (Eds.), *New directions in attribution research* (Vol. 2). Hillsdale, N.J.: Lawrence Erlbaum Associates, 1978.

Leet-Pelligrini, H. M. Conversational dominance as a function of gender and expertise. In H. Giles, W. P. Robinson, & P. M. Smith (Eds.), *Language: Social psychological perspectives*. Oxford: Pergamon, 1980.

Levinson, S. Universals in sociolinguistics. *Working papers in linguistics*. Cambridge: University of Cambridge, 1978.

Lind, E. A., & O'Barr, W. M. The social significance of speech in the courtroom. In H. Giles & R. N. St. Clair (Eds.), *Language and social psychology*. Oxford: Blackwell, 1979.

Manis, J. G., & Meltzer, B. N. *Symbolic interaction: A reader in social psychology*. Boston: Allyn and Bacon, 1967.

Mead, G. H. *Mind, self and society*. Chicago: University of Chicago Press, 1934.

Miller, G., & Steinberg, M. *Between people: A new analysis of interpersonal communication*. Chicago: Science Research Associate, 1975.

Moscovici, S. Society and theory in social psychology. In J. Israel & H. Tajfel (Eds.), *The context of social psychology: A critical assessment*. London: Academic Press, 1972.

Norman, W. T. Toward an adequate taxonomy of personality attributes: Replicated factor structure in peer nomination personality ratings. *Journal of Abnormal and Social Psychology*, 1963, *66*, 574–584.

O'Keefe, B., & Delia, J. Psychological and interactional dimensions of communicative development. In H. Giles & R. N. St. Clair (Eds.), *Recent advances in language, communication and social psychology*. London: Lawrence Erlbaum Associates, in press.

Osgood, C., Suci, G., & Tannenbaum, P. H. *The measurement of meaning*. Urbana: University of Illinois Press, 1957.

Platt, J. A model for polyglossia and multilingualism. *Language in Society*, 1977, *6*, 361–378.

Price, R., & Bouffard, D. L. Behavioral appropriateness and situational constraint as dimensions of social behavior. *Journal of Personality and Social Psychology*, 1974, *30*, 579–586.

Robinson, W. P., Giles, H., & Smith, P. M. Epilogue. In H. Giles, W. P. Robinson, & P. M. Smith (Eds.), *Language: Social psychological perspectives.* Oxford: Pergamon, 1980.

Roloff, M., & Berger, C. R. *Social cognition and communication.* Beverly Hills, Calif.: Sage, 1983.

Rommetveit, R. *On message structure.* London: Wiley, 1974.

Rosenberg, S., & Jones, R. A method for investigating and representing a person's implicit theory of personality: Theodore Dreiser's view of people. *Journal of Personality and Social Psychology,* 1972, *22,* 372–386.

Rosenberg, S., & Sedlak, A. Structural representations of implicit personality theory. In L. Berkowitz (Ed.), *Advances in experimental social psychology* (Vol. 6). New York: Academic Press, 1972.

Ryan, E. B. Why do low-prestige language varieties persist? In H. Giles & R. N. St. Clair (Eds.), *Language and social psychology.* Oxford: Blackwell, 1979.

St. Clair, R. N. The contexts of language. In R. N. St. Clair & H. Giles (Eds.), *The social and psychological contexts of language.* Hillsdale, N.J.: Lawrence Erlbaum Associates, 1980.

St. Clair, R. N. Symbolic interactionism and linguistic theory. In R. Haller (Ed.), *Proceedings of the mid-America linguistics conference.* Lincoln: University of Nebraska Press, 1982.

St. Clair, R. N., & Giles, H. (Eds.) *The social and psychological contexts of language.* Hillsdale, N.J.: Lawrence Erlbaum Associates, 1980.

Sampson, E. E. Psychology and the American ideal. *Journal of Personality and Social Psychology,* 1977, *35,* 767–782.

Schenkein, J. Identity negotiations in conversation. In J. Schenkein (Ed.), *Studies in the organization of conversational interaction.* New York: Academic Press, 1978.

Scherer, K. R., & Giles, H. (Eds.) *Social markers in speech.* Cambridge: Cambridge University Press, 1979.

Scotton, C. M. Strategies of neutrality: Language choice in uncertain situations. *Language,* 1976, *52,* 919–941.

Scotton, C. M. Codeswitching as a "safe choice" in choosing a lingua franca. In W. McCormack & S. Wurm (Eds.), *Language and society: Anthropological issues.* The Hague: Mouton, 1979.

Scotton, C. M. Explaining linguistic choices as identity negotiations. In H. Giles, W. P. Robinson, & P. M. Smith (Eds.), *Language: Social psychological perspectives.* Oxford: Pergamon, 1980.

Smith, P. M., Giles, H., & Hewstone, M. Sociolinguistics: A social psychological perspective. In R. N. St. Clair & H. Giles (Eds.), *The social and psychological contexts of language.* Hillsdale, N.J.: Lawrence Erlbaum Associates, 1980.

Smith, P. M., Giles, H., & Hewstone, M. New horizons in the study of speech and social situations. In B. Bain (Ed.), *The social genesis of language.* New York: Plenum, in press.

Steiner, I. D. Whatever happened to the group in social psychology? *Journal of Experimental Social Psychology,* 1974, *10,* 94–108.

Stephenson, G. M. Intergroup bargaining and negotiation. In J. C. Turner & H. Giles (Eds.), *Intergroup behavior.* Oxford: Blackwell, 1981.

Street, R. L., Jr., & Giles, H. Speech accommodation theory: A social cognitive approach to language and speech behavior. In M. Roloff & C. R. Berger (Eds.), *Social cognition and communication.* Beverly Hills, Calif.: Sage, 1983.

Suls, J. M., & Miller, R. L. *Social comparison processes.* New York: Wiley, 1977.

Tajfel, H. Experiments in a vacuum. In J. Israel & H. Tajfel (Eds.), *The context of social psychology: A critical assessment.* London: Academic Press, 1972.

Tajfel, H. Social identity and intergroup behavior. *Social Science Information,* 1974, *13,* 65–93.

Tajfel, H. (Ed.). *Differentiation between social groups.* London: Academic Press, 1978.

Tajfel, H., & Turner, J. C. An integrative theory of intergroup conflict. In W. G. Austin & S. Worchel (Eds.), *The social psychology of intergroup relations.* Monterey, Calif.: Brooks/Cole, 1979.

Taylor, D. M., & Giles, H. At the cross roads of research into language and ethnic relations. In H. Giles & B. Saint-Jacques (Eds.), *Language and ethnic relations.* Oxford: Pergamon, 1979.

Taylor, D. M., & Royer, L. Group processes affecting anticipated language choice in intergroup relations. In H. Giles, W. P. Robinson, & P. M. Smith (Eds.), *Language: Social psychological perspectives.* Oxford: Pergamon, 1980.

Thakerar, J. N., Giles, H., & Cheshire, J. Psychological and linguistic parameters of speech accommodation theory. In C. Fraser & K. R. Scherer (Eds.), *Advances in the social psychology of language.* Cambridge: Cambridge University Press, 1982.

Turner, J. C., & Brown, R. J. Social status, cognitive alternatives and intergroup behavior. In H. Tajfel (Ed.), *Differentiation between social groups.* London: Academic Press, 1978.

Turner, J. C., & Giles, H. (Eds.) *Intergroup behavior.* Oxford: Blackwell, 1981.

Wish, M. Subjects' expectations about their own interpersonal communication: A multidimensional approach. *Personality and Social Psychology Bulletin*, 1975, *1*, 501–504.

Wish, M. Dimensions of dyadic communication. In S. Weitz (Ed.), *Nonverbal communication*, 2nd Ed. New York: Oxford University Press, 1978.

Wish, M., Deutsch, M., & Kaplan, S. J. Perceived dimensions of interpersonal relations. *Journal of Personality and Social Psychology*, 1976, *33*, 409–420.

Wish, M., & Kaplan, S. J. Toward an implicit theory of interpersonal communication. *Sociometry*, 1977, *40*, 234–246.

Yamamoto, A. Communication in culture spaces. In W. McCormack & S. Wurm (Eds.), *Language and society: Anthropological issues*. The Hague: Mouton, 1979.

IV

Conclusions

11. The Future of Social Psychology: Taking the Past to Heart

JOSEPH M. F. JASPARS
University of Oxford

THE PAST

The Family Tree of Social Psychology

Many studies were devoted to the academic exercise of defining social psychology (Allport 1968; Grauman 1969; Sherif 1936). To what extent, however, were such attempts to demarcate a scientific territory futile enterprises, serving mainly to justify university positions or textbooks in social psychology?

As a prologue to a substantive discussion of problems in social psychology one might, therefore, like Brown (1965), consider "hawking and spitting" as the only reasonable introduction. "Statements of intent are so often belied by subsequent action . . . that one prefers to let intention be discovered by what is done" (22). Brown admitted he could not abstract from a list of topics studied by social psychologists a logical class defining the proper domain of social psychology. Unlike other social psychologists, Brown did not regard this inability as a problem. After all, biology did not begin with a good definition of life, nor did linguistics have, at first, a good definition of language. The boundaries of formal studies are, according to Brown, seldom sharply defined, and definitions reflect mainly historically determined divisions of labor.

Ten years later, Brown (Brown and Herrnstein 1975) frankly admitted that the search for a logical classification in (social) psychology is fruitless. The relations between the meanings of words and concepts (and *social psychology* is, first of all, a word) are better conceived of as family resemblances. It is easy to see that various social psychological research questions are interrelated and resemble each other like members of a conceptual family. However, it is impossible to decide, other than arbitrarily, which questions or problems belong to the family of social psychological issues because no characteristic is common to them all.

The best hope seems to lie in an analysis of historical, conceptual, or empirical relations revealing either the theoretical or practical family structure of a particular discipline. Analyses for definitions of such concepts as *social* or *group* and *attitude* (Jaspars 1973) show that in these cases at least two independent conceptual dimensions appear to exist.

Authors thus vary widely in using the concept *social* when trying to define social psychology or social behavior. It is not just that some social psychologists use a wider concept of *social* than do others; it is also a question of what is meant by a *stimulus* in social psychology and to what extent one wants to ascribe intentionality to human behavior. As Grauman (1969) has pointed out, the notion of a stimulus in social psychology differs from the *stimulus* concept in psychophysics.

In social psychology, a stimulus is often seen as having motivational properties. Stimulus is usually defined in terms of the response following it and is not considered as a sufficient cause for that response. In addition to the dubious conception of other people, their behavior, and the products of their actions as stimuli, the term *social* is sometimes used to describe behavior that in some unspecified way refers to or is related to other people or the social environment. Berger and Lambert (1968), emphasizing the distinction between those two conceptions, concluded that social psychologists study three types of social behavior: behavior determined by social antecedents; behavior as a response to social stimuli; and behavior that is both. Although it is questionable whether we are dealing with conceptually independent distinctions (a stimulus giving rise to a response also is a determinant of that response), it might make practical sense to accept such a differentiation because it allows for a reasonable and perhaps generally acceptable description of the focus of interest of social psychology: the study of behavioral (inter)dependence, social interaction, or human relations.

Nobody maintains the universal validity of correlations or causal relations between the behavior of individuals discovered in the field or in the laboratory. Such relationships usually depend on variations in the physical or natural environment, the cultural and social structure of which the individuals are part, and on differences within individuals (over time) and between individuals.

The problem, then, is that, apart from the value of our focal social psychological research, we have never developed research or a theory about the transformation or universal findings to apply to particular individuals or special cultural or structural situations. This is remarkable because the problem of the relationship between social interaction, individual behavior, and group phenomena (culture, social structure, and social change) is an old one concerned with the difficult relationship between sociology and psychology, which itself gave birth to social psychology as a separate discipline.

Comte's Dilemma

It is customary to point out that social psychology came into being as an academic discipline in 1908, when McDougall (1908) and Ross (1908) published the first two social psychology textbooks. Although the appearance of a first textbook is an arbitrary choice for marking the birthdate of a scientific discipline, the choice for social psychology is also misleading.

The least one might expect in granting McDougall and Ross a special place in the history of social psychology is that their work be regarded as crucial or important for the discipline's development. This is not the case for McDougall or Ross. McDougall's work does not reflect the development in psychology or the social sciences around the turn of the century, nor does his textbook contain a program followed up by later researchers. McDougall regarded his book only as a propaedeutic to social psychology. He agrees with some of his critics at the time, who remarked that "he [McDougall] seems to do a great deal of packing in preparation for a journey on which he never starts." Such preparatory and programmatic discussions about the nature and task of social psychology occurred on a wider scale than we now realize and certainly a lot earlier than social psychology's first textbooks.

Allport (1968) probably pushed the foundations of social psychology as an academic discipline further back than anyone by arguing that the origin of social psychology can be traced to Comte's conception of "la morale; as the true final science which would be able to systematize the special knowledge of our individual nature by virtue of an appropriate combination of [the] two points of view, the biological and the sociological" (Allport 1968, 48).

As Samuelson recently pointed out (Samuelson 1974), Allport may have been guilty of creating an origin myth in order to "validate and legitimize present views [of social psychology] by showing that a great thinker 'discovered' these, our truths, a hundred years ago," which then proves "that our questions are 'perennial' ones" (Samuelson 1974, 223). Samuelson rightly points out that Allport distorted Comte and his work by mentioning only his preoccupation with formal, methodological, perennial questions and neglecting the ideological function evident from his social political doctrine.

Historians of sociology (Becker and Barnes 1966), less myopic in this respect, have not overlooked that Comte's most important work was a blueprint for social reform of a peculiar kind. By emphasizing the political and ideological side of Comte's life and work, Samuelson is, however, also misleading. He does not pay much attention to the religious almost messianic and therefore not realistic character of Comte's political plans.

The justification for mentioning Comte as a forerunner of social psychology lies in the combination of messianic social expectations and important (social) scientific questions his work exhibits. Social psychology's history and prehistory show that this dilemma has never been completely absent in psychology and related social sciences, but it has appeared, for good reasons, repeatedly in an acute form in social psychology.

Although Allport's view of Comte's work is too restricted and scholarly, Comte was concerned with the relation between the individual and society. His organismic theory of society, history, and social personality as it related to action, intelligence, and feeling was borrowed from the phrenologist Gall. More importantly, he clearly stated that social amelioration depended on the conformity of the fundamental characteristics of human nature and the principles of sociology.

The reader who doubts the social role of the scientific study of the individual in Comte's views should read the catalog of supreme duties Comte assigned to his positivist priests. Comte's priests judged the worth of each member of society and, relying primarily on suggestion, attempted to place each person in society according to individual merits and capacities. The important point, however, is that the priests in Comte's positivist state would not possess any temporal power. This fact, of course, goes directly against Samuelson's political interpretation of Comte's work and makes Comte's state "an odd combination of religious and intellectual idealism with benevolent though partly nonpolitical paternalism in the interest of organic welfare" (Becker and Barnes 1966, 590).

Comte's messianic expectations of the scientific study of people and society were and are shared to some extent by many psychologists and social scientists. At the end of the nineteenth century, Brentano (1874) spoke about psychology as the science of the future that would determine human existence even more than the natural sciences. McDougall regarded psychology as the essential foundation on which all social sciences, including ethics, must rest. American pragmatism as developed by Dewey equated value and truth of scientific concepts and theories with its usefulness for society. Moreno saw himself on an equal footing with Jesus and Marx, regarding sociometry as important for society as the New Testament and scientific socialism (Moreno 1934).

The disillusion following such high hopes for a better world based on the social sciences and psychology made these disciplines religion's natural successor as the scapegoat of modern society. It is difficult to understand the recent criticism of social psychology if one does not consider these optimistic social expectations that have been part of social psychology from the beginning.

The turning point in the social sciences probably came with Weber's (1904) defence of a value-free methodology for the social sciences, which argued that such expectations were unfounded. Social scientists should not be regarded as visionaries and prophets whose revelations could or would save the world. The contemporary radical and humanistic movements in social psychology aiming to bring social emancipation or individual salvation indicate that various notions of a socially relevant psychology still have some characteristics of political, ideological, and religious movements.

The Task of Social Psychology

Comte's dilemma is also reflected in the development of social psychology in a more important intrascientific way. Social psychology's emergence as a separate discipline around the turn of the century is related to the relationship between the study of the individual and the study of society, between psychology and sociology. The Durkheim (1895)-Tarde (1903) debate clearly expressed the two fundamentally opposing views about this relationship for the first time. Durkheim viewed society as a reality *sui generis;* Tarde defended the individual as the alpha and the omega of the social system (Lukes 1973).

As Farr (1980) recently pointed out, Wundt's Volkerpsychologie, which he separated from individual psychology, may have influenced the sociological tradition in social psychology more than we have realized. But at the same time, Wundt also influenced Moede, whose experimental group psychology was a direct social extension of Wundt's psychophysics (Moede 1920).

From the beginning, social psychology attempted to individualize sociology, as in Tarde's instrumental psychology, or to socialize psychology, as in Moede's experimental group psychology. From this viewpoint, one can regard the history of social psychology as a development in which the burden of this integrative task has led to a gradual narrowing of the social reality to be studied and a widening of the study of individual behavior. These trends eventually reduced society to another individual and social psychology to the study of social interaction. The integrative task of social psychology was thus simplified, and it also became possible to use the experimental method. The consequence of this development was, of course, that an important part of social psychology's primary task could not be accomplished, resulting in psychologists and sociologists' losing interest in the results of social psychological research, especially because the relevance of social psychological research for the study of social issues became questionable.

This situation can be illustrated with an analysis of sociological, psychological, and social psychological journals around 1960. Figure 11-1 presents a simplified representation of the most important information exchanges (reference) of the ten journals most often cited in the *Annual Review of Psychology* chapters on social psychology. The

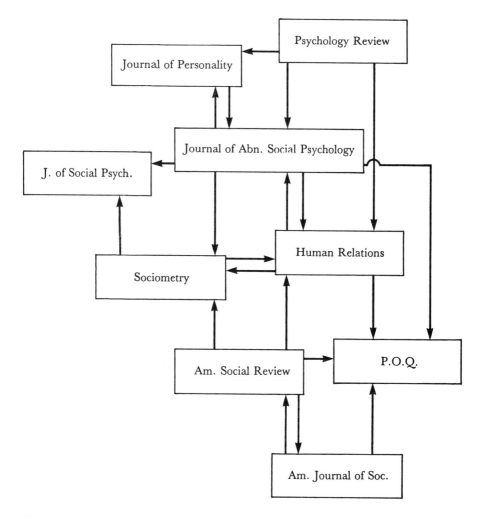

Figure 11-1. Sociogram of Journal Relations

information flow is strongly asymmetrical. The academic social psychological journals refer to each other and to sociological and psychological journals, but the reverse flow of information is less pronounced. Academic or experimental social psychology appears to be trying to integrate ideas or findings from sociology and psychology, but less interest appears among sociologists and psychologists for the results of this work.

The same asymmetrical pattern appears in social psychology between experimental and applied research. Such applied journals as

Public Opinion Quarterly and *Journal of Social Psychology* use much of the experimental work published in the central academic journals, but these journals do not refer to the applied journals in their own publications. Experimental social psychology at the beginning of the 1960s solved Comte's dilemma, which interested only academic social psychology. The solution was obtained by miniaturizing the social environment so it could be studied in the laboratory. This practice at first gave social psychology some scientific respectability, but it eventually created considerable dissatisfaction and disillusionment.

The key position of experimental social psychology in this development can be appreciated only if one realizes that social psychologists were also always concerned with the psychological study of such social issues as prejudice, the effect of mass media, political behavior, mental health, job satisfaction, and educational problems. This interest is not evident from the most important social psychological journals. The percentage of experimental studies in *Journal of Personality and Social Psychology* rose from 30 percent in 1944 to 89 percent in 1969, a tendency opposite to that in psychology in general. Psychological textbooks since the beginning of this century have devoted less attention to straightforward experimental psychology and more to social psychology.

This trend does not coincide with the trend in scientific journals, which have always devoted more attention to socially oriented psychology than to experimental psychology. The strategy of experimental social psychologists appears successful in the sense that writers of introductory psychology textbooks now find social psychological studies scientific enough to be included in a general introduction to the field.

Against the background of these past developments, some contemporary movements in social psychology can be interpreted as renewed attempts to integrate the study of the individual and society. The experimental approach in social psychology requiring a form of social reality that can be manipulated as an independent variable evokes at least two basic criticisms. One criticism is directed at the neglect of everything social but not able to be manipulated in an experimental study. A second criticism is directed at the model of people and the philosophy of science underlying the experimental approach in social psychology. Recent developments in social psychology can be described as different combinations of these two basic forms of criticism of the dominant experimental social psychology. On the one hand, these critical developments are concerned with a further socialization of social psychology; on the other hand, critical attempts are made to humanize social psychology.

THE PRESENT

The Social Relevance of Social Psychology

Much recent criticism in social psychology originated in Western Europe and is directed at social psychology as it developed in the United States (Israel and Tajfel 1972). The European Association of Experimental Social Psychology, founded with the support of some prominent American social psychologists, a few years ago published a critical analysis of contemporary social psychology with a strong anti-American bent. An American reviewer described it as a biting of the now faltering American hand that fed it.

The sharpest criticism of American social psychology probably appeared in the German *Zeitschrift fur Sozialpsychologie* (Holzkamp 1976). The beginnings of an integration of Marxist philosophy and social psychology could be noticed both in Eastern and Western Europe (Hiebsch and Vorweg 1972). It is remarkable that even a number of typical American developments in social psychology originated in the European scientific tradition. The humanistic tradition, which in social psychology is strongly related to the training movement, the influence of symbolic interactionism, and ethnomethodology are examples (Farr 1980). The most recent American developments in this respect are probably the renewed interest in cross-cultural research (Triandis 1976) and the application of system theory (McGuire 1967).

Contemporary attempts to resocialize social psychology are manifest in at least three different approaches. First, a number of mainly Western European social psychologists tried to introduce macrosociological variables in experimental social psychology.

Society is brought into the laboratory. It suffices here to refer to Moscovici's work on minority group influence and the work by Tajfel and his colleagues on intergroup relations (Moscovici 1976; Tajfel 1978). Taylor and Brown's (1979) recent discussion of this work and replies by Moscovici (1979) and Tajfel (1979) indicate that this approach involves more than introducing new social variables in traditional social psychological experiments. It is also a different theoretical approach, which, as Moscovici indicates, goes back to the question of society or the individual, sociology or psychology. Taylor and Brown opted for Tard's viewpoint, whereas Moscovici placed himself in the Durkheim tradition, descending, if necessary, from the social to the individual level. Tajfel also favored a similar position. He argued that a clear distinction must be made between individualistic theories and theories concerned with socially shared patterns of individual behavior.

The facts that the individual is the building block of the theory and that measurement occurs at the individual level do not mean that all the relevant theoretical concepts are of an individual kind. Individual actions may constitute social reality, but this does not mean that one can understand or explain the social behavior of individuals by referring to the psychological processes involved in constructing the social system without considering the reality sui generis the system represents. or less homogeneous social situations. They also indicated this notion understand without a social concept like anomie.

The second important point is that neither Moscovici nor Tajfel dealt with sociological concepts as such but with the shared or collective representations of a reality social in origin. Apart from the constructional aspect of social reality, this view offers two novel approaches for social psychology. One approach deals with the representational aspect of the social world. The other approach is primarily concerned with the consequences of the collective nature of these representations.

Jaspars and Fraser (1983) pointed out for the first time that such representations are relevant for making distinctions among groups of individuals and not for differentiating among individuals within more or less homogeneous social situations. They also indicated this notion of social attitudes was advocated by Thomas and Znaniecki (1928) to understand the problems of Polish peasants in America. Since then, however, the concept of attitude has been completely individualized in American social psychology and converted into a personality trait.

The second contemporary attempt to resocialize social psychology appeared in the work of a number of Marxist social psychologists. They primarily attempted to unmask the ideological foundation and societal function of the dominant tradition in social psychology by showing that experimental social psychological research does not concern itself with the historically developed social class system. In doing so, this research has supported the capitalistic system. In its purest, historical materialistic form, this approach is represented best in Plon (1974).

Holzkamp's emancipatory social psychology also shows great affinity with the Marxist approach (Holzkamp 1976). Holzkamp presents the clearest radical attempt to resocialize social psychology. According to Holzkamp, social psychology's tasks are to investigate the contradiction between the appearance of pleasant everyday life and the antagonistic class structure and to make the oppressed class aware of these contradictions. Research prepares for these tasks by creating controlled situations in which phenomena examplary for practical situations can be studied in detail. In short, social psychology is a plea for applied research with a political purpose. Society is not brought into the laboratory, but experiments are made into an integral part of political action. The obvious danger is making social psychological research of partisan thinking that would be self-defeating from a scientific point of view.

Note, therefore, that the Eastern European version of Marxist social psychology usually distinguishes carefully between ideology and social psychology (Hiebsch and Vorweg 1972).

The current self-criticism in American social psychology is well known. The ethical implications of social psychological experimentation, the methodological problems produced by demand characteristics, and experimenter expectancy effects have been discussed at length (Orne 1962) and appear to have led to interpersonal experiments in more naturalistic settings, just as in the ethological tradition, more evident in some European work (Argyle 1969).

The most important criticism, however, comes from McGuire, Gergen, and Triandis, who appear to attach much significance to the historical, social, and cultural relativity of a lot of past social psychological research. McGuire (1973) looks for a solution in applying more advanced experimental designs and techniques of analysis. He suggests that the bridge between experimental social psychology and the study of complex social issues can be built with the use of computer simulation techniques.

Gergen (1973, 1985) is, of course, more pessimistic, giving up the pretense of a general social psychology and ruling out the critical testing of hypotheses by experimentation. At most, experiments may be useful to explicate biosocial relationships, alter our consciousness of the way things are, demonstrate the viability of certain theoretical viewpoints, or be of some service in social reform.

Triandis (1976) is equally critical of current experimental social psychology, but he is not as pessimistic as Gergen. Triandis essentially appears to believe that cross-cultural research of variables that are culture general but that can be operationalized in a culture-specific way can offer a solution. This general theory of social behavior interprets behavior as function of habits and intentions and also considers differences among individuals, situations, and types of behavior. To determine the importance of each factor, Triandis proposes an analysis of the subjective interpretations people give to the social situation.

The Humanistic Critique of Social Psychology

Contemporary criticism of experimental social psychology is not limited to a critique of the minimal social character of most social psychological research. It is also directed, as pointed out, at the philosophy of science and at the anthropological presuppositions underlying the experimental approach in social psychology. The supposedly mechanistic model of people, the Humean conception of causality, and the logical positivistic methodology are the focus of the most severe criticism (Harré and Secord 1972).

This criticism, of course, is not new nor is it specifically directed at social psychology. It is remarkable that only recently has this criticism been significant in social psychology. There has never been anything like an idiographic, *verstehende*, phenomenological, or existential social psychology; this does not mean, of course, that no attention has been paid to social psychological questions in phenomenological philosophy or psychology. The belated impact of a philosopher like Schutz is a case in point.

Such current versions of humanistic approaches to the study of social behavior as symbolic interactionism, ethnomethodology, and ethogenics appear to have limited appeal for most mainstream social psychologists. One reason many social psychologists are not impressed by the criticism and alternatives offered is not that they disagree with the fundamental issues raised by these approaches, but that they feel they have already gone a long way in accommodating these criticisms in their research and that accepting the sometimes extremely subjective methodological alternatives would be counterproductive.

As Zajonc (1968) pointed out, "the physical and objective properties of social stimulation and incentives have always been assumed to be less significant for the analysis of social behavior than their subjective counterparts" (222). Despite the strong experimental tradition in recent social psychological research, it is hard to find theories or experiments in social psychology adhering strictly to a mechanistic model of people. I agree with Broadbent (1973) that much of this criticism is based on an outdated conception of mechanistic-causal approaches to human behavior.

In a comprehensive historical study, Fleming (1967) showed how one central concept of social psychology, attitude, has come "to embody a new conception of man, a redefinition of the distinctively human to encompass the impact of the last hundred years upon men's views of themselves" (288). In line with this argument, Braginski and Braginski (1974) argued that solutions for many of psychology's problems are in social psychology.

This is not to say that experimental social psychology has no problems; rather, social psychology's main problem is not its mechanistic, causal, neopositivistic approach. Social psychology is perhaps the last area of psychology to deserve this criticism. A careful analysis of the humanistic critique of the experimental approach in social psychology (Holzkamp 1976; Harré and Secord 1972; Semin and Manstead 1979) shows that the minimal social situation, created in experiments, is objected to. Such situations are not representative of social life in general because they are a historical partition, reduced and unstable (Holzkamp 1976), or because they are anonymous (Harré 1979) and evoke nomic social behavior (Semin and Manstead 1979). Such situations allow us to get away with simple, reductionistic explanations of social behavior. We may have learned, as McGuire (1973) argued, to be finders of situations in which our hypotheses can be demonstrated as tautologically true" (450). However, this criticism is ultimately not a humanistic critique of experimental social psychology that treats people as objects, but a criticism of the restrictive and limited social situations we have investigated. As such, the humanistic critique of experimental social psychology is basically the same as the criticism raised by authors concerned with the resocialization of social psychology.

The crucial problem for a viable social psychology still appears to be integrating the study of people and society, of the individual and the wider social context, of psychology and sociology. Yet, the objection to which most critics agree is clear. The social relevance of social psychology is limited because the results of social psychological research cannot claim to possess even a modest degree of universality, mainly because they have been obtained in situations not representative of social life in general.

Gergen's (1978) recent reappraisal of experimentation in social psychology best illustrates this point. "To the extent that natural, social, or subjective circumstances are altered, empirical findings may fluctuate. . . . Theoretical statements resting on such a shifting data base may thus be of circumscribed validity across time" (518). To elucidate, Gergen considers a more or less established principle in contemporary social psychology with immense experimental support: Attraction toward another is a positive function of O's similarity to P. Gergen shows convincingly that many alterations can occur affecting the universality of the similarity attraction "law."

This pessimistic view of experimentation's function is perhaps naïve. Gergen seems to expect that the similarity attraction law as developed in laboratory experiments should hold invariantly, irrespective of alterations in natural, social, and subjective circumstances. It is doubtful that any laws in the human or physical sciences are universal in this sense. The fact that birds fly does not contradict the law of gravity. We must send astronauts to the moon to find the natural circumstances in which Newton's gravitational law can be demonstrated. Only after centuries of experimentation could the gravitational constant G be determined accurately. It is not easy to measure very tiny forces in the presence of the much larger perturbing forces because of all of the other matter in the universe.

This celebrated example from the physical sciences is cited not to argue that this is the model to which we should or could aspire, but to indicate the magnitude of the task to be accomplished with respect to social psychological "laws." First, we should note that Newton's gravitational law is more complex than its crude social analogue because it considers factors other than the distance between physical objects. Second, the constancy of G depends on the physical units of mass, length, and time used.

Even if a more sophisticated attraction similarity law were formulated that would take other major factors into account, and even if such a law could be expressed in some acceptable psychological units of measurement, it is unlikely that the coefficient(s) of the function describing the relationship between attraction and similarity would be constant. Rather than despair and argue that such a law cannot be formulated, we might ask whether the variations in our attraction similarity function are purely random or whether they are in some systematic way related to the circumstances in which attraction and similarity are observed.

The problem is, of course, that we cannot answer this question unless we have some ways of describing and classifying the circumstances that can affect our social psychological law. What is needed is a psychological taxonomy of social situations incorporating at least the major relevant variations in circumstances. Such an approach is, in fact, an old one, already advocated by John Stuart Mill. He spoke of the need for principia media or axiomata media to relate the empirical laws resulting from simple observations to the highest generalizations. Axiomatic media, according to Mill, indicate to what extent historical or geographical reality limited the conditions for the universal laws.

Is it possible to develop such a taxonomy? Yes, I believe it is. Several indications point in this direction. In fact, several such taxonomies, at different levels of generality, have emerged in recent social psychological literature. First are attempts to study the effects of interpersonal situations in a more systematic way than before. The work by Argyle and colleagues (Argyle, Furnham, and Graham 1981) is the clearest development in this direction. Second, a number of social psychologists are concerned with the impact of social structure on social behavior. Several examples of this development have been mentioned. Finally, Triandis and Berry's recent work (1980) shows a similar development at the cross-cultural level.

THE FUTURE

Taking the Past to Heart

Nothing is so foolhardy as trying to predict the future of one's discipline. This task is perhaps best left to those who have had a major impact on the field so we would at least have the advantage of a possible self-fulfilling prophecy.

I must admit, however, that the first publication I edited was a special issue of a Dutch student journal on the future of psychology.

Most contributors graciously consented to speculate about the future. It is superfluous to add that now, twenty years later, their predictions do not make much sense. Of course, no one foresaw the student revolution of 1968–1969 and its impact on the social sciences or specifically on the crisis in (social) psychology. No authors predicted the popularity of the training movement or the rise of humanistic psychology. Judging from this experience, it is apparently impossible to predict future developments in a particular area of psychology, let alone to predict whether and when major advances will occur.

Nevertheless, perhaps we can take the past to heart in planning for the future. We can ask ourselves when social psychology seemed to advance in a significant way and why such progress was possible at the time.

I do not know of any serious sociology of knowledge or a history of science study with the development of social psychology as its subject matter. The only study with some relevance to the issue is an analysis by Deutsch, Platt, and Senghaas (1971a) of the conditions favoring major advances in social science. Although the study has been criticized for biased sampling of advances, its major conclusion appears to hold. "What seems to have worked best [in social science] were small teams in large places—a spatial concentration of stimulation and support, a plurality of persons, organizations and initiatives and some communication with the world of practical needs" (Deutsch, Platt, and Senghaas 1971b, 451).

The obvious social psychological candidate is, of course, Lewin; in fact, he is the only social psychologist whose work is included in the list of major advances. Lewin happened to be in the right places at the right time; also his unique integration of theory and applied work classified him among the major contributors of the social sciences.

As Deutsch, Platt, and Senghaas (1971a) show, this kind of integration appears typical for much important work in the social sciences. According to the authors, major contributors appear to be able to begin with a practical and concrete problem; they then raise it to a high level of abstraction and can formulate a technology giving the sounded theory a wider application. In psychology, Freud had this ability. In social psychology, Lewin is the clearest example. If proof is needed beyond the well-known editions of Lewin's papers (Lewin 1938, 1951) the reader should see his first published paper after his dissertation (Lewin 1917), which deals with the landscape of war. Someone who can, in the battlefield trenches, develop a chapter on the phenomenology of the landscape must have the ability Deutsch, Platt, and Senghaas regard as typical for major contributors in the social sciences.

Although I do not want to dwell on Lewin's work in and contributions to social psychology, I propose it as a possible strategy for future research in social psychology. The credo of such a social psychology would be to develop and extend explanations of social behavior and eventually, perhaps, more general theories by the comparative study of social behavior in a variety of real-life situations. Although laboratory situations might be included among the situations to be studied, a distinction must be made between experimental studies, whose aim is to resolve theoretical issues, and (laboratory) research, which is concerned with miniature replications of social reality. Experimental studies are concerned mainly with questions of internal validity (Cook and Campbell 1976); for laboratory studies, external validity is more important.

This distinction is important because applying theoretical notions developed and tested in the laboratory to a particular situation requires knowing the effect of the situation as a whole on the phenomena one is interested in without necessarily being able to specify precisely the situational aspects responsible for the effect. The field variables necessary for classifying social situations are therefore not necessarily the same as the universal variables used to formulate the theory in a general way.

Some problems must be resolved to follow such a strategy. First, it may not be immediately evident that we can observe every form of behavior in all situations. Argyle (1975) argued that "certain aspects of behaviour are measurable and common to all situations—e.g., amount of talk, gaze, proximity. These can be predicted from equations in the tradition of Newtonian mechanics and Gas Laws. But there are other aspects of behaviour like what people say, which moves they make at chess and what they do at a party, which have to be treated somewhat differently. I shall argue that a 'generative rules' approach, as used in linguistics is more appropriate and that we have to deal with discrete entities [of behavior, situations and perhaps persons] rather like the discrete units in genetics or chemistry" (175).

Although Argyle's distinction seems to indicate a serious problem for cross-situational generalizations, this is not the crucial issue; an important part of genetics is concerned with continuous variation as the result of genetic differences of a discrete nature. For general laws in psychology, aspects of behavior and situations need not be described on common dimensions. In other words, if we were to describe the stimuli in terms of their psychological effect, we could regard these situations as functionally equivalent.

Social psychology, of course, is not so simple. In psychophysical experiments, a smell will lead more or less to the same response on different presentations; in social encounters, however, the same gesture may provoke different reactions depending on the situation in which it occurs. For this reason, we have tried to define stimuli or situations in social psychology in terms of subjective representations rather than in terms of objective features. One cannot generalize from a situation where people turn wooden blocks around for either $1.00 or $20.00 to a situation in which the end of the world is predicted, unless one has a concept such as cognitive dissonance. Once we can describe situations in psychological terms, we can formulate more general laws of social behavior.

Lewin was a master in this respect. When he tried to answer such a practical question as, "Why do people eat what they eat," he did not analyze it in terms of moves, or props, but in terms of social and economic channels, gate sections, and gatekeepers; this process allowed him to generalize to such other situations as discrimination against minorities. To do so, the critical issue is "that of finding the actual gatekeepers. . . . This requires," Lewin added, "essentially a sociological analysis" (Lewin, 1951, 186).

Such translations and analyses are essential if we want to compare social behavior in complex social situations. Many concepts in social psychology can be fruitfully applied in a variety of situations. However, it behooves us to develop systemically the situational dictionary required. At the same time, a psychological taxonomy of situations is needed to be able to generalize.

Such a difficult double task depends to a large extent on the imagination of individual researchers. We are not completely in the dark when describing situations. Research in other areas of psychology and in other social and biological sciences provides a wealth of information about social behavior not always formulated in a different language. Translations are possible, and taxonomies are available at several levels of social organization.

To illustrate this point, consider three things: some taxonomic proposals, various research strategies and methods of analysis, and some examples of relations between social behavior as studied in social psychology and other areas of psychology and social sciences.

Psychological Taxonomies of Social Situations

An applied taxonomy. To generalize social psychological findings developed in vacuo to social behavior in situation, it makes sense to take a pragmatic view and start by finding out to what kind of situations social psychologists usually try to apply their knowledge. We may never be able to predict how certain relationships will vary across the whole social universe, but if we can develop useful knowledge for certain practical problems, we will achieve some degree of integration.

Social psychologists have long concerned themselves with many social issues, but the results of applied research have rarely been incorporated in academic social psychology. The final volume of the *Handbook of Social Psychology* and the *Journal of Social Issues* are full of relevant social psychological research, but we have not compared the findings emerging from different fields of application and studied how these findings could be related to each other and to the results of laboratory research. It would be a valuable exercise, as a start, simply to try to teach general social psychology based purely on the results of applied research. It would force us to come to grips with the differences and the similarities of social behavior in various areas of application.

To do so, I analyzed the applied work of social psychologists in the Netherlands (Jaspars 1975; 1977). The analysis was instigated by the serendipitous observation that Dutch social psychologists appear to hold multiple memberships in various sections of the Netherlands Institute for Psychologists. The strongest associations appear to exist with clinical, organizational, and developmental psychology, in that order. General research is in the fourth place; interest in experimental psychology rates lowest. Over and above the affiliations, the associated interests of Dutch social psychologists exhibit a clear structure.

A simple nonmetric multidimensional scaling analysis revealed three clusters of interest. These clusters reflect the main applied affiliations of social psychologists: a clinical-educational-developmental cluster, an industrial-vocational guidance cluster, and a research-experimental psychology cluster. The latter represents academic social psychology; the two other clusters clearly are two opposed broad fields of application.

To make experimental social psychology more social in a practical sense, one could want to generalize to those two main areas. Some integration of applied social psychology could probably be achieved easiest within rather than between the two main fields of application. From a practical viewpoint, one would wish to see taxonomies and translations developed in each area. The field of educational-developmental-clinical applications would first require an interpersonal or relational taxonomy, dealing with situations as they occur in the family, the classroom, and the clinic. The field of organizational and industrial social psychology would also require a taxonomy at the group, organizational, or institutional level, essentially dealing with the effects of social structure on social psychology at an intermediate level.

The analysis does not show the need for a taxonomy above the institutional level; this is to be expected because we dealt only with the most frequent applications of social psychology in one country. Extrapolating from this analysis, it seems obvious that we also need a taxonomy at the societal level that can consider the effect of the social system in its cultural and structural aspects.

Taxonomies of social situations. Attempts have been made recently to develop taxonomies at various levels of generality. The greatest progress has probably been achieved in analyzing situations at the level of interpersonal encounters as they occur in everyday life. To a large extent, this development appears to be the outcome of the P x S debate. This debate argues that variation in social behavior is largely a function of the situation and the interaction between person and situation variables.

Although these conclusions are not entirely warranted by the research evidence (Furnham and Jaspars 1982), much can be gained by attempting to specify in a systematic way the situational influences determining behavior. The first relevant research was undertaken some time ago (Cattell 1963; Mann 1959). Only recently, however, have various taxonomies of this kind been proposed. Pervin (1978) reviewed most of these proposals, pointing out many difficulties. The meager substantive results of empirical studies do not appear to add a clear taxonomy of interpersonal situations. To the extent that these situational taxonomies are based on multidimensional scaling or multivariate analysis of perceived behavioral effects situations, this is not surprising because fact or analytic studies of individual differences in behavior, formally equivalent to this approach of classifying situations, have not led to an agreed-on universal taxonomy of personality traits except at the highest second or third order-level of factorial structure. It seems reasonable to predict, therefore, that a generally applicable interpersonal taxonomy will not be more complex than the personal taxonomy consisting of such factors as extroversion, anxiety, and intelligence.

Some results in the literature already point in that direction. Insel and Moos (1974) proposed a three-dimensional classification in terms of relationship, personal development, and system maintainance or change. Mehrabian and Russell (1974) suggested that situations can be classified along dimensions of semantic meaning similar to those identified by Osgood et al. (1957): pleasure, arousal, and dominance. Forgas (1976) uncovered such dimensions as friendly-unfriendly, knowledge of how to behave, and degree of organization for everyday situations of Oxford students. Magnusson (1971) and Pervin (1976) presented a more complex taxonomy, encompassing five dimensions with some similarity to Osgood's factors.

A serious problem with most studies using self-reports or ratings of abstractly described situations is that the results may reflect semantic similarity rather than behavioral equivalence. Most studies also have not described the situations in terms of the behavior they elicit. A proper analysis should show a double structure of situations and responses or behavior to be able to make the translation from objective environmental classification to a psychological taxonomy, which might be in studies of social behavior.

At least two such studies have appeared, although their data are not analyzed as indicated above. Moreover, these studies do not deal with actual behavior but with judgments of appropriateness or applicability

of several behavior patterns in a variety of situations (Price and Bouffard 1974; Argyle, Graham, Campbell, and White 1979). The substantive contribution of these studies is still limited. It is not surprising to
find subjects think writing appropriate for a classroom situation and
kissing for a date or that one should show positive affection at a wedding but not when making a complaint.

Additional analysis of the results in these studies shows in principle
what such a double structure of situations and behavioral responses
might look like. Figure 11–2 represents the outcome of a nonmetric
multidimensional scaling analysis of Price's (1975) summarized data.
The analysis could have been performed on Price and Bouffard's (1974)
complete situation-behavior matrix using any H.D.S. computer-program
available for the analyzing of such data, but it suffices for illustration
to present the summary results.

Figure 11–2 shows the major situations Price identified as regions
with equal preference for the four types of behavior he found (Coombs
1964). The distances between any position in these regions and the
various points representing the behavior patterns indicate the degree
appropriateness of the behavior in the situation. The figure shows that
we can describe the same behavior-situation space either in behavioral
or in situational terms and at the same time can relate the two descriptions to each other. The space itself presents the translation needed to

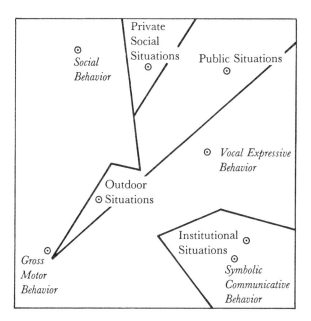

Figure 11–2. Isotonic Regions of Situational Appropriateness for Various
Forms of Social Behavior (after Price 1975; Price & Bouffard 1974).

incorporate the findings in a more general social psychological theory. We might thus describe Price's results as showing two basic situational distinctions, such as outdoors situations (lower left) versus indoors situations, and private vs institutional situations, a situation he applies mainly to indoor situations. In terms of behavior elicited, we distinguish between motor behavior and social behavior and a second dimension indicating differences between various forms of social behavior.

The suggestion following from this analysis is if one were interested, for example, in the relationship between similarity and attraction (see Gergen 1978), the relationships might be different in private social situations as compared to institutional situations. However, we can now include the difference between the situations in terms of the behavioral dimension distinguishing them.

This example indicates another important point. It would be advantageous to characterize the behavioral dimension conceptually so the distinction could be directly related to the theory from which we want to derive general statements applicable to both types of situations. This is not a necessary requirement and may not be possible because the distinctions emerging from situational analysis may differ from those developed in the laboratory. To the extent that the behavioral dimensions, implicit in situational differences, are distinct from those already available, we must extend our theories.

One obstacle in the further expanse of social psychological theories developed in vacuo is the occurrence of interaction effects due to the combination of situational or field variables and universal variables. One can easily imagine that a study's complexity would increase so rapidly with the inclusion of more than one field variable that any analysis would be impractical.

It seems, however, that we have so far not paid enough attention to the precise nature of interaction effects that occur. Situations affect both the probability of occurrence of certain behavior patterns (a main effect that does not threaten generalizability) and also the variance of the behavior exhibited by persons in a situation. Such differences in variance will lead to interaction effects, but these effects are not a serious problem for generalizing across situations because standardizing scores or, in general, transforming the measurement scale can solve this problem. This does not mean that differences in behavioral variance between situations are simply artifacts. This may be so in certain studies; but in general, one major psychological effect of situations is that they act as constraints or amplifiers of existing differences. The notion that behavior is more well governed in certain situations than in others (Argyle et al. 1979) is compatible with this idea.

We can go beyond this aspect in a more refined analysis of interactional effects. The study by Argyle et al. (1979) illustrates this point. Argyle et al. show that certain rules have a more general application than other rules, irrespective of the situation, and, on the other hand, that certain situations are more rule-governed than other situations. If one considers their results insofar as they cannot be explained by these two main effects, we find the applicability of rules to the various situations is strongly related. For complaint and interview situations, we find almost the same ranking of applicability, whereas we find the opposite ordering for friendly chats and hostess-wedding-dates situations.

This finding implies a strong interaction between situations and rule application, but it is a completely predictable interaction because the double structure of rules and situations appears to be one-dimensional. If one knows how the rules apply to one situation, one knows how they apply to all situations. Only when the taxonomy of situations is multidimensional is a more complex model necessary for generalization across situations representing different dimensions.

So far, we have discussed only interpersonal taxonomies. However, situations cannot be described solely in relational terms. Sets of interpersonal relations defining small groups, organizations, and social structure can be differentiated along attribute dimensions unique to each level. Parallel but not unrelated distinctions are being made with respect to the cultural aspects—both material and unmaterial—of social systems at each level. Structural and cultural taxonomies of this kind have not been developed in any systematical way. There is, however, a relevant social psychological, sociological, and anthropological literature.

The most systematic approach at all levels probably comes from Cattell, who used factor analytic methods to describe differences in individual behavior and differences between small groups and nations. Cattell's results (see, e.g., Cattell 1950) are of dubious value given the quality of the data on which his analyses are based. In a comprehensive study of small groups, Cattell and Stice (1960) developed a taxonomy for describing group situations of fourteen factors. Some factors suggest plausible distinctions at group level (morale, procedure, orientation, etc.), but many factors appear to reflect only the various instruments (questionnaires, observations, objective tests) used in the study. Moreover, much variance captured by Cattell and Stice's fourteen factors must be error variance.

Since the reliability of many measures is abysmally low, sometimes negative, I have reanalyzed the data of the Cattell and Stice study, removing or combining unreliable measures and analyzing results first for each instrument before proceeding to an overall analysis. Admittedly, much information is lost in this way, but in view of the data's quality this does not seem a great loss. The result is a two-dimensional solution. The two dimensions are readily interpretable as productivity and cohesiveness, which have been described in group dynamics literature before and since Cattell's study. The interesting point in Cattell's study is, however, that both group dimensions are also reflected at the interpersonal and the individual level. This is not so surprising because Cattell and Stice worked with groups of individuals who came together for the first time in the laboratory. This productivity at the group level appears to parallel individual prominence (intelligence) and task-oriented interaction, whereas cohesiveness of groups was higher in groups of extrovert and nonanxious individuals who had positive relations with each other.

Real-life groups seem to require a more extensive taxonomy than the one developed in group dynamics. In an unpublished study, Jaspars (1964) collected reports about 180 real groups such as school children, sports teams, work groups, student fraternities, military units, and study groups from persons who were members of those groups at the time of the study or had been members of those groups in the past. A group description questionnaire was developed in a pilot study using carefully selected group characteristics from the work by many other researchers.

Principal component analysis of the data led, after varimax rotation, to eight readily interpretable dimensions such as: formal-informal, stability, exclusiveness, cohesiveness, the position of the group in the organization, intimacy, power of the group over its members, and degree of stratification. The original group classification from which the study started (sports teams, work groups, etc.) could easily be differentiated using the eight factors taxonomy. Second-order analysis produced the two-dimensional solution represented in Figure 11-3, along with the positions of the eight factors.

As seen in Figure 11-3, the main distinction is between the power, stability, and formality of military units and school classes on the one hand and the instability and informality of sports teams and fraternities. Study and work groups, occupying an intermediate position, are cohesive but not exclusive. The dimensions show some similarity to the dimensions generally reported in the group literature, but I want to emphasize that we are dealing here with a second-order analysis that disregards variations between groups of the same type, so some group dimensions collapse.

The study's purposes were to develop a taxonomy of small groups in real life and to discover the relationship between the factors differentiating the groups and the productivity and cohesiveness of the groups. To give two illustrations: high school classes with a high degree of cohesion had a low level of productivity, whereas work groups of students were more productive when they were stratified. To the extent that group productivity is a simple function of individual productivity, different factors appear to determine productive behavior, depending on the group situation in which the individual happens to be operating.

At a higher level of social organization, the necessity for studying social behavior in its social context has been stated repeatedly. The

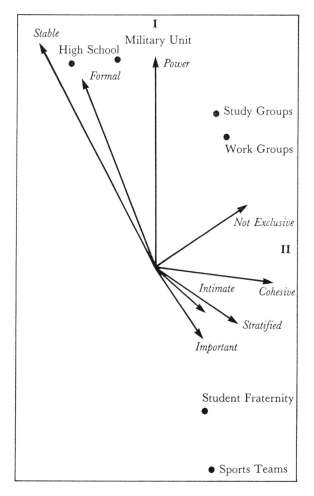

Figure 11-3. Small Group Taxonomy: Second Order Analysis (Source: Jaspars 1964.)

work by Moscovici (1981) on social representations and by Tajfel (1982) on intergroup relations has been mentioned. In both approaches, the search for a taxonomy is not a major issue, and it is questionable whether a taxonomy can be achieved here. Moscovici (personal communication) apparently suspects that a few major representations may be of overriding importance, but these representations cannot easily be interrelated since they are characterized primarily by their content. Tajfel's studies of the intergroup relations also show that an attempt is first made to understand how such relations develop in relation to such psychological processes as trying to establish a social identity through social comparison. By including genuine social variables in the theory, the question of a taxonomy for explaining a particular social phenomenon becomes less important.

The strongest advocates for higher level taxonomy are cross-cultural psychologists. Triandis (1976) and Berry (1979) best represent a social psychology attempting to achieve universal formulations that can be locally applied. Berry (1975) presented an ecological approach to cross-cultural psychology. His ambitious model of six major components, each a whole model in itself, is too complex to describe here. Yet it is important to emphasize that so far the cross-cultural psychologists have presented conceptual frameworks allowing them first to systematize their own empirical research, although both approaches also can encompass other research findings. However, the cross-cultural psychologists do not present a cultural taxonomy, although such a taxonomy would be compatible with their general models of social behavior.

In another paper, Berry (1979) emphasized a view similar to one in this chapter. To test the limits of current theory, he argued that collecting and comparing many local examples are necessary. Although Berry recognized dimensions for comparison other than cross-cultural ones, he emphasized the universal features of social and cultural life proposed by Malinowski (1944) and Murdock (1945).

Berry is, of course, aware of the emic-etic distinction as applied to anthropology and the problems of comparability. He nevertheless believes that a cross-cultural comparative approach is possible based on the work of these anthropologists. One important feature from the point of view of developing an empirically based taxonomy for culture is that Murdock's proposal for seventy-three universals received some empirical support in factor analytic studies of empirical observations of cultural variation (Sawyer and Levine 1966). Perhaps we should again mention the pioneering research of Cattell et al. (1979) that developed a theory and taxonomy for cultural and political-economic psychology. However, Cattell recognized some difficulties with these early studies, so his results cannot be regarded as a firm basis for cultural taxonomies. Cattell also appeared more interested in explaining macrosociological phenomena, such as war, with the aid of these taxonomies than in explaining individual social behavior.

Attempts to explain social behavior as a function of large cultural differences are in Berry's work. The clearest example is his well-known study of perceptual discrimination, field-dependence, and conformity in two subsistence-level societies: the Temne people of Sierra Leone and the Eskimos of Baffin Island. In one part of the study, the degree of food accumulation and socialization practices in the two cultures were used to predict conformity differences between them. It was predicted that such cultural differences would lead to low conformity in the case of hunting or fishing people, whereas food accumulators like the Temne would show a high level of conformity. The study's result confirmed the hypothesis that subsistence-level societies tend to produce the degree of conformity required by their economies.

From the comparative point of view, the study also illustrated the combined effect of a universal and field variable in social behavior. In the conformity study, Berry varied, as in the original Asch (1956) study, the difference in length of the lines to be compared with the standard line. We know from experimental conformity studies that increasing the size of the discrepancy between the source and the receiver in a social influence situation increases the effect of a communication, at least up to a certain point. The assumption of such a relationship underlies most social influence models. Berry found that this relationship remained unaffected in both the Eskimo and Temne samples. As a matter of fact, the effect of a difference in length of two *mm*'s is half as large as the high difference in culture. Because no statistical interaction appears between the cultural field variable and the social psychological discrepancy variable in their effect on the conformity behavior, it is easy to generalize across cultures in this case.

Berry's (1976) later extension of this study showed that the variation in degree of independence characterizing an individual's relationship to his or her group norms could be predicted reasonably well across seventeen subsistence-level cultures.

THE COMPARATIVE ANALYSIS OF BEHAVIOR

If we assume that it is possible to develop situational taxonomies in terms of the behavioral effects of situations, we have not solved all the problems involved in a comparative analysis of social behavior. As pointed out, different situations may have similar behavioral effects and similar situations may lead to different responses. To achieve at least a roughly one-to-one correspondence between situational characteristics and social behavior, we substitute subjective representations for the objective description of the situation. This equivalence problem has been most acute in cross-cultural studies.

Triandis's approach resolved the problem essentially along the cognitive lines just suggested. He made subjective culture the central concept of his model (Triandis et al. 1972). Berry and Dasen (1974) distinguished functional and metric equivalence as well as conceptual equivalence. Functional equivalence of behavior in Berry's sense is the same as behavioral equivalence of situations discussed above; metric equivalence refers to second-order similarity of the kind discussed in relation to Steven's power law.

Whatever form our initial observations take, we have essentially an off-diagonal data matrix relating elements of two different sets (stimuli-responses, situations-behaviors, situations-subjective interpretations, subjectively interpreted situations-behavior) to each other. This data matrix must be analyzed. Taxonomic studies have usually applied some form of multivariate analysis or multidimensional scaling to either situations or responses; but the analysis of both sets of elements can proceed simultaneously, revealing a double structure that allows us to translate situations in behavioral equivalents. Although the results of such an analysis are interesting, it does not suffice if we are interested in generalizing statements about social behavior across a variety of situations.

A different type of analysis would be to establish the degree of generalizability by ANOVA techniques as developed in the 1950s and used by interactionist social psychologists (Endler and Magnusson 1976). However, we are not interested only in the generalizability of responses or behaviors across situations; we first want to predict situational transformations of universal social psychological relationships. To do so, we must add to our situation-response matrix the factor describing differences between individuals to complete the person-situation-response (P.S.R.) data set. Following traditional analysis of variance models, we can decompose the total behavior variance into variance components due to main effects of persons, situations, responses, and their interaction effects:

$$V_{B_{PRS}} = V_P + V_r + V_S + V_{Pr} + V_{Ps} + V_{SR} + V_{PSR} + V_e$$

Where

$V_{B_{PRS}}$ = total variance of behavior

V_P, V_r, V_S = variance of components corresponding with persons responses and situations

V_{Pr}, V_{PS}, V_{SR}, V_{PSR} = interaction variances

V_e = error component

Although not customary, we can interpret the variances associated with P as expressing social psychological relationships. If the P factor refers to a classification of Ss in an experiment according to the extent to which they have been frustrated, and if we observe a variety of aggressive responses (R) in different situations (S), then a main effect of P indicated an overall relationship between frustration and aggression irrespective of the specific nature of the aggressive response or the situation in which the response is observed. The various interaction effects, then, indicate to what extent the relationship holds for specific forms of aggressive behavior or for specific situations or for a combination of both. If it were possible to vary persons, situations, and behavioral responses at will, there would be a generalization problem because we would at least in theory always specify the degree to which certain relationships could or could not be generalized.

However, there may be a confounding of independent variables. The behavior repertoire may be different in different situations, as pointed out by Argyle (1976). The most obvious S, R, confounding in the case of cultural variables with such ranging implications is the problem of translation equivalence (Berry 1976). For instance, physical aggression may be a common reaction to frustration in game-like situations, whereas verbal aggression might occur predominantly in debates. Similar confounding can occur in other combinations of independent variables.

When we are interested in the effect of cultural variables on social behavior, it may be impossible, as Jahoda (1979) argued, experimentally to create differences with respect to the P variable in certain cultures. In a traditional village community, it would be inconceivable to use a confederate in a conformity study because everyone knows everybody else. How would we know, in the case of verbal aggression, which responses are equivalent across cultures? Finally, there is the possibility of the P factor's being confounded with the R factor. If the person variable were age, we would be confronted with the well-known problem of not being able to observe the same responses in young children and in adults. This problem is, of course, more serious in comparisons across species.

In view of these difficulties, one might abandon hope of being able to make general statements about social behavior, even if it is in theory possible, as shown, to include situational transformations in such statements. Such a pessimistic conclusion is not justified. A solution to the general problem can be found in an elaboration of Lewin's formulation that behavior is a function of the person and the situation. Interactionist social psychologists have attempted to determine the impact of situational, personal, and response mode differences on behavior, by directly analyzing the P.S. or the P.S.R. data matrix. Another solution would be, however, to ask how a P.S. matrix could be generated. The previous discussion implicitly answers this question.

We have, on one hand, been discussing relationships between social behavior (e.g., aggression) and theoretically relevant P variables (e.g., frustration), which may or may not be manipulated or created in the laboratory. The results of such studies constitute a P.R. matrix. On the other hand, we have discussed behavioral taxonomies of social situations and have illustrated such taxonomies. The data in these studies constitute an S.R. matrix. The question now is whether we can predict the P.S. matrix, reflecting how people will react in particular situations, since we know how they react in general or under laboratory conditions and what reactions are likely to occur in particular situations.

The solution in terms of matrix algebra operations is that:

PS – PR. SR

where

> PS = person-situation matrix describing the relationships between person variables and behavior in particular situations
>
> PR = person-response matrix describing the relationships between person variables and particular responses
>
> SR = situation-response matrix describing the relationships between situational variables and particular responses

If we interpret PS as B, SR as S, and PR as P, in Lewin's terminology, we have a more specific and precise formulation of this general statement:

B = P x S

The situation interpreted here as a behavioral taxonomy now acts as a transformation matrix, which, multiplied by the universal social behavior matrix, generates the situational behavior matrix.

To illustrate this point, we can use the experimental social psychology example that similarity leads to attraction, the generality of which Gergen (1973) rightly doubts. How could we treat this finding in the model just proposed? To predict whether similarity will lead to attraction in particular circumstances, we need a taxonomy of the situations to which we want to apply our general experimental finding. For the sake of simplicity, assume the relevant situations can be distinguished along the dimension formal-informal, corresponding to the results of the recent study of Argyle and his students (Argyle et al. 1979). Predicting the attraction behavior of similar and dissimilar persons in formal and informal situations now takes the form shown in Table 11-1.

The values in each cell are fictitious but not arbitrary. The B (PS) matrix reveals that similarity affects attraction, but apparently the effect is stronger in informal situations as compared with formal situations. That is, there is an interaction of the theoretical person variable and the situational variable. Note that this interaction is the result of the combination of two main effects: a main effect of the situation on attraction and a main effect of the theoretical variable on attraction.

TABLE 11-1
Situational Transformation of the Similarity-Attraction Law
(Fictitious Data)

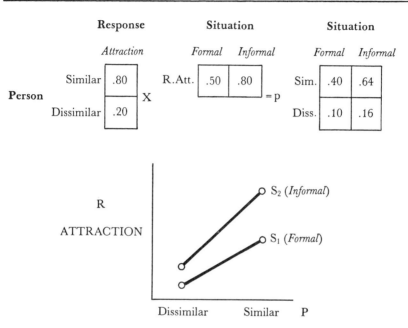

This simple example does not consider more complex relationships, but the approach can be generalized to more than one response. Interpreting the behavior matrix becomes more difficult in that case because we would have to assume that various response models can be combined into a single overall measure. If we had used the frustration-aggression example, we might have wanted to measure aggression in a number of different ways (verbal, physical). An overall measure of aggression in a variety of situations would make sense only if we had shown that specific aggressive responses showed positive intercorrelations within and across one person and situation variables.

In addition, the comparative approach here can be used in different ways. The first application would be the one described, where universal relationships developed through theoretically relevant experimentation are combined with information from a behavioral taxonomy of situations to predict social behavior in specific situations. If we also have observations of the behavior in those situations, we can test our predictions directly.

Certain studies may not have a taxonomy but have only experimental findings on the one hand and field observations on the other hand. The matrix formulation suggests that we can now find the taxonomic transformation, by solving the matrix equation for S. Thus:

$$S = (P'P)^{-1} \; P'B$$

The third application follows directly from the previous extension. We have information about social behavior in a variety of real-life situations and also a taxonomy. This allows us to formulate universal relationships by solving the equation for P, where:

$$P = PS' \; (SS')^{-1}$$

These abstract propositions are not as far-fetched as they appear on the basis of the presentation given here.

In experimental social psychology many experiments on coalition formation (Caplow 1956) seemed to favor a minimal resource theory or a minimal winning theory. It is first argued that parties will coalesce that have just enough resources together to form a majority. The theory is based on the parity norm that coalition partners accept a distribution of outcomes in proportion to their combined resources.

Although most laboratory experiments have ignored the content or issues involved in the social process of forming coalitions, these studies should at least be applicable to political coalition formation. The question is, can one generalize from the laboratory to the parliament? To make such a generalization, we need field studies about political coalition formation.

Such studies have been done. De Swaan (1973), analyzing cabinet formations in nine European parliaments after 1919, showed that a minimal range theory best predicted the coalitions formed. The minimal range theory asserts that coalescing parties have a minimal difference with regard to their political orientation. Such a theory has, of course, obvious parallels in social psychology, where the similarity-attraction paradigm and balance theory would make similar predictions.

It is easy to see how the results from experimental studies that neglected the political orientation factor can be combined with either a political taxonomy or another social psychological theory to predict the actual coalition in European parliaments.

A Wilke et al. (1973) experimental study did just that; since Wilke's results are similar to De Swaan's, I will use these data to illustrate the comparative approach. Table 11-2 presents the results obtained by Wilke et al.

Predicting the political coalitions formed in Wilke's study is the basis of a political taxonomy. The universal factor of resource or power distribution is simple in this particular case because the marginal values in Table 11-2 can be used as measures of the theoretical power variable

TABLE 11-2
Coalitions Formed for Different Combinations of Power and Political Orientation, after Wilke et al. 1973

Resource combinations	Center-right	Center-left	Left-right	
40-30	15.5	7.7	0.0	23.0
40-20	17.4	16.1	0.6	34.0
30-20	15.5	25.2	1.9	43.0
	48.0	49.0	2.5	99.9

and the political field variable. Multiplying the appropriate values yields predicted values that correlate .89 with the observed coalitions formed.

Wilke et al. also found, however, a significant interaction effect not predictable from the main effects of power and political orientation. This implies that we would have to include an additional theoretical and an additional taxonomic variable in our model. This can easily be done by following the same procedure for the residual matrix. Combining the results of the second analysis with those of the first led to a perfect fit of the predicted and the observed values, except for rounding errors. The results obtained are presented in Table 11-3.

As seen in Table 11-3, the first response vector corresponds with intuitive ideas and theoretical notions about the likelihood of certain combinations of resources or political orientations occurring. Center-right and center-left coalitions are more likely to occur, and minimum resource theory accords with the results presented for PR.

Note, however, that predictions by various minimum resource models are not close to the power distribution of coalitions found by Wilke et al. Although the principle appears to operate, it apparently is not as strong as several theories suggest. It thus is reasonable to consider other minimum resource models than those currently proposed in the literature.[1] The need for a second power or resource vector to explain political coalition formation indicates that a minimum resource theory is not sufficient to explain the coalitions formed, even if we consider the political taxonomy. Apparently a factor works against minimum resource coalitions and in favor of maximum resource coalitions. The absolute amount of joint power also determines the choice of coalition partners.

A similar analysis is possible with the political taxonomy or the minimum range theory. Obviously, the formation of adjacent coalitions is more likely than the nonadjacent left-right coalition, and center-right

TABLE 11-3
Political Coalition Formation as a Function of
Power and Political Orientation (after Wilke et al. 1973)

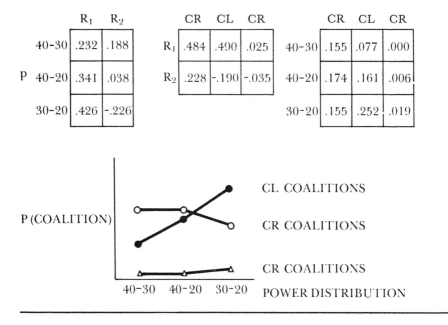

	R₁	R₂			CR	CL	CR			CR	CL	CR
40-30	.232	.188		R₁	.484	.490	.025		40-30	.155	.077	.000
P 40-20	.341	.038		R₂	.228	-.190	-.035		40-20	.174	.161	.006
30-20	.426	-.226							30-20	.155	.252	.019

coalitions also were not surprising in the political climate of the Netherlands at the time of the study.

This example illustrated that it is possible to predict situational transformations of general social psychological laws and also that we can infer such universal theoretical formulations from behavior observed in specific situations by a comparative analysis. It is surprising that this approach has not been developed in social psychology. It is an important approach in the study of law, anthropology, political sciences, and general psychology. In psychology, the comparative approach has become identified with the comparative study of human and animal behavior, although the notion of a comparative psychology also originally included cross-cultural and developmental comparative studies (Werner 1952).

Much general knowledge can be gained from studying social behavior in a variety of situations—either applied situations or cross-cultural studies. However, the large gap between the applied-interpersonal level and the cross-cultural level could be fruitfully studied by a comparative approach. Transformations of behavioral regularities as a function of institutional, structural, and subcultural factors have not been studied in a systematic fashion. A comparative study of social behavior could lead to a later integration of various fields of application and ultimately, perhaps, to a general psychology that is neither socially irrelevant nor theoretically trivial.

ENDNOTE

1. A simple minimum resource model for a 4-3-2 power distribution which does fit well is, however, easy to formulate. Assuming proportional distribution of outcomes after coalition formation, it is first assumed that coalition partners decide on the basis of the ratio of the outcomes for several partners and secondly that the probabilities of forming a coalition for any two parties are different. The prediction in the case of Wilke's study would be .25, .23, .42, for 40-30, 40-20, and 30-20, respectively.

REFERENCES

Allport, G. The historical background of modern social psychology. In G. Lindzey & E. Aronson (Eds.), *The handbook of social psychology* (Vol. 1), 1968.

Argyle, M. *Social interaction.* London: Methuen 1969.

Argyle, M. Do personality traits exist? *New Behaviour*, 1975, *3*, 176–179.

Argyle, M. Personality and social behaviour. In R. Harré (Ed.), *Personality.* Oxford: Blackwell, 1976.

Argyle, M. Furnham, A., & Graham J. *Social situations.* Cambridge: Cambridge University Press, 1981.

Argyle, M., Graham, J., Campbell, A., & White, P. The rules of different situations. *New Zealand Psychologist*, 1979, *8*, 13–22.

Asch, S. Studies of independence and conformity: A minority of one against a unanimous group. *Psychological Monograph*, 1956, *70* (9, Whole No. 416).

Becker, H., & Barnes, H. *Social thought from lore to science.* New York: Dover, 1966.

Berger, S., & Lambert, W. Stimulus-response theory in contemporary social psychology. L. G. Lindzey, & E. Aronson (Eds.), *The handbook of social psychology* (Vol. 1), Cambridge, Mass.: Addison-Wesley, 1968.

Berry, J. An ecological approach to cross-cultural psychology. *Netherland Journal of Psychology*, 1975, *30*, 51–84.

Berry, J. *Human ecology and cognitive style*. New York: Wiley, 1976.

Berry, J. A cultural ecology of social behaviour. In L. Berkowitz (Ed.), *Advances in experimental social psychology* (Vol. 12), 1979.

Berry, J., & Dasen, P. (Eds.). *Culture and cognition: Readings in cross-cultural psychology*. London: Methuen, 1974.

Braginski, B., & Braginski, D. *Mainstream psychology. A critique*. New York: Holt, Rinehart, 1974.

Bretano, F. *Psychologie vom empirischer stardpurkte*. Heidelberg, 1874.

Broadbent, D. *In defense of empirical psychology*. London: Methuen, 1973.

Brown, R., & Herrnstein, R. *Psychology*. London: Methuen, 1975.

Brown, R., Herrnstein, R. *Psychology*. London: Methuen, 1975.

Caplow, T. A theory of coalitions in the triad. *American Sociological Review*, 1956, *21*, 489–493.

Cattell, R. The principal culture patterns discoverable in the syntal dimensions of existing nations. *Journal of Social Psychology*, 1950, *32*, 215–253.

Cattell, R. Formulating the environmental situation in behaviour theory. In S. Sells (Ed.), *Stimulus determinants of behaviour*. New York: Ronald Press, 1963.

Cattell, R., Graham, R., & Wolwer, R. The reassessment of the factorial cultural dimensions of modern nations. *Journal of Social Psychology* 1979, *108*, 241–258.

Cattell, R., & Stice, G. *The dimensions of groups and their relations to the behaviour of members*. Champaign, Ill.: I.P.A.I., 1960.

Coombs, C. *A theory of data*. New York: Wiley, 1964

Cook, T., & Campbell, D. The design and conduct of quasi-experiments and true experiments in field settings. In M. Dunnette (Ed.), *Handbook of industrial organizational psychology*. New York: Rand McNally, 1976.

DeSwaan, A. *Coalition theories and cabinet formations*. Amsterdam: Elsevier, 1973.

Deutsch, K., Platt, J., & Senghaas, D. Conditions favouring major advances in social science. *Science,* 1971, *172*, 450–459. (a)

Deutsch, K., Platt, J., & Senghaas, D. Letter in reply. *Science*, 1971, *172*, 1192. (b).

Durkheim, E. *The rules of sociological meaning*. 1895. (Translated by S. Solomay and J. Mueller, Chicago: Chicago University Press, 1938.)

Endler, N., & Magnusson D. Toward an interactional psychology of personality. *Psychological Bulletin*, 1976, *83*, 956–974.

Farr, R. On reading Darwin and discovering social psychology. In R. Gilmour and S. Duck (Eds.), *The development of social psychology*. London: Academic Press, 1980.

Fleming, D. Attitude: The history of a concept. *Perspectives in American History*, 1967, *1*, 287–365.

Forgas, J. The perception of social episodes: Categorical and dimensional representations in two different social milieus. *Journal of Personality and Social Psychology*, 1976, *34*, 199–209.

Furnham, A., & Jaspars, J. Interactionism in psychology: A critical analysis of the S-R Inventories. Unpublished paper, 1982.

Gergen, K. Social psychology as history. *Journal of Personality and Social Psychology*, 1973, *26*, 309–320.

Gergen, K. Experimentation in social psychology: A reappraisal. *European Journal of Social Psychology*, 1978, *8*, 507–527.

Gergen, K. Towards intellectual audacity in social psychology. In R. Gilmour & S. Duck, *The development of social psychology*. London: Academic Press, 1980.

Grauman, C. *Handbuch der psychologie*. Gottingen: Hogrefe, 1969.

Harré, R. *Social being*. Oxford: Blackwell, 1979.

Harré, R., & Secord P. *The explanation of social behaviour*. Oxford: Blackwell, 1972.

Hiebsch, H., & Vorweg, M. *Einfuhrung in die Marxistische sozial psychologie*. Berlin: Wissendhaften, 1972.

Holzkamp, K. *Kritische psychologie*. Hamburg: Fischer Taschenbuch Verlay, 1976.

Insel, P., & Moos, R. Psychological environments: Expanding the scope of human ecology. *American Psychologist*, 1974, *29*, 179–188.

Israel, J., & Tajfel, H. (Eds.). *The context of social psychology*. London: Academic Press, 1972.

Jahoda, G. A cross-cultural perspective on experimental social psychology. *Personality and Social Psychology Bulletin*, 1979, *5*, 142–148.

Jaspars, J. M. F. De analyse van groepskumunikus. Unpublished manuscript, 1964.

Jaspars, J. M. F. The case against attitudes. Opening address to the BPS Social Psychology Conference, 1973.

Jaspars, J. M. F. The Future of social Psychology Paper presented at the Bielefeld Conference, EAESP, 1975.

Jaspars, J. M. F. Sociale psychologie. In K. Soudijn & H.B. Bergman (Eds.), *Ontorkhelisgen in de psychologie*. Boom: Meppel, 1977.

Jaspars, J. M. F., & Fraser, C. Attitudes as collective representations. In S. Moscovici & R. Farr (Eds.), *Social representations*. Cambridge: Cambridge University Press, 1983.

Lewin, K. Krieglandschaft. *Zeitschaft fur angewandte psychologie*, 1917, *12*, 440-447.

Lewin, K. *A dynamic theory of personality*. New York: McGraw-Hill, 1938.

Lewin, K. *Field theory in social science*. New York: Harper, 1951.

Lukes, S. *Emile Durkheim. His life and work: A historical and critical study*. Harmonsworth: Penguin, 1973.

McDougall, W. *An introduction to social psychology*. London: Methuen, 1908.

Magnusson, D. An analysis of situational dimensions. *Perceptual and Motor Skills*, 1971, *32*, 851-867.

Malinowski, B. *A scientific theory of culture*. Chapel Hill: University of North Carolina Press, 1944.

Mann, R. A review of the relationship between personality and performance in small groups. *Psychological Bulletin*, 1959, *56*, 241-270.

McGuire, W. Some impending reorientations in social psychology. *Journal of Experimental Social Psychology*, 1967, *3*, 124-129.

McGuire, W. The yin and yang of process in social psychology. *Journal of Personality and Social Psychology*, 1973, *26*, 446-456.

Mehrabian, A., & Russell, J. *An approach to environmental psychology*. Cambridge, Mass.: M.I.T. Press, 1974.

Moede, W. *Experimentelle massenpsychologie*. Leipsig: S. Hirzel, 1920.

Moreno, J. *Who shall survive?* Washington, D.C.: NHD Publishing Co., 1934.

Moscovici, S. *Social influence and social change*. London: Academic Press, 1976.

Moscovici, S. A rejoinder. *British Journal of Social and Clinical Psychology*, 1979, *18*, 181.

Moscovici, S. Personal Communication, 1980.

Moscovici, S. On social representations. In J. Forgas (Ed.), *Social cognition: Perspectives on everyday understanding*. London: Academic Press, 1981.

Murdock, G. The common denominator of cultures. In R. Linton (Ed.), *The science of man in the world crisis*. New York: Macmillan, 1945.

Orne, M. On the social psychology of the social psychology experiment. *American Psychologist*, 1962, *17*, 776-783.

Osgood, C., Suci, G., & Tannenbaum, P. *The measurement of meaning*. Urbana: University of Illinois Press, 1957.

Pervin, L. A free-response description approach to the analysis of person-situation interaction. *Journal of Personality and Social Psychology*, 1976, *34*, 365-374.

Pervin, L. Definitions, measurement and classifications of stimuli, situations and environments. *Human ecology*, 1978, *6*, 71–105.

Plon, M. On the meaning of the notion of conflict and its study in social psychology. *European Journal of Social Psychology*, 1974, *4*, 389–436.

Price, R. The taxonomic classification of behaviours and situations and the problem of behaviour-environment congruence. *Human Relations*, 1975, *27*, 567–585.

Price, R., & Bouffard, D. Behavioural appropriateness and situational constraints as dimensions of social behaviour. *Journal of Personality and Social Psychology*, 1974, *30*, 579–586.

Ross, E. *Social psychology*. New York: Macmillan, 1908.

Samuelson, F. History, origin, myth, and ideology: Comte's "discovery" of social psychology. *Journal for the Theory of Social Behaviour*, 1974, *4*, 217–231.

Sawyer, J., & Levine, R. Cultural dimensions: A factor analysis of the world ethnographic sample. *American Anthropologist*, 1966, *68*, 708–731.

Semin, G., & Manstead, A. Social psychology: Social or psychological? *British Journal of Social and Clinical Psychology*, 1979, *18*, 191–202.

Sherif, M. *The psychology of social norms*. New York: Harper and Row, 1936.

Tajfel, H. *Differentiation between social groups: Studies in the social psychology of intergroup relations*. London: Academic Press, 1978.

Tajfel, H. Individuals and groups in social psychology. *British Journal of Social and Clinical Psychology*, 1979, *18*, 183–190.

Tajfel, H. Social psychology of intergroup relations. *Annual Review of Psychology*, 1982, *33*, 1–39.

Tarde, G. *The laws of imitation*. New York: Holt, 1903.

Taylor, D., & Brown, R. Towards a more social social psychology. *British Journal of Social and Clinical Psychology*, 1979, *18*, 173–180.

Thomas, W., & Znaniecki, F. *The Polish peasant in Europe and America*. Boston: R. Badger, 1928.

Triandis, H. Social psychology and cultural analysis. In L. Strickland, F. Aboud, & K. Gergen (Eds.), *Social psychology in transition*. New York: Plenum Press, 1976.

Triandis, H., & Berry, W. *Handbook in cross-cultural psychology* (Vol. 1). London: Allyn and Bacon, 1980.

Triandis, H., Vassiliou, V., Tanaka, Y., & Sharmingham, A. *The analysis of subjective culture*. New York: Wiley, 1972.

Weber, M. *The methodology of the social sciences*. New York: Free Press, 1904.

Werner, H. The concept of development from a comparative and organomic point of view. In D. Harris (Ed.), *The concept of development.* Minneapolis: Minneapolis Press, 1952.

Wilke, H., Meertens, R., & Steur, T. Uncertainty and power inversion in coalition formation. *British Journal of Social and Clinical Psychology,* 1973, *12,* 38–45.

Zajonc, R. Cognitive theories in social psychology. In G. Lindzey & E. Aronson (Eds.), *The handbook of social psychology* (Vol. 1). Cambridge, Mass.: Addison-Wesley, 1968.

Index

A

Absolute consistency, 19
Accounts, 161–163
Activity specificity, 224
Actor-observer differences, 55, 72
Algebra, 298, 300
Alpha and beta press, 12
American sociology, 135. (*See also* Sociology)
Analytic models, 155
ANOVAs
 four-way, 70–72
 three-way, 63–70
 two-way, 54–63
Anxiety, 15, 24, 31–33, 49, 123
Archaeology, 208
Architectural history, 217
Assessing situations, 29, 169
Attribution theory, 65

B

Behavior
 consistency of, 1, 16, 19–21, 28, 35, 104–105
 desirable, 91
 difficult, 172–176
 dimensions of, 177, 249, 290
 imaginary, 62
 settings of, 211, 215–216
 sexual, 116–117
Behavior settings, 211, 215, 216
Behavioral sequences, 93
Behavior theory, 15
Biblical curse, 210

Biological basis of personality, 4
Biosocial theory of personality, 12
Biosphere, 12
Bystander effect, 245

C

Chemistry, 215
Classrooms, 140
Coalition formation, 302
Cognitive models of speech determinants, 252
Coherence, 60
Collective definition of the situation, 137
Commons dilemma, 5, 191
Conditioning
 eyelid, 112
 Pavlovian, 111, 114, 116
Consistency,
 absolute, 19
 relative, 19
Consistency of behavior, 1, 16, 19–21, 28, 35, 104, 105
Constituents of place, 216, 217
Contemporary research problems, 199
Content variables, 18
Cooperation dilemmas, 195
Coping strategies, 202
Correlational methods, 22, 23
Cross-cultural comparisons, 106–108, 296–297
Cross-sectional studies, 21
Crowding, 33, 34
Cultural definitions, 141